Shojo Beat

kimi ni todoke
From Me to You

Vol. 5

Story & Art by
Karuho Shiina

Volume 5

Contents

Story Thus Far

Sawako Kuronuma has always been a loner. Though not by choice, this optimistic 15-year-old can't seem to make any friends. Stuck with the unfortunate nickname "Sadako" after the haunting movie character, rumors about her summoning spirits have been greatly exaggerated. With her shy personality and scary looks, most of her classmates would barely talk to her, much less look into her eyes for more than three seconds lest they be cursed. Drawn out of her shell by her popular classmate Shota Kazehaya, Sawako is no longer an outcast in class. And with her new friends Ayane and Chizu, she's finally leading a more normal teenage life. Sawako is also befriended by one of the cutest girls in school, Kurumi, who asks Sawako to help her date Kazehaya. Sawako tells her she can't do it—and later realizes that her special feelings for Kazehaya must be love! Kurumi plans to quash Sawako's friendship with Kazehaya, but Yano figures out that Kurumi is the one who spread the vicious rumors that involved not only Sawako but Chizu and Ayane as well. Sawako is shocked, but empathizes with Kurumi's feelings for Kazehaya...

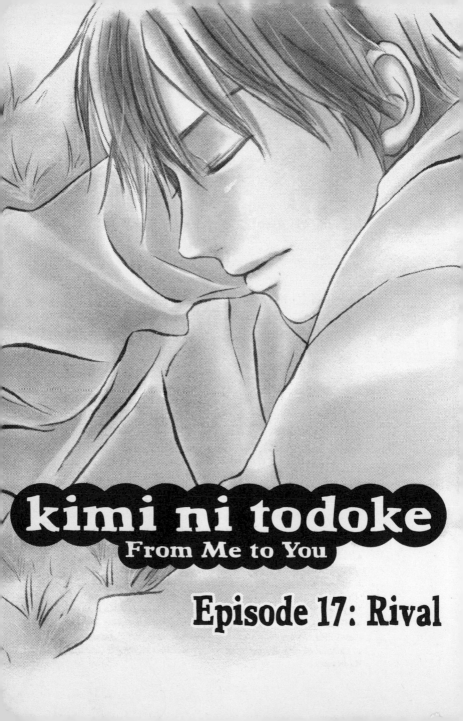

kimi ni todoke
From Me to You

Episode 17: Rival

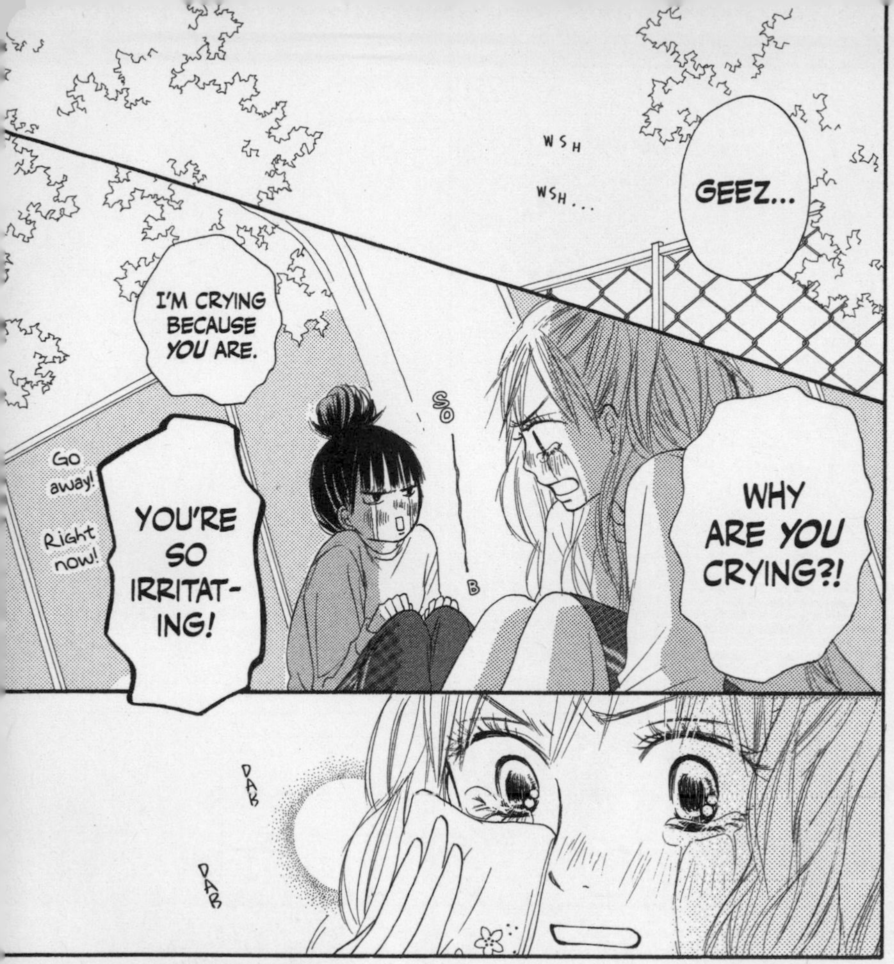
GEEZ...
WSH
WSH...
WHY ARE YOU CRYING?!
SOB
I'M CRYING BECAUSE YOU ARE.
YOU'RE SO IRRITATING!
Go away! Right now!
DAB
DAB

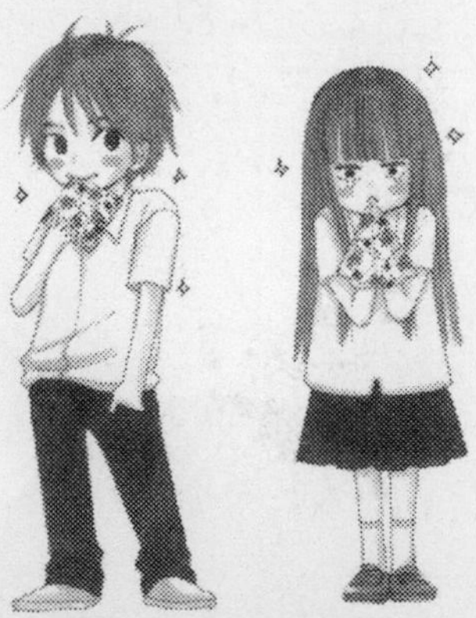

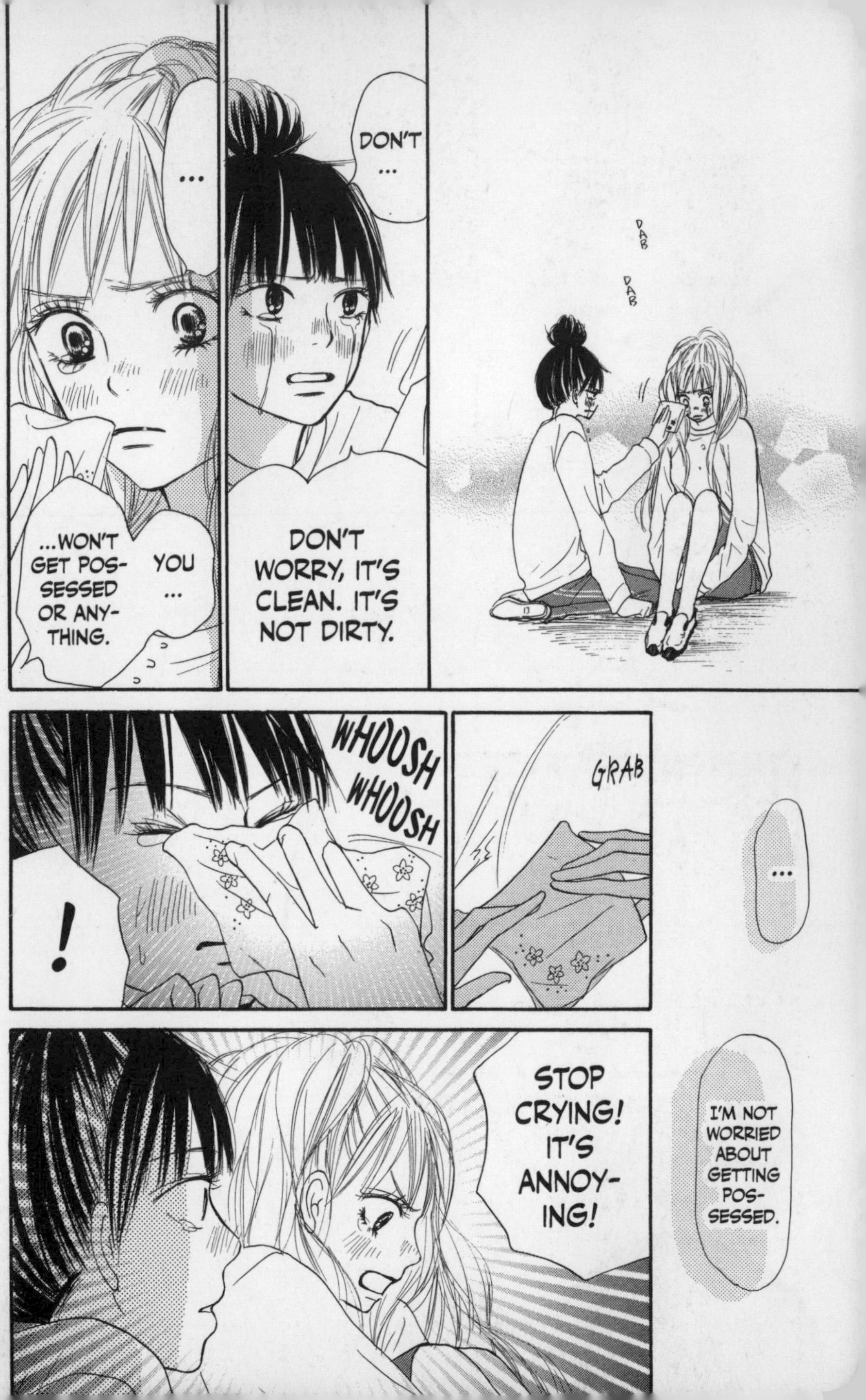
DAB
DAB
DON'T ...
DON'T WORRY, IT'S CLEAN. IT'S NOT DIRTY.
...
YOU ...
...WON'T GET POS-SESSED OR ANY-THING.
...
GRAB
WHOOSH WHOOSH
!
I'M NOT WORRIED ABOUT GETTING POS-SESSED.
STOP CRYING! IT'S ANNOY-ING!

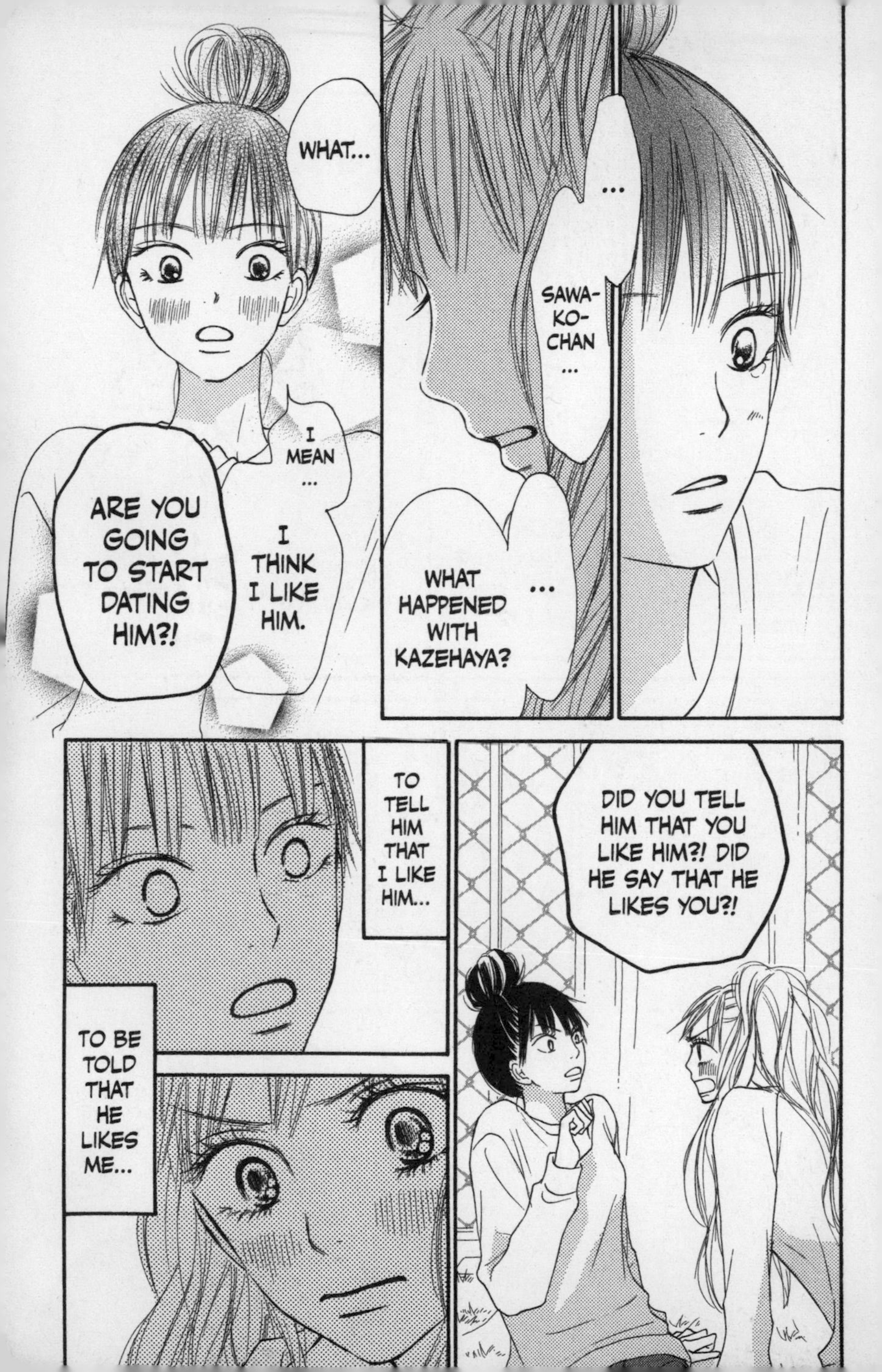
...
SAWA-KO-CHAN...
WHAT HAPPENED WITH KAZEHAYA?
...
WHAT...
I MEAN...
I THINK I LIKE HIM.
ARE YOU GOING TO START DATING HIM?!
DID YOU TELL HIM THAT YOU LIKE HIM?! DID HE SAY THAT HE LIKES YOU?!
TO TELL HIM THAT I LIKE HIM...
TO BE TOLD THAT HE LIKES ME...

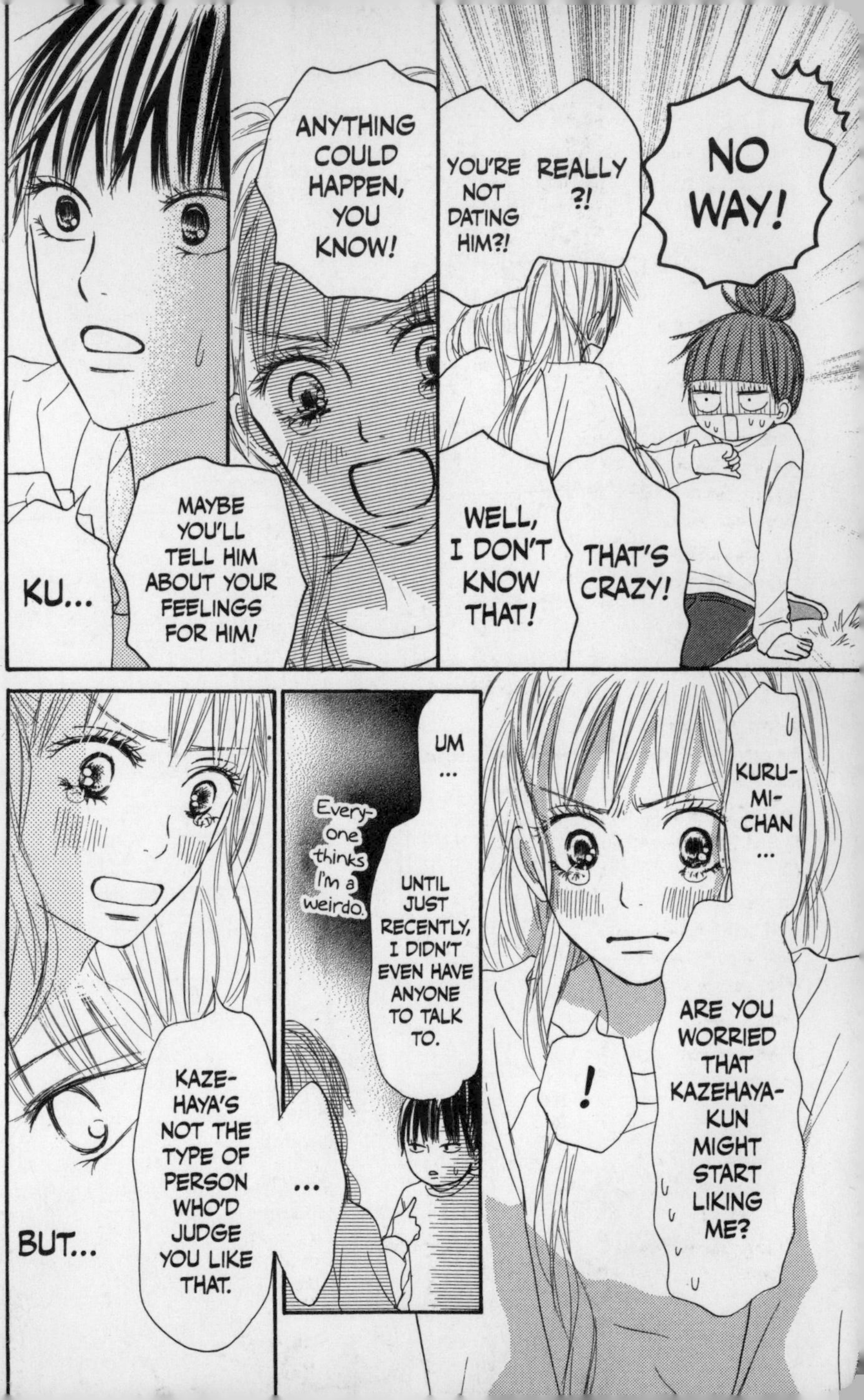
NO WAY!
REALLY ?!
YOU'RE NOT DATING HIM?!
THAT'S CRAZY!
WELL, I DON'T KNOW THAT!
ANYTHING COULD HAPPEN, YOU KNOW!
MAYBE YOU'LL TELL HIM ABOUT YOUR FEELINGS FOR HIM!
KU...
KURU-MI-CHAN ...
ARE YOU WORRIED THAT KAZEHAYA-KUN MIGHT START LIKING ME?
!
UM ...
UNTIL JUST RECENTLY, I DIDN'T EVEN HAVE ANYONE TO TALK TO.
Every-one thinks I'm a weirdo.
...
KAZE-HAYA'S NOT THE TYPE OF PERSON WHO'D JUDGE YOU LIKE THAT.
BUT...

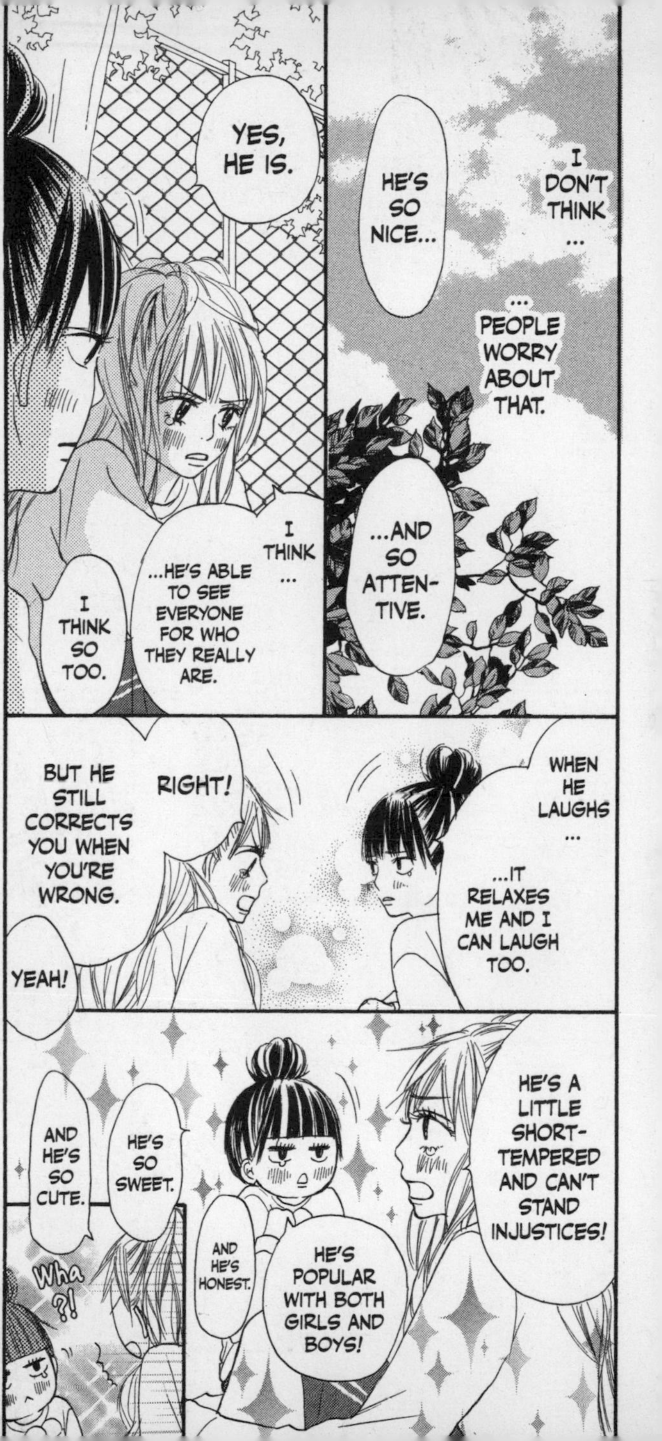
I DON'T THINK...
...PEOPLE WORRY ABOUT THAT.
HE'S SO NICE...
...AND SO ATTEN-TIVE.
YES, HE IS.
I THINK...
...HE'S ABLE TO SEE EVERYONE FOR WHO THEY REALLY ARE.
I THINK SO TOO.
WHEN HE LAUGHS...
...IT RELAXES ME AND I CAN LAUGH TOO.
RIGHT!
BUT HE STILL CORRECTS YOU WHEN YOU'RE WRONG.
YEAH!
HE'S A LITTLE SHORT-TEMPERED AND CAN'T STAND INJUSTICES!
HE'S POPULAR WITH BOTH GIRLS AND BOYS!
AND HE'S HONEST.
HE'S SO SWEET.
AND HE'S SO CUTE.
Wha?!

KARUPIN on JAPAN 1

Hello! How are you doing? ✿

If this is your first time reading this comic, nice to meet you! If you've been reading, thank you for your support!

My name is Shiina Karuho. Nice to meet you. ✧

Every time I write self-introductions, I feel like they are so annoying. Do you feel the same way when you read them?

Maybe I'll naturally change. Maybe I never will.

I'm confused.
What month is it? I don't know. What day of the week is it?

I have no idea.

Women are such weak creatures...

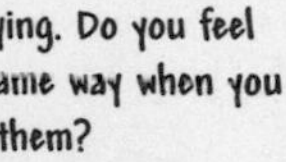
What was I writing about?

I apologize to all women. I'm sorry...

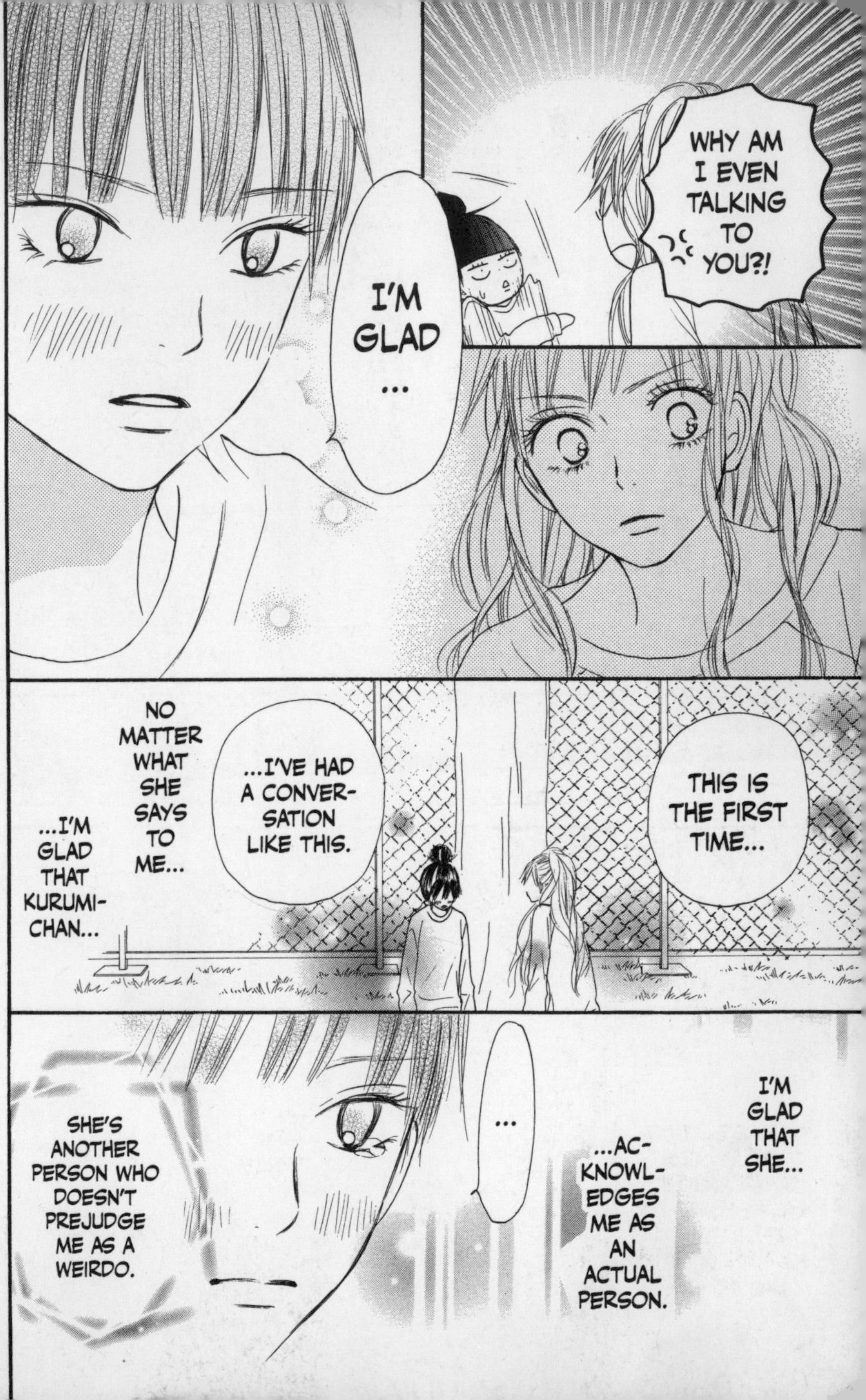
WHY AM I EVEN TALKING TO YOU?!
I'M GLAD ...
THIS IS THE FIRST TIME...
...I'VE HAD A CONVERSATION LIKE THIS.
NO MATTER WHAT SHE SAYS TO ME...
...I'M GLAD THAT KURUMI-CHAN...
I'M GLAD THAT SHE...
...ACKNOWLEDGES ME AS AN ACTUAL PERSON.
...
SHE'S ANOTHER PERSON WHO DOESN'T PREJUDGE ME AS A WEIRDO.

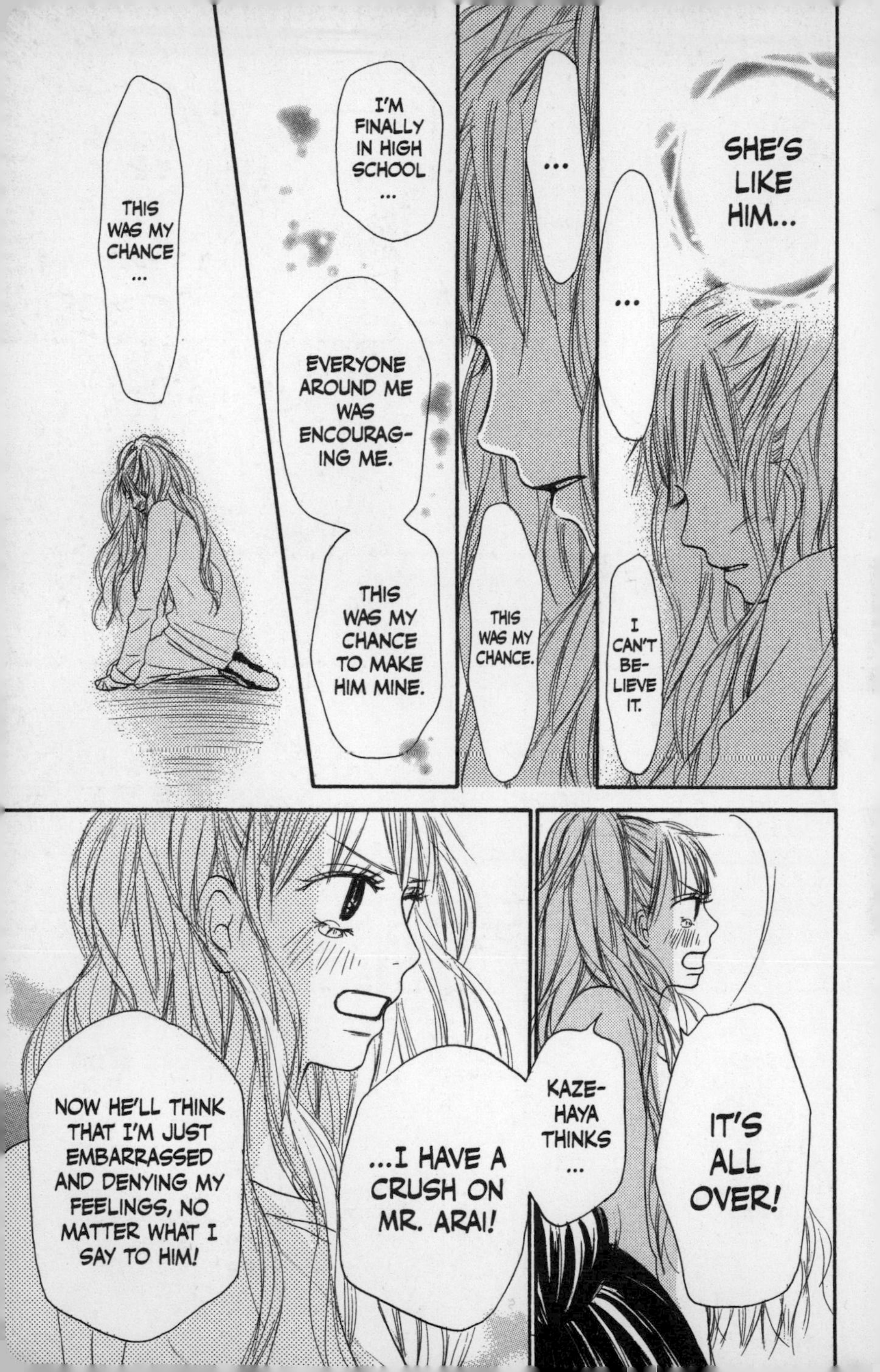
SHE'S LIKE HIM...
...
I CAN'T BELIEVE IT.
...
THIS WAS MY CHANCE.
I'M FINALLY IN HIGH SCHOOL ...
EVERYONE AROUND ME WAS ENCOURAGING ME.
THIS WAS MY CHANCE TO MAKE HIM MINE.
THIS WAS MY CHANCE ...
IT'S ALL OVER!
KAZEHAYA THINKS ...
...I HAVE A CRUSH ON MR. ARAI!
NOW HE'LL THINK THAT I'M JUST EMBARRASSED AND DENYING MY FEELINGS, NO MATTER WHAT I SAY TO HIM!

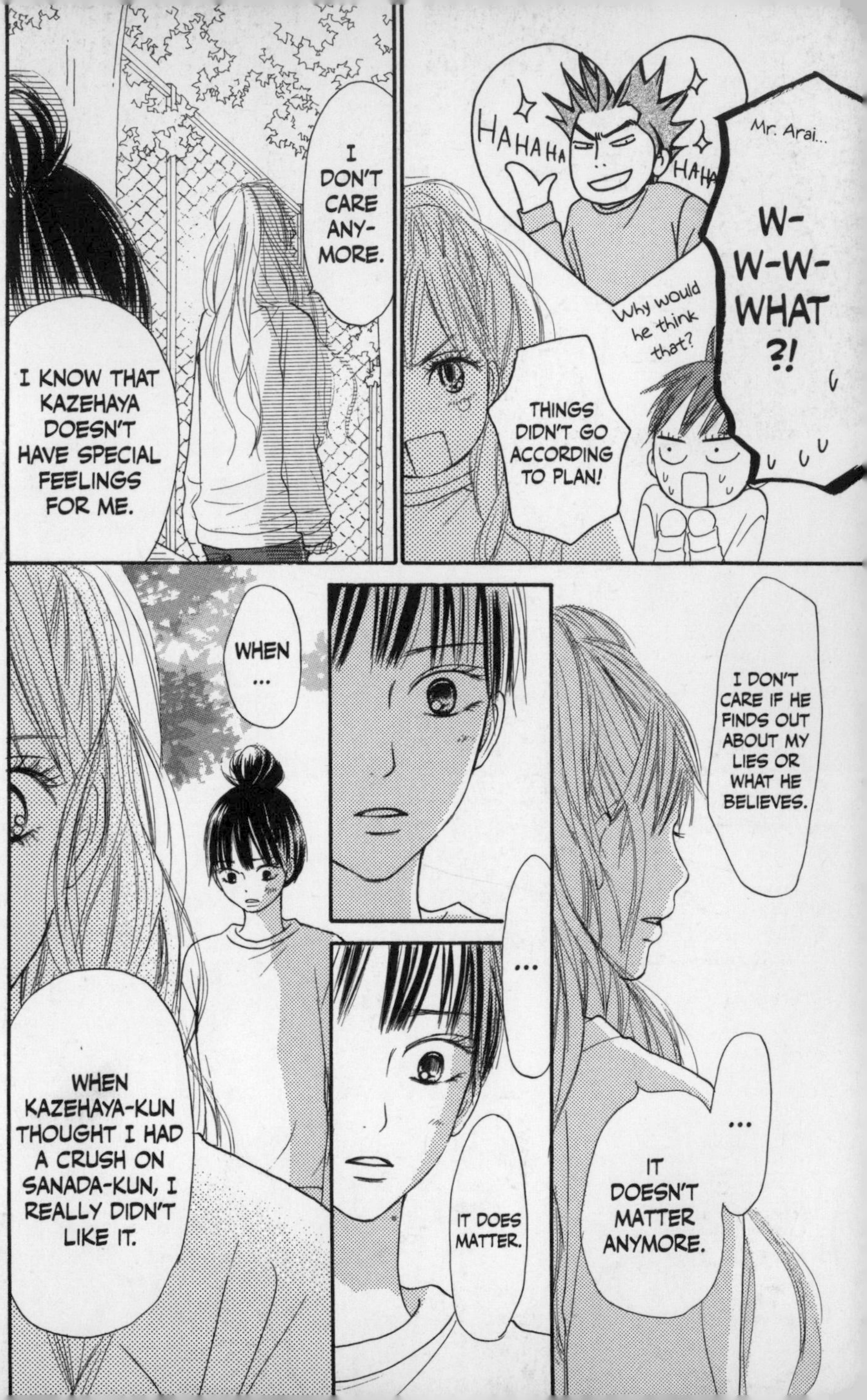
Mr. Arai...
W-W-W-WHAT?!
HAHAHA HAHA
Why would he think that?
THINGS DIDN'T GO ACCORDING TO PLAN!
I DON'T CARE ANYMORE.
I KNOW THAT KAZEHAYA DOESN'T HAVE SPECIAL FEELINGS FOR ME.
I DON'T CARE IF HE FINDS OUT ABOUT MY LIES OR WHAT HE BELIEVES.
...
...
IT DOESN'T MATTER ANYMORE.
IT DOES MATTER.
WHEN ...
WHEN KAZEHAYA-KUN THOUGHT I HAD A CRUSH ON SANADA-KUN, I REALLY DIDN'T LIKE IT.

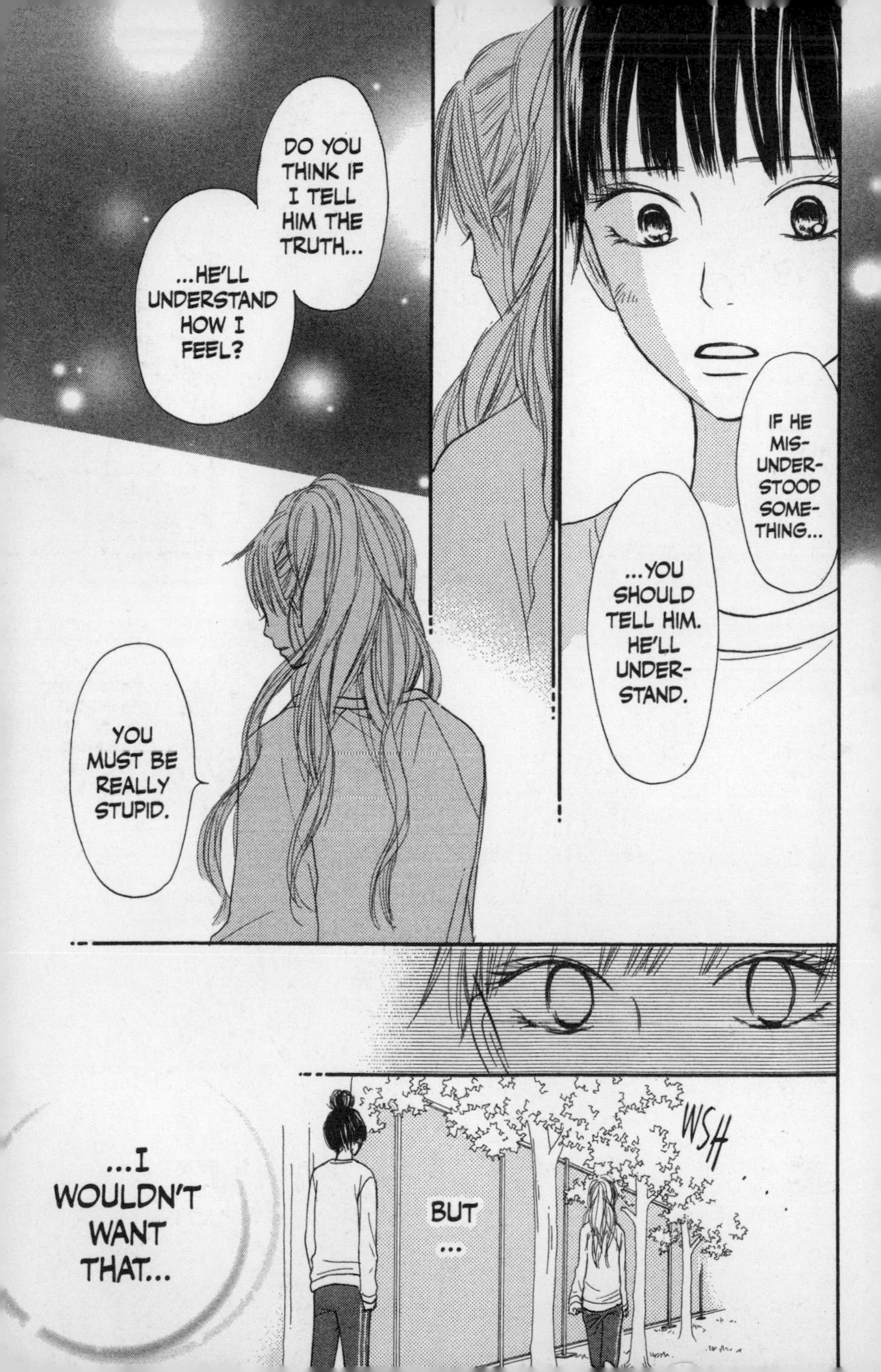
IF HE MIS-UNDER-STOOD SOME-THING...
...YOU SHOULD TELL HIM. HE'LL UNDER-STAND.
DO YOU THINK IF I TELL HIM THE TRUTH...
...HE'LL UNDERSTAND HOW I FEEL?
YOU MUST BE REALLY STUPID.
WSH
BUT...
...I WOULDN'T WANT THAT...

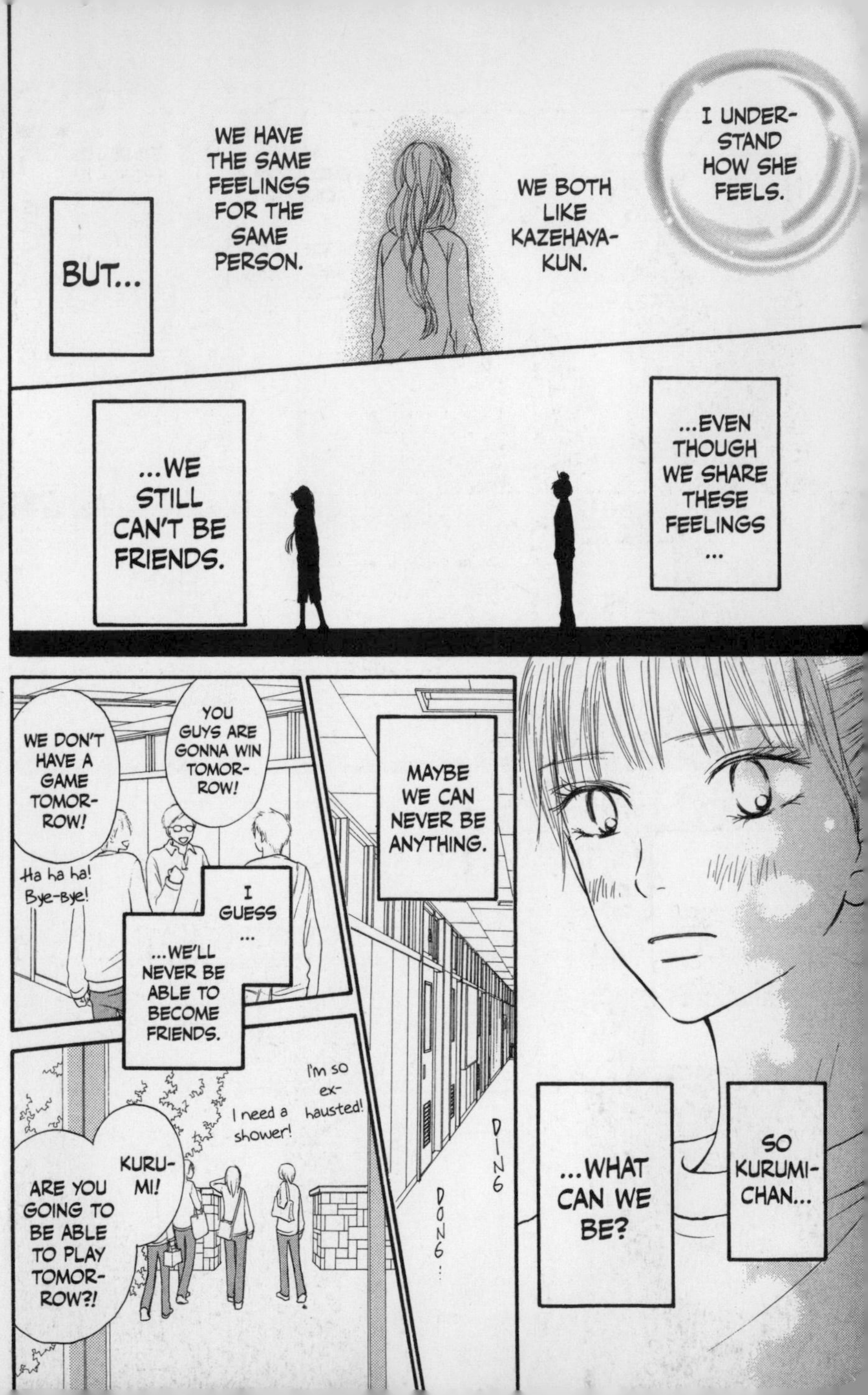
I UNDER-STAND HOW SHE FEELS.
WE BOTH LIKE KAZEHAYA-KUN.
WE HAVE THE SAME FEELINGS FOR THE SAME PERSON.
BUT...
...EVEN THOUGH WE SHARE THESE FEELINGS ...
...WE STILL CAN'T BE FRIENDS.
SO KURUMI-CHAN...
...WHAT CAN WE BE?
MAYBE WE CAN NEVER BE ANYTHING.
DING
DONG...
YOU GUYS ARE GONNA WIN TOMOR-ROW!
WE DON'T HAVE A GAME TOMOR-ROW!
Ha ha ha! Bye-bye!
I GUESS ...
...WE'LL NEVER BE ABLE TO BECOME FRIENDS.
I'm so ex-hausted!
I need a shower!
KURU-MI!
ARE YOU GOING TO BE ABLE TO PLAY TOMOR-ROW?!

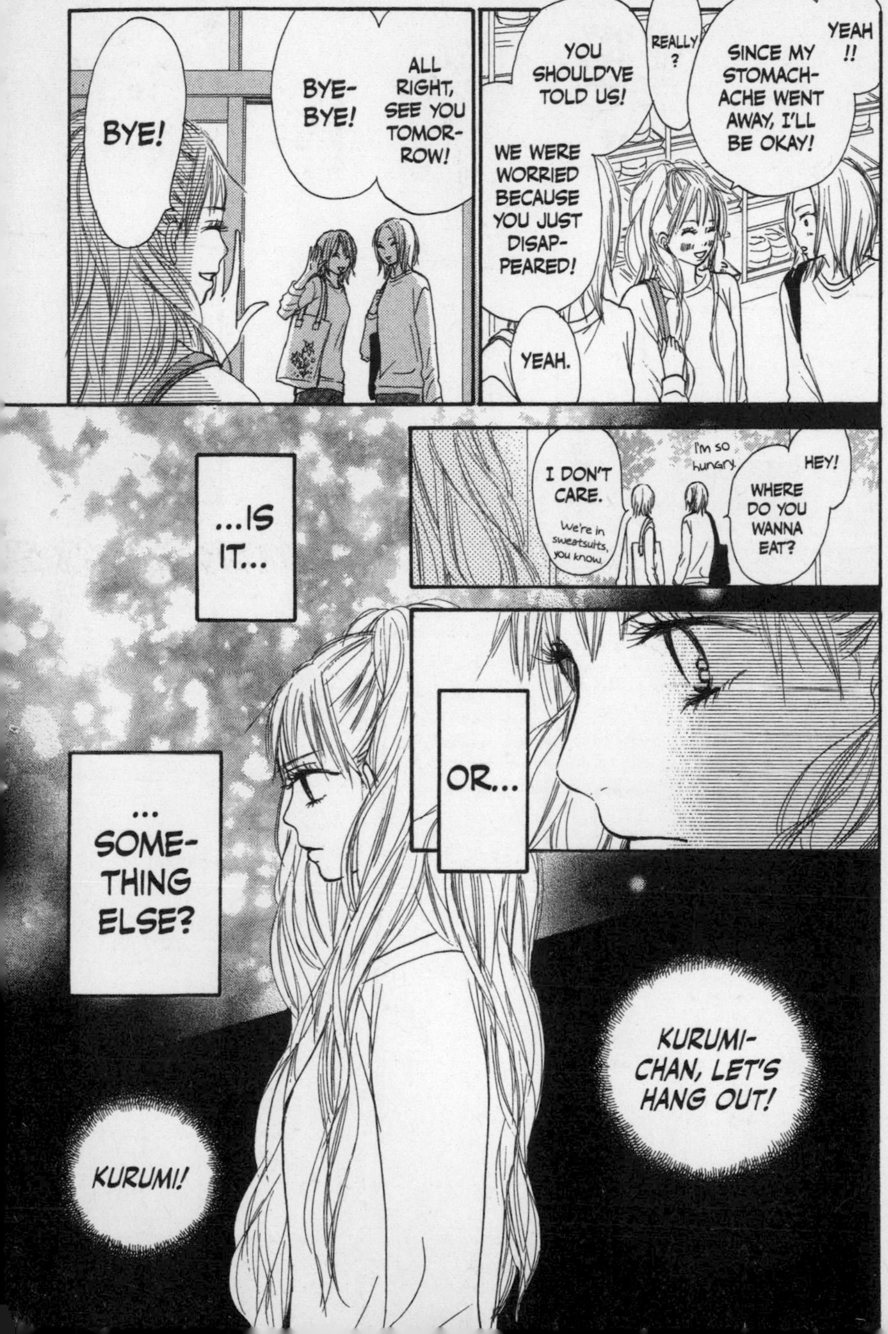
YEAH !!
SINCE MY STOMACH-ACHE WENT AWAY, I'LL BE OKAY!
REALLY ?
YOU SHOULD'VE TOLD US!
WE WERE WORRIED BECAUSE YOU JUST DISAP-PEARED!
YEAH.
ALL RIGHT, SEE YOU TOMOR-ROW!
BYE-BYE!
BYE!
HEY!
WHERE DO YOU WANNA EAT?
I'm so hungry.
I DON'T CARE.
We're in sweatsuits, you know.
...IS IT...
OR...
... SOME-THING ELSE?
KURUMI-CHAN, LET'S HANG OUT!
KURUMI!

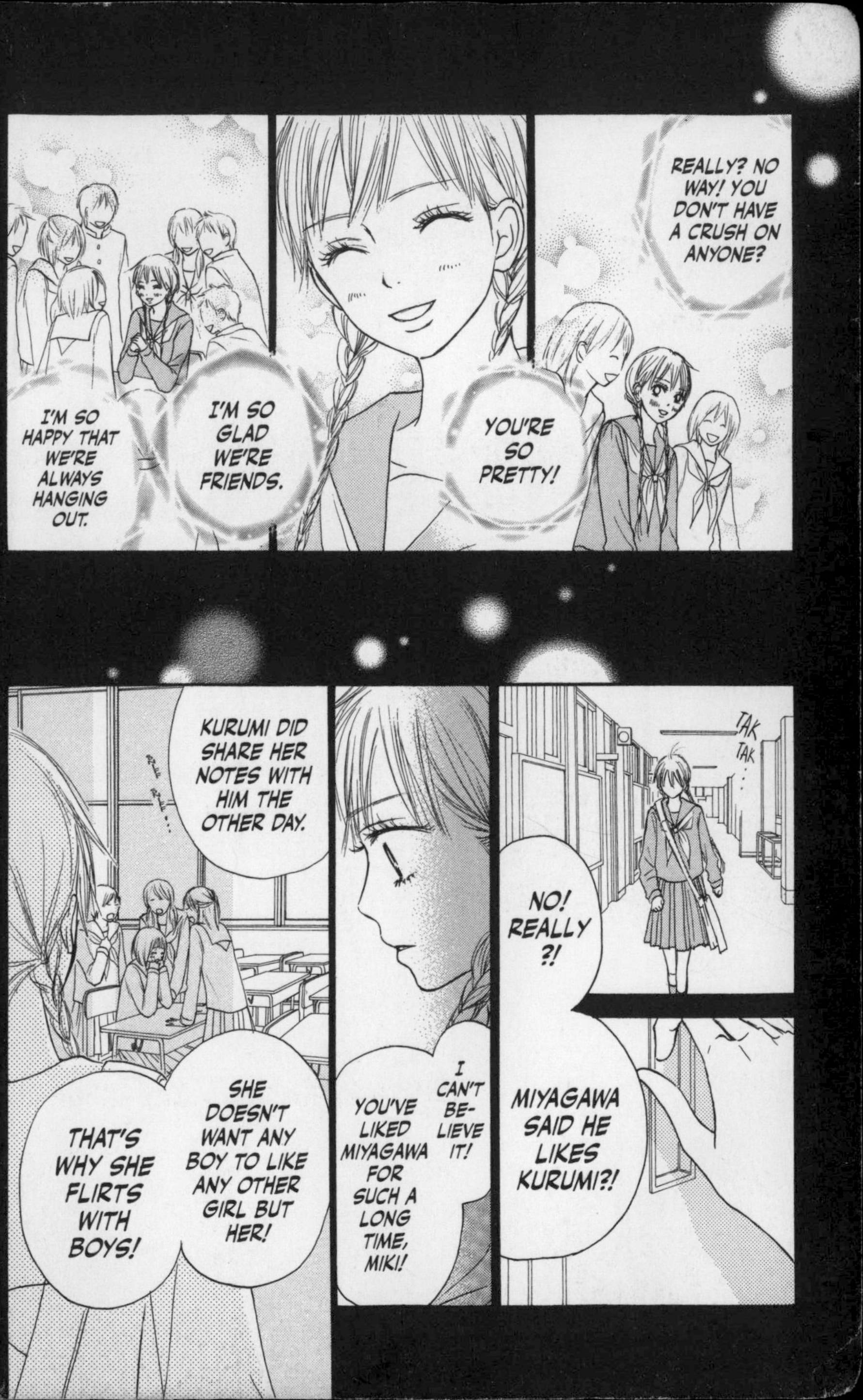
REALLY? NO WAY! YOU DON'T HAVE A CRUSH ON ANYONE?
YOU'RE SO PRETTY!
I'M SO GLAD WE'RE FRIENDS.
I'M SO HAPPY THAT WE'RE ALWAYS HANGING OUT.
TAK TAK...
NO! REALLY?!
MIYAGAWA SAID HE LIKES KURUMI?!
I CAN'T BE-LIEVE IT!
YOU'VE LIKED MIYAGAWA FOR SUCH A LONG TIME, MIKI!
KURUMI DID SHARE HER NOTES WITH HIM THE OTHER DAY.
SHE DOESN'T WANT ANY BOY TO LIKE ANY OTHER GIRL BUT HER!
THAT'S WHY SHE FLIRTS WITH BOYS!

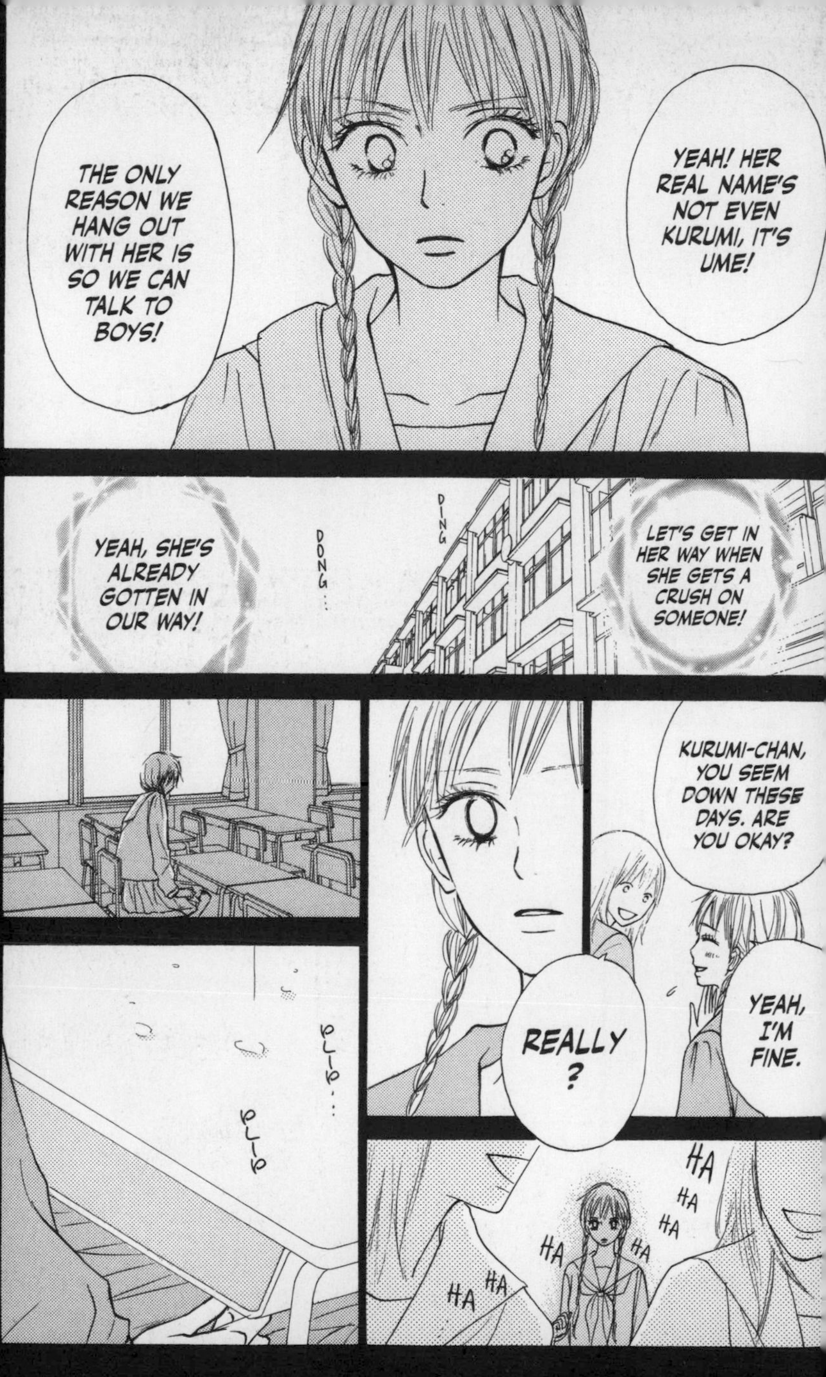

YEAH! HER REAL NAME'S NOT EVEN KURUMI, IT'S UME!
THE ONLY REASON WE HANG OUT WITH HER IS SO WE CAN TALK TO BOYS!
LET'S GET IN HER WAY WHEN SHE GETS A CRUSH ON SOMEONE!
DING
DONG...
YEAH, SHE'S ALREADY GOTTEN IN OUR WAY!
KURUMI-CHAN, YOU SEEM DOWN THESE DAYS. ARE YOU OKAY?
YEAH, I'M FINE.
REALLY?
HA HA HA HA HA HA HA HA
PLIP...
PLIP

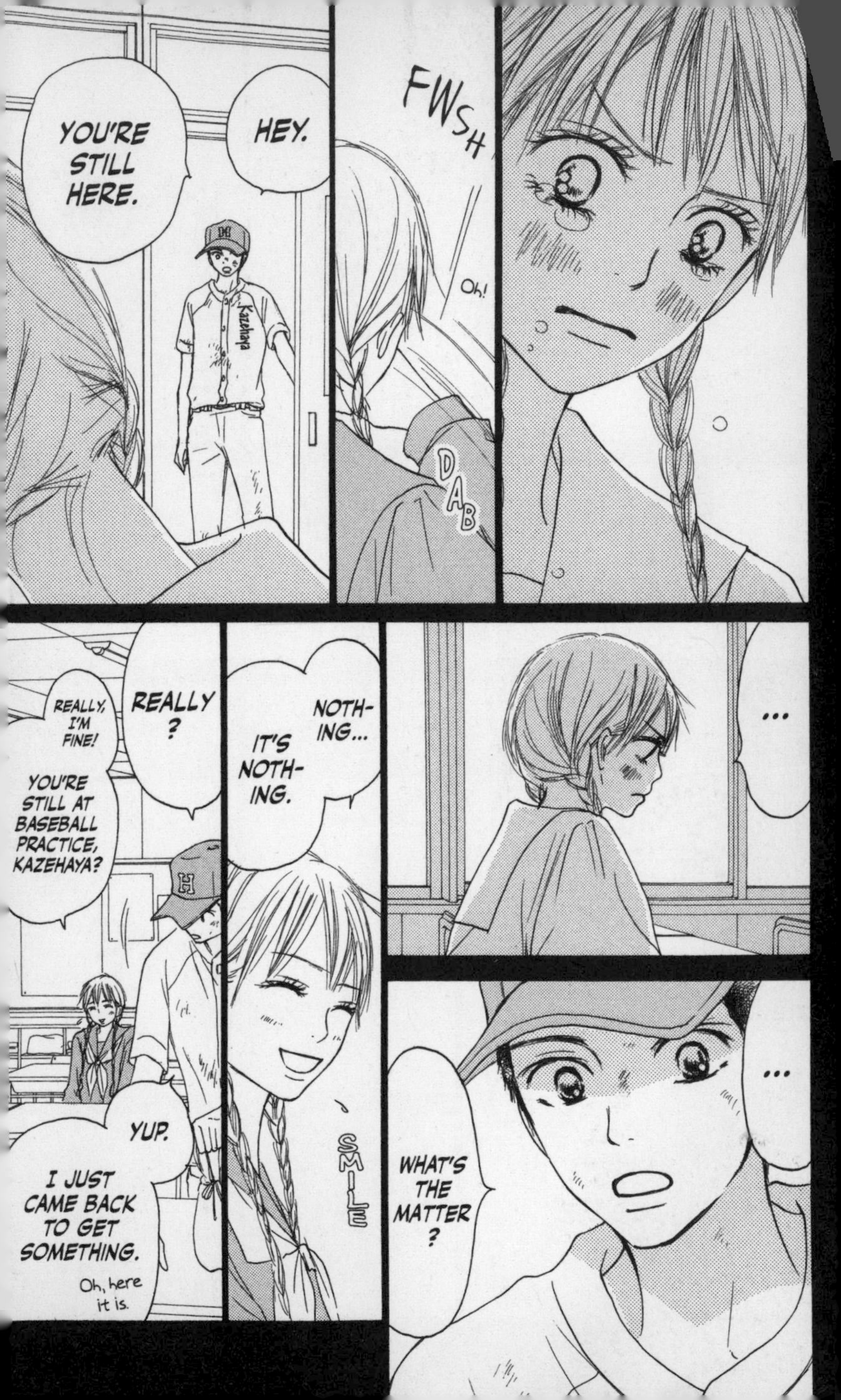
FWSH
Oh!
DAB
HEY.
YOU'RE STILL HERE.
Kazehaya
...
...
WHAT'S THE MATTER?
NOTHING...
IT'S NOTHING.
SMILE
REALLY?
REALLY, I'M FINE!
YOU'RE STILL AT BASEBALL PRACTICE, KAZEHAYA?
YUP.
I JUST CAME BACK TO GET SOMETHING.
Oh, here it is.

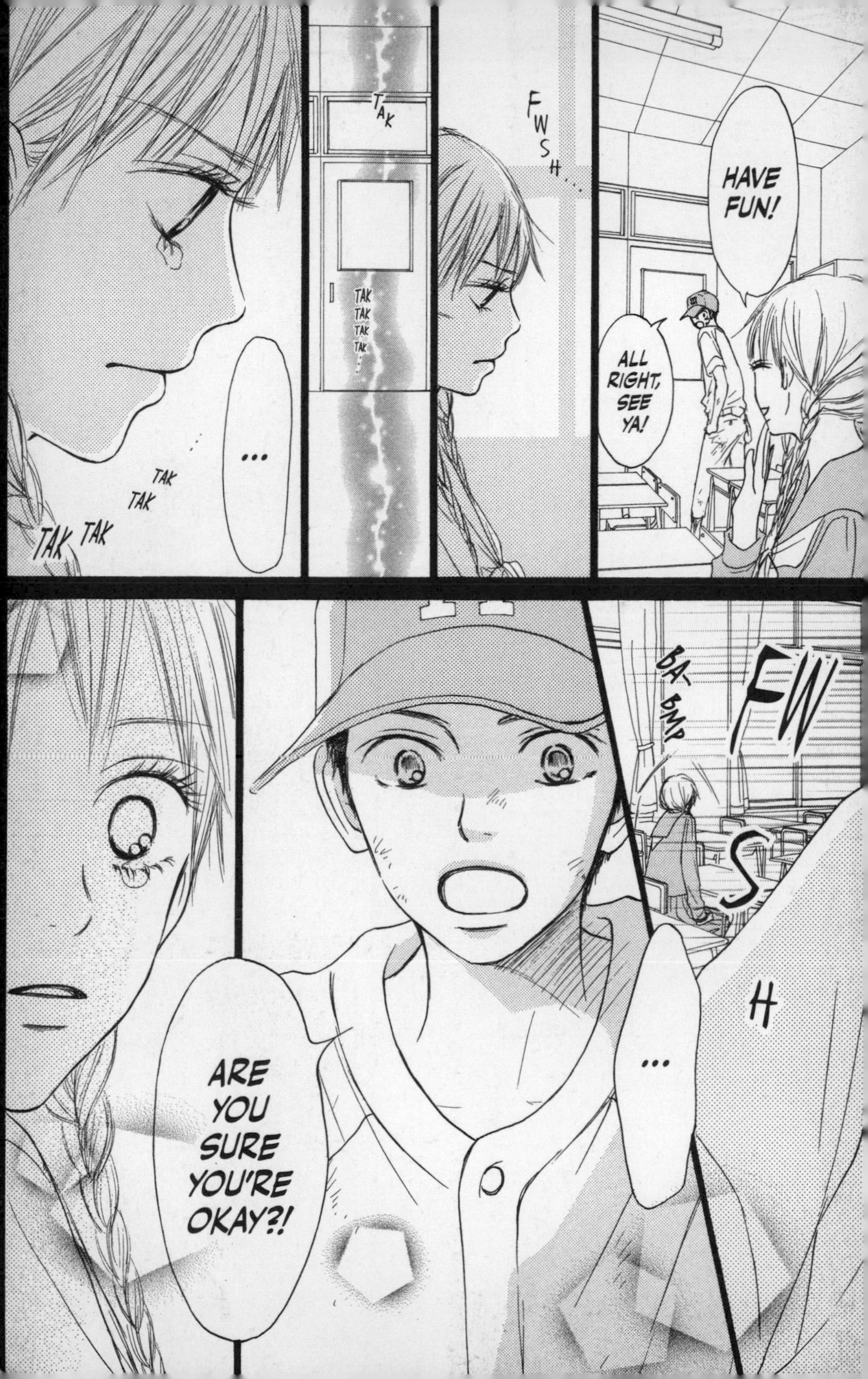
HAVE FUN!
ALL RIGHT, SEE YA!
FWSH...
TAK
TAK TAK TAK TAK...
...
...
TAK TAK TAK TAK
BA-BMP
FWSH
...
ARE YOU SURE YOU'RE OKAY?!

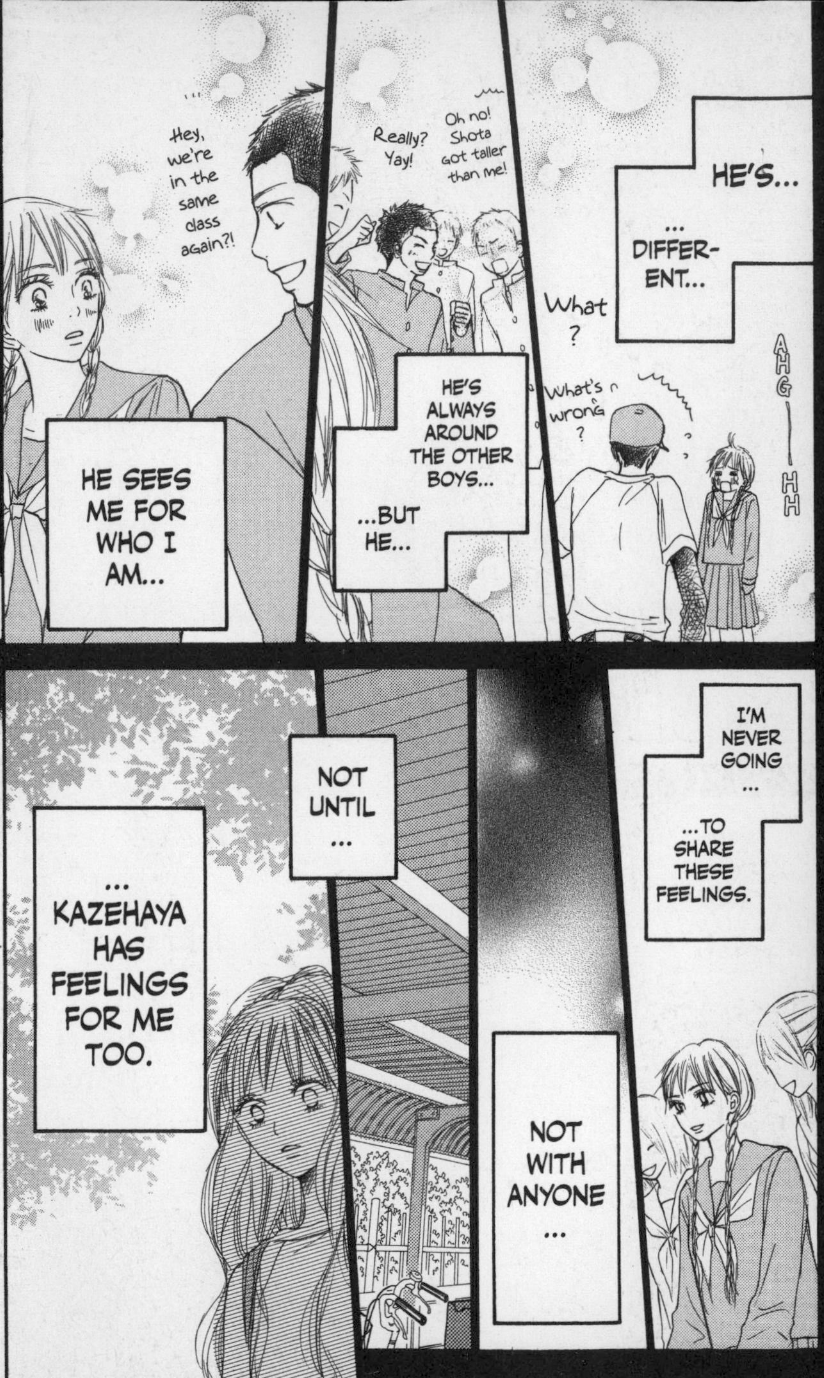
HE'S...
... DIFFER-ENT...
AHG—HH
What?
What's wrong?
Oh no! Shota got taller than me!
Really? Yay!
HE'S ALWAYS AROUND THE OTHER BOYS...
...BUT HE...
...
Hey, we're in the same class again?!
HE SEES ME FOR WHO I AM...
I'M NEVER GOING ...
...TO SHARE THESE FEELINGS.
NOT WITH ANYONE ...
NOT UNTIL ...
... KAZEHAYA HAS FEELINGS FOR ME TOO.

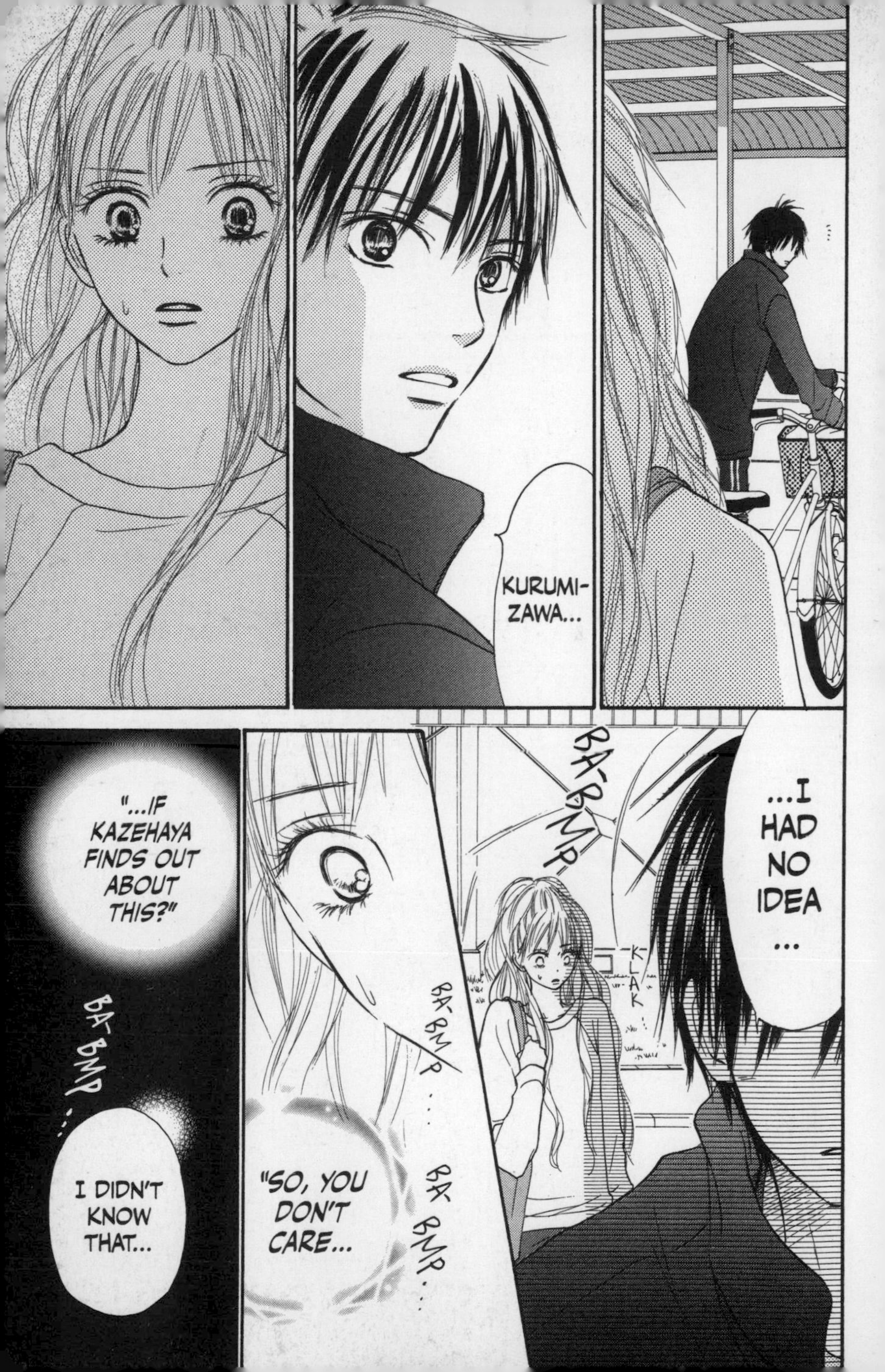
KURUMI-
ZAWA...
...I HAD NO IDEA ...
BA-BMP
KLAK
BA-BMP...
BA-BMP...
"SO, YOU DON'T CARE...
"...IF KAZEHAYA FINDS OUT ABOUT THIS?"
BA-BMP...
I DIDN'T KNOW THAT...

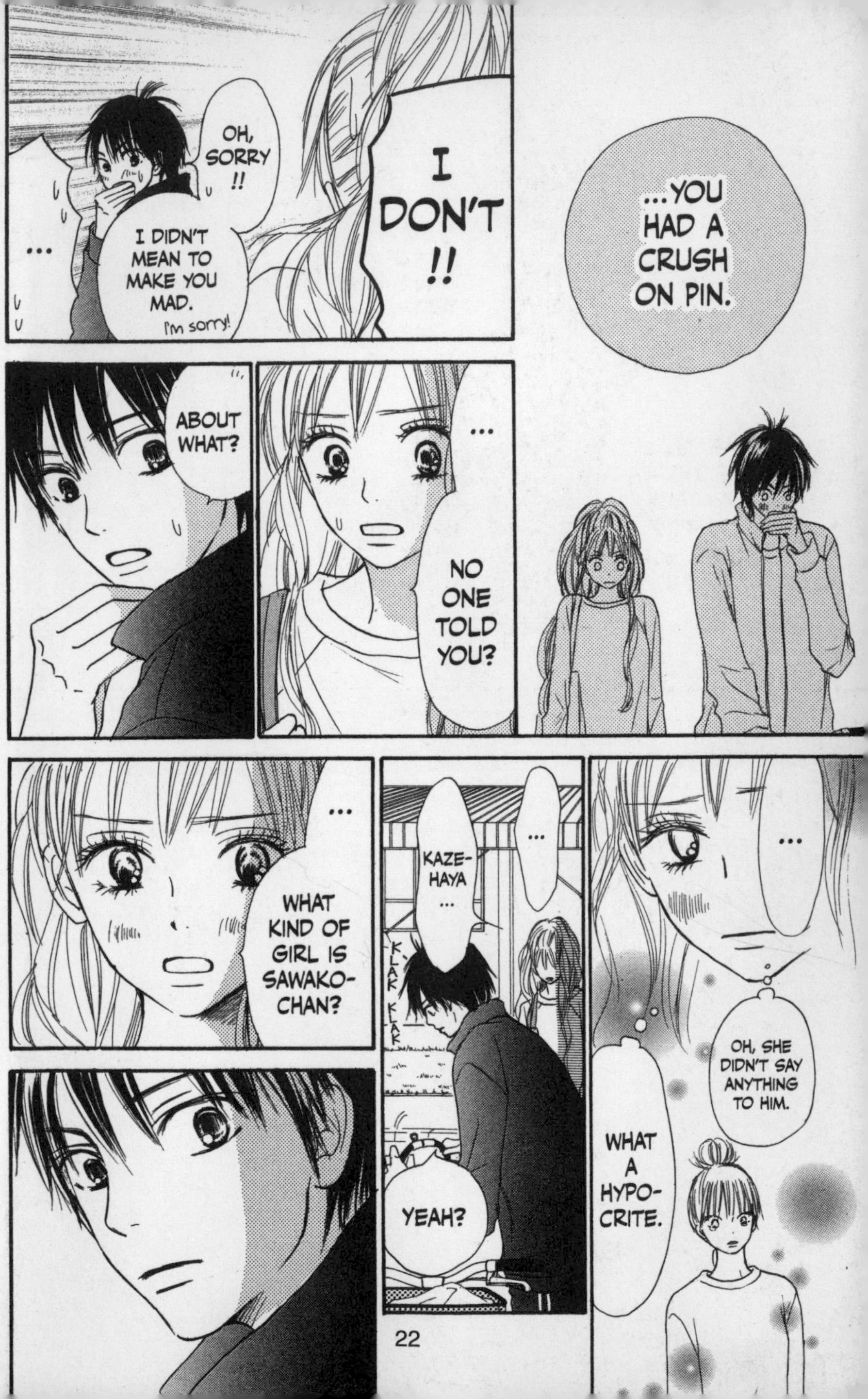
...YOU HAD A CRUSH ON PIN.
I DON'T!!
OH, SORRY!!
I DIDN'T MEAN TO MAKE YOU MAD.
I'm sorry!
...
...
NO ONE TOLD YOU?
ABOUT WHAT?
...
OH, SHE DIDN'T SAY ANYTHING TO HIM.
WHAT A HYPOCRITE.
...
KAZEHAYA...
KLAK KLAK
YEAH?
...
WHAT KIND OF GIRL IS SAWAKO-CHAN?

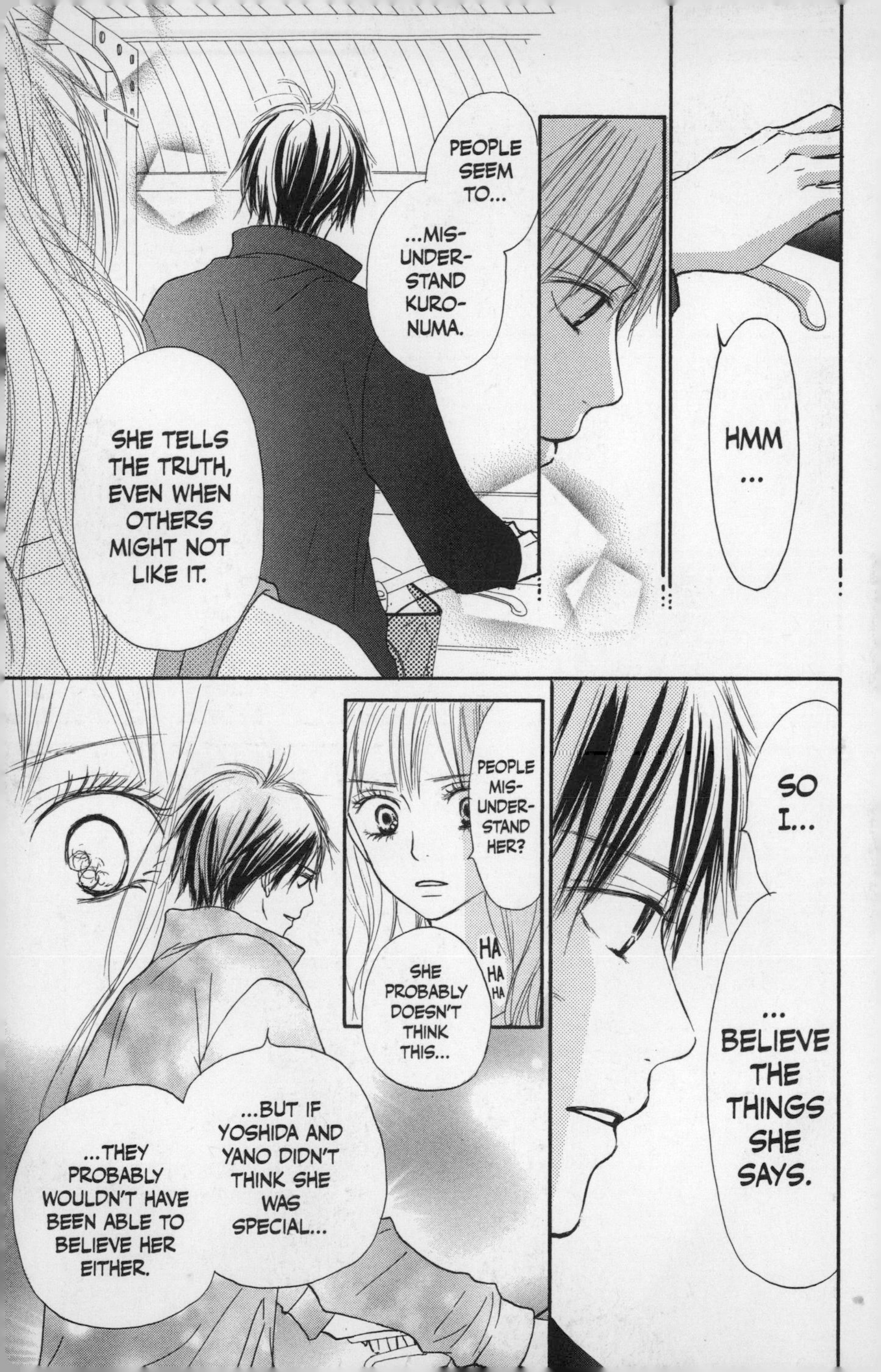
HMM ...
PEOPLE SEEM TO...
...MIS-UNDER-STAND KURO-NUMA.
SHE TELLS THE TRUTH, EVEN WHEN OTHERS MIGHT NOT LIKE IT.
SO I...
... BELIEVE THE THINGS SHE SAYS.
PEOPLE MIS-UNDER-STAND HER?
HA HA HA
SHE PROBABLY DOESN'T THINK THIS...
...BUT IF YOSHIDA AND YANO DIDN'T THINK SHE WAS SPECIAL...
...THEY PROBABLY WOULDN'T HAVE BEEN ABLE TO BELIEVE HER EITHER.

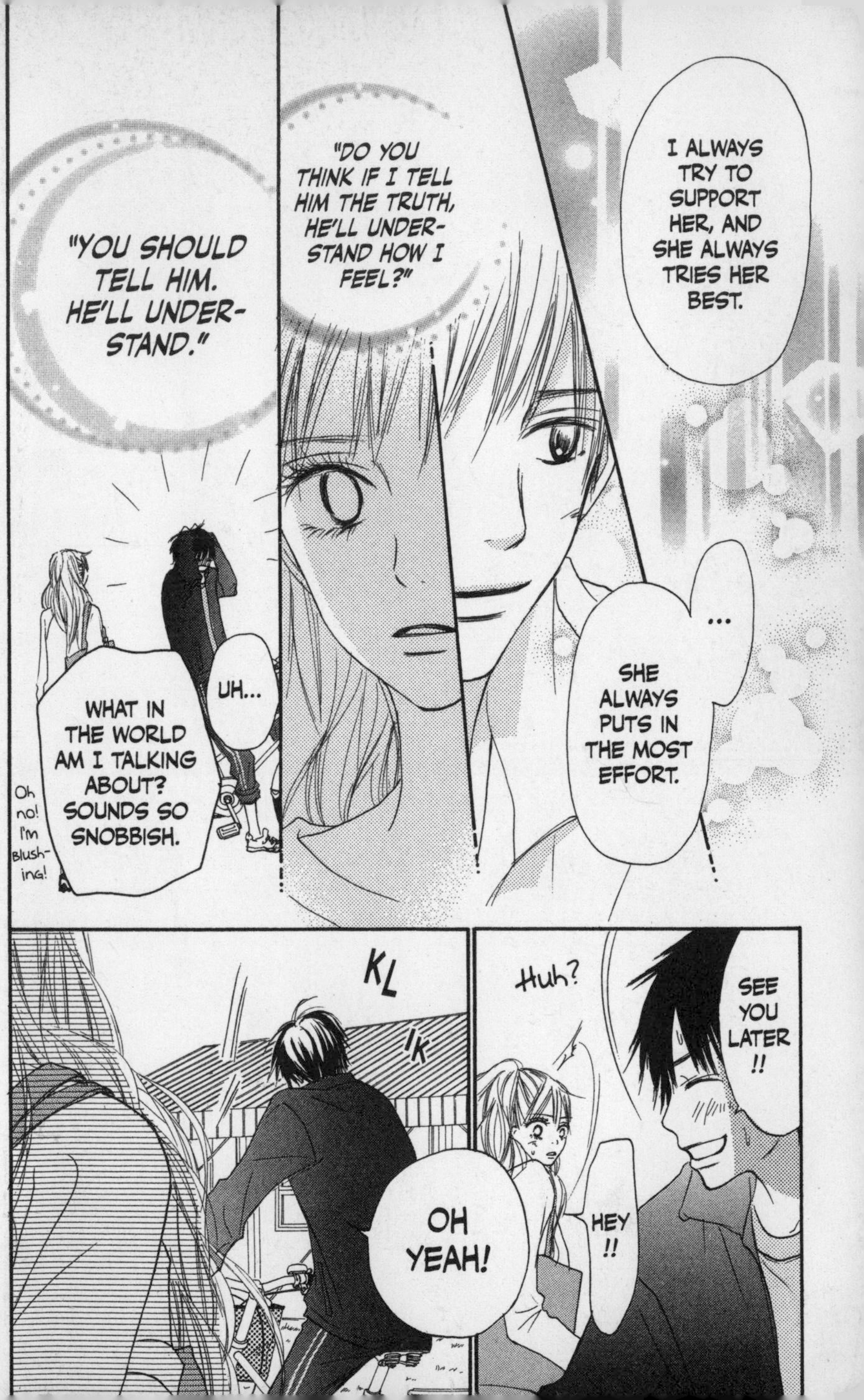
I ALWAYS TRY TO SUPPORT HER, AND SHE ALWAYS TRIES HER BEST.
...
SHE ALWAYS PUTS IN THE MOST EFFORT.
"DO YOU THINK IF I TELL HIM THE TRUTH, HE'LL UNDER-STAND HOW I FEEL?"
"YOU SHOULD TELL HIM. HE'LL UNDER-STAND."
UH...
WHAT IN THE WORLD AM I TALKING ABOUT? SOUNDS SO SNOBBISH.
Oh no! I'm Blush-ing!
SEE YOU LATER !!
Huh?
HEY !!
KLIK
OH YEAH!

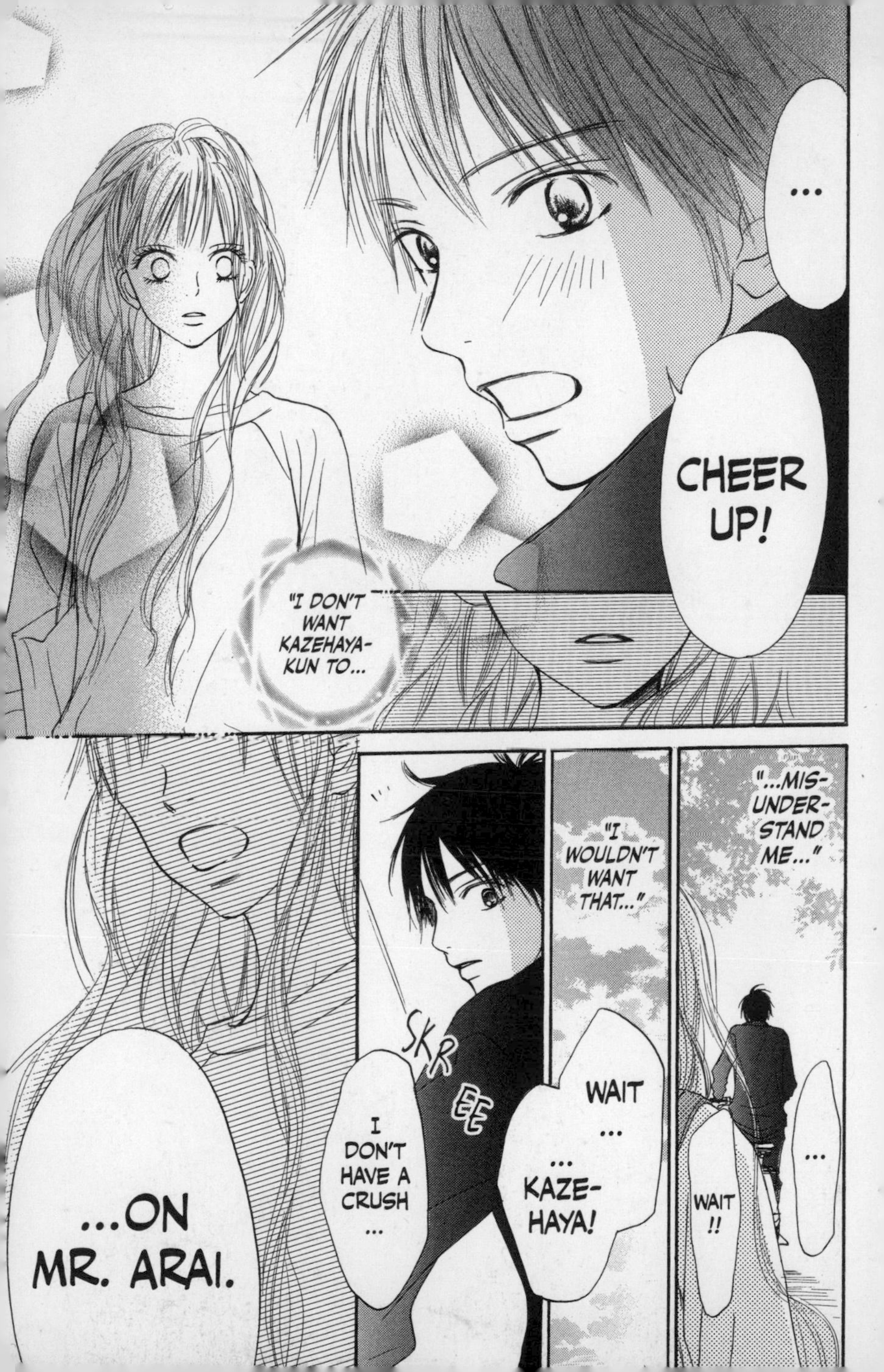
...
CHEER UP!
"I DON'T WANT KAZEHAYA-KUN TO...
"...MIS-UNDERSTAND ME..."
...
WAIT !!
"I WOULDN'T WANT THAT..."
WAIT ... ... KAZE-HAYA!
SKREEE
I DON'T HAVE A CRUSH ...
...ON MR. ARAI.

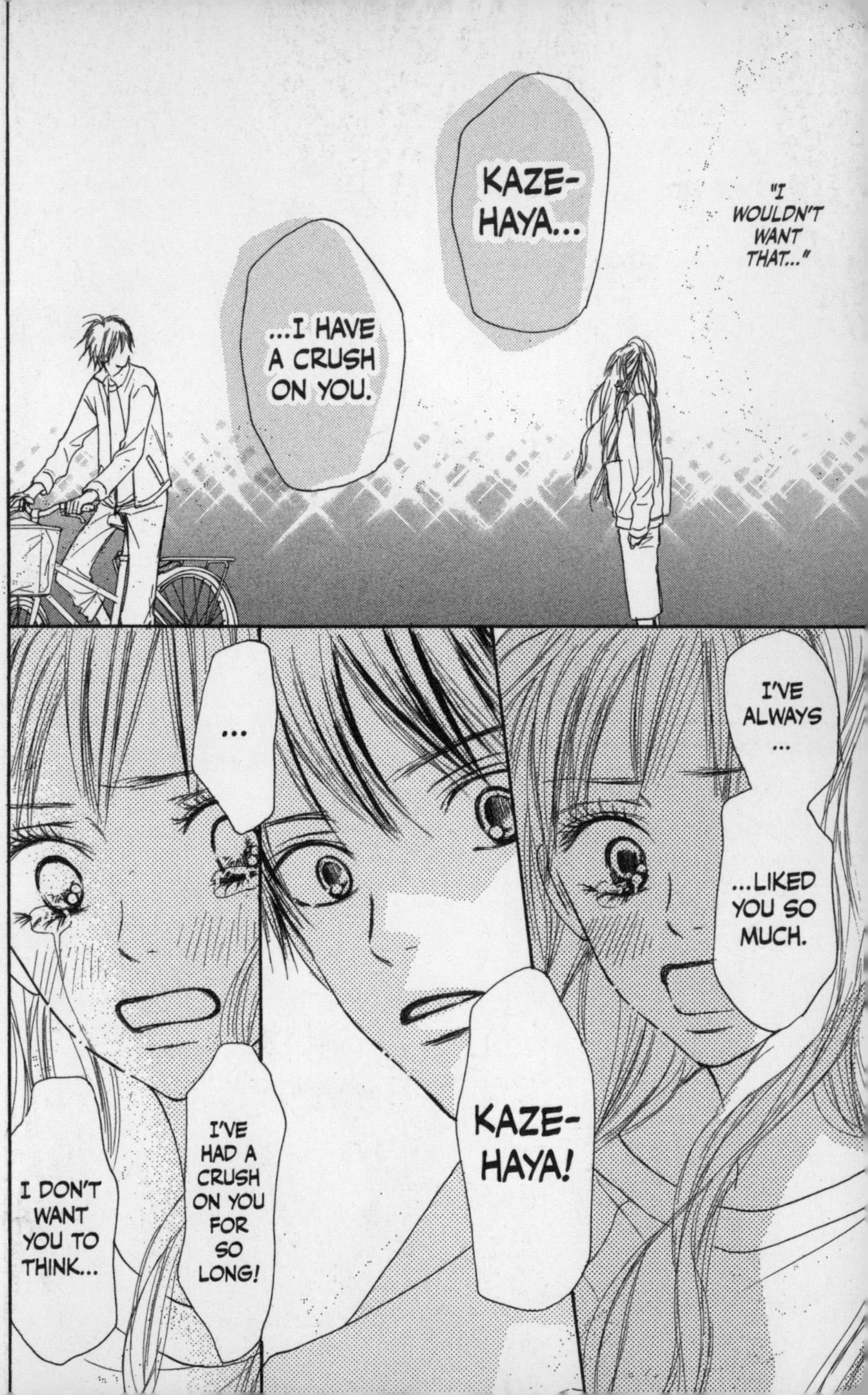
"I WOULDN'T WANT THAT..."
KAZE-HAYA...
...I HAVE A CRUSH ON YOU.
I'VE ALWAYS ...
...LIKED YOU SO MUCH.
KAZE-HAYA!
...
I'VE HAD A CRUSH ON YOU FOR SO LONG!
I DON'T WANT YOU TO THINK...

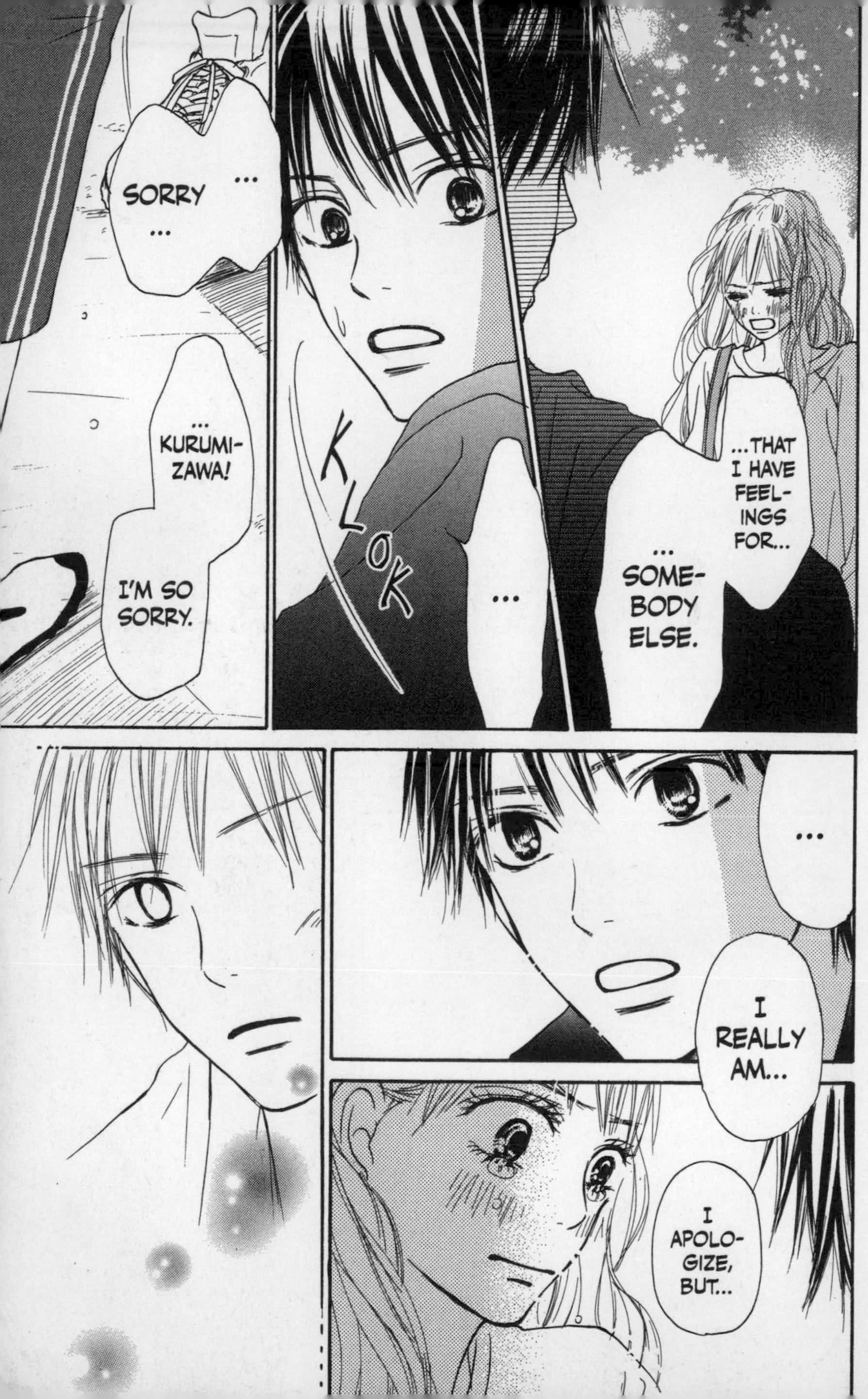
...THAT I HAVE FEELINGS FOR...
...SOMEBODY ELSE.
KLOK
...
...SORRY...
...KURUMIZAWA!
I'M SO SORRY.
...
I REALLY AM...
I APOLOGIZE, BUT...

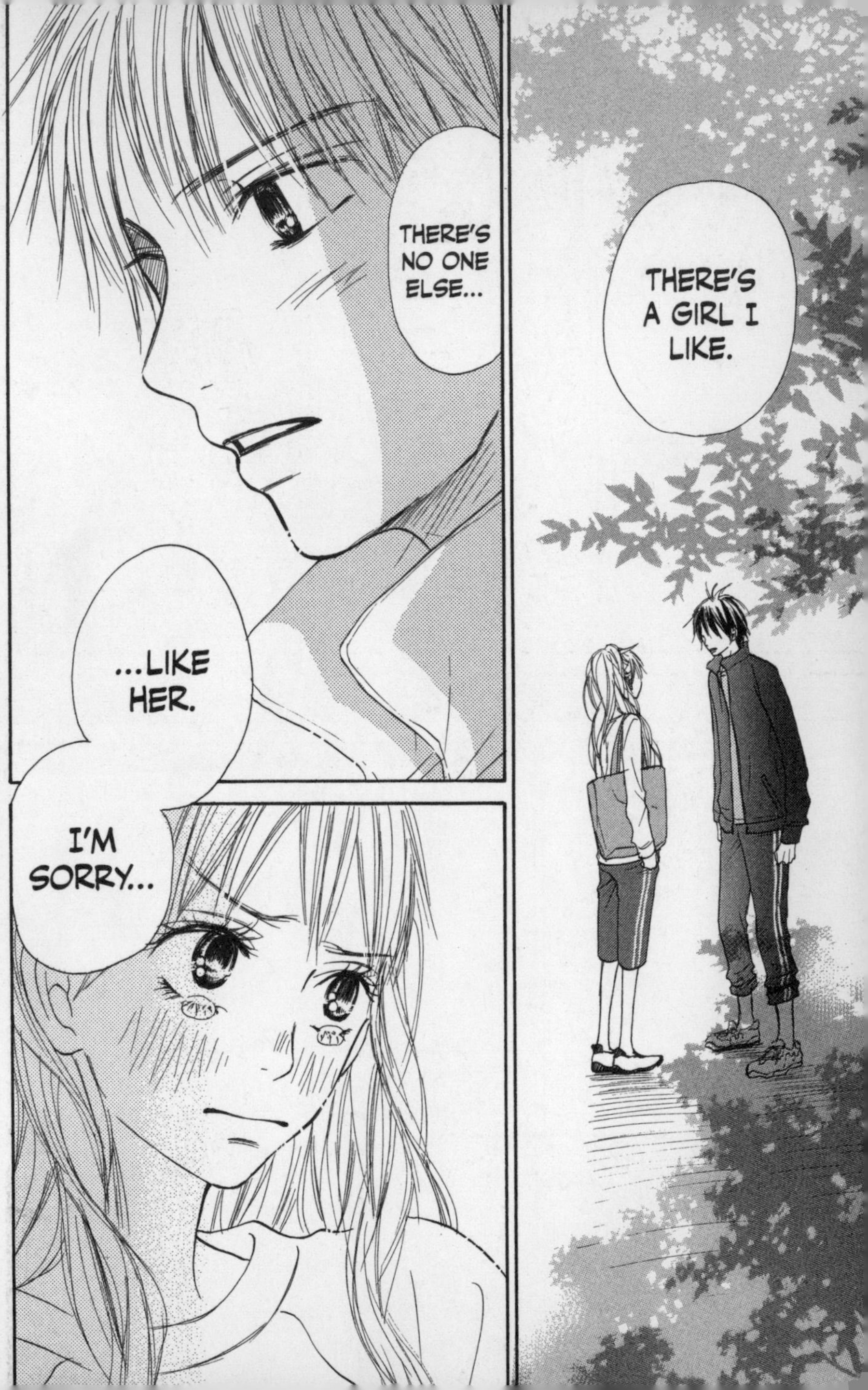
THERE'S A GIRL I LIKE.
THERE'S NO ONE ELSE...
...LIKE HER.
I'M SORRY...

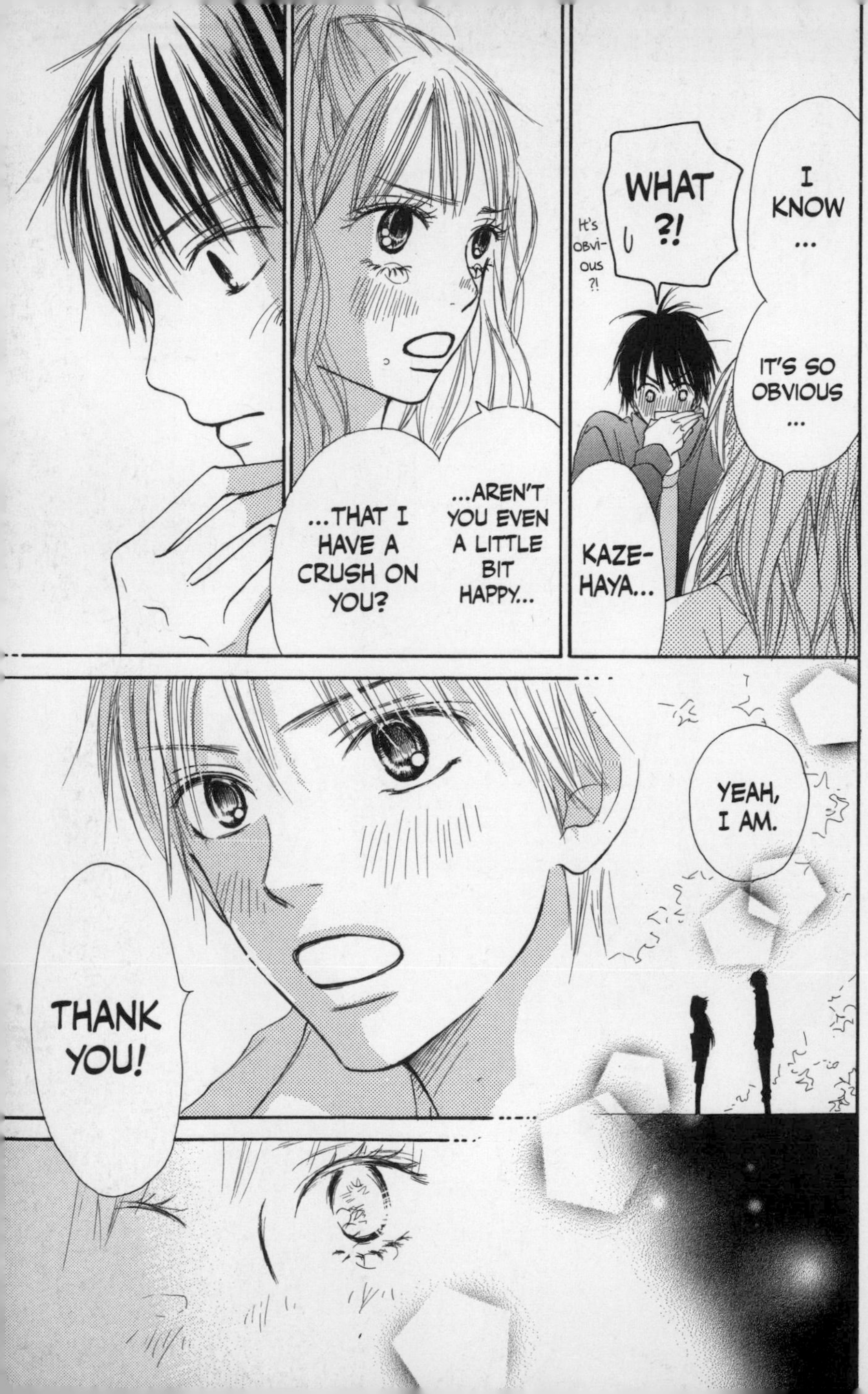
I KNOW...
IT'S SO OBVIOUS...
WHAT?!
It's obvious?!
KAZE-HAYA...
...AREN'T YOU EVEN A LITTLE BIT HAPPY...
...THAT I HAVE A CRUSH ON YOU?
YEAH, I AM.
THANK YOU!

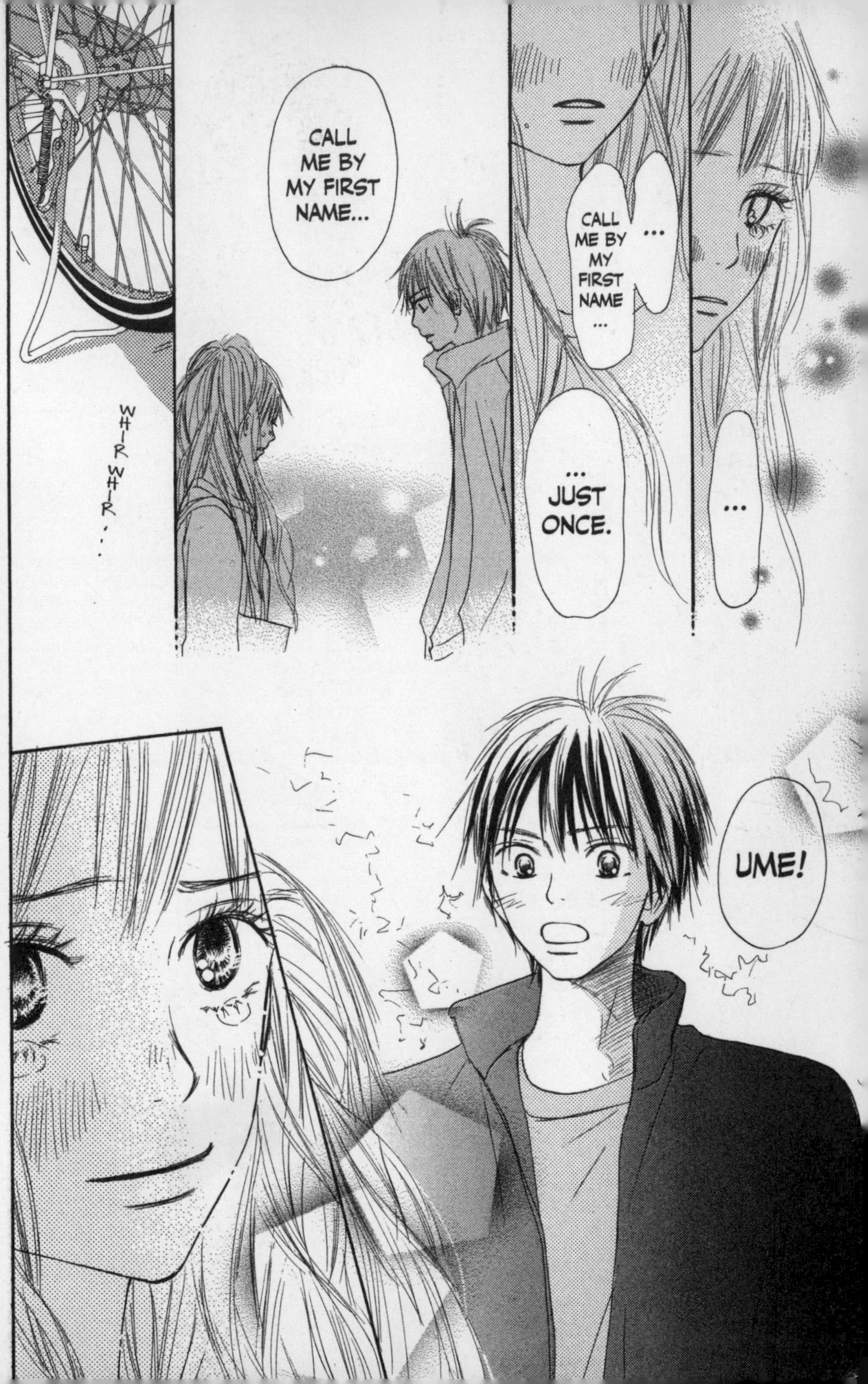
...
CALL ME BY MY FIRST NAME ...
...
... JUST ONCE.
CALL ME BY MY FIRST NAME...
WHIR WHIR..
UME!

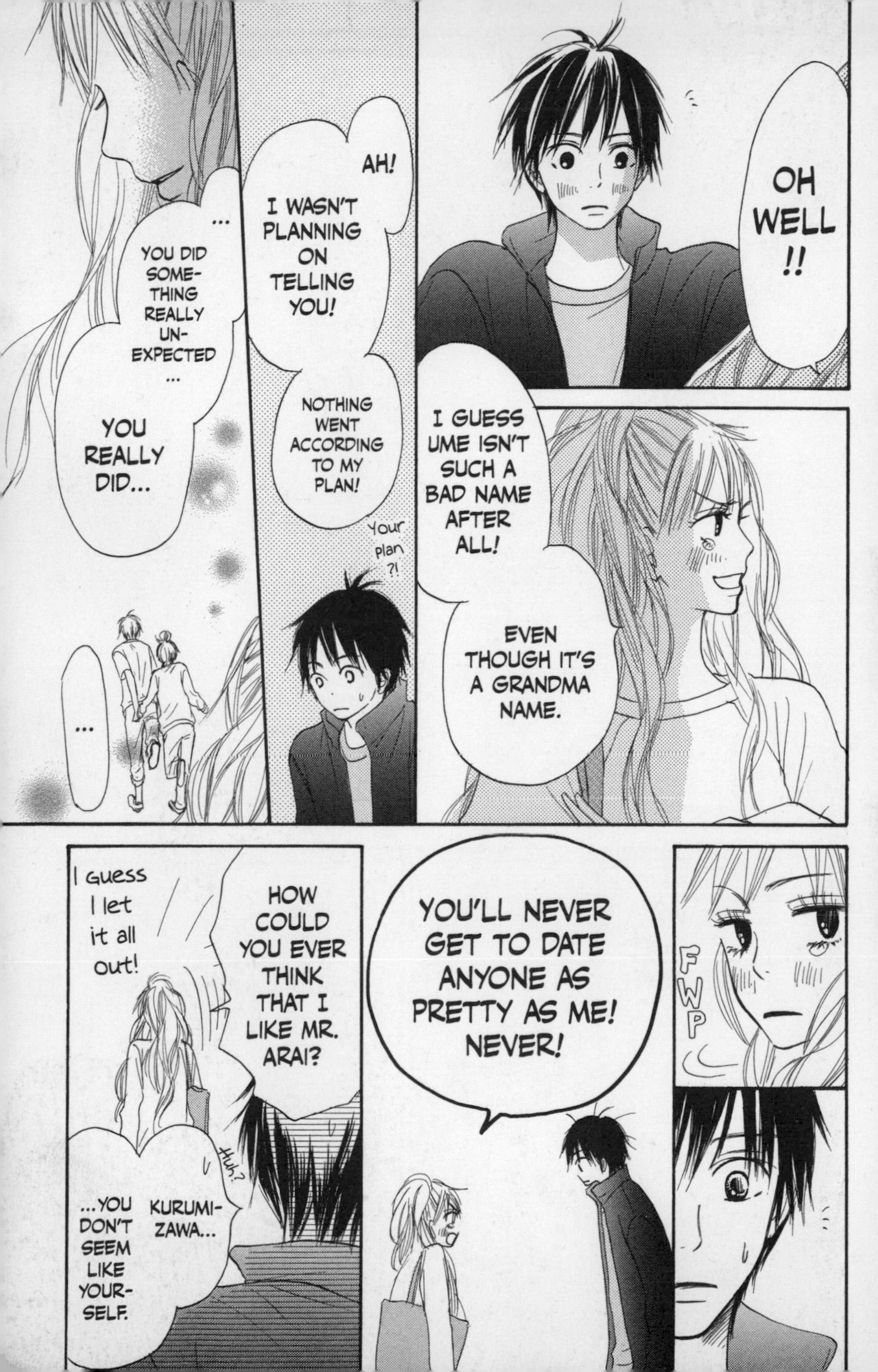
OH WELL !!
I GUESS UME ISN'T SUCH A BAD NAME AFTER ALL!
EVEN THOUGH IT'S A GRANDMA NAME.
AH!
I WASN'T PLANNING ON TELLING YOU!
NOTHING WENT ACCORDING TO MY PLAN!
Your plan ?!
...
YOU DID SOMETHING REALLY UNEXPECTED ...
YOU REALLY DID...
...
FWP
YOU'LL NEVER GET TO DATE ANYONE AS PRETTY AS ME! NEVER!
HOW COULD YOU EVER THINK THAT I LIKE MR. ARAI?
I guess I let it all out!
Huh?
KURUMIZAWA...
...YOU DON'T SEEM LIKE YOURSELF.

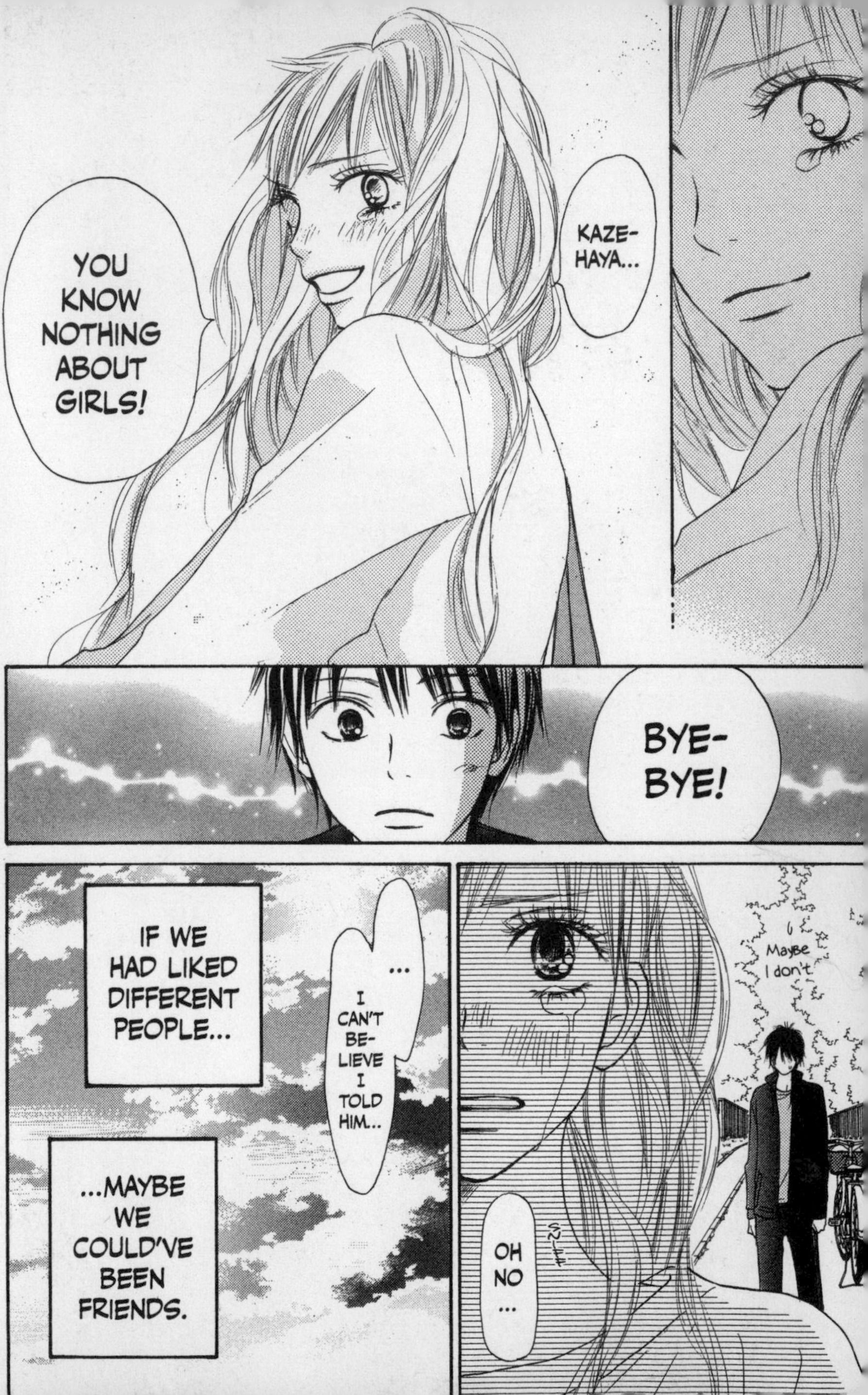
KAZE-HAYA...
YOU KNOW NOTHING ABOUT GIRLS!
BYE-BYE!
Maybe I don't
OH NO ...
... I CAN'T BE-LIEVE I TOLD HIM..
IF WE HAD LIKED DIFFERENT PEOPLE...
...MAYBE WE COULD'VE BEEN FRIENDS.

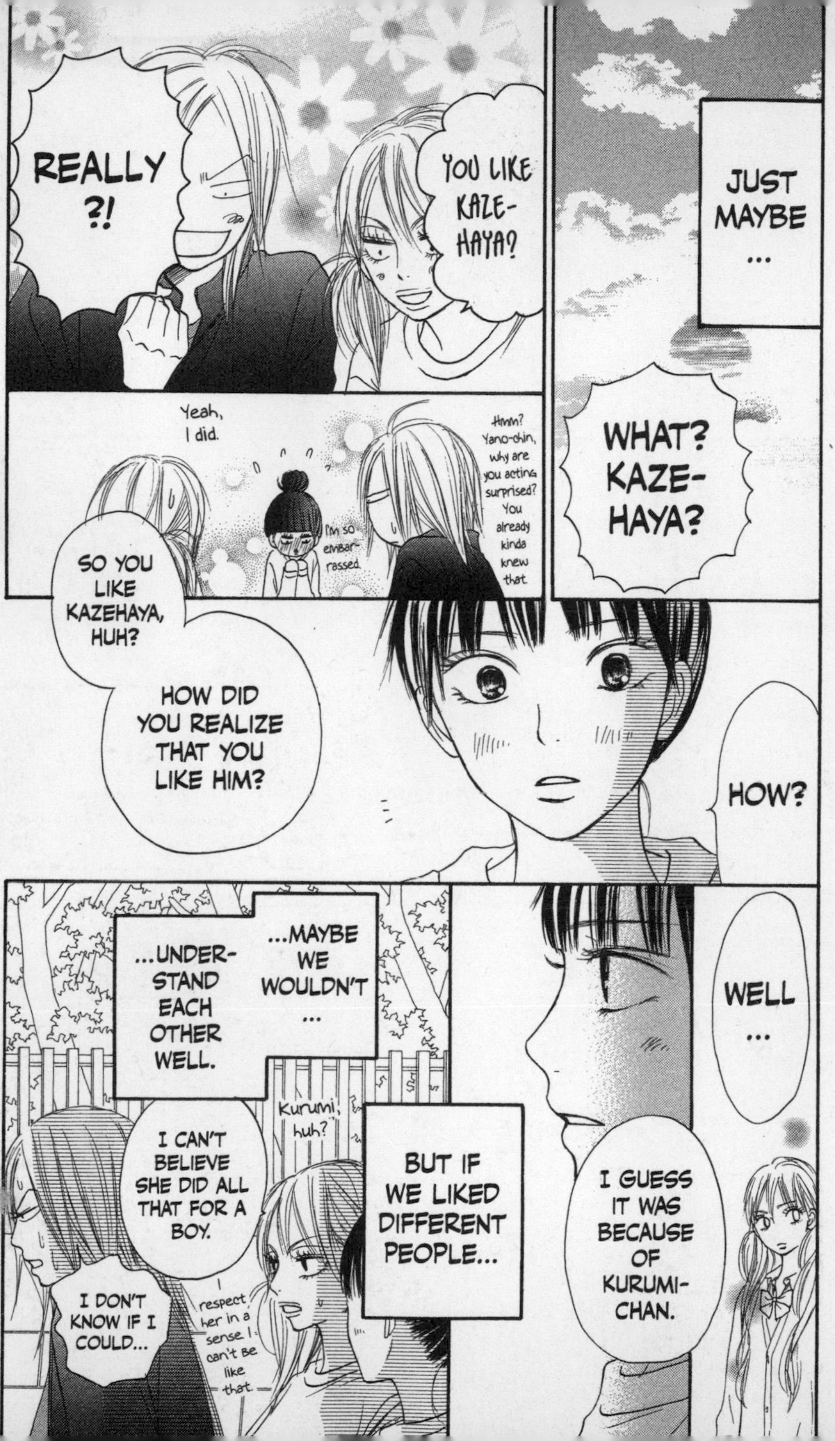
JUST MAYBE ...
WHAT? KAZE-HAYA?
YOU LIKE KAZE-HAYA?
REALLY ?!
Hmm? Yano-chin, why are you acting surprised? You already kinda knew that.
I'm so embarrassed
Yeah, I did.
SO YOU LIKE KAZEHAYA, HUH?
HOW DID YOU REALIZE THAT YOU LIKE HIM?
HOW?
WELL ...
I GUESS IT WAS BECAUSE OF KURUMI-CHAN.
BUT IF WE LIKED DIFFERENT PEOPLE...
...MAYBE WE WOULDN'T ...
...UNDER-STAND EACH OTHER WELL.
Kurumi, huh?
I CAN'T BELIEVE SHE DID ALL THAT FOR A BOY.
I respect her in a sense. I can't be like that.
I DON'T KNOW IF I COULD...

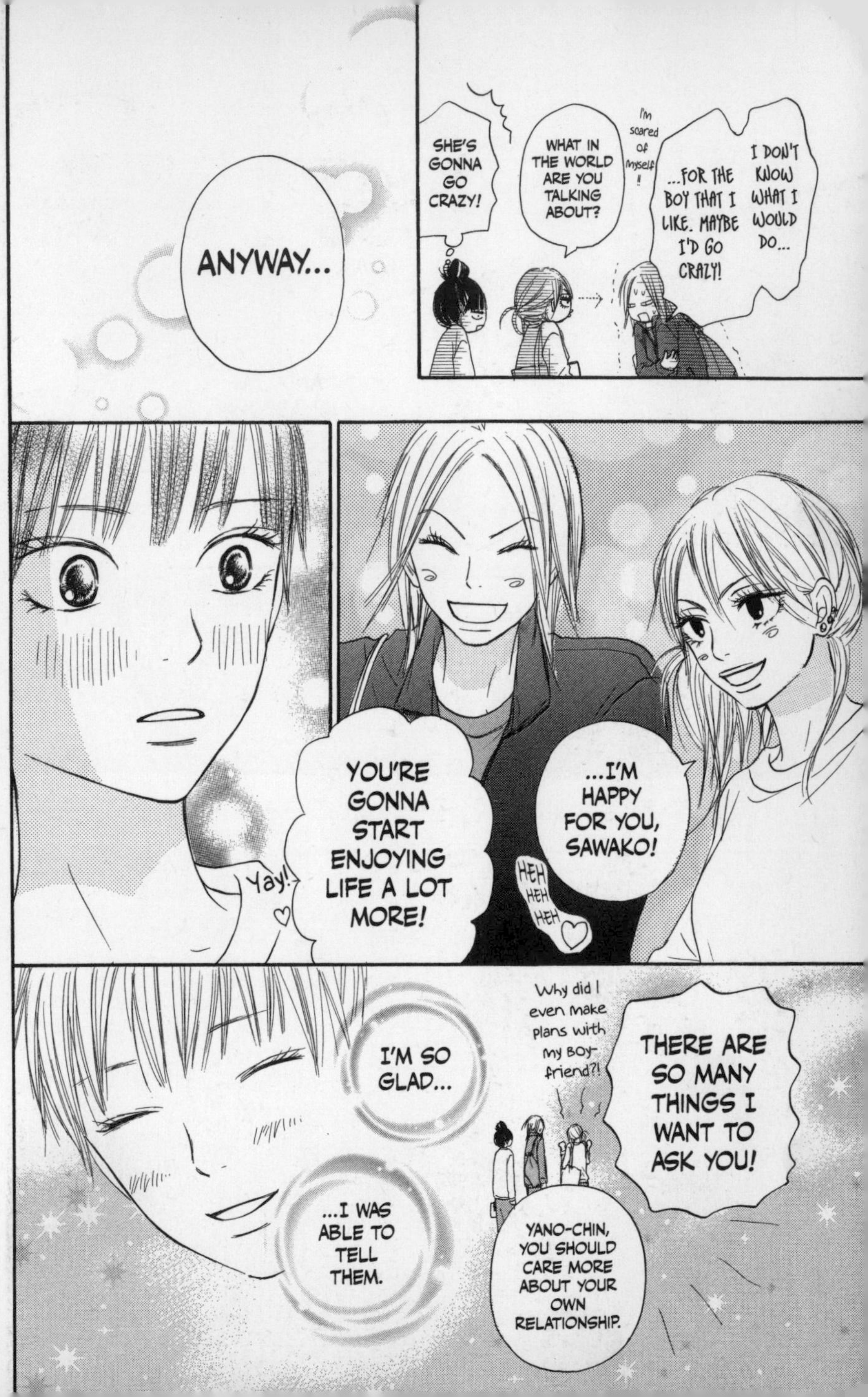
I DON'T KNOW WHAT I WOULD DO...
...FOR THE BOY THAT I LIKE. MAYBE I'D GO CRAZY!
I'm scared of myself!!
WHAT IN THE WORLD ARE YOU TALKING ABOUT?
SHE'S GONNA GO CRAZY!
ANYWAY...
...I'M HAPPY FOR YOU, SAWAKO!
HEH HEH HEH
YOU'RE GONNA START ENJOYING LIFE A LOT MORE!
Yay!
THERE ARE SO MANY THINGS I WANT TO ASK YOU!
Why did I even make plans with my boy-friend?!
YANO-CHIN, YOU SHOULD CARE MORE ABOUT YOUR OWN RELATIONSHIP.
I'M SO GLAD...
...I WAS ABLE TO TELL THEM.

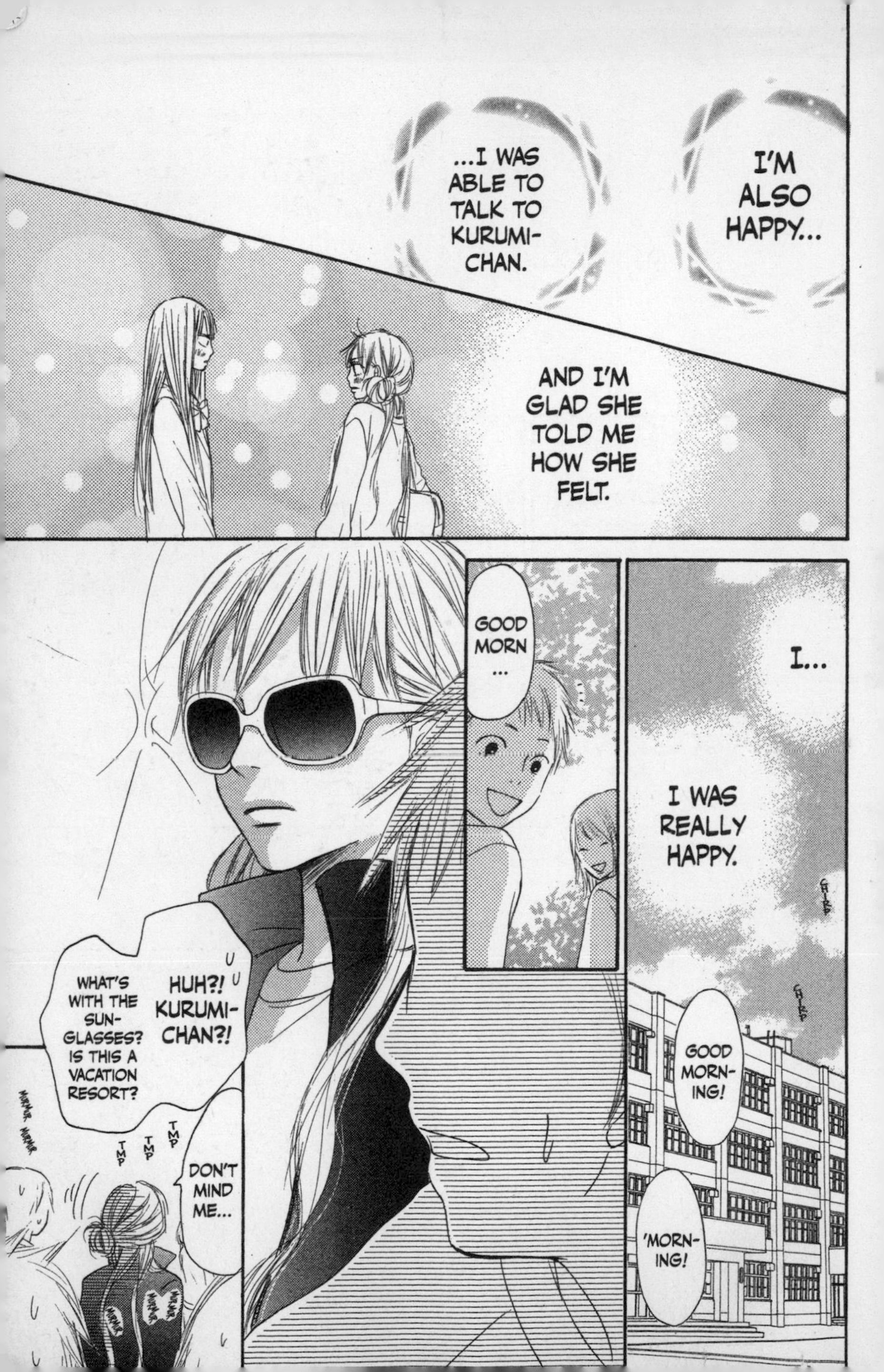
I'M ALSO HAPPY...
...I WAS ABLE TO TALK TO KURUMI-CHAN.
AND I'M GLAD SHE TOLD ME HOW SHE FELT.
I...
I WAS REALLY HAPPY.
CHIRP
CHIRP
GOOD MORNING!
'MORNING!
GOOD MORN...
HUH?! KURUMI-CHAN?!
WHAT'S WITH THE SUNGLASSES? IS THIS A VACATION RESORT?
TMP TMP TMP
MURMUR MURMUR
DON'T MIND ME...

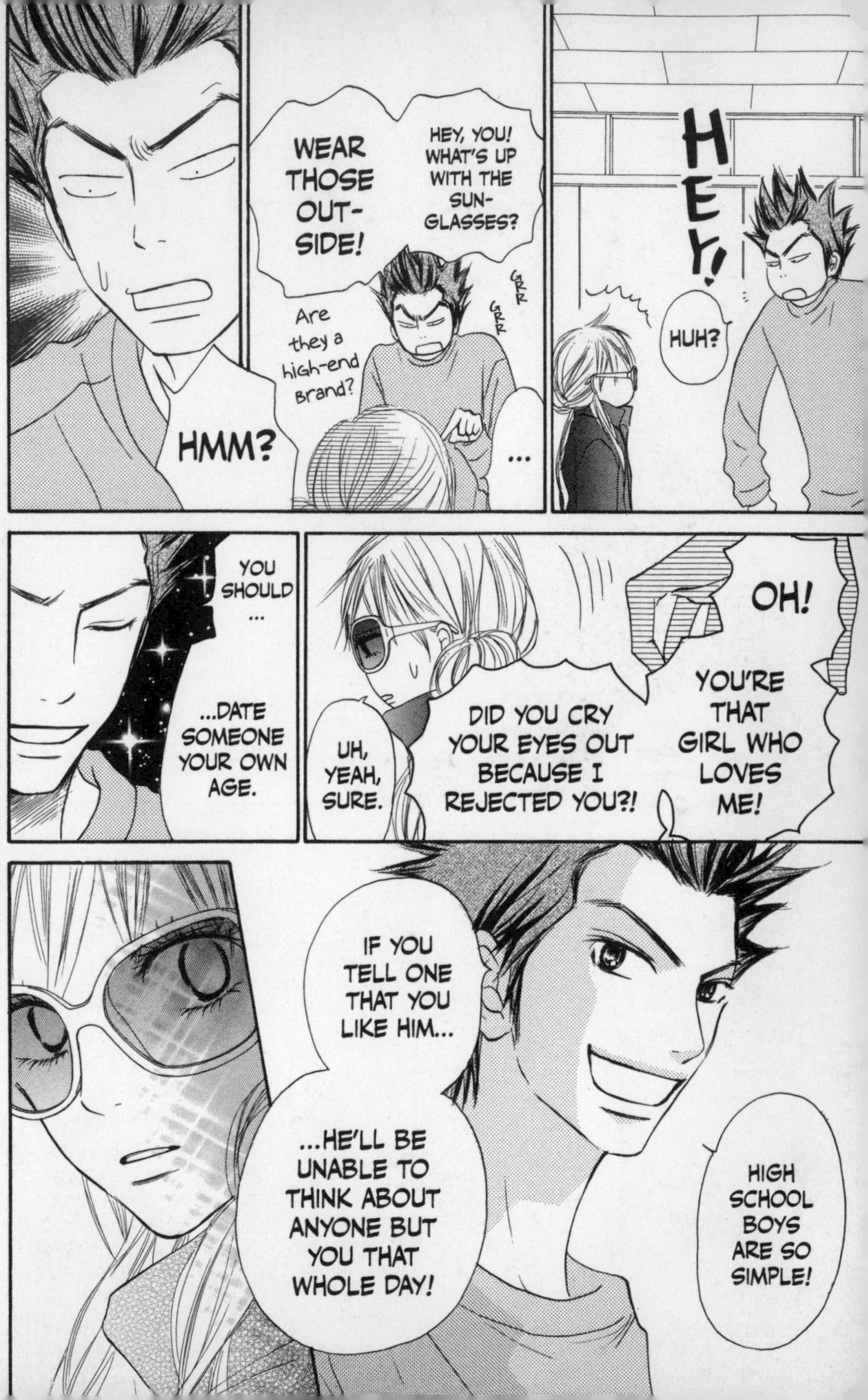
HEY!
HUH?
HEY, YOU! WHAT'S UP WITH THE SUN-GLASSES?
WEAR THOSE OUT-SIDE!
GRR GRR
Are they a high-end Brand?
...
HMM?
OH!
YOU'RE THAT GIRL WHO LOVES ME!
DID YOU CRY YOUR EYES OUT BECAUSE I REJECTED YOU?!
UH, YEAH, SURE.
YOU SHOULD ...
...DATE SOMEONE YOUR OWN AGE.
HIGH SCHOOL BOYS ARE SO SIMPLE!
IF YOU TELL ONE THAT YOU LIKE HIM...
...HE'LL BE UNABLE TO THINK ABOUT ANYONE BUT YOU THAT WHOLE DAY!

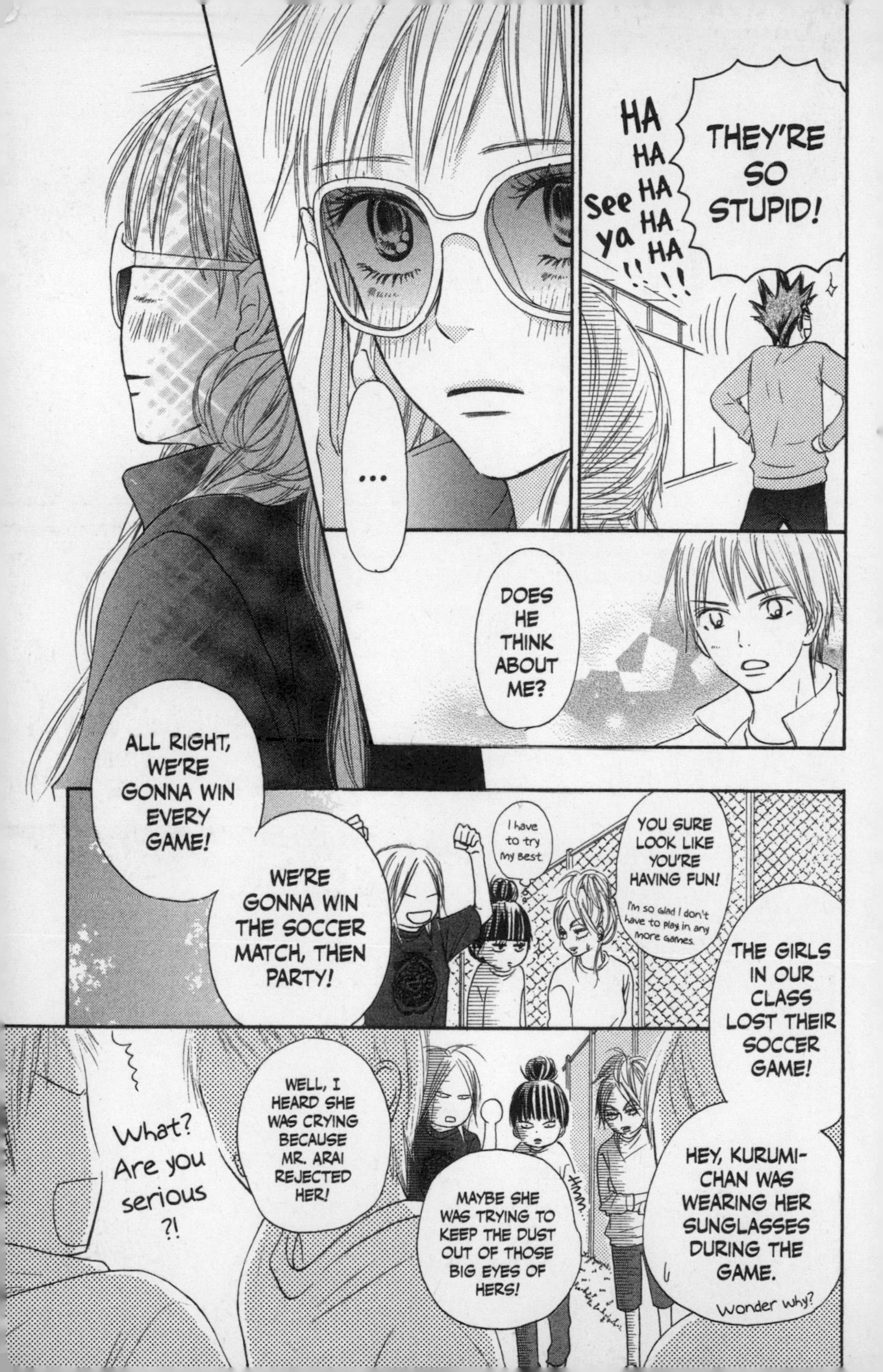
THEY'RE SO STUPID!
HA HA HA HA HA!!
See ya!!
...
DOES HE THINK ABOUT ME?
YOU SURE LOOK LIKE YOU'RE HAVING FUN!
I'm so glad I don't have to play in any more games.
I have to try my best.
ALL RIGHT, WE'RE GONNA WIN EVERY GAME!
WE'RE GONNA WIN THE SOCCER MATCH, THEN PARTY!
THE GIRLS IN OUR CLASS LOST THEIR SOCCER GAME!
HEY, KURUMI-CHAN WAS WEARING HER SUNGLASSES DURING THE GAME.
Wonder why?
Hmm...
MAYBE SHE WAS TRYING TO KEEP THE DUST OUT OF THOSE BIG EYES OF HERS!
WELL, I HEARD SHE WAS CRYING BECAUSE MR. ARAI REJECTED HER!
What? Are you serious ?!

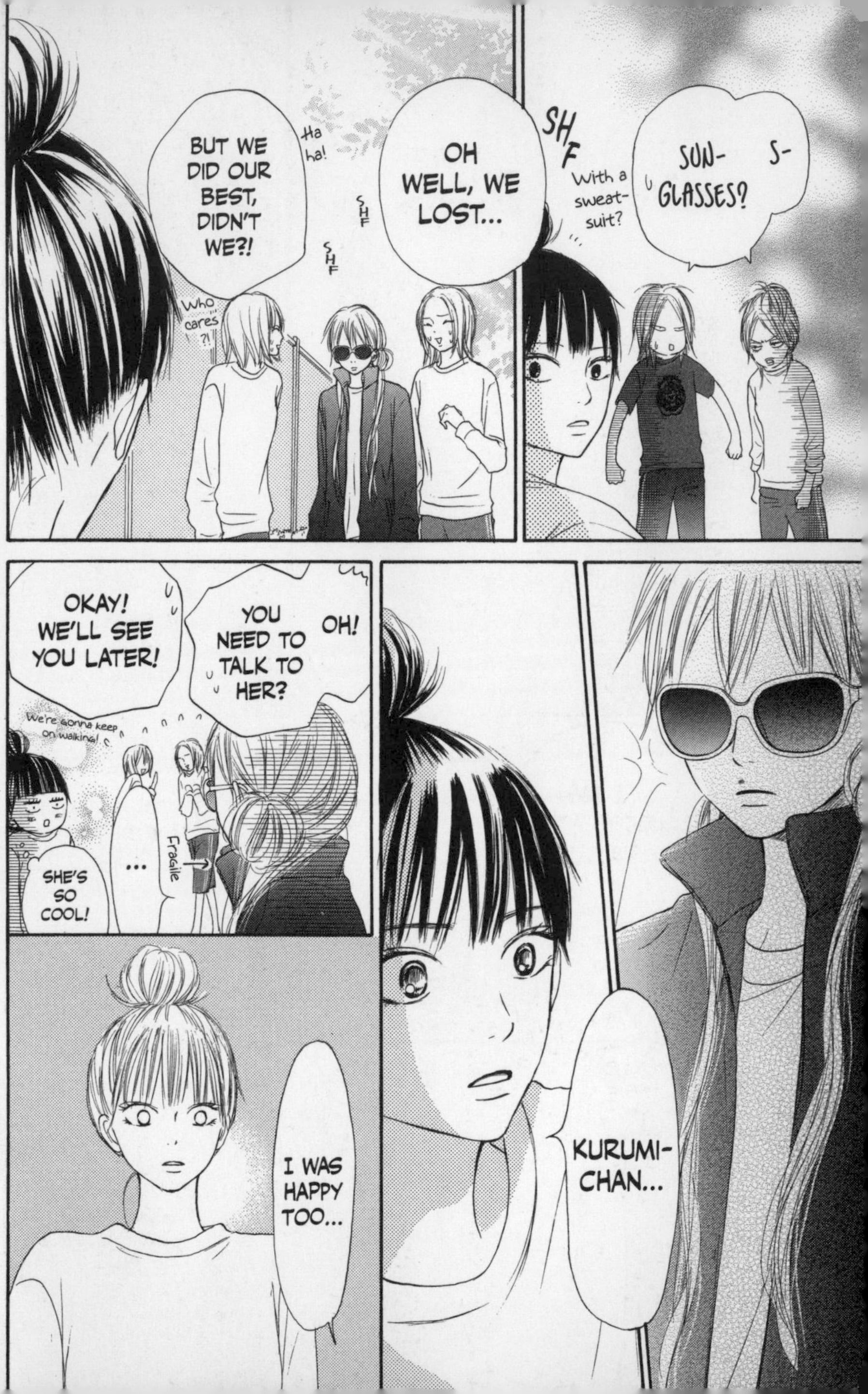
S-
SUN-GLASSES?
SHF
With a sweat-suit?
OH WELL, WE LOST...
Ha ha!
SHF
BUT WE DID OUR BEST, DIDN'T WE?!
SHF
Who cares?!
KURUMI-CHAN...
OH!
YOU NEED TO TALK TO HER?
OKAY! WE'LL SEE YOU LATER!
We're gonna keep on walking!
...
Fragile
SHE'S SO COOL!
I WAS HAPPY TOO...

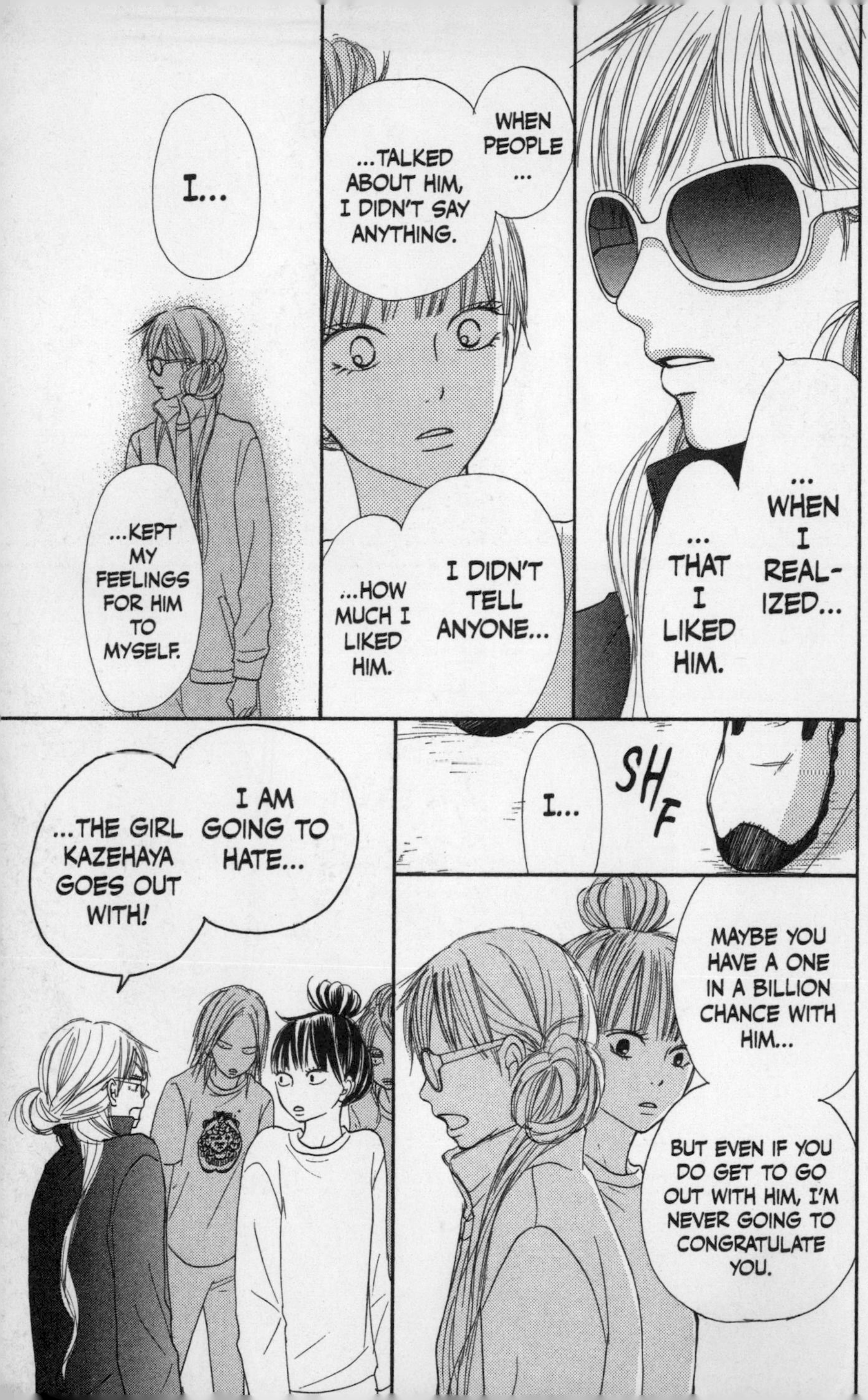
...WHEN I REALIZED...
...THAT I LIKED HIM.
WHEN PEOPLE...
...TALKED ABOUT HIM, I DIDN'T SAY ANYTHING.
I DIDN'T TELL ANYONE...
...HOW MUCH I LIKED HIM.
I...
...KEPT MY FEELINGS FOR HIM TO MYSELF.
SHF
I...
MAYBE YOU HAVE A ONE IN A BILLION CHANCE WITH HIM...
BUT EVEN IF YOU DO GET TO GO OUT WITH HIM, I'M NEVER GOING TO CONGRATULATE YOU.
I AM GOING TO HATE...
...THE GIRL KAZEHAYA GOES OUT WITH!

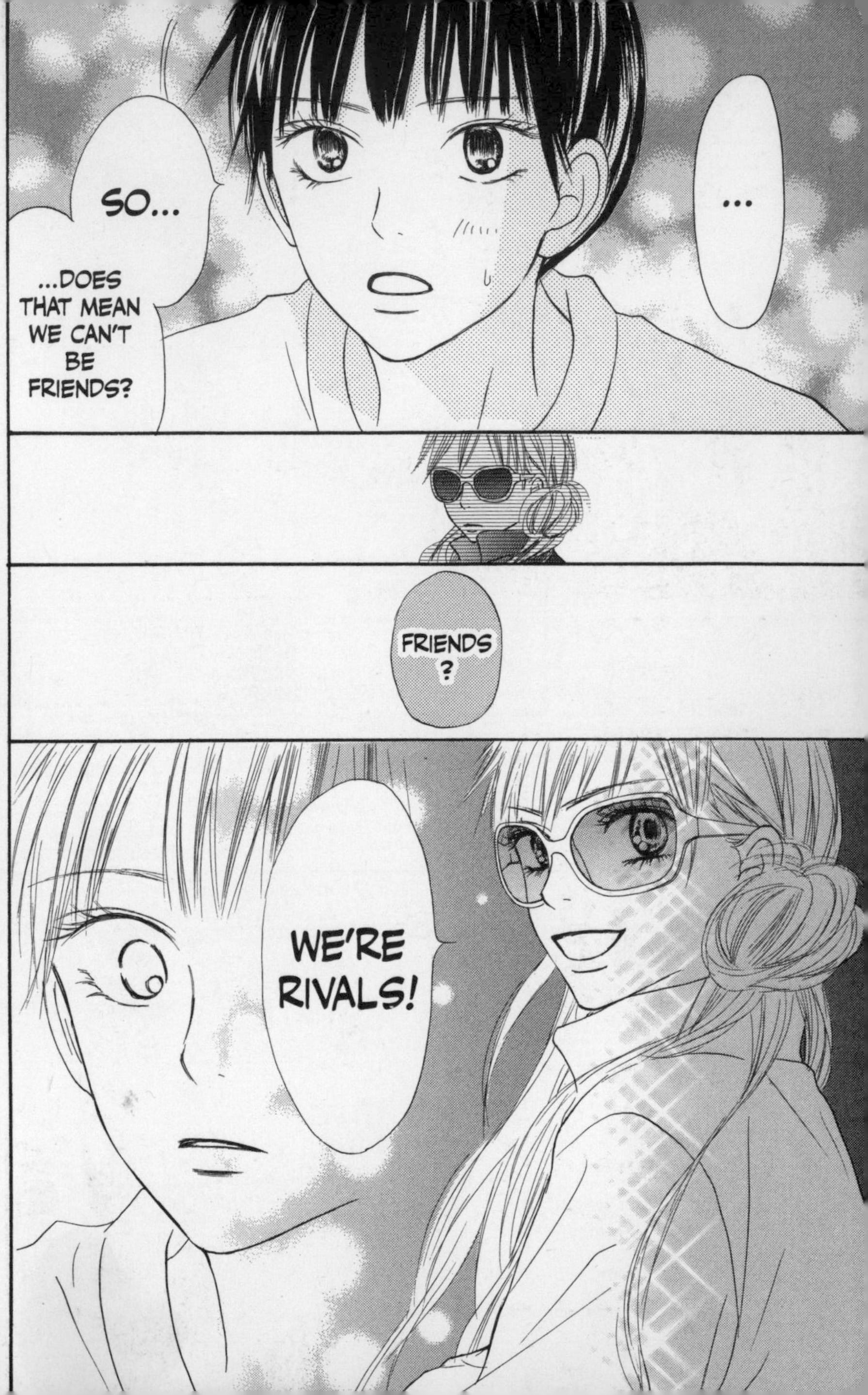
...
SO...
...DOES THAT MEAN WE CAN'T BE FRIENDS?
FRIENDS ?
WE'RE RIVALS!

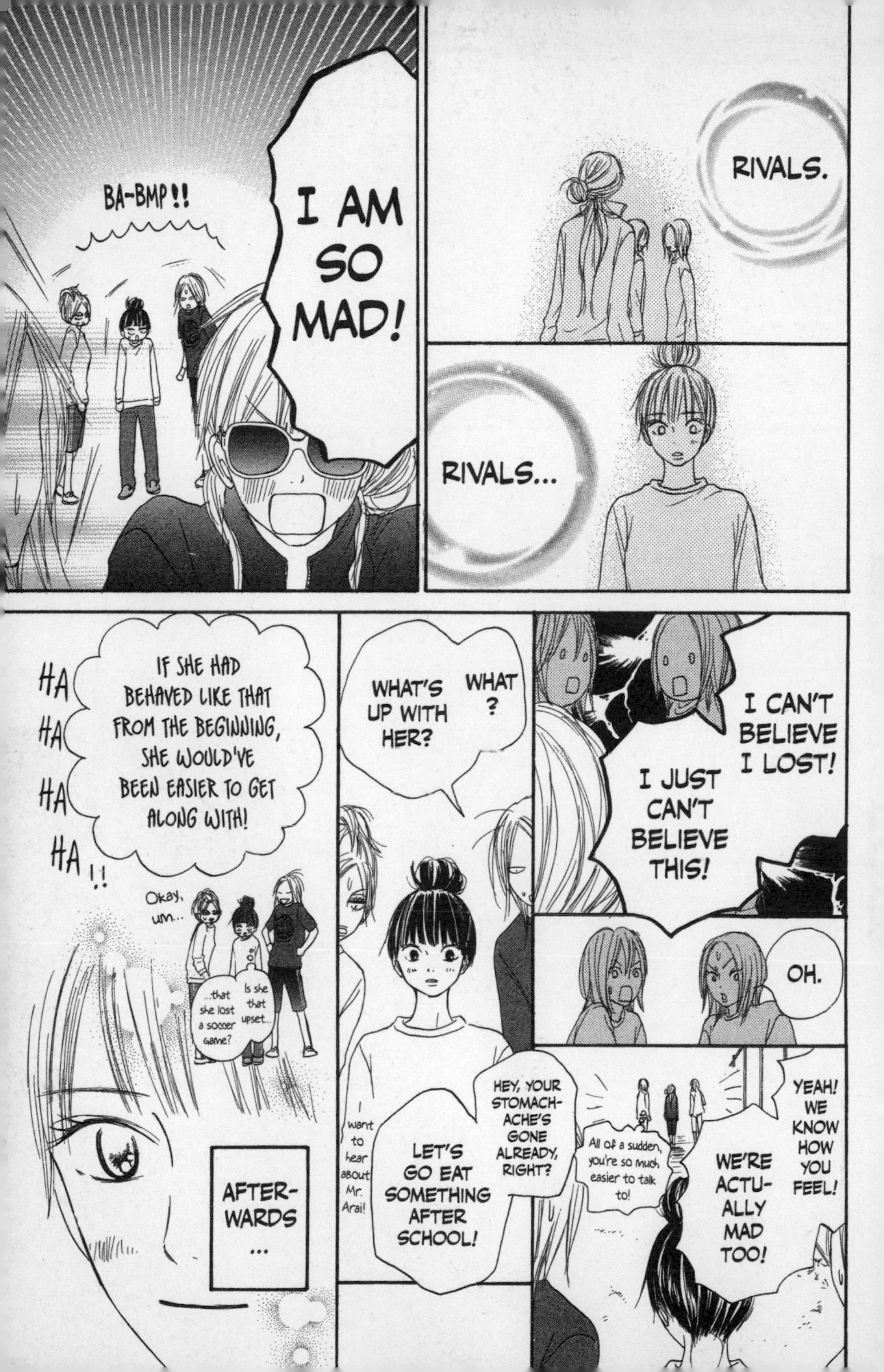
RIVALS.
RIVALS...
I AM SO MAD!
BA-BMP!!
I CAN'T BELIEVE I LOST!
I JUST CAN'T BELIEVE THIS!
OH.
YEAH! WE KNOW HOW YOU FEEL!
WE'RE ACTU-ALLY MAD TOO!
All of a sudden, you're so much easier to talk to!
HEY, YOUR STOMACH-ACHE'S GONE ALREADY, RIGHT?
WHAT?
WHAT'S UP WITH HER?
LET'S GO EAT SOMETHING AFTER SCHOOL!
I want to hear about Mr. Arai!
HA HA HA HA!!
IF SHE HAD BEHAVED LIKE THAT FROM THE BEGINNING, SHE WOULD'VE BEEN EASIER TO GET ALONG WITH!
Okay, um...
Is she that upset...
...that she lost a soccer game?
AFTER-WARDS...

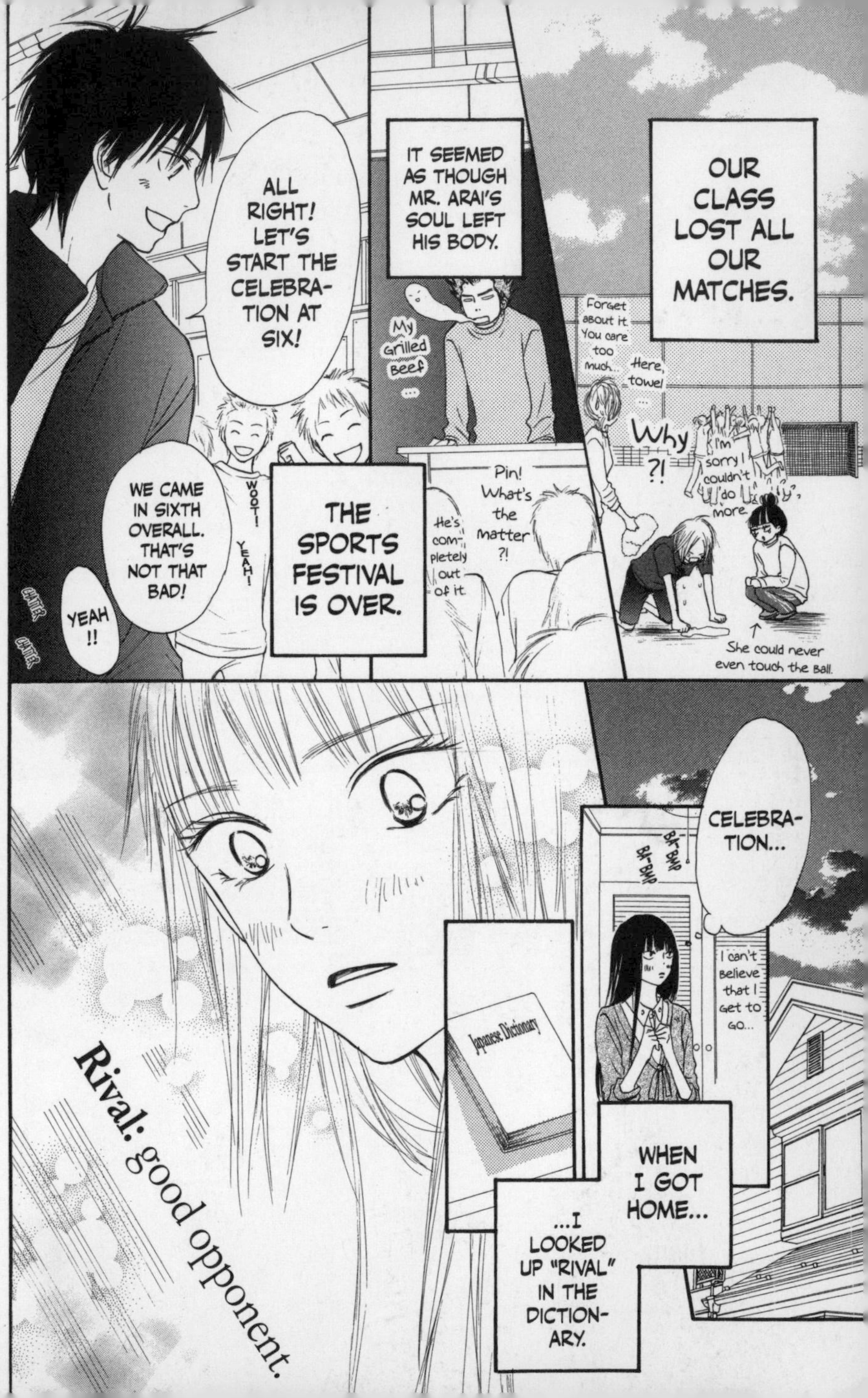
OUR CLASS LOST ALL OUR MATCHES.
Forget about it. You care too much...
Here, towel ...
Why ?!
I'm sorry I couldn't do more
She could never even touch the Ball.
IT SEEMED AS THOUGH MR. ARAI'S SOUL LEFT HIS BODY.
My Grilled Beef ...
Pin! What's the matter ?!
He's completely out of it.
THE SPORTS FESTIVAL IS OVER.
ALL RIGHT! LET'S START THE CELEBRATION AT SIX!
WOOT!
YEAH!
WE CAME IN SIXTH OVERALL. THAT'S NOT THAT BAD!
YEAH !!
CHATTER CHATTER
CELEBRATION...
BA-BMP BA-BMP
I can't Believe that I get to go...
WHEN I GOT HOME...
...I LOOKED UP "RIVAL" IN THE DICTIONARY.
Japanese Dictionary
Rival: good opponent.

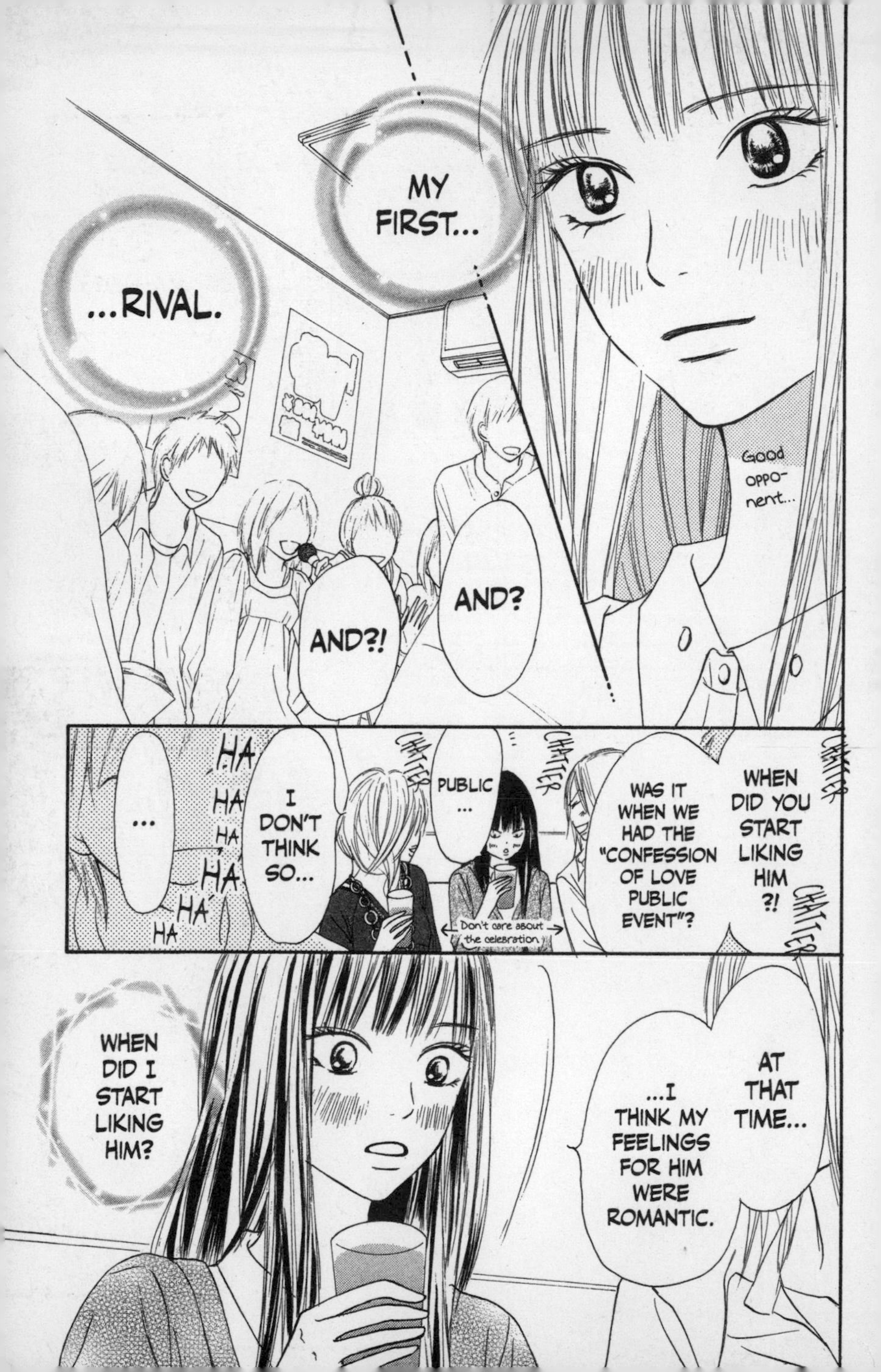
MY FIRST...
...RIVAL.
Good oppo-nent...
AND?
AND?!
CHATTER
WHEN DID YOU START LIKING HIM?!
CHATTER
WAS IT WHEN WE HAD THE "CONFESSION OF LOVE PUBLIC EVENT"?
CHATTER
PUBLIC...
CHATTER
Don't care about the celebration
I DON'T THINK SO...
HA HA HA HA HA HA HA
...
AT THAT TIME...
...I THINK MY FEELINGS FOR HIM WERE ROMANTIC.
WHEN DID I START LIKING HIM?

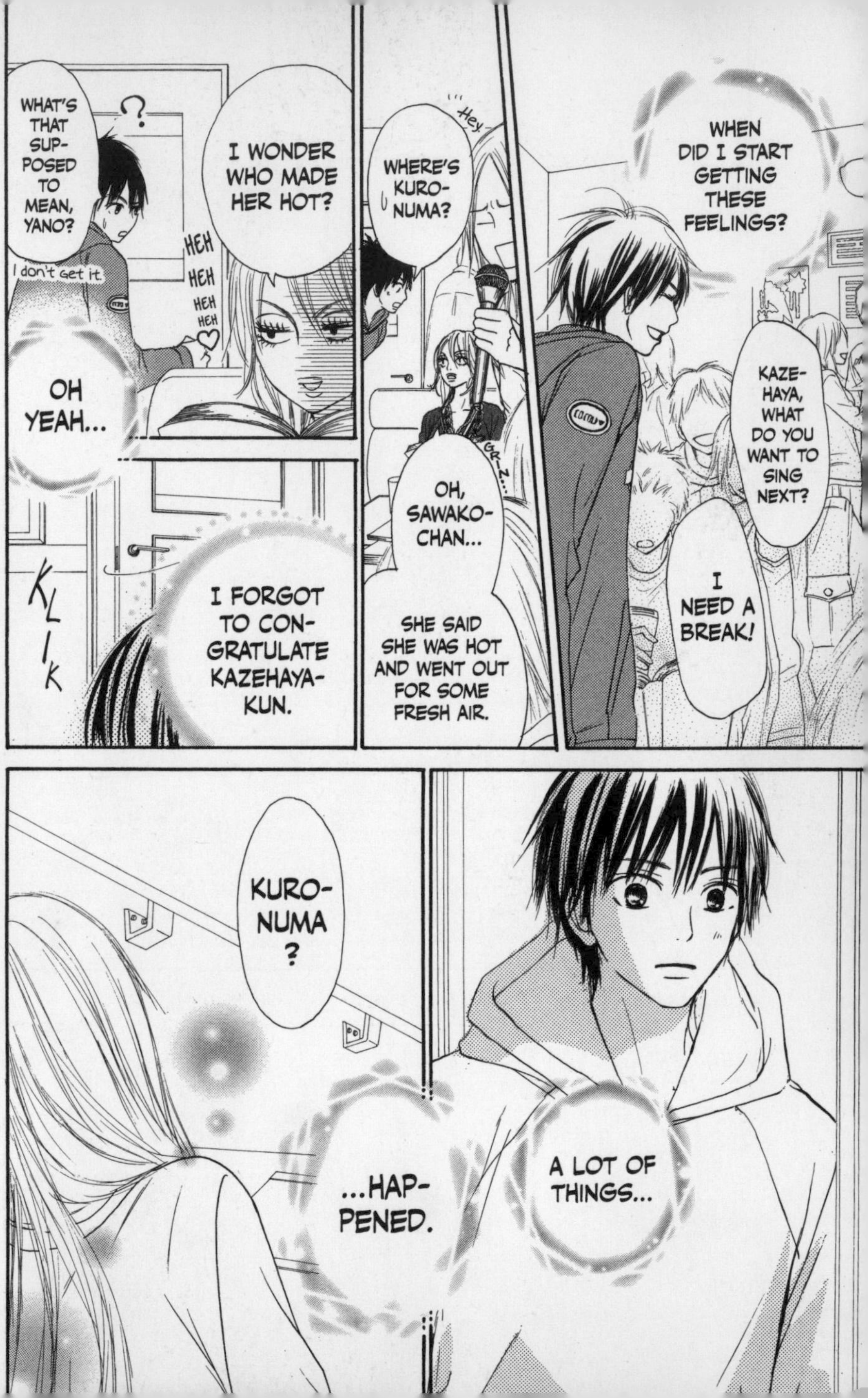
WHEN DID I START GETTING THESE FEELINGS?
KAZEHAYA, WHAT DO YOU WANT TO SING NEXT?
I NEED A BREAK!
Hey
WHERE'S KURONUMA?
GRIN...
OH, SAWAKO-CHAN...
SHE SAID SHE WAS HOT AND WENT OUT FOR SOME FRESH AIR.
I WONDER WHO MADE HER HOT?
HEH HEH HEH HEH
WHAT'S THAT SUPPOSED TO MEAN, YANO?
I don't get it.
OH YEAH...
I FORGOT TO CONGRATULATE KAZEHAYA-KUN.
KLIK
A LOT OF THINGS...
...HAPPENED.
KURONUMA?

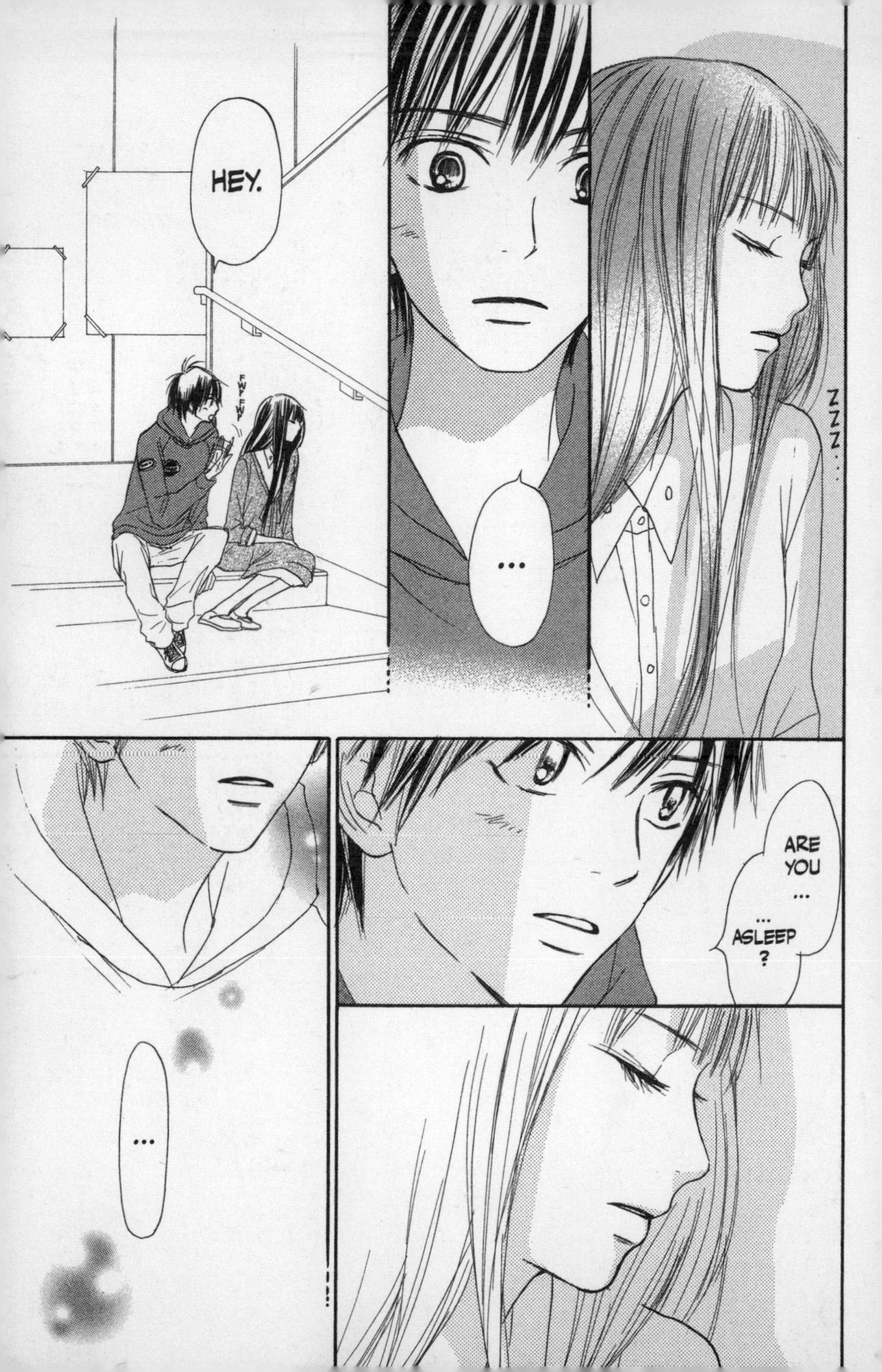
ZZZ...
...
HEY.
FWP FWP
ARE YOU ... ... ASLEEP?
...

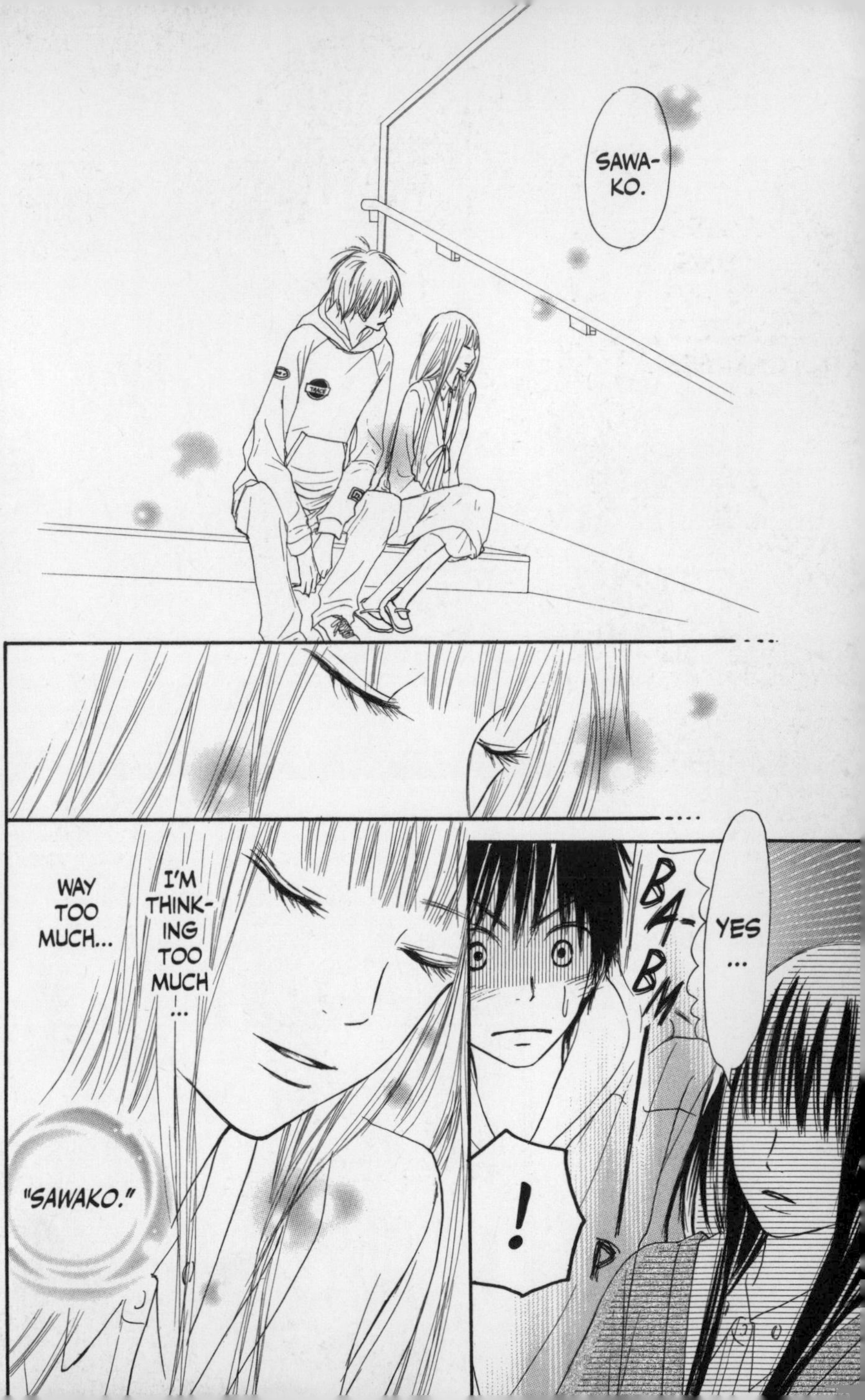
SAWA-KO.
YES ...
BA-BM
!
P
I'M THINKING TOO MUCH!...
WAY TOO MUCH...
"SAWAKO."

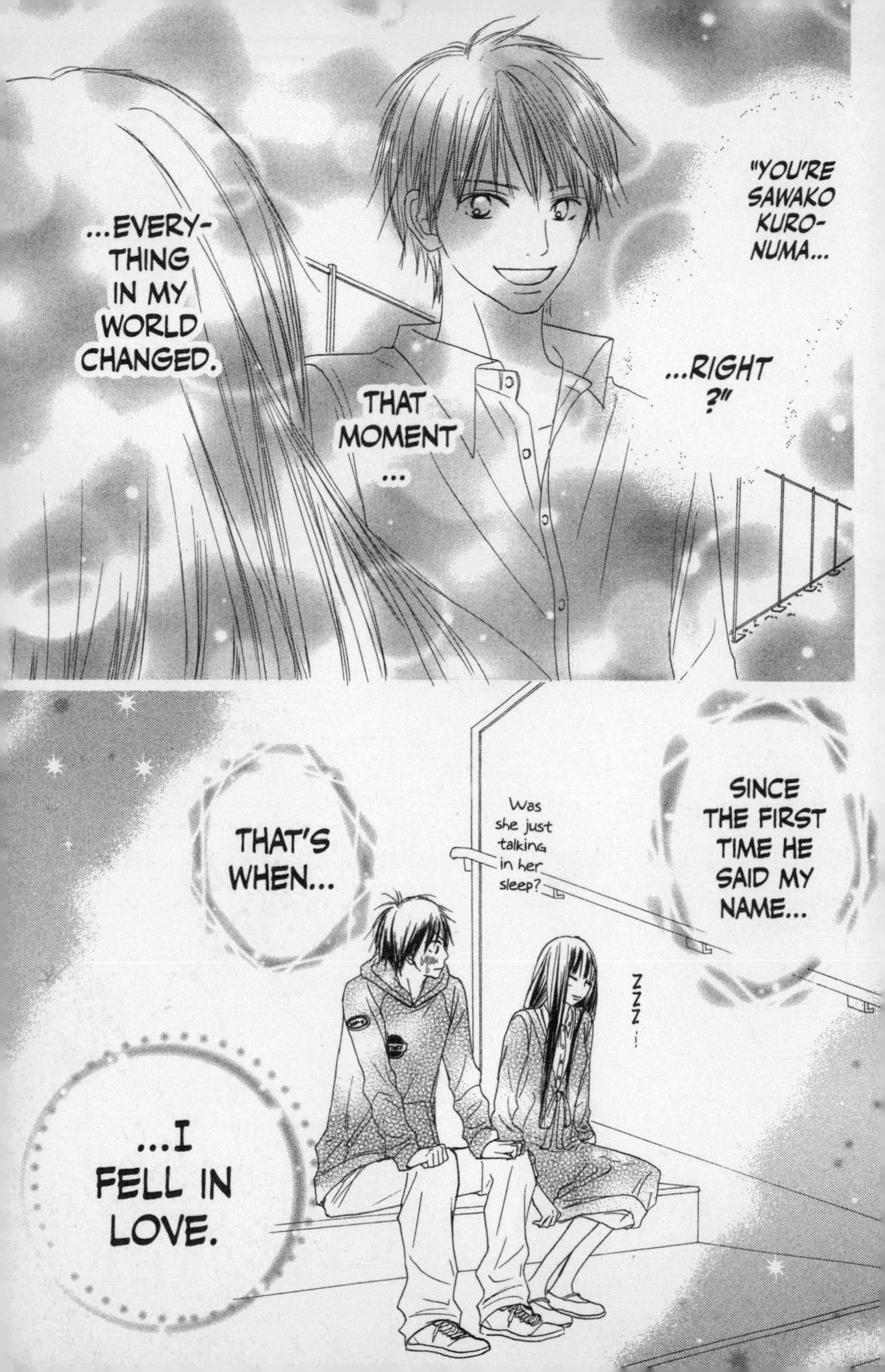
"YOU'RE SAWAKO KURO-NUMA...
...RIGHT?"
THAT MOMENT...
...EVERY-THING IN MY WORLD CHANGED.
SINCE THE FIRST TIME HE SAID MY NAME...
Was she just talking in her sleep?
ZZZ
THAT'S WHEN...
...I FELL IN LOVE.

♥ Episode 18: Weekend

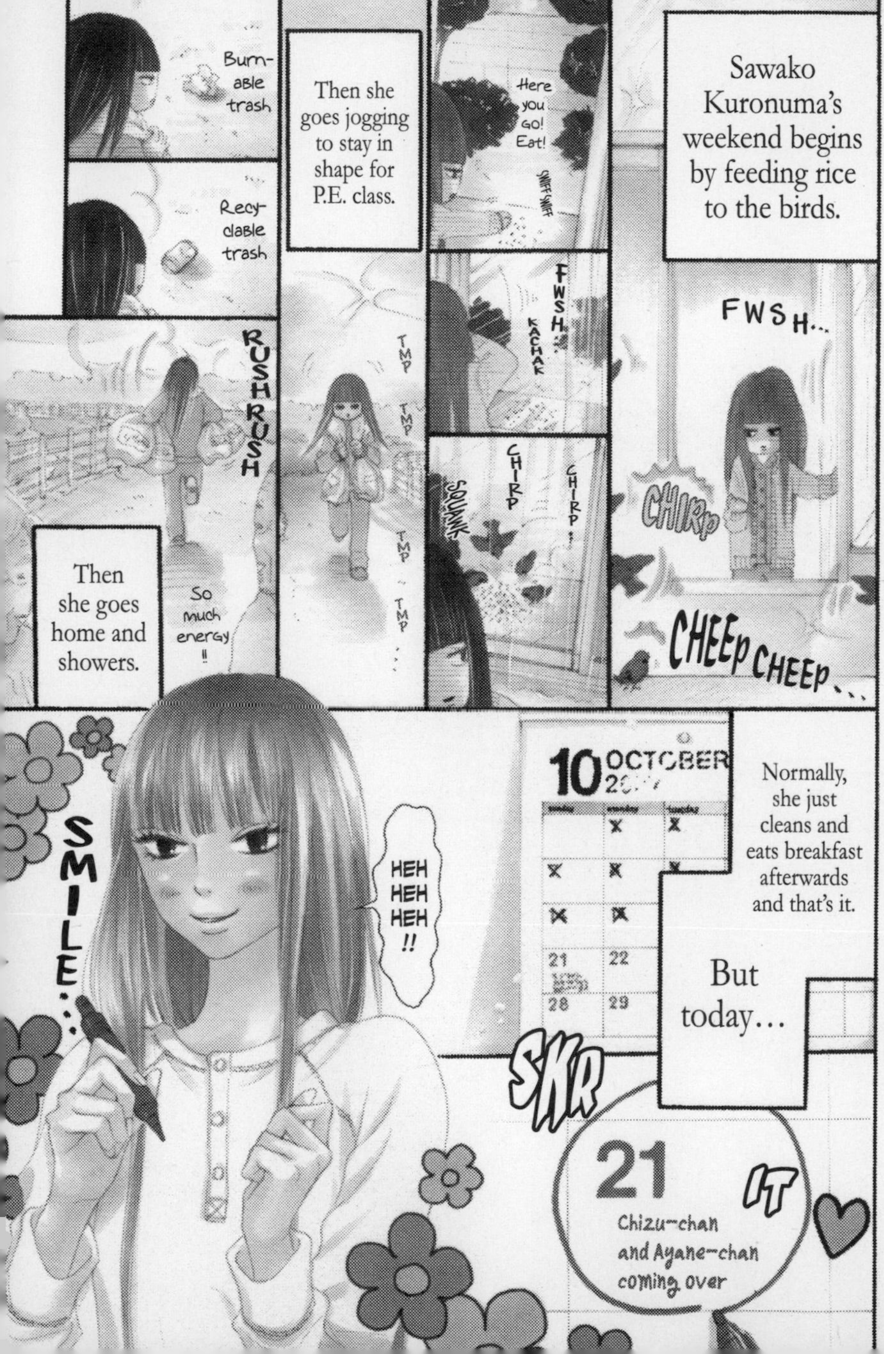
Sawako Kuronuma's weekend begins by feeding rice to the birds.
FWSH...
CHIRP
CHEEP CHEEP...
Here you GO! Eat!
SNIFF SNIFF
FWSH...
KACHAK
CHIRP
CHIRP
SQUAWK
Then she goes jogging to stay in shape for P.E. class.
TMP
TMP
TMP
TMP...
Burn-able trash
Recy-clable trash
RUSH RUSH
Then she goes home and showers.
So much energy!!
Normally, she just cleans and eats breakfast afterwards and that's it.
But today...
10 OCTOBER
21
22
28
29
SKR
21
Chizu-chan and Ayane-chan coming over
IT
HEH HEH HEH!!
SMILE...

Episode 18: Weekend

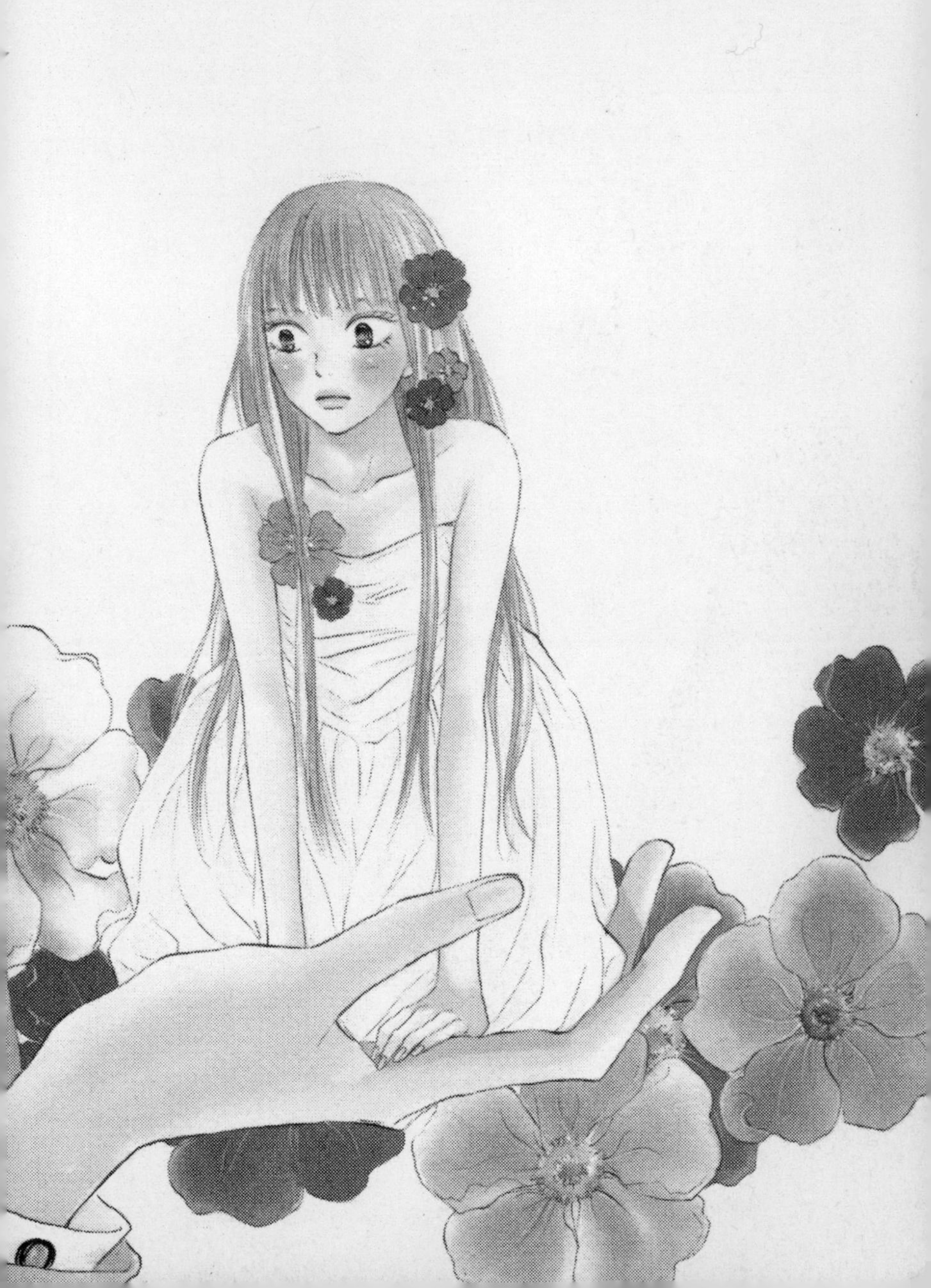

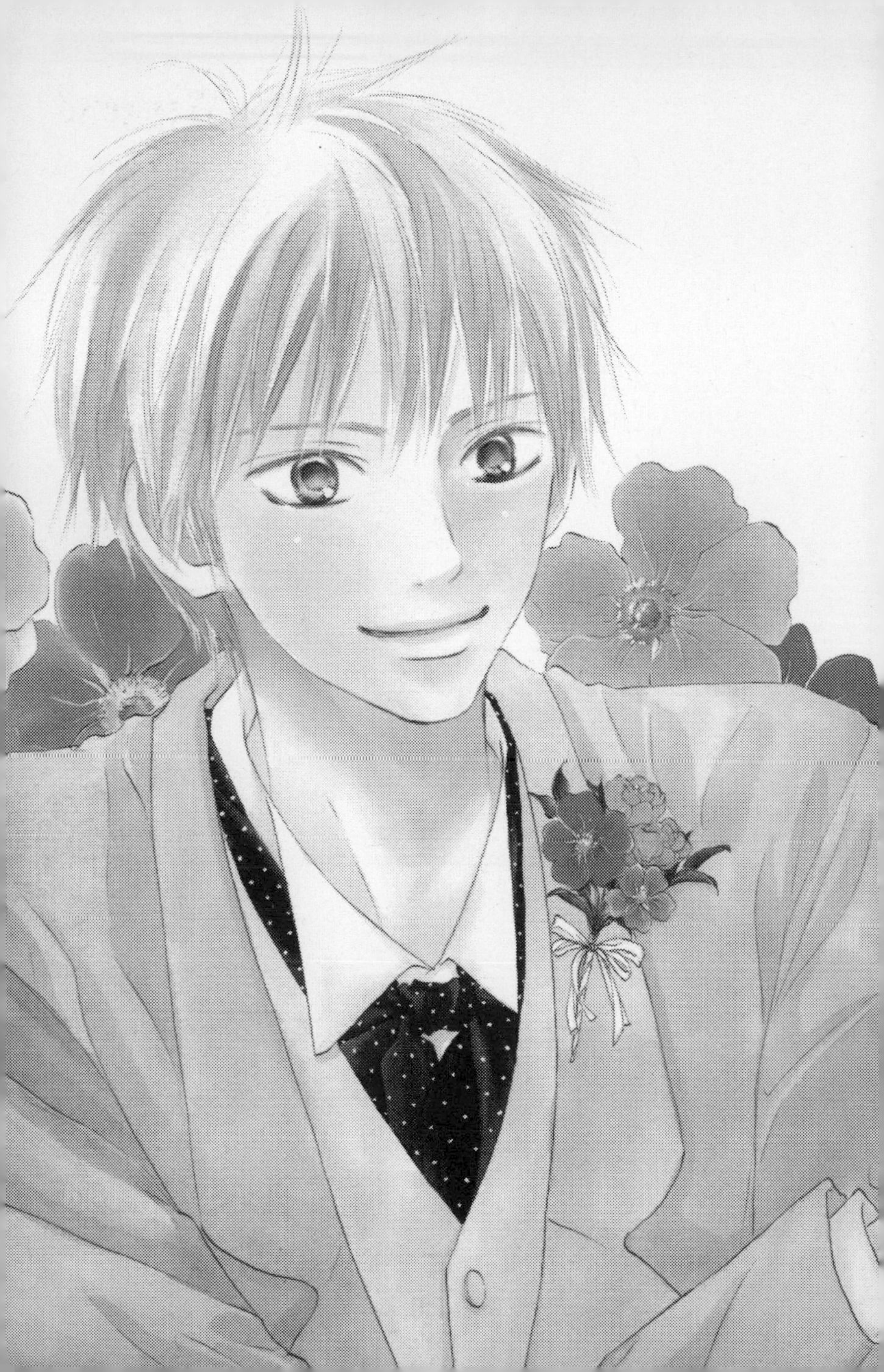

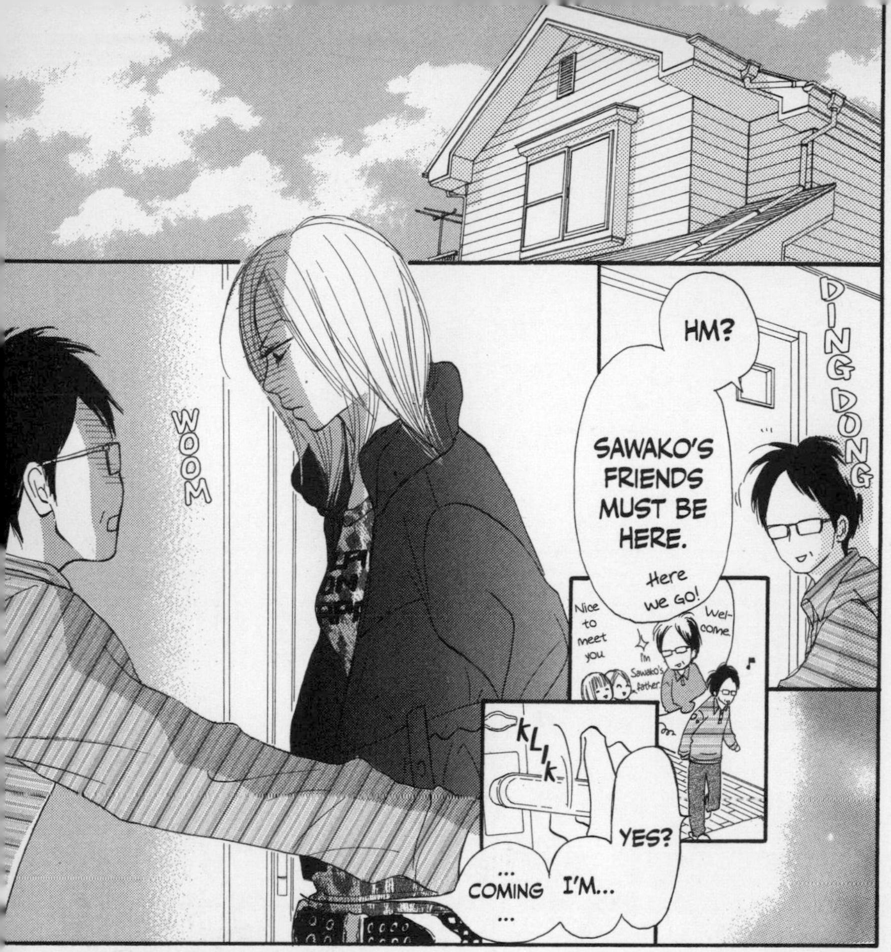
DING DONG
HM?
...
SAWAKO'S FRIENDS MUST BE HERE.
Here we GO!
Wel-come
I'm Sawako's father
Nice to meet you
KLIK
YES?
I'M... ...COMING...
WOOM

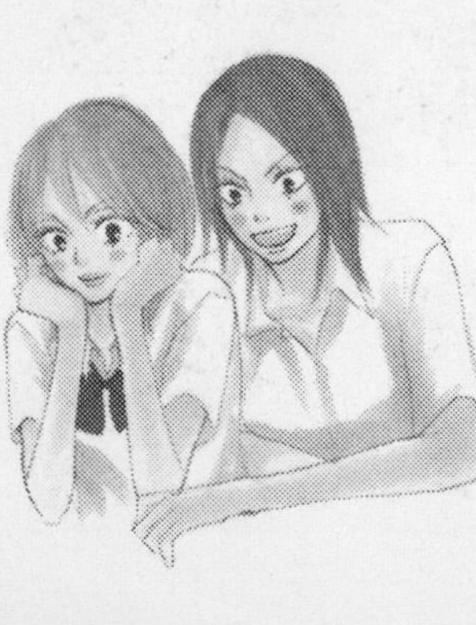

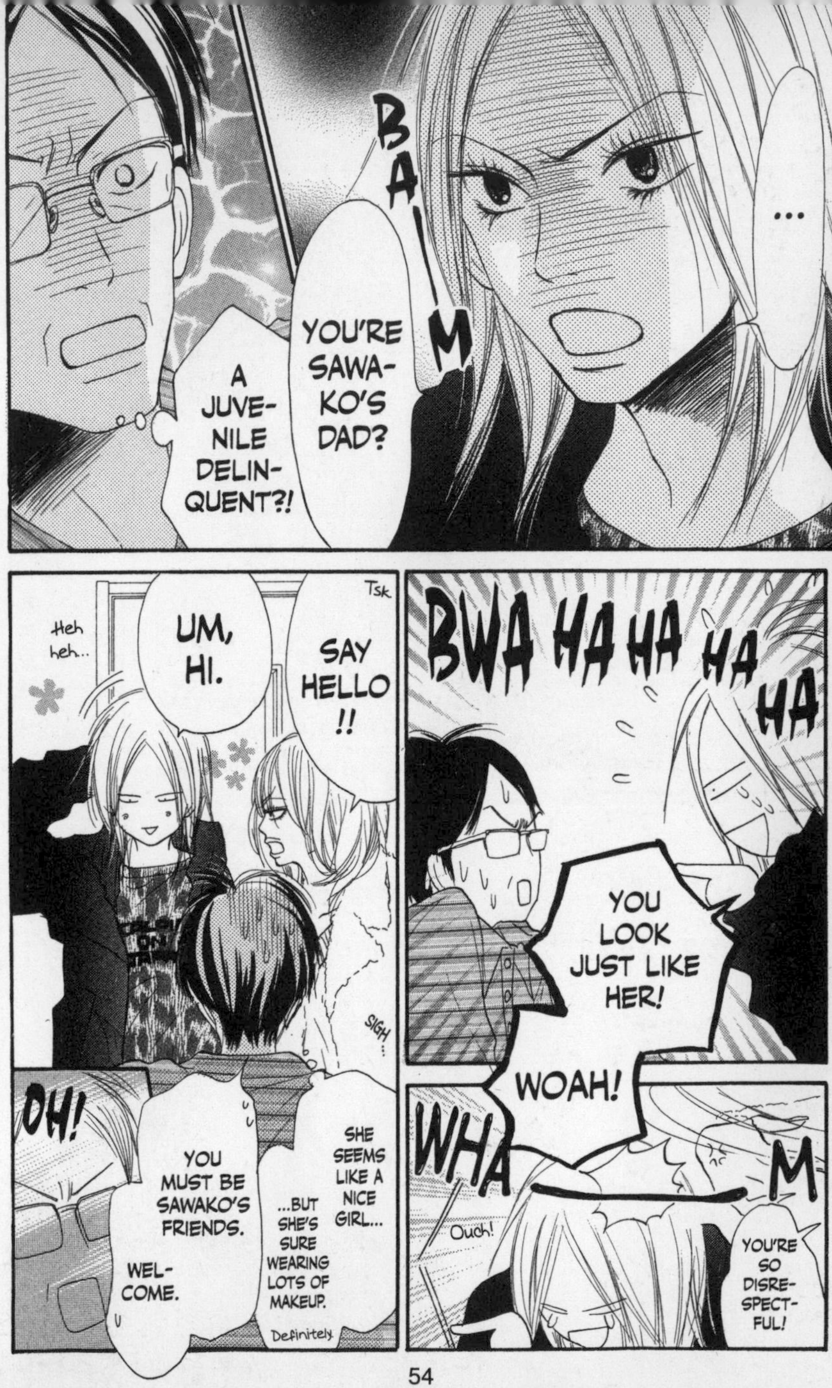
...
BAM
YOU'RE SAWAKO'S DAD?
A JUVENILE DELINQUENT?!
BWA HA HA HA HA HA
YOU LOOK JUST LIKE HER!
Tsk
SAY HELLO!!
UM, HI.
Heh heh...
SIGH...
WOAH!
WHAM
Ouch!
YOU'RE SO DISRESPECTFUL!
OH!
SHE SEEMS LIKE A NICE GIRL...
...BUT SHE'S SURE WEARING LOTS OF MAKEUP.
Definitely.
YOU MUST BE SAWAKO'S FRIENDS.
WELCOME.

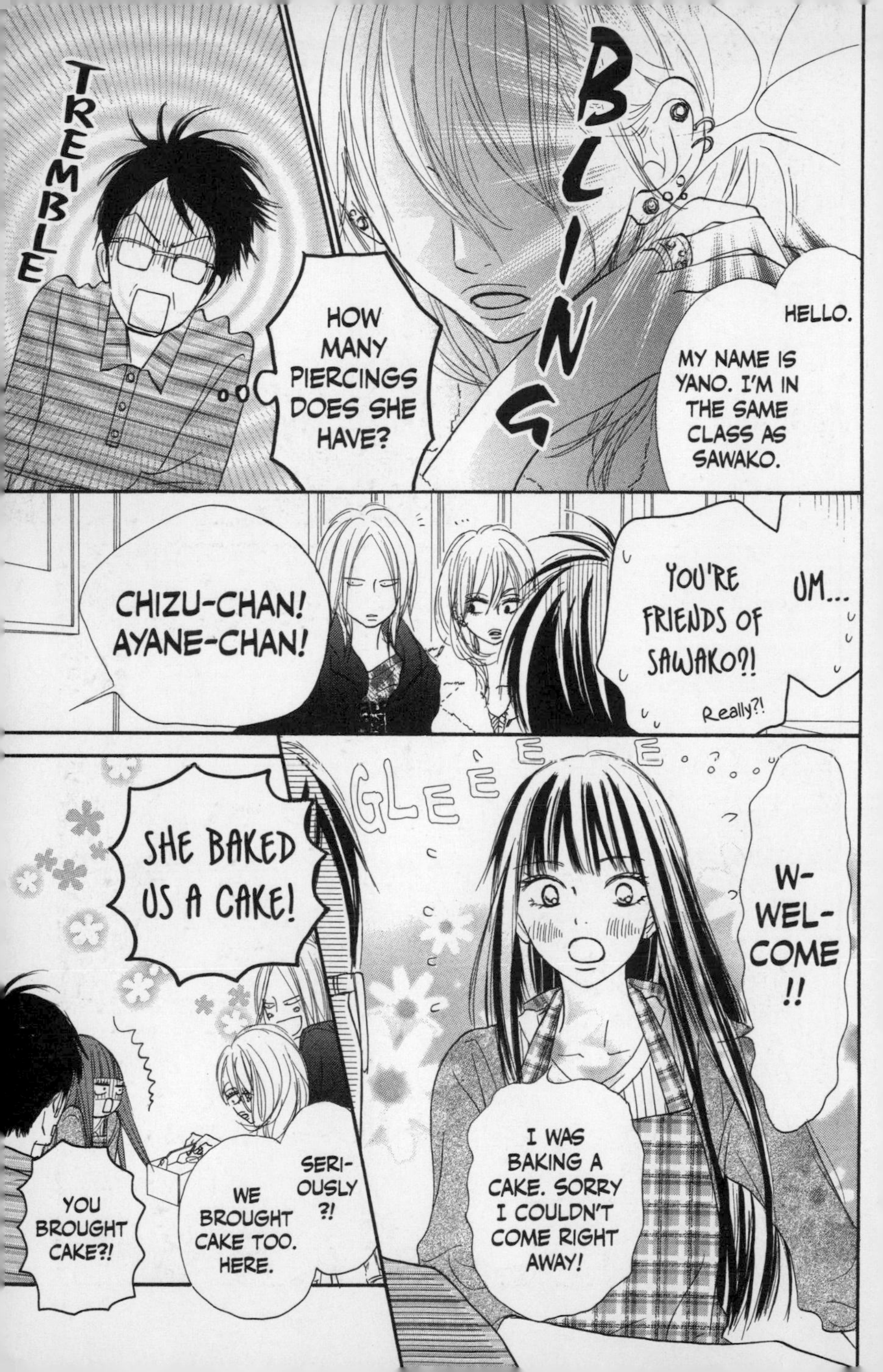
BLING
HELLO.
MY NAME IS YANO. I'M IN THE SAME CLASS AS SAWAKO.
TREMBLE
HOW MANY PIERCINGS DOES SHE HAVE?
UM...
YOU'RE FRIENDS OF SAWAKO?!
Really?!
CHIZU-CHAN! AYANE-CHAN!
GLEEEE
W-WEL-COME!!
I WAS BAKING A CAKE. SORRY I COULDN'T COME RIGHT AWAY!
SHE BAKED US A CAKE!
SERI-OUSLY?!
WE BROUGHT CAKE TOO. HERE.
YOU BROUGHT CAKE?!

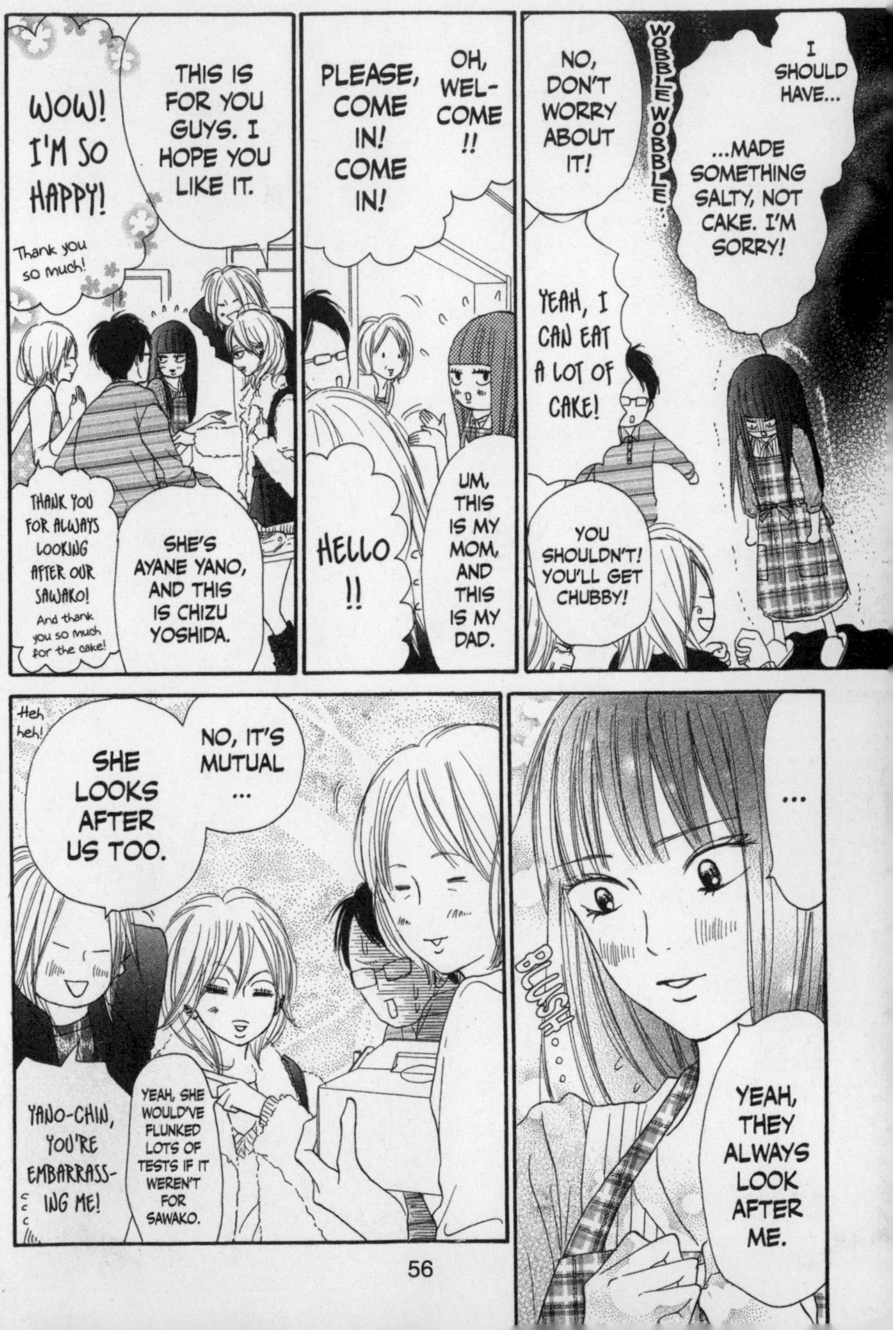
I SHOULD HAVE...
...MADE SOMETHING SALTY, NOT CAKE. I'M SORRY!
WOBBLE WOBBLE
NO, DON'T WORRY ABOUT IT!
YEAH, I CAN EAT A LOT OF CAKE!
YOU SHOULDN'T! YOU'LL GET CHUBBY!
OH, WEL-COME!!
PLEASE, COME IN! COME IN!
UM, THIS IS MY MOM, AND THIS IS MY DAD.
HELLO!!
THIS IS FOR YOU GUYS. I HOPE YOU LIKE IT.
WOW! I'M SO HAPPY!
Thank you so much!
SHE'S AYANE YANO, AND THIS IS CHIZU YOSHIDA.
THANK YOU FOR ALWAYS LOOKING AFTER OUR SAWAKO!
And thank you so much for the cake!
...
BLUSH
YEAH, THEY ALWAYS LOOK AFTER ME.
Heh, heh!
NO, IT'S MUTUAL...
SHE LOOKS AFTER US TOO.
YEAH, SHE WOULD'VE FLUNKED LOTS OF TESTS IF IT WEREN'T FOR SAWAKO.
YANO-CHIN, YOU'RE EMBARRASSING ME!

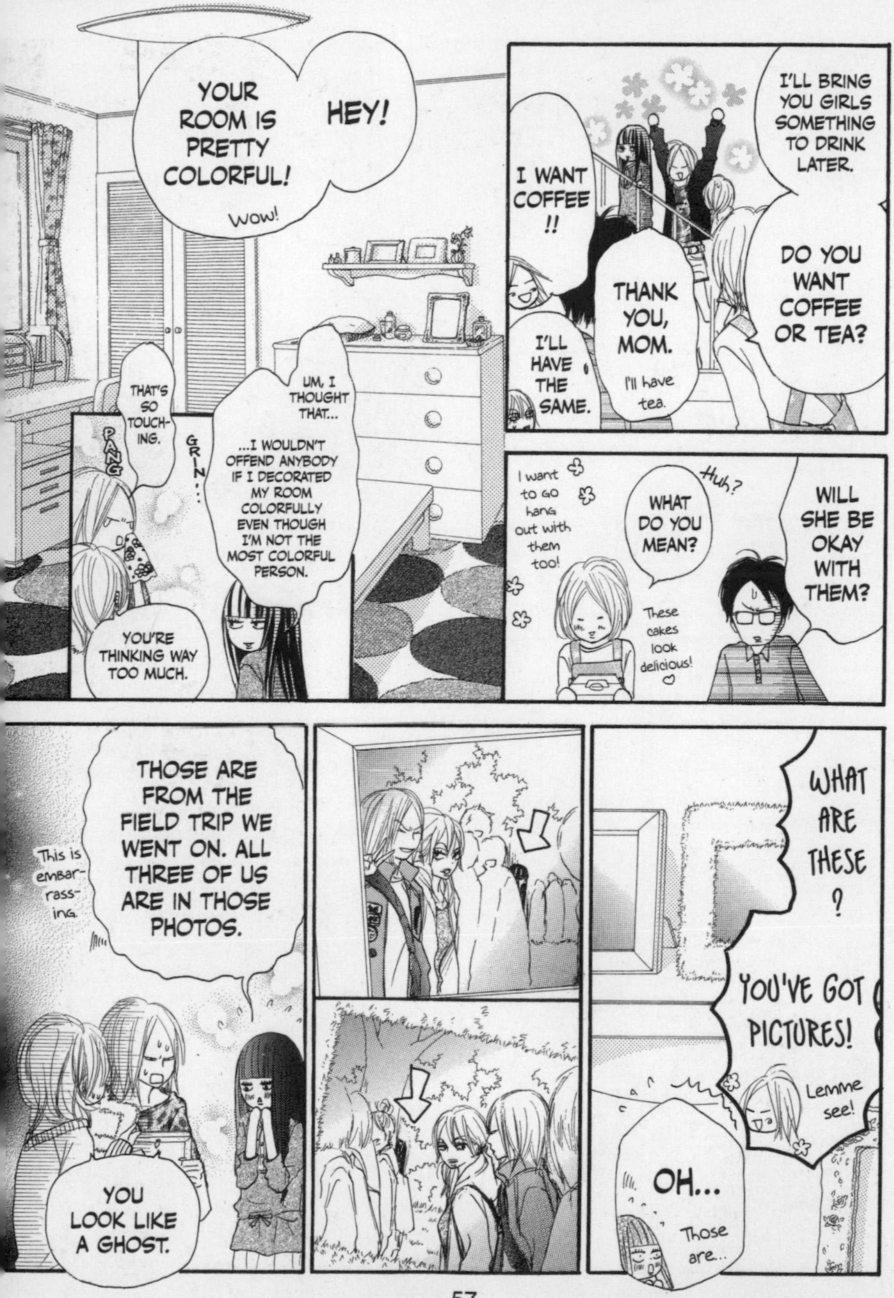
I'LL BRING YOU GIRLS SOMETHING TO DRINK LATER.
DO YOU WANT COFFEE OR TEA?
I WANT COFFEE!!
THANK YOU, MOM.
I'll have tea.
I'LL HAVE THE SAME.
WILL SHE BE OKAY WITH THEM?
Huh?
WHAT DO YOU MEAN?
I want to go hang out with them too!
These cakes look delicious!
HEY!
YOUR ROOM IS PRETTY COLORFUL!
Wow!
UM, I THOUGHT THAT...
...I WOULDN'T OFFEND ANYBODY IF I DECORATED MY ROOM COLORFULLY EVEN THOUGH I'M NOT THE MOST COLORFUL PERSON.
THAT'S SO TOUCHING.
GRIN...
PANG
YOU'RE THINKING WAY TOO MUCH.
WHAT ARE THESE?
YOU'VE GOT PICTURES!
Lemme see!
OH...
Those are...
THOSE ARE FROM THE FIELD TRIP WE WENT ON. ALL THREE OF US ARE IN THOSE PHOTOS.
This is embarrassing.
YOU LOOK LIKE A GHOST.

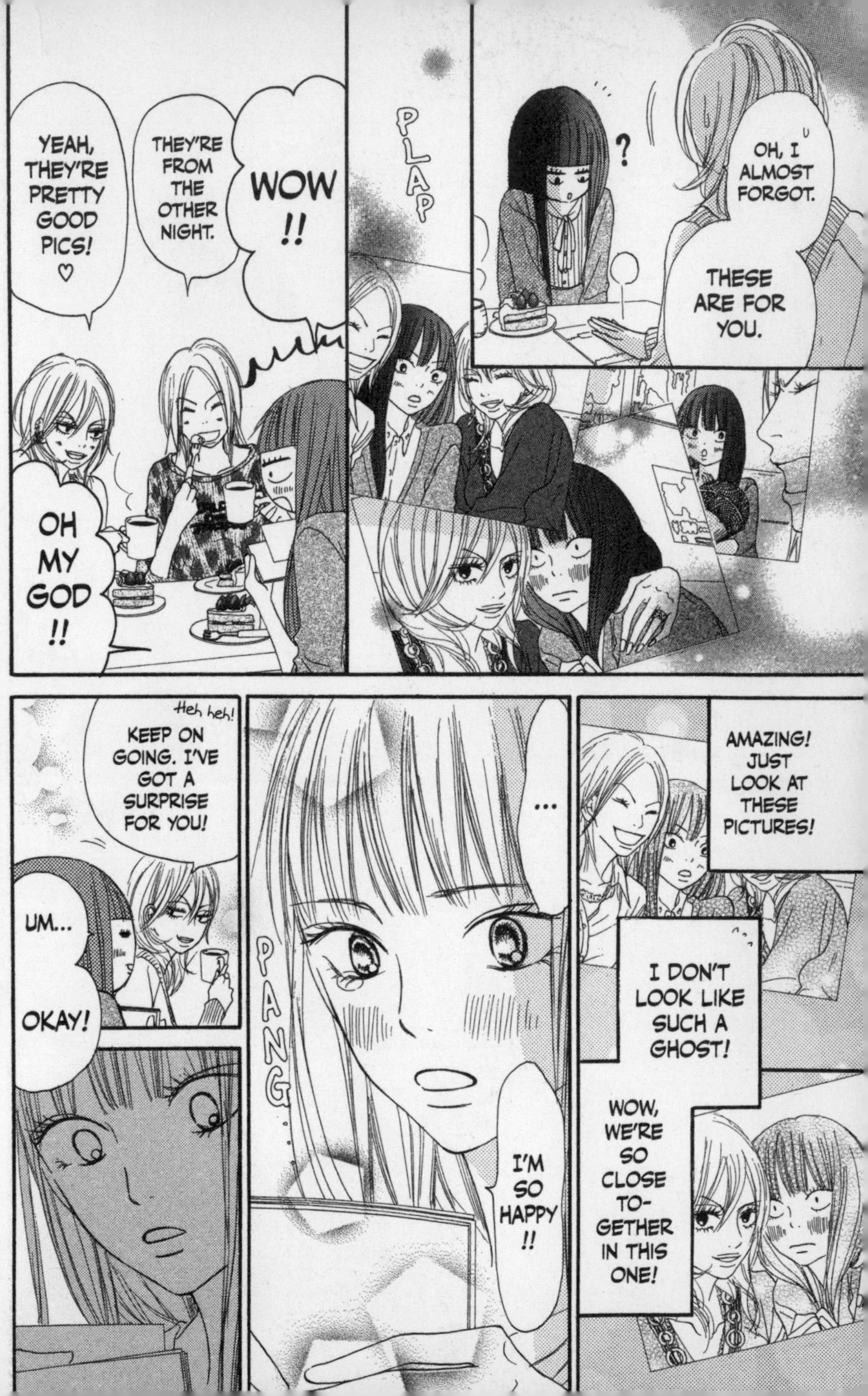
OH, I ALMOST FORGOT.
THESE ARE FOR YOU.
?
PLAP
WOW !!
THEY'RE FROM THE OTHER NIGHT.
YEAH, THEY'RE PRETTY GOOD PICS! ♡
OH MY GOD !!
AMAZING! JUST LOOK AT THESE PICTURES!
I DON'T LOOK LIKE SUCH A GHOST!
WOW, WE'RE SO CLOSE TO-GETHER IN THIS ONE!
...
PANG
I'M SO HAPPY !!
Heh heh!
KEEP ON GOING. I'VE GOT A SURPRISE FOR YOU!
UM...
OKAY!

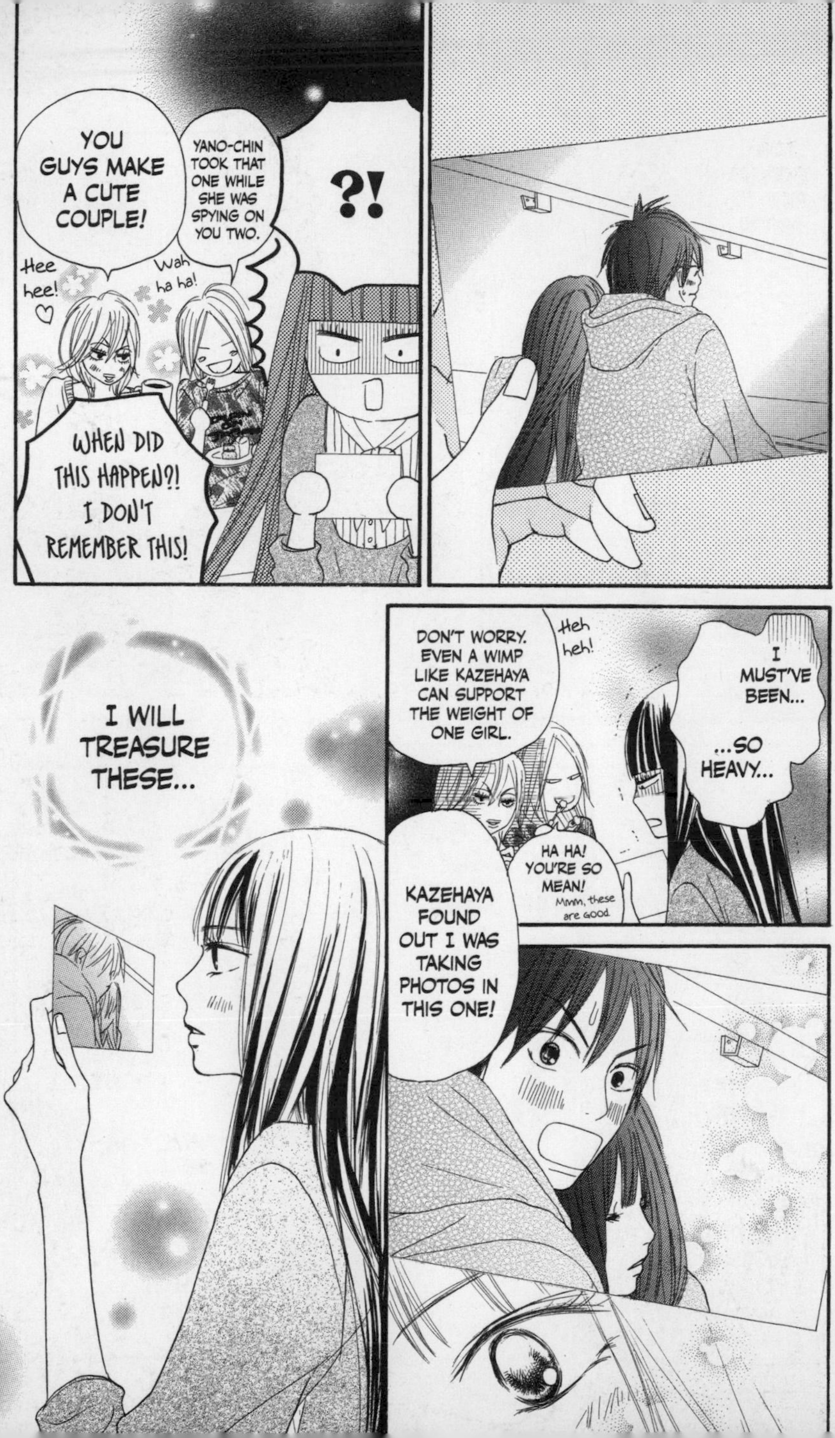
?!
YANO-CHIN TOOK THAT ONE WHILE SHE WAS SPYING ON YOU TWO.
Wah ha ha!
YOU GUYS MAKE A CUTE COUPLE!
Hee hee! ♡
WHEN DID THIS HAPPEN?! I DON'T REMEMBER THIS!
I MUST'VE BEEN...
...SO HEAVY...
Heh heh!
DON'T WORRY. EVEN A WIMP LIKE KAZEHAYA CAN SUPPORT THE WEIGHT OF ONE GIRL.
HA HA! YOU'RE SO MEAN!
Mmm, these are good
KAZEHAYA FOUND OUT I WAS TAKING PHOTOS IN THIS ONE!
I WILL TREASURE THESE...

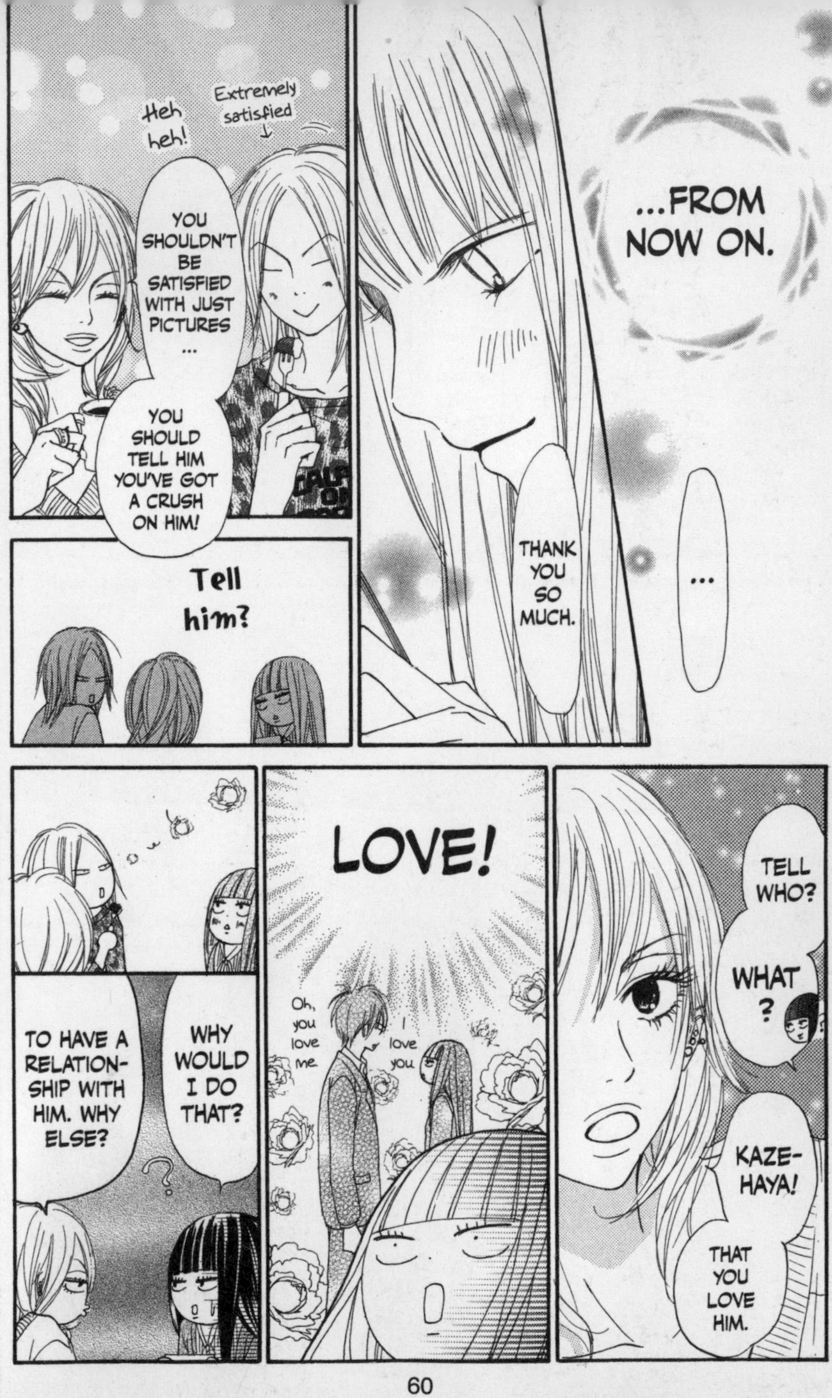
...FROM NOW ON.
...
THANK YOU SO MUCH.
Extremely satisfied
Heh heh!
YOU SHOULDN'T BE SATISFIED WITH JUST PICTURES ...
YOU SHOULD TELL HIM YOU'VE GOT A CRUSH ON HIM!
Tell him?
TELL WHO?
WHAT?
KAZE-HAYA!
THAT YOU LOVE HIM.
LOVE!
I love you
Oh, you love me.
WHY WOULD I DO THAT?
TO HAVE A RELATION-SHIP WITH HIM. WHY ELSE?

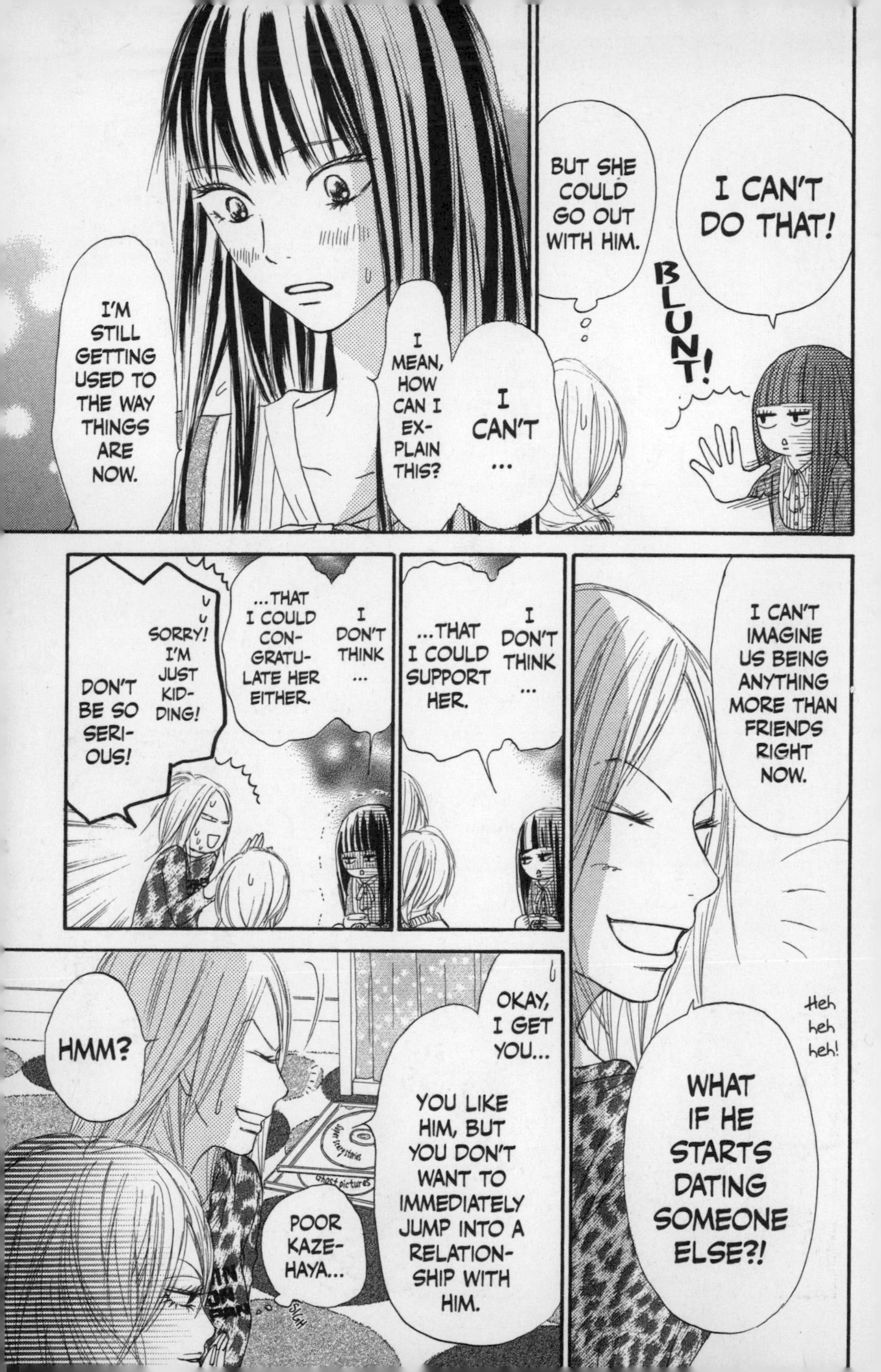
I CAN'T DO THAT!
BLUNT!
BUT SHE COULD GO OUT WITH HIM.
I CAN'T ...
I MEAN, HOW CAN I EXPLAIN THIS?
I'M STILL GETTING USED TO THE WAY THINGS ARE NOW.
I CAN'T IMAGINE US BEING ANYTHING MORE THAN FRIENDS RIGHT NOW.
Heh heh heh!
WHAT IF HE STARTS DATING SOMEONE ELSE?!
I DON'T THINK ...
...THAT I COULD SUPPORT HER.
I DON'T THINK ...
...THAT I COULD CONGRATULATE HER EITHER.
SORRY! I'M JUST KIDDING!
DON'T BE SO SERIOUS!
OKAY, I GET YOU...
YOU LIKE HIM, BUT YOU DON'T WANT TO IMMEDIATELY JUMP INTO A RELATIONSHIP WITH HIM.
HMM?
Super scary stories
Ghost pictures
POOR KAZEHAYA...
SIGH

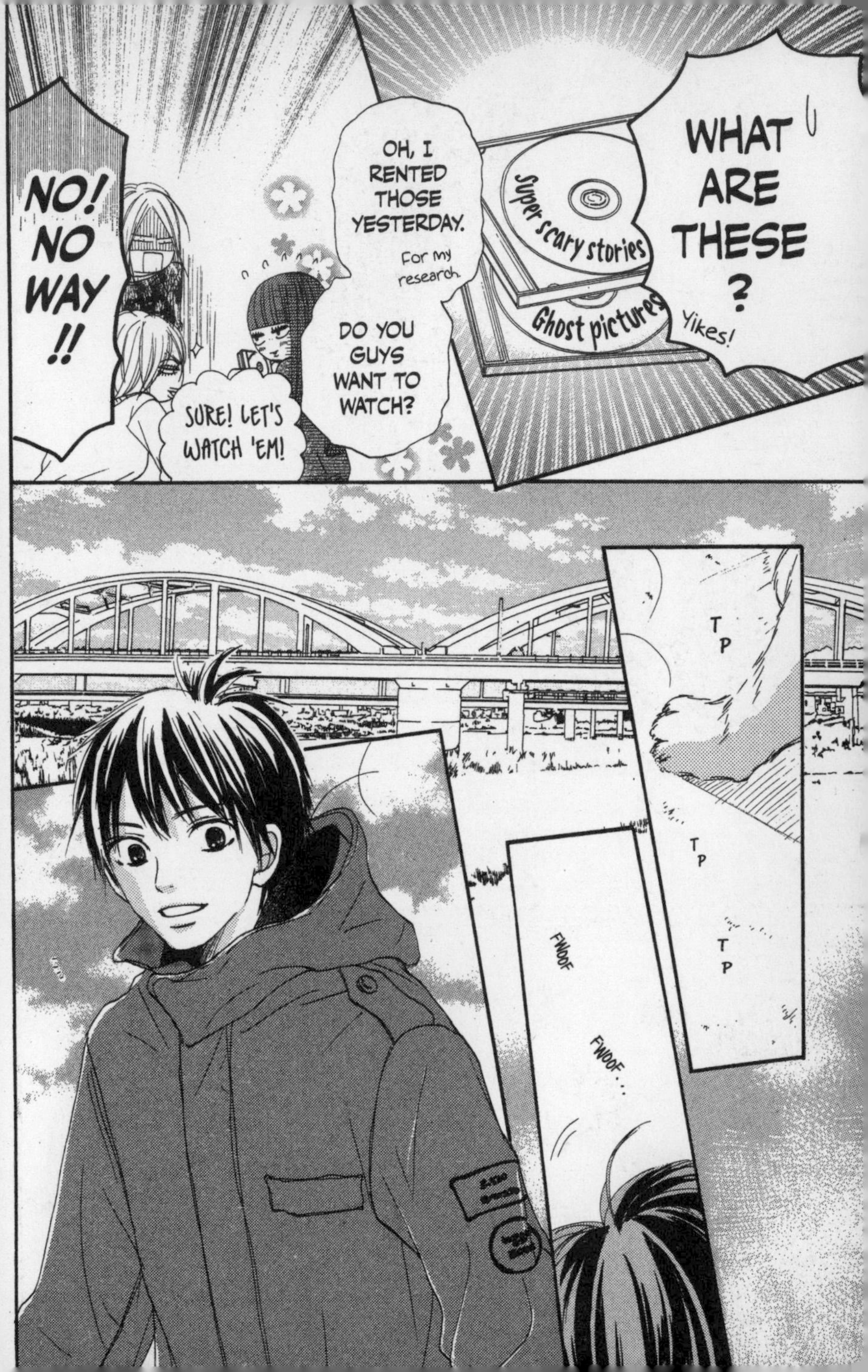
WHAT ARE THESE?
Super scary stories
Ghost pictures
Yikes!
OH, I RENTED THOSE YESTERDAY.
For my research.
DO YOU GUYS WANT TO WATCH?
SURE! LET'S WATCH 'EM!
NO! NO WAY!!
TP
TP
TP
FWOOF
FWOOF...

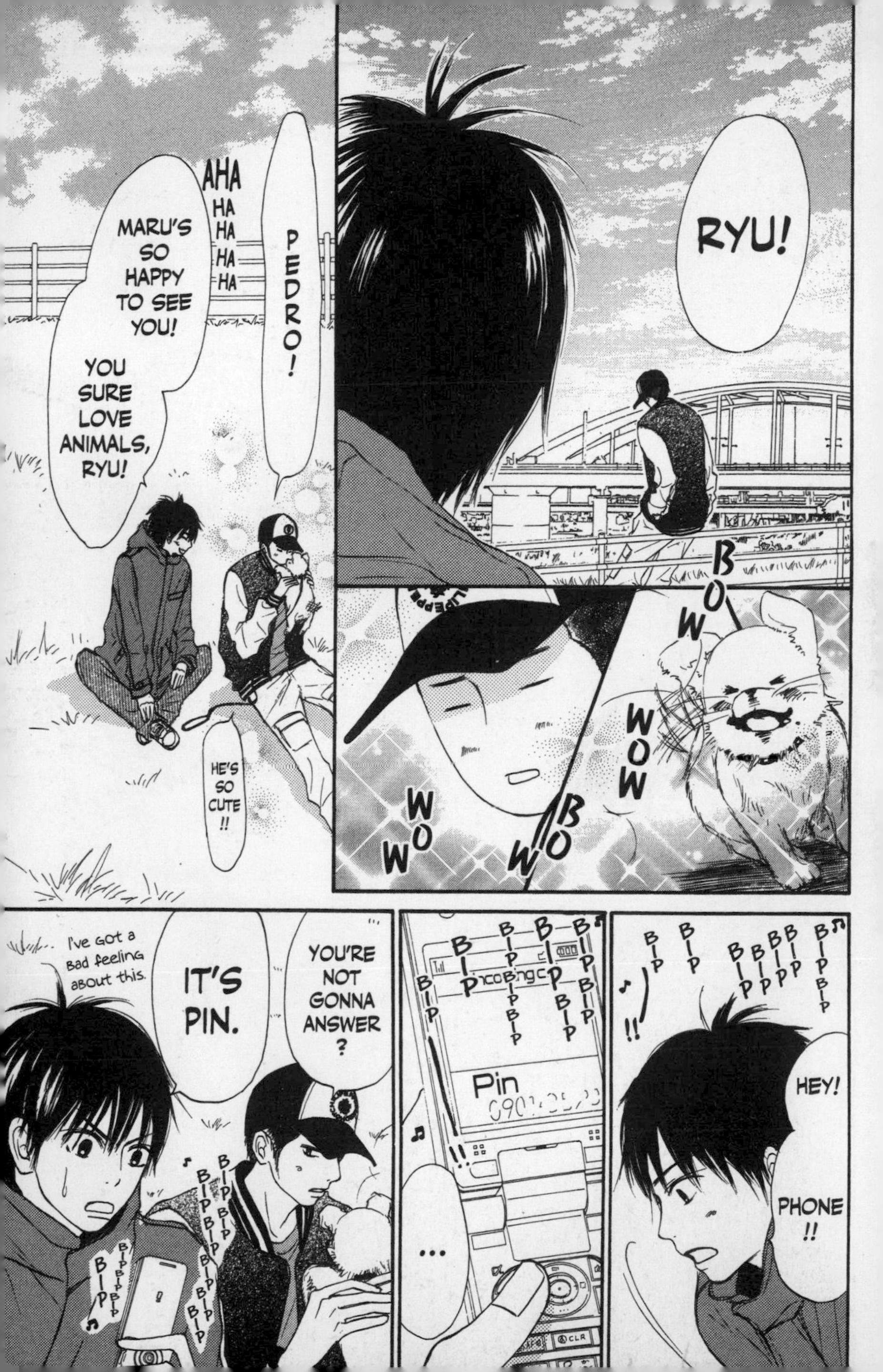
RYU!
BOW WOW
WOW WOW
BOW WOW
WOW WOW
PEDRO!
AHA HA HA HA HA
MARU'S SO HAPPY TO SEE YOU!
YOU SURE LOVE ANIMALS, RYU!
HE'S SO CUTE!!
BIP BIP BIP BIP BIP BIP
♪ !!
HEY!
PHONE!!
BIP BIP BIP BIP BIP BIP BIP BIP BIP BIP BIP BIP
Pin
...
YOU'RE NOT GONNA ANSWER?
IT'S PIN.
I've got a bad feeling about this.
BIP BIP BIP BIP BIP BIP BIP BIP BIP BIP BIP

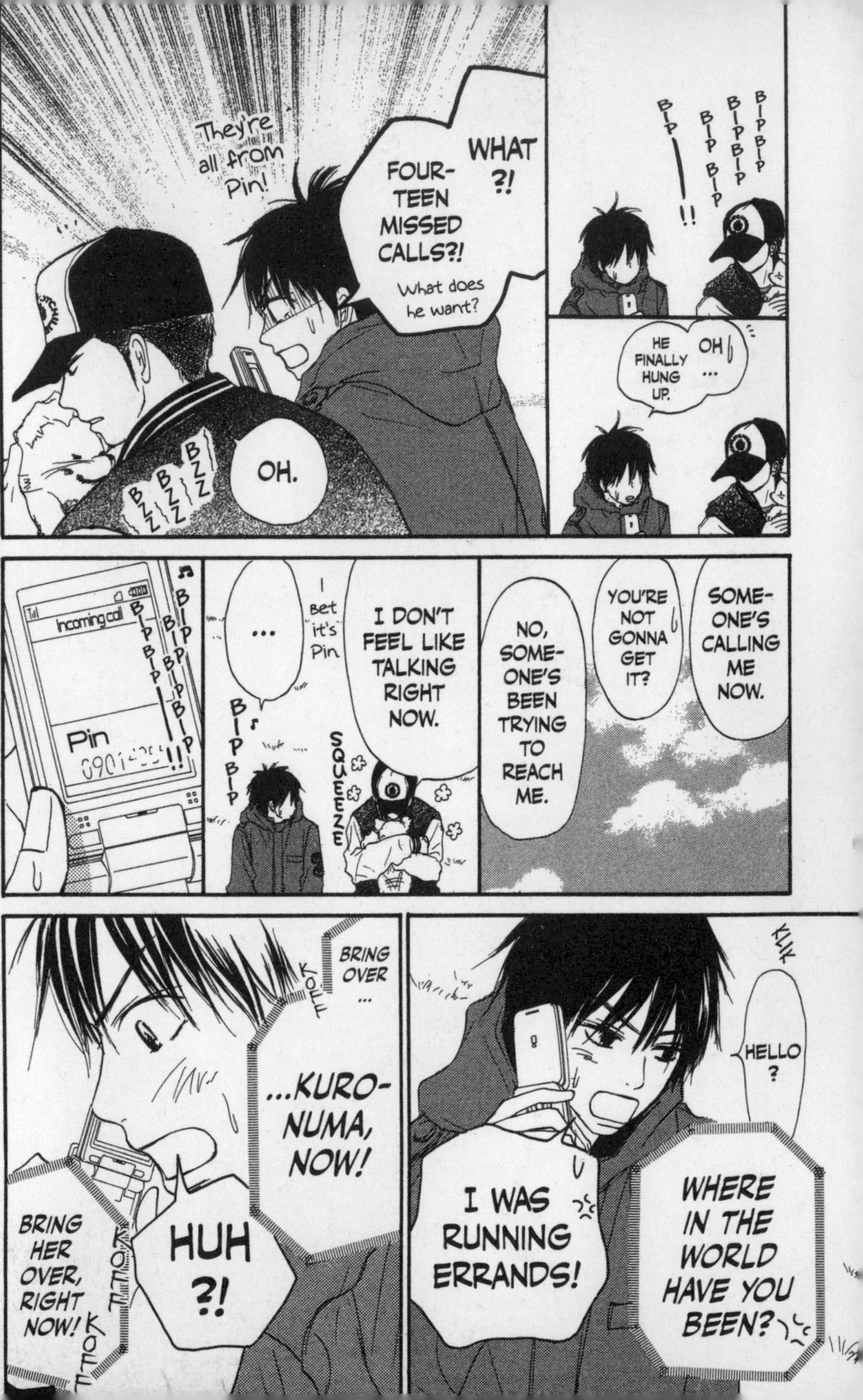
BIP BIP BIP BIP
BIP BIP BIP
BIP—!!
OH...
HE FINALLY HUNG UP.
WHAT?!
FOURTEEN MISSED CALLS?!
What does he want?
They're all from Pin!
OH.
BZZ BZZ BZZ
SOMEONE'S CALLING ME NOW.
YOU'RE NOT GONNA GET IT?
NO, SOMEONE'S BEEN TRYING TO REACH ME.
I DON'T FEEL LIKE TALKING RIGHT NOW.
I bet it's Pin.
...
BIP BIP
SQUEEZE
Incoming call
Pin
BIP BIP BIP—!!
BIP BIP BIP BIP
KLIK
HELLO?
WHERE IN THE WORLD HAVE YOU BEEN?
I WAS RUNNING ERRANDS!
BRING OVER...
KOFF
...KURONUMA, NOW!
HUH?!
BRING HER OVER, RIGHT NOW!
KOFF KOFF

KARUPIN on JAPAN 2

I would like to tell you about the handmade stamps that I've been receiving. They're crafted so beautifully. They're amazing! I want to introduce them in the order received.

Sawako Stamp ①

Hiromi-chan, who helps us out every month, made the Sawako stamp! It's so cute! The flowers around Sawako were specially crafted by Hiromi-chan! It's made out of an eraser, intricately designed, and so much cuter than the Sawako that I draw!

It comes with a handmade box!

Hiromi is soothingly beautiful.

The box is cute too...

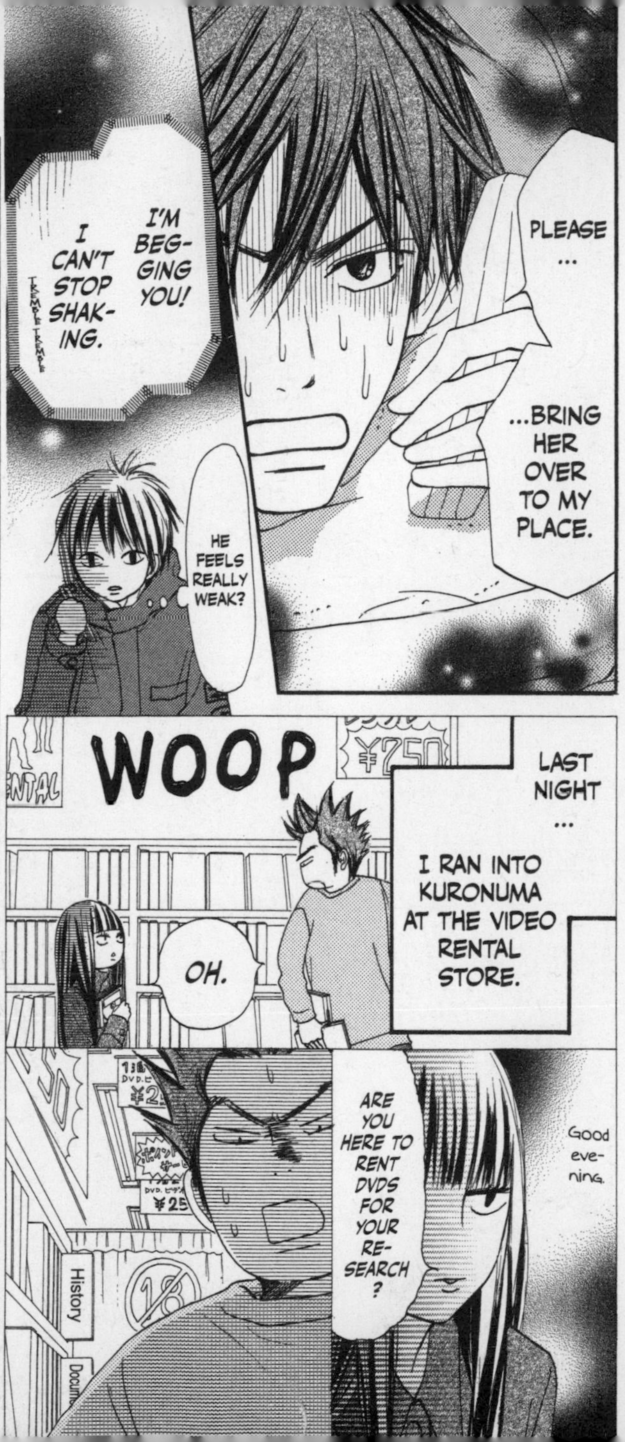
PLEASE ...
...BRING HER OVER TO MY PLACE.
I'M BEG-GING YOU!
I CAN'T STOP SHAK-ING.
TREMBLE TREMBLE
HE FEELS REALLY WEAK?
LAST NIGHT ...
I RAN INTO KURONUMA AT THE VIDEO RENTAL STORE.
WOOP
¥250
OH.
Good eve-ning.
ARE YOU HERE TO RENT DVDS FOR YOUR RE-SEARCH?
History

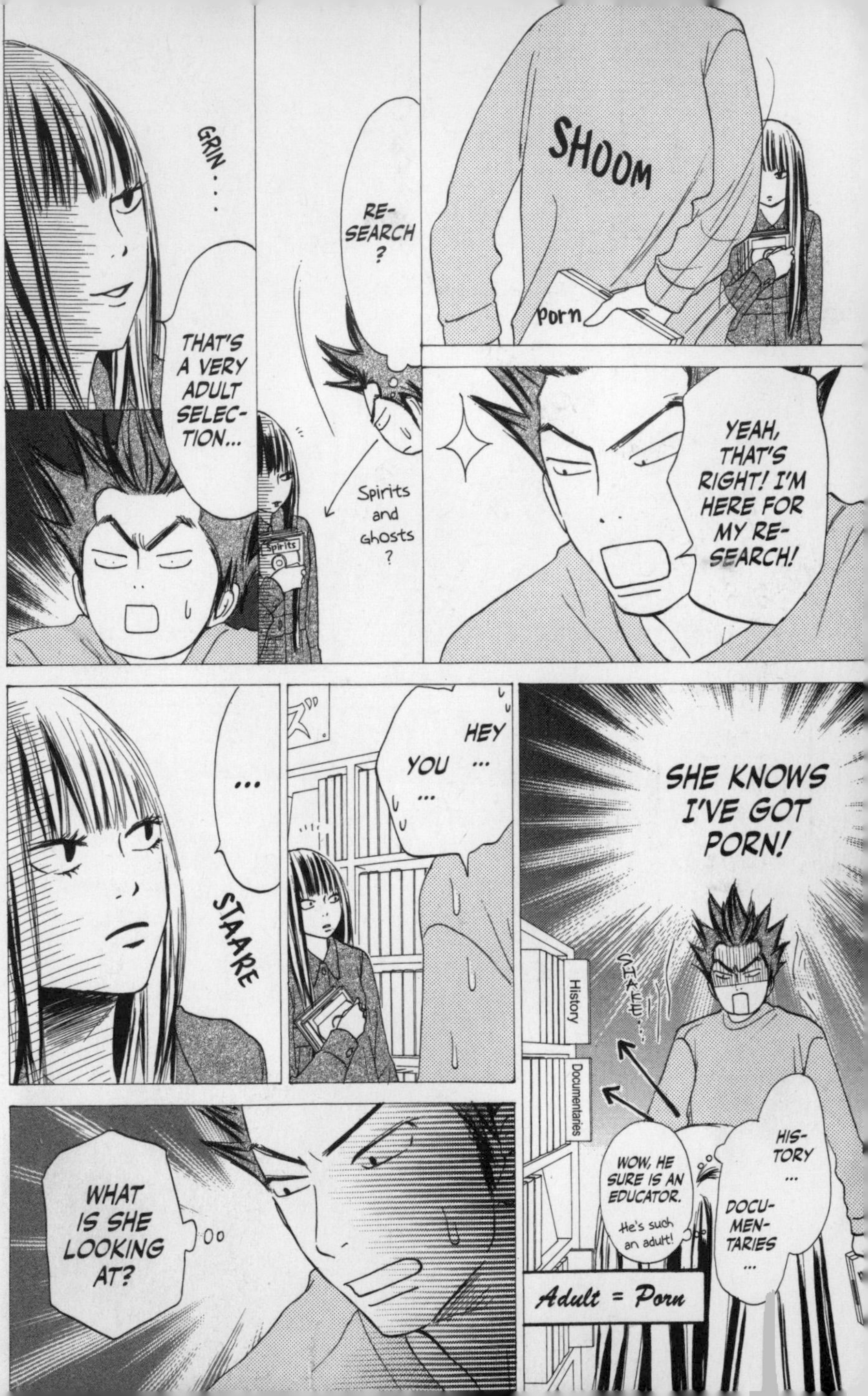
SHOOM
Porn
YEAH, THAT'S RIGHT! I'M HERE FOR MY RE-SEARCH!
RE-SEARCH?
Spirits and ghosts?
Spirits
GRIN...
THAT'S A VERY ADULT SELEC-TION...
SHE KNOWS I'VE GOT PORN!
SHAKE...
History
Documentaries
HIS-TORY... DOCU-MEN-TARIES...
WOW, HE SURE IS AN EDUCATOR.
He's such an adult!
Adult = Porn
HEY YOU...
...
STAARE
WHAT IS SHE LOOKING AT?

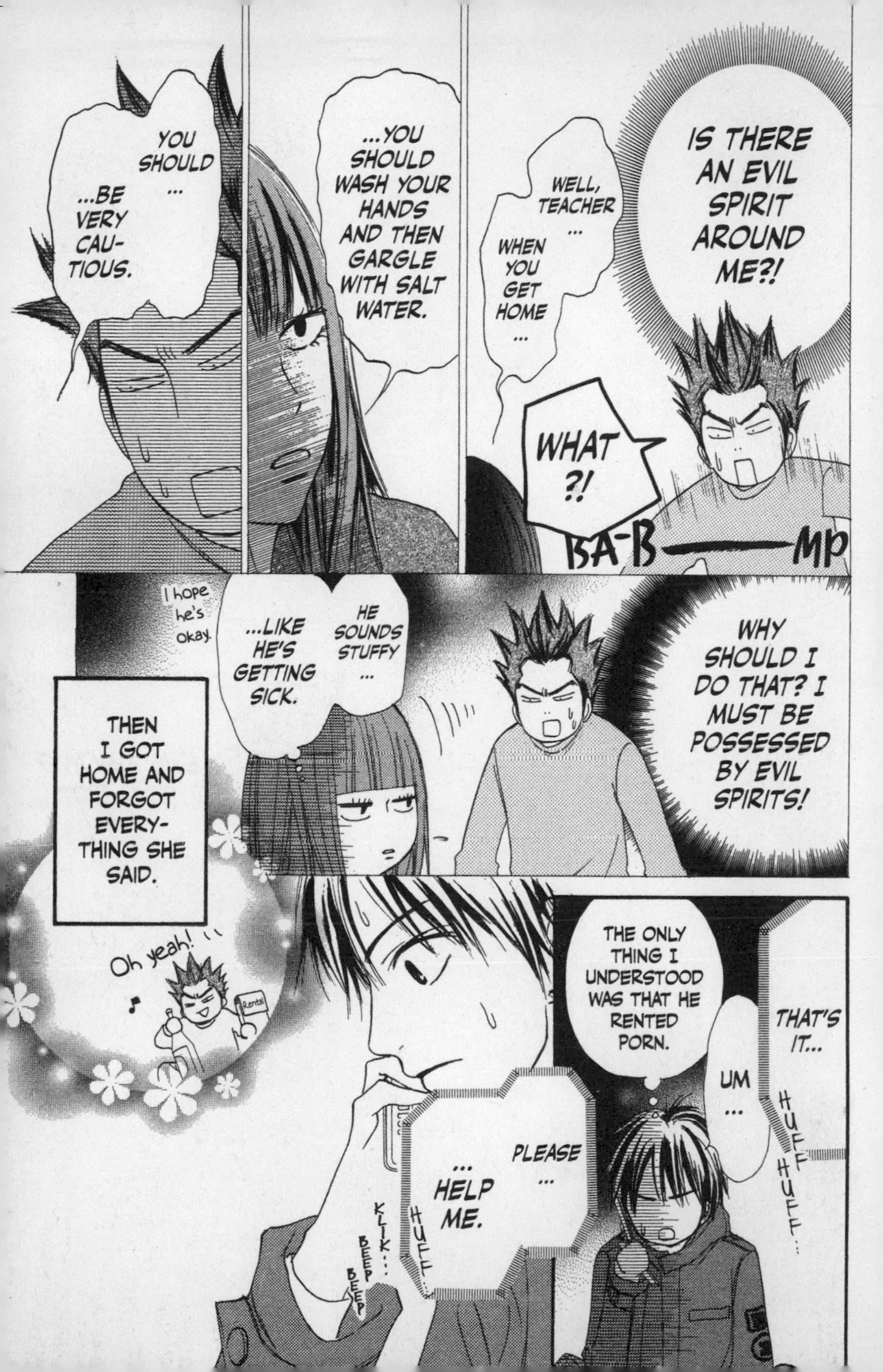
IS THERE AN EVIL SPIRIT AROUND ME?!
WELL, TEACHER ... WHEN YOU GET HOME ...
WHAT?!
BA-B——MP
...YOU SHOULD WASH YOUR HANDS AND THEN GARGLE WITH SALT WATER.
YOU SHOULD ... ...BE VERY CAU-TIOUS.
WHY SHOULD I DO THAT? I MUST BE POSSESSED BY EVIL SPIRITS!
HE SOUNDS STUFFY ...
...LIKE HE'S GETTING SICK.
I hope he's okay.
THAT'S IT...
HUFF HUFF HUFF...
THE ONLY THING I UNDERSTOOD WAS THAT HE RENTED PORN.
UM ...
THEN I GOT HOME AND FORGOT EVERY-THING SHE SAID.
Oh yeah!
Rental
PLEASE ...
... HELP ME.
HUFF...
KLIK...
BEEP BEEP

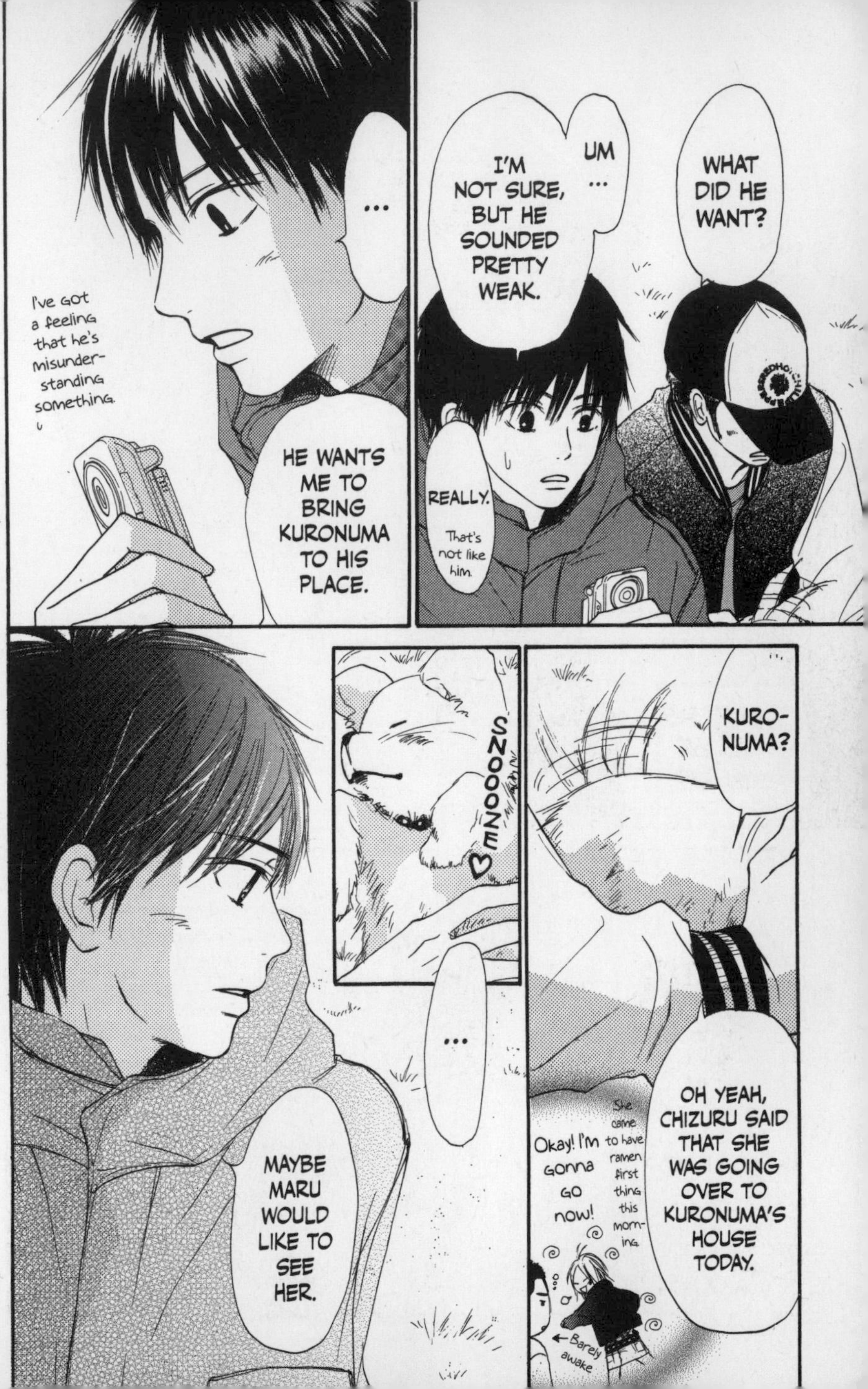
WHAT DID HE WANT?
UM ...
I'M NOT SURE, BUT HE SOUNDED PRETTY WEAK.
REALLY.
That's not like him.
...
HE WANTS ME TO BRING KURONUMA TO HIS PLACE.
I've got a feeling that he's misunderstanding something.
KURO-NUMA?
OH YEAH, CHIZURU SAID THAT SHE WAS GOING OVER TO KURONUMA'S HOUSE TODAY.
She came to have ramen first thing this morning.
Okay! I'm gonna go now!
← Barely awake
SNOOOOZE ♥
...
MAYBE MARU WOULD LIKE TO SEE HER.

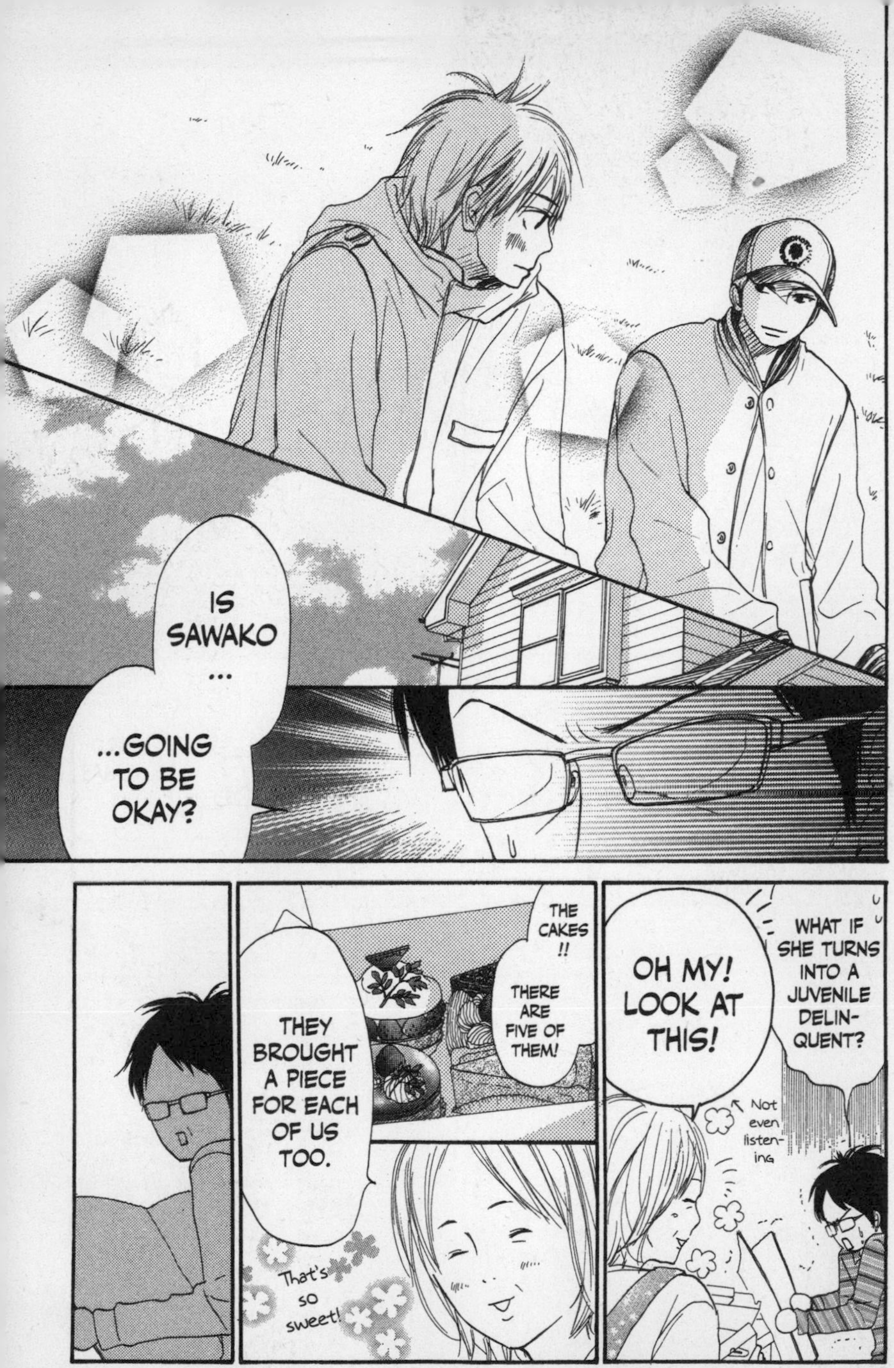
IS SAWAKO ...
...GOING TO BE OKAY?
WHAT IF SHE TURNS INTO A JUVENILE DELIN-QUENT?
OH MY! LOOK AT THIS!
Not even listen-ing
THE CAKES !!
THERE ARE FIVE OF THEM!
THEY BROUGHT A PIECE FOR EACH OF US TOO.
That's so sweet!

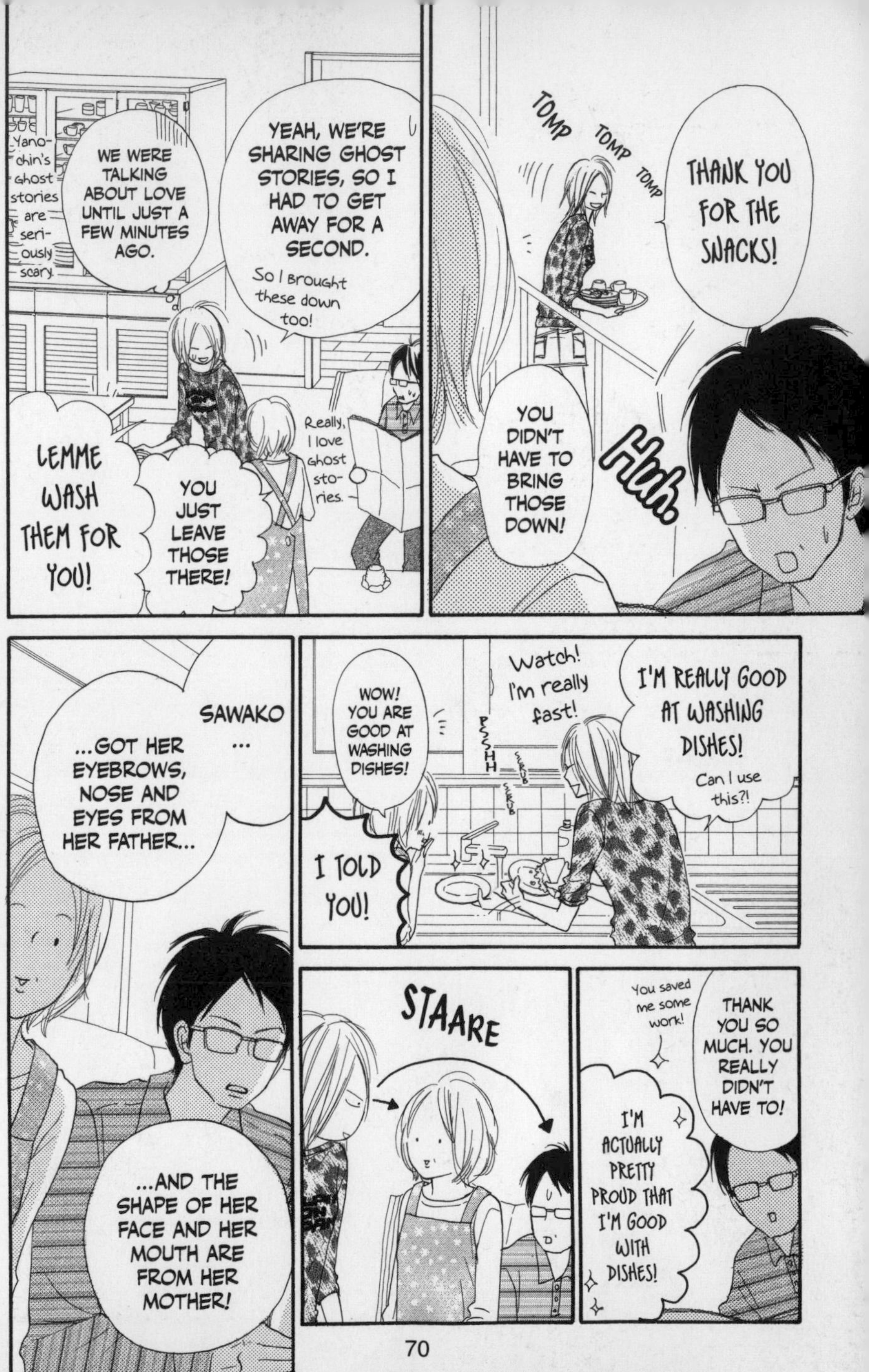
TOMP TOMP TOMP
THANK YOU FOR THE SNACKS!
YOU DIDN'T HAVE TO BRING THOSE DOWN!
Huh.
YEAH, WE'RE SHARING GHOST STORIES, SO I HAD TO GET AWAY FOR A SECOND.
So I brought these down too!
WE WERE TALKING ABOUT LOVE UNTIL JUST A FEW MINUTES AGO.
Yano-chin's ghost stories are seriously scary.
Really, I love ghost stories.
YOU JUST LEAVE THOSE THERE!
LEMME WASH THEM FOR YOU!
I'M REALLY GOOD AT WASHING DISHES!
Can I use this?!
Watch! I'm really fast!
PSSHH
SKRUB SKRUB
WOW! YOU ARE GOOD AT WASHING DISHES!
I TOLD YOU!
THANK YOU SO MUCH. YOU REALLY DIDN'T HAVE TO!
You saved me some work!
I'M ACTUALLY PRETTY PROUD THAT I'M GOOD WITH DISHES!
STAARE
SAWAKO...
...GOT HER EYEBROWS, NOSE AND EYES FROM HER FATHER...
...AND THE SHAPE OF HER FACE AND HER MOUTH ARE FROM HER MOTHER!

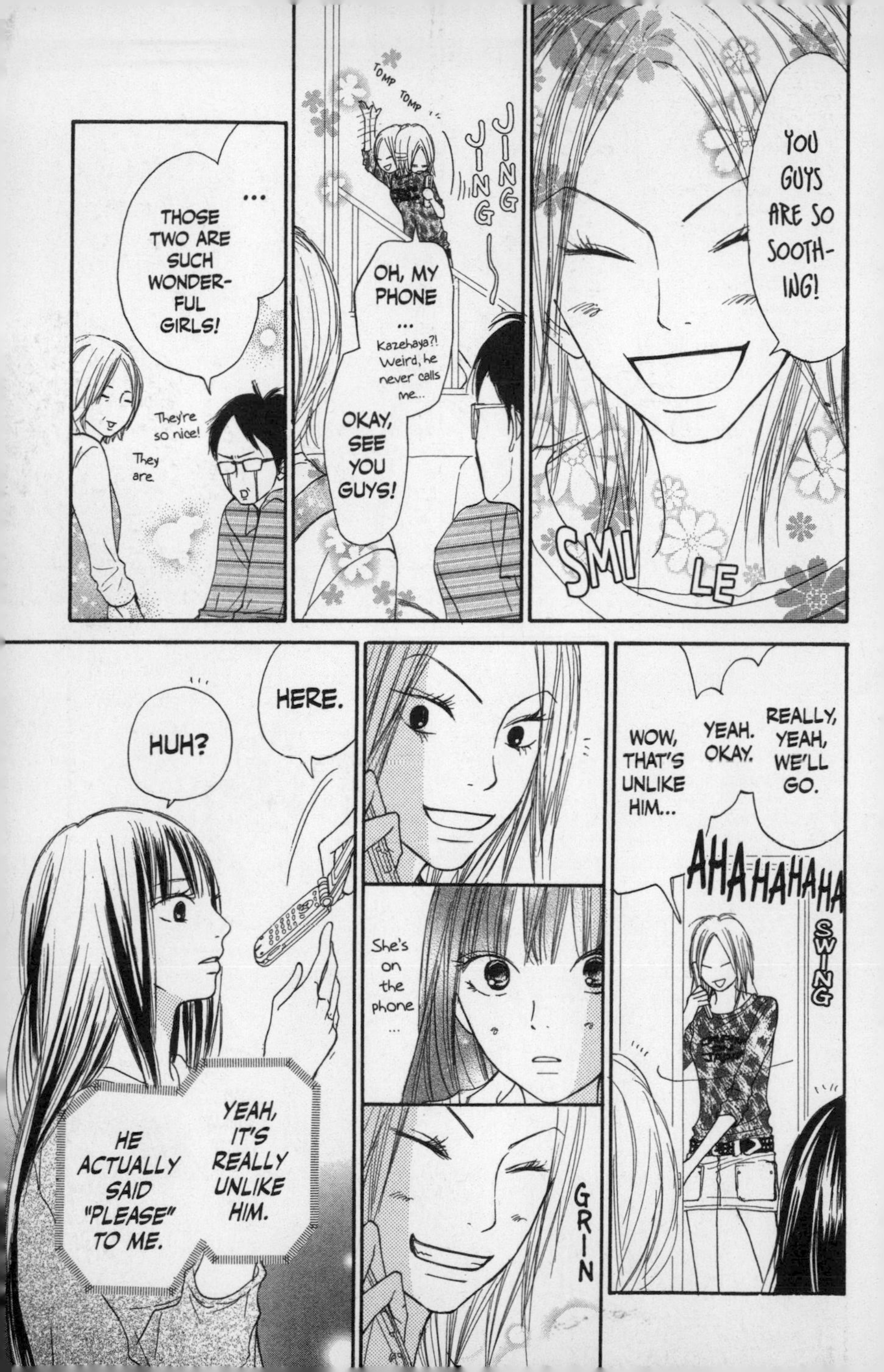
YOU GUYS ARE SO SOOTHING!
SMILE
TOMP TOMP
JING JING
OH, MY PHONE...
Kazehaya?! Weird, he never calls me...
OKAY, SEE YOU GUYS!
...
THOSE TWO ARE SUCH WONDERFUL GIRLS!
They're so nice!
They are.
REALLY, YEAH, WE'LL GO.
YEAH. OKAY.
WOW, THAT'S UNLIKE HIM...
AHAHAHAHA
SWING
She's on the phone...
GRIN
HERE.
HUH?
YEAH, IT'S REALLY UNLIKE HIM.
HE ACTUALLY SAID "PLEASE" TO ME.

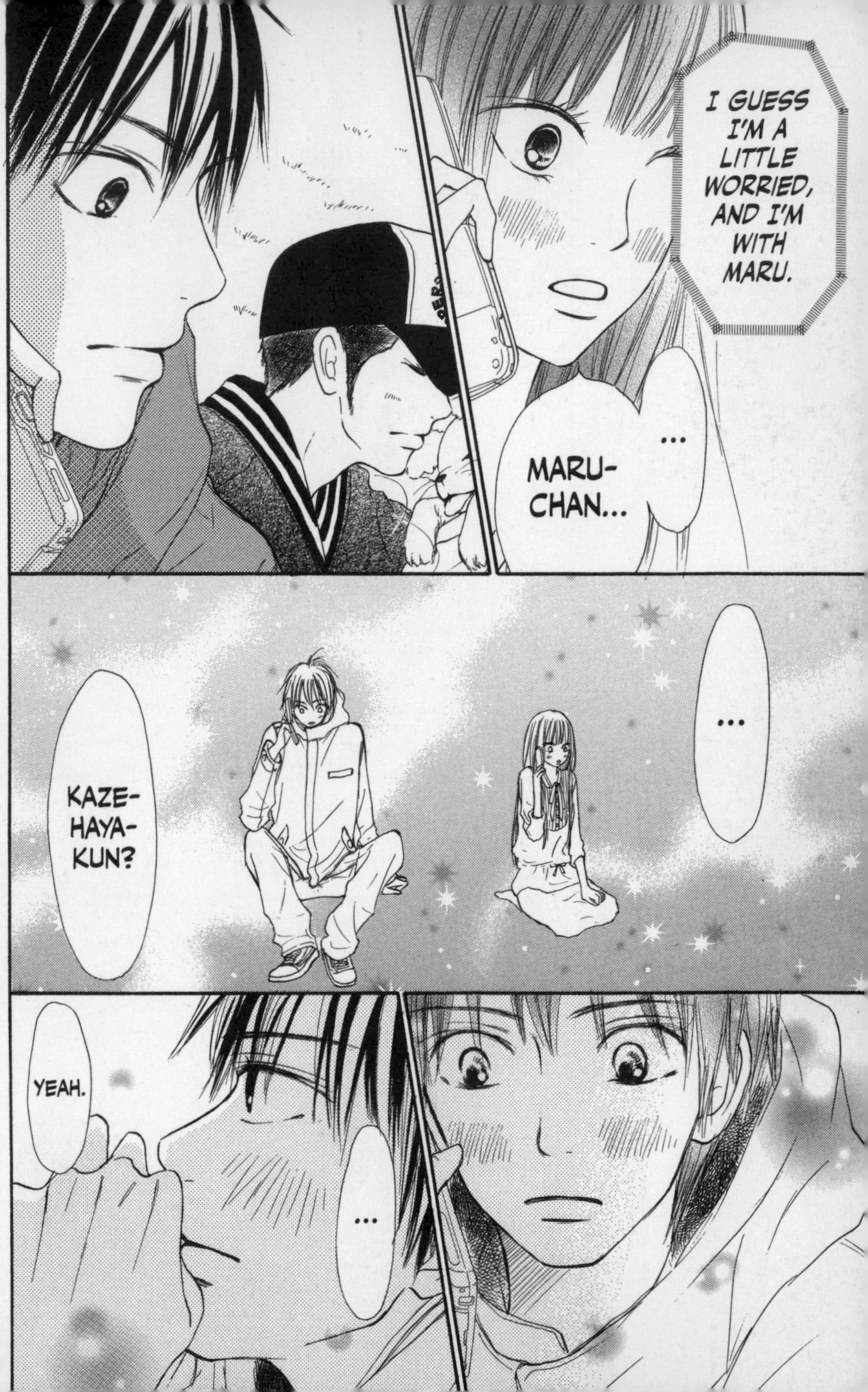
I GUESS I'M A LITTLE WORRIED, AND I'M WITH MARU.
...
MARU-CHAN...
...
KAZE-HAYA-KUN?
...
YEAH.

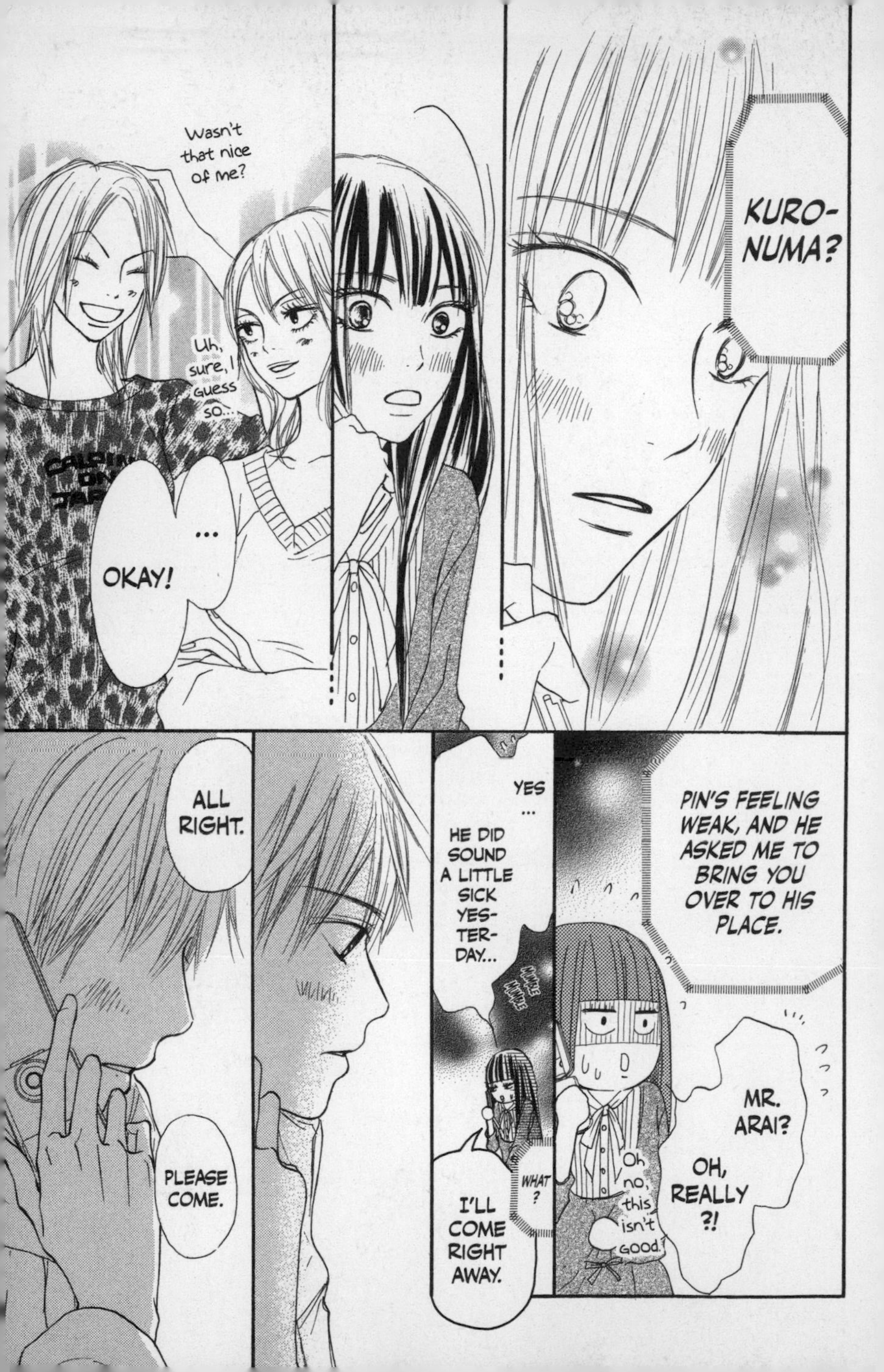
KURO-NUMA?
Wasn't that nice of me?
Uh, sure, I guess so...
... OKAY!
PIN'S FEELING WEAK, AND HE ASKED ME TO BRING YOU OVER TO HIS PLACE.
MR. ARAI?
OH, REALLY?!
Oh no, this isn't good.
YES...
HE DID SOUND A LITTLE SICK YES-TER-DAY...
MUMBLE MUMBLE
WHAT?
I'LL COME RIGHT AWAY.
ALL RIGHT.
PLEASE COME.

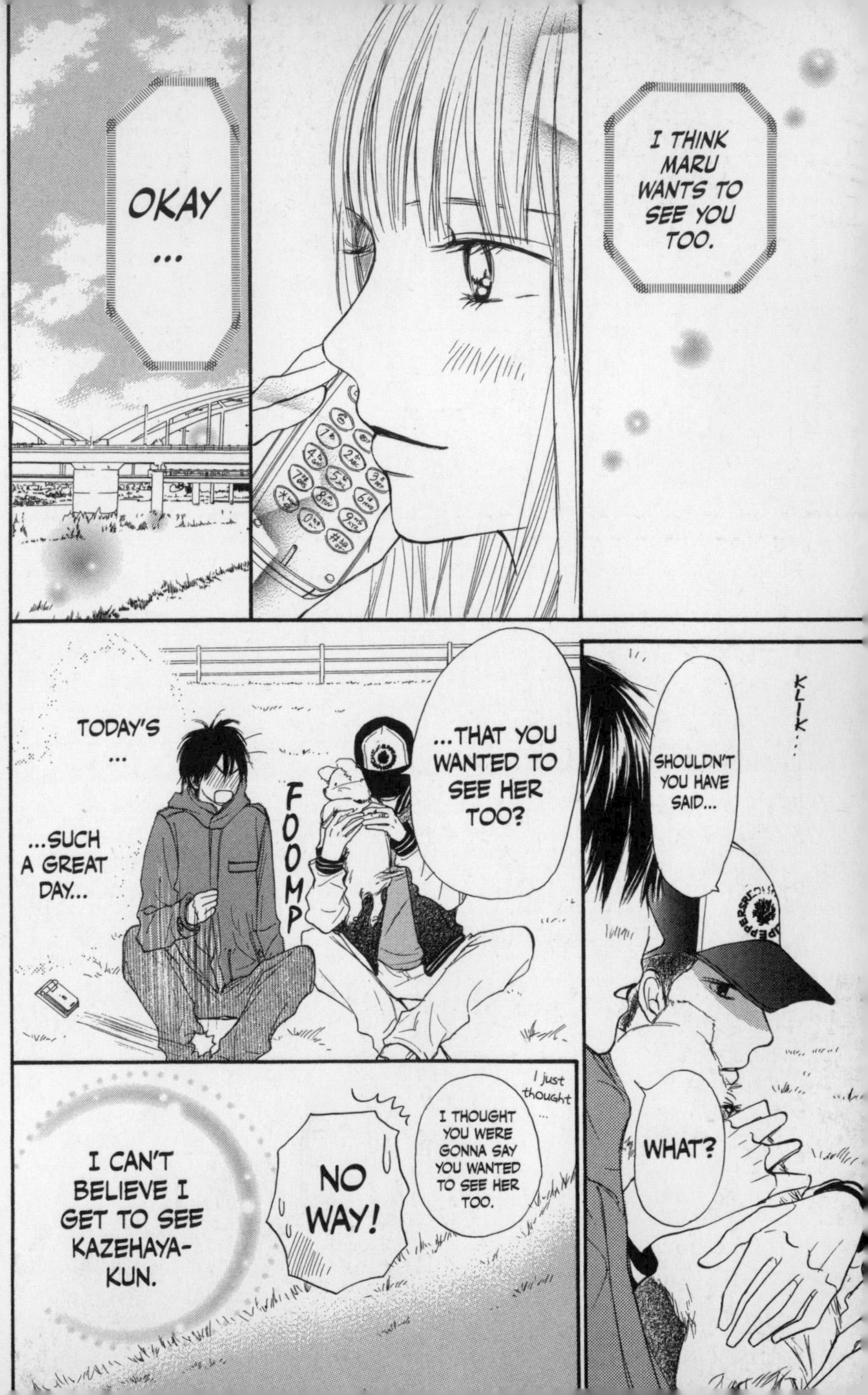

I THINK MARU WANTS TO SEE YOU TOO.
OKAY ...
KLIK..
SHOULDN'T YOU HAVE SAID...
...THAT YOU WANTED TO SEE HER TOO?
FOOOMP
TODAY'S ...
...SUCH A GREAT DAY...
WHAT?
I just thought ...
I THOUGHT YOU WERE GONNA SAY YOU WANTED TO SEE HER TOO.
NO WAY!
I CAN'T BELIEVE I GET TO SEE KAZEHAYA-KUN.

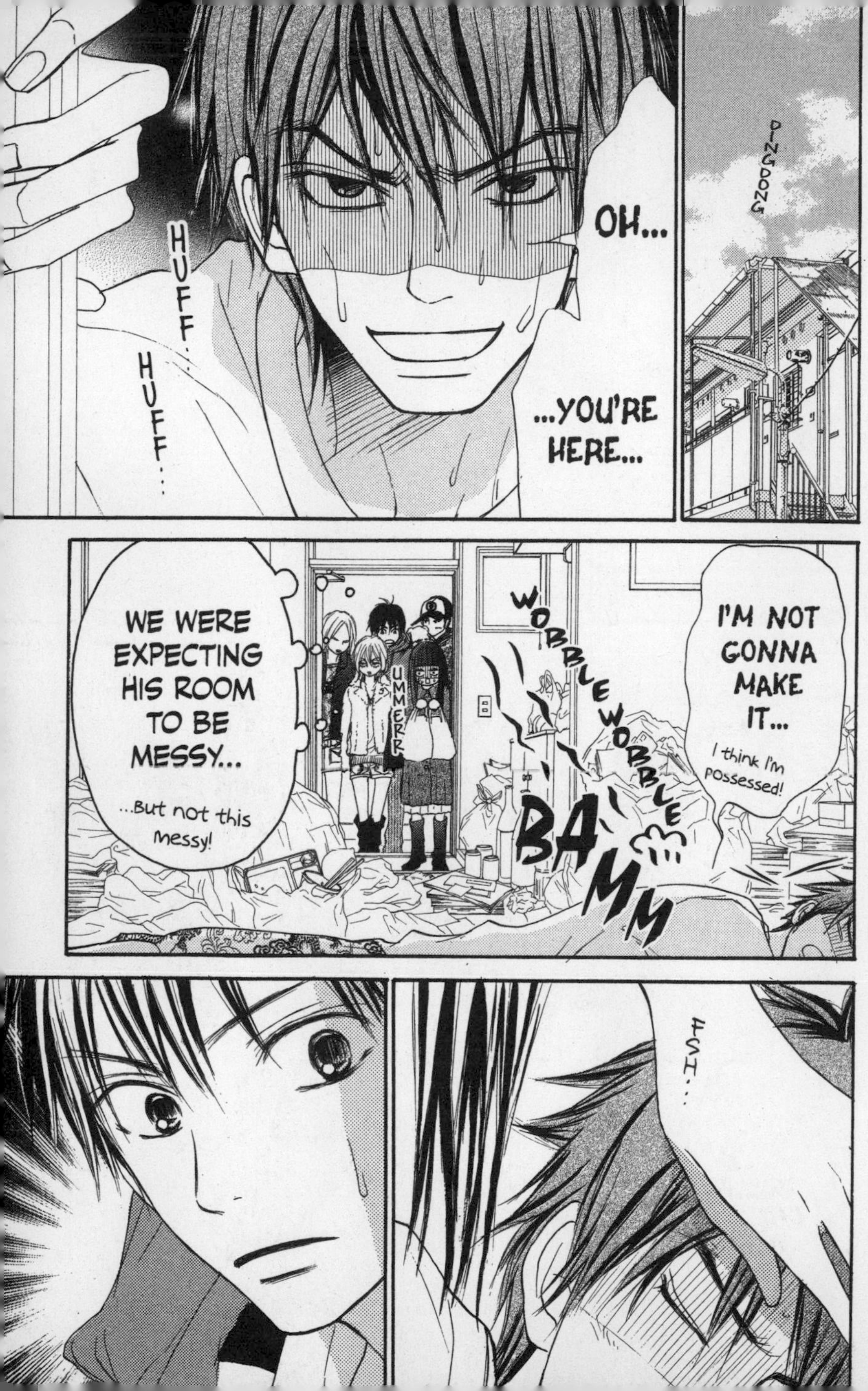
DING DONG
OH...
...YOU'RE HERE...
HUFF...
HUFF...
I'M NOT GONNA MAKE IT...
I think I'm possessed!
WOBBLEWOBBLE
BAMM
UMMERR
WE WERE EXPECTING HIS ROOM TO BE MESSY...
...But not this messy!
FSH...

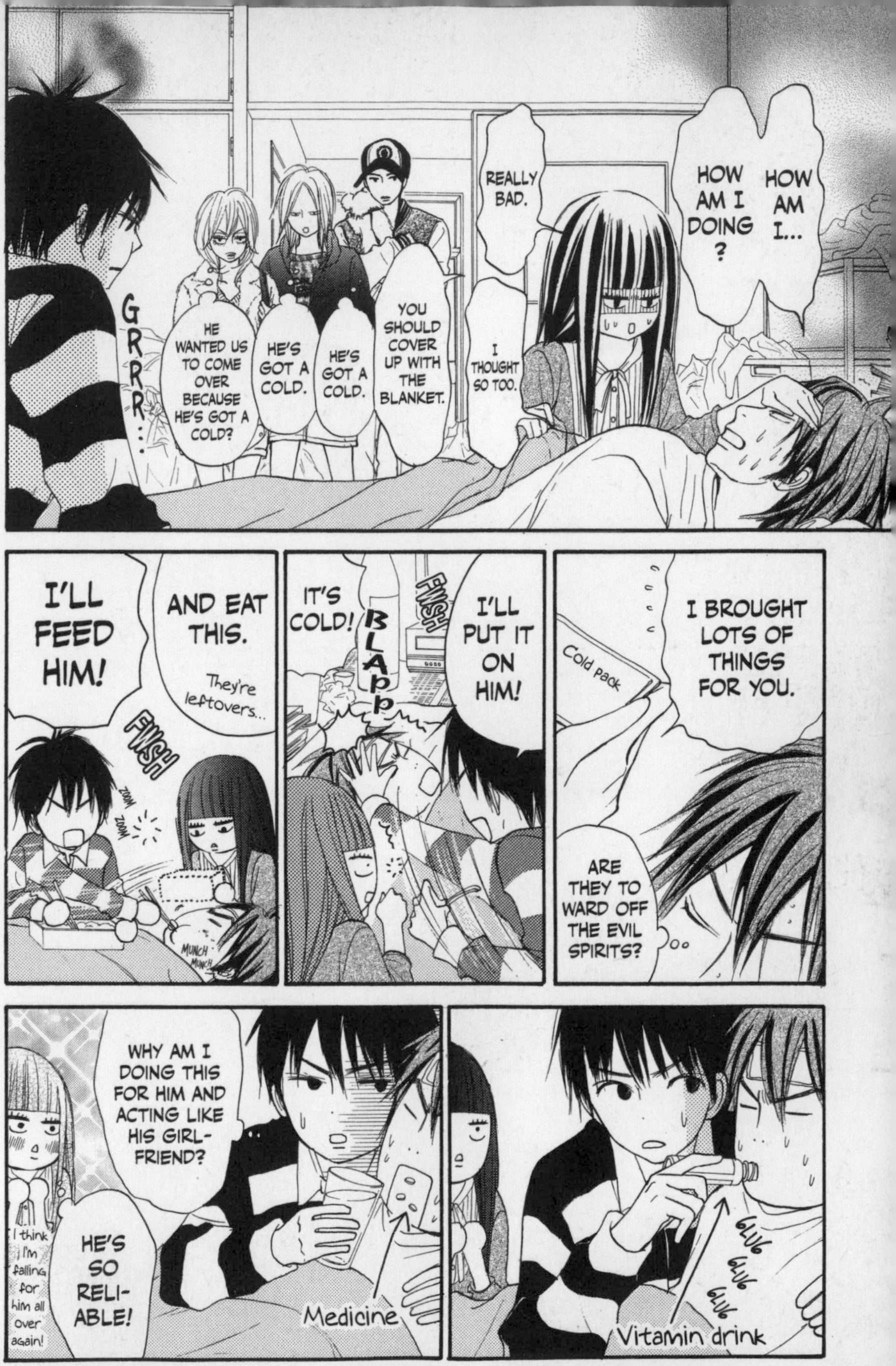
HOW AM I...
HOW AM I DOING?
REALLY BAD.
I THOUGHT SO TOO.
YOU SHOULD COVER UP WITH THE BLANKET.
HE'S GOT A COLD.
HE'S GOT A COLD.
HE WANTED US TO COME OVER BECAUSE HE'S GOT A COLD?
GRRR...
I BROUGHT LOTS OF THINGS FOR YOU.
Cold pack
ARE THEY TO WARD OFF THE EVIL SPIRITS?
I'LL PUT IT ON HIM!
FWSH
IT'S COLD!
BLAPP
AND EAT THIS.
They're leftovers...
I'LL FEED HIM!
FWSH
ZOOM ZOOM
MUNCH MUNCH
GLUG GLUG GLUG
Vitamin drink
WHY AM I DOING THIS FOR HIM AND ACTING LIKE HIS GIRL-FRIEND?
HE'S SO RELI-ABLE!
I think I'm falling for him all over again!
Medicine

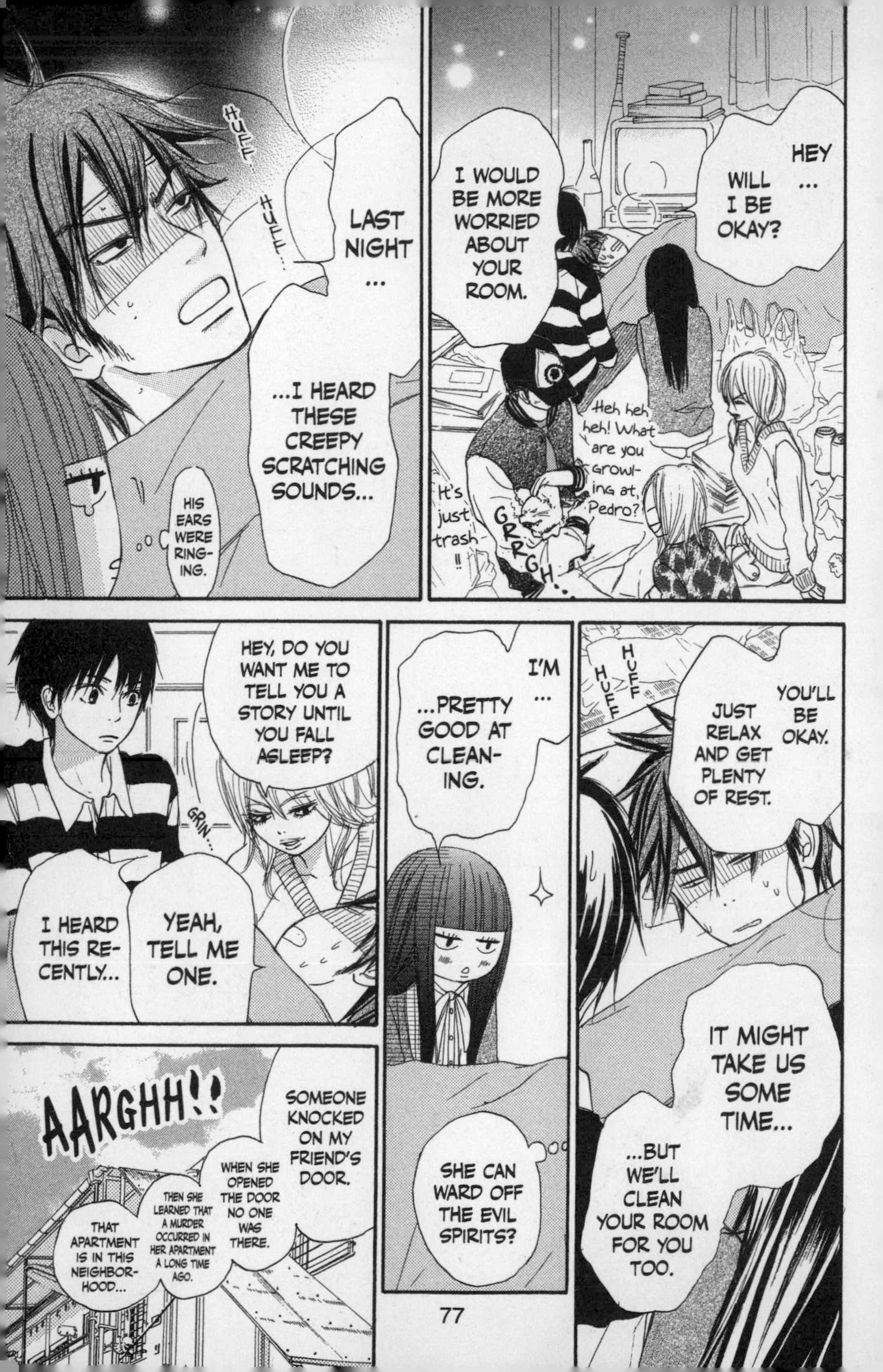
HEY ... WILL I BE OKAY?
I WOULD BE MORE WORRIED ABOUT YOUR ROOM.
Heh heh heh! What are you growl-ing at, Pedro?
It's just trash!!
GRRGH..
HUFF... HUFF...
LAST NIGHT ...
...I HEARD THESE CREEPY SCRATCHING SOUNDS...
HIS EARS WERE RING-ING.
YOU'LL BE OKAY.
JUST RELAX AND GET PLENTY OF REST.
HUFF HUFF
IT MIGHT TAKE US SOME TIME...
...BUT WE'LL CLEAN YOUR ROOM FOR YOU TOO.
I'M ...
...PRETTY GOOD AT CLEAN-ING.
SHE CAN WARD OFF THE EVIL SPIRITS?
HEY, DO YOU WANT ME TO TELL YOU A STORY UNTIL YOU FALL ASLEEP?
GRIN...
YEAH, TELL ME ONE.
I HEARD THIS RE-CENTLY...
SOMEONE KNOCKED ON MY FRIEND'S DOOR.
WHEN SHE OPENED THE DOOR NO ONE WAS THERE.
THEN SHE LEARNED THAT A MURDER OCCURRED IN HER APARTMENT A LONG TIME AGO.
THAT APARTMENT IS IN THIS NEIGHBOR-HOOD...
AARGHH!!

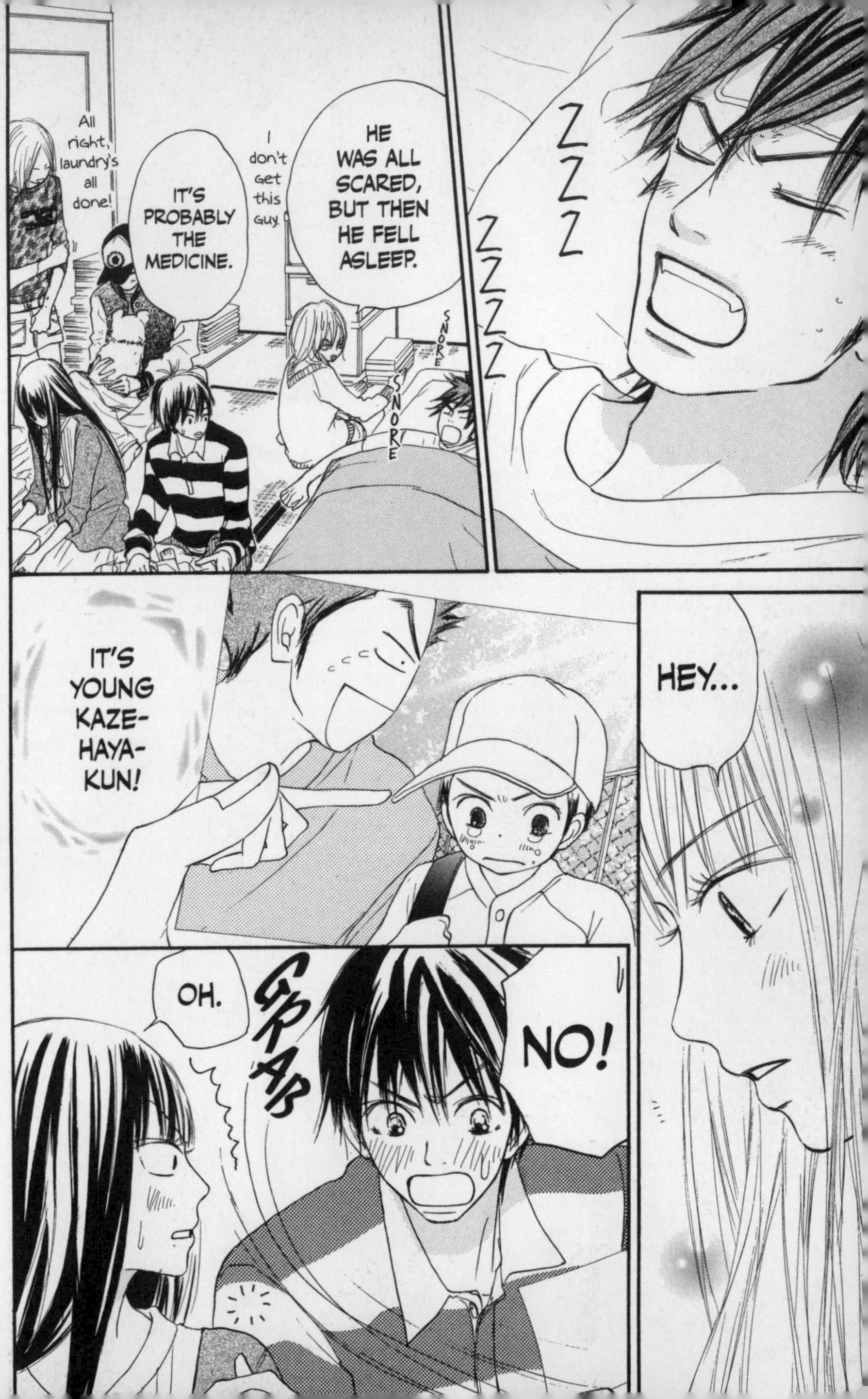

Z Z Z
Z Z Z Z
HE WAS ALL SCARED, BUT THEN HE FELL ASLEEP.
SNORE
SNORE
I don't get this guy.
IT'S PROBABLY THE MEDICINE.
All right, laundry's all done!
HEY...
IT'S YOUNG KAZE-HAYA-KUN!
NO!
GRAB
OH.

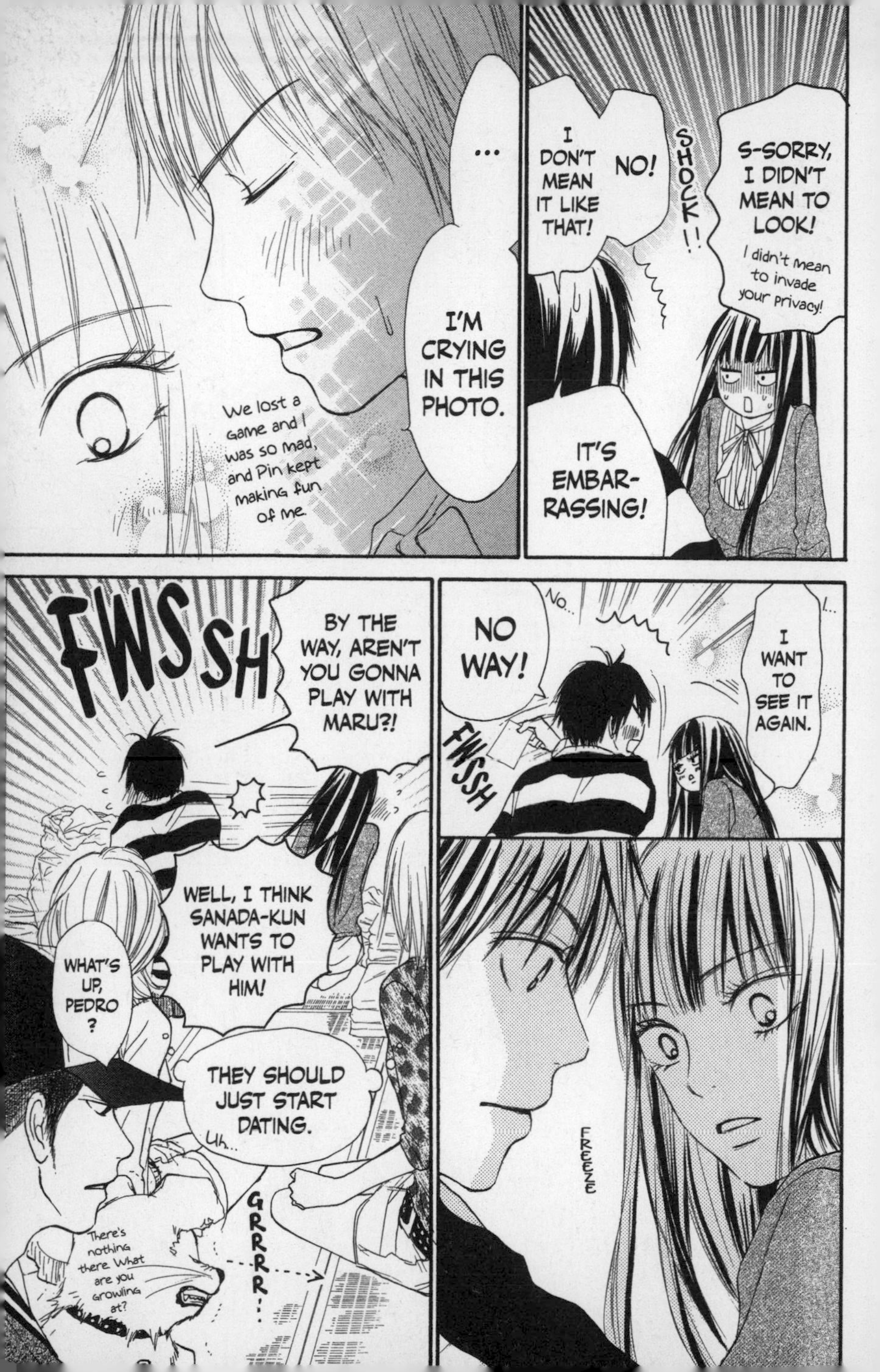
S-SORRY, I DIDN'T MEAN TO LOOK!
I didn't mean to invade your privacy!
SHOCK!!
NO!
I DON'T MEAN IT LIKE THAT!
IT'S EMBARRASSING!
...
I'M CRYING IN THIS PHOTO.
We lost a game and I was so mad, and Pin kept making fun of me.
I...
I WANT TO SEE IT AGAIN.
No...
NO WAY!
FWSSH
FREEZE
FWSSH
BY THE WAY, AREN'T YOU GONNA PLAY WITH MARU?!
WELL, I THINK SANADA-KUN WANTS TO PLAY WITH HIM!
WHAT'S UP, PEDRO?
THEY SHOULD JUST START DATING.
Uh...
GRRRR...
There's nothing there What are you growling at?

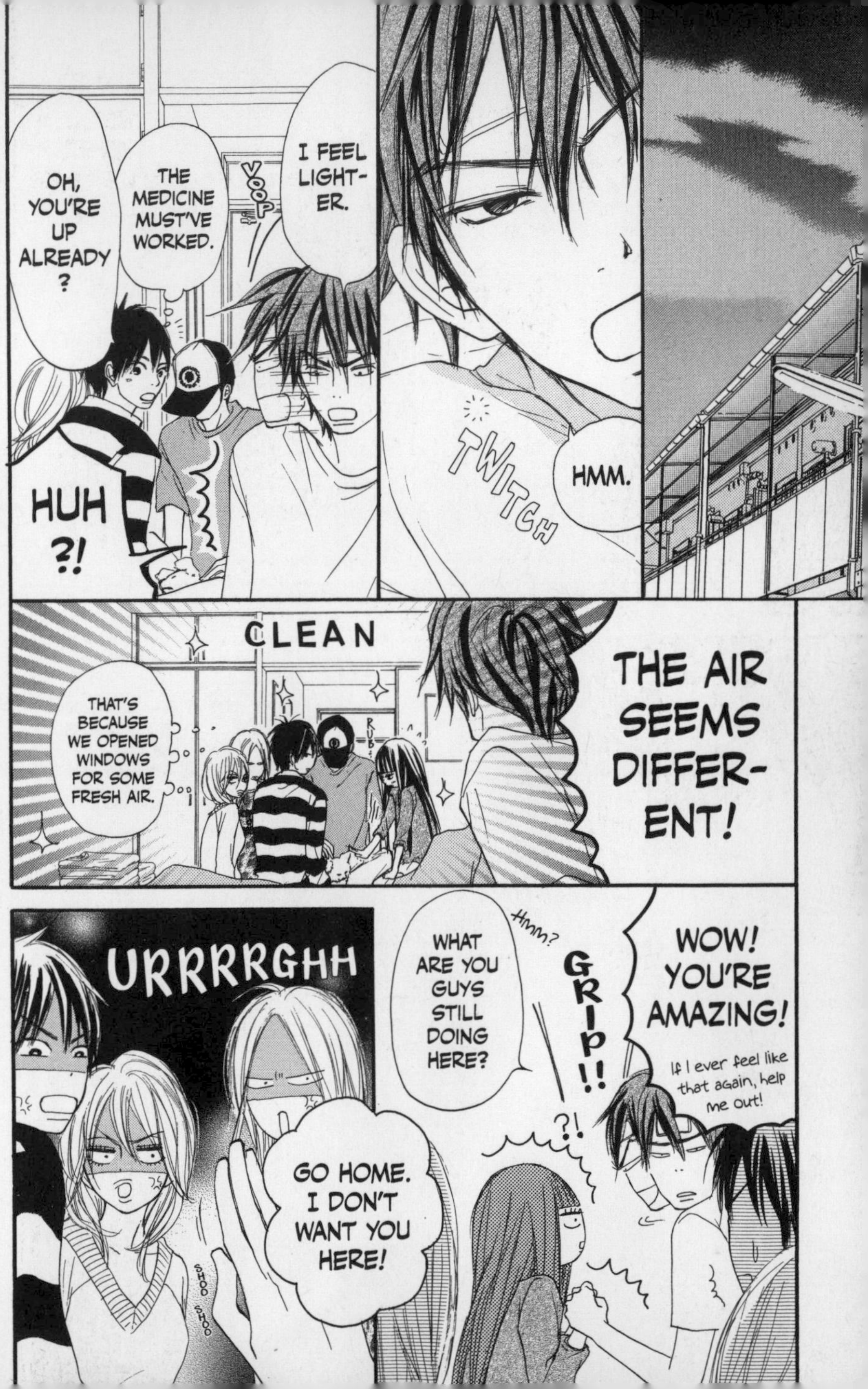
HMM.
TWITCH
I FEEL LIGHTER.
VOOP
THE MEDICINE MUST'VE WORKED.
OH, YOU'RE UP ALREADY?
HUH?!
THE AIR SEEMS DIFFERENT!
CLEAN
RUB
THAT'S BECAUSE WE OPENED WINDOWS FOR SOME FRESH AIR.
WOW! YOU'RE AMAZING!
If I ever feel like that again, help me out!
GRIP!!
Hmm?
WHAT ARE YOU GUYS STILL DOING HERE?
?!
URRRRGHH
GO HOME. I DON'T WANT YOU HERE!
SHOO SHOO

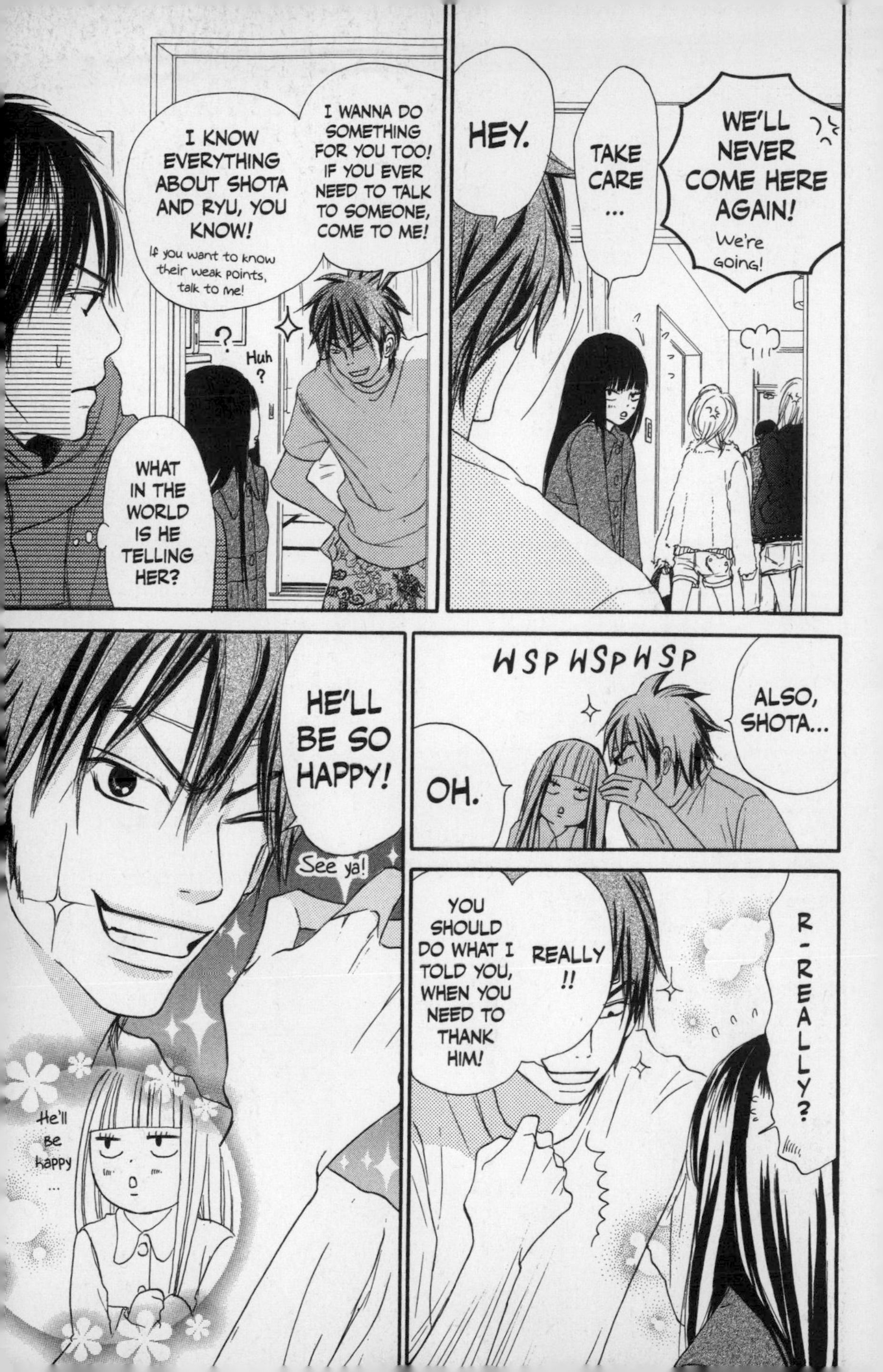
WE'LL NEVER COME HERE AGAIN!
We're going!
TAKE CARE...
HEY.
I WANNA DO SOMETHING FOR YOU TOO! IF YOU EVER NEED TO TALK TO SOMEONE, COME TO ME!
I KNOW EVERYTHING ABOUT SHOTA AND RYU, YOU KNOW!
If you want to know their weak points, talk to me!
Huh?
WHAT IN THE WORLD IS HE TELLING HER?
WSP WSP WSP
ALSO, SHOTA...
OH.
R-REALLY?
REALLY!!
YOU SHOULD DO WHAT I TOLD YOU, WHEN YOU NEED TO THANK HIM!
HE'LL BE SO HAPPY!
See ya!
He'll be happy...

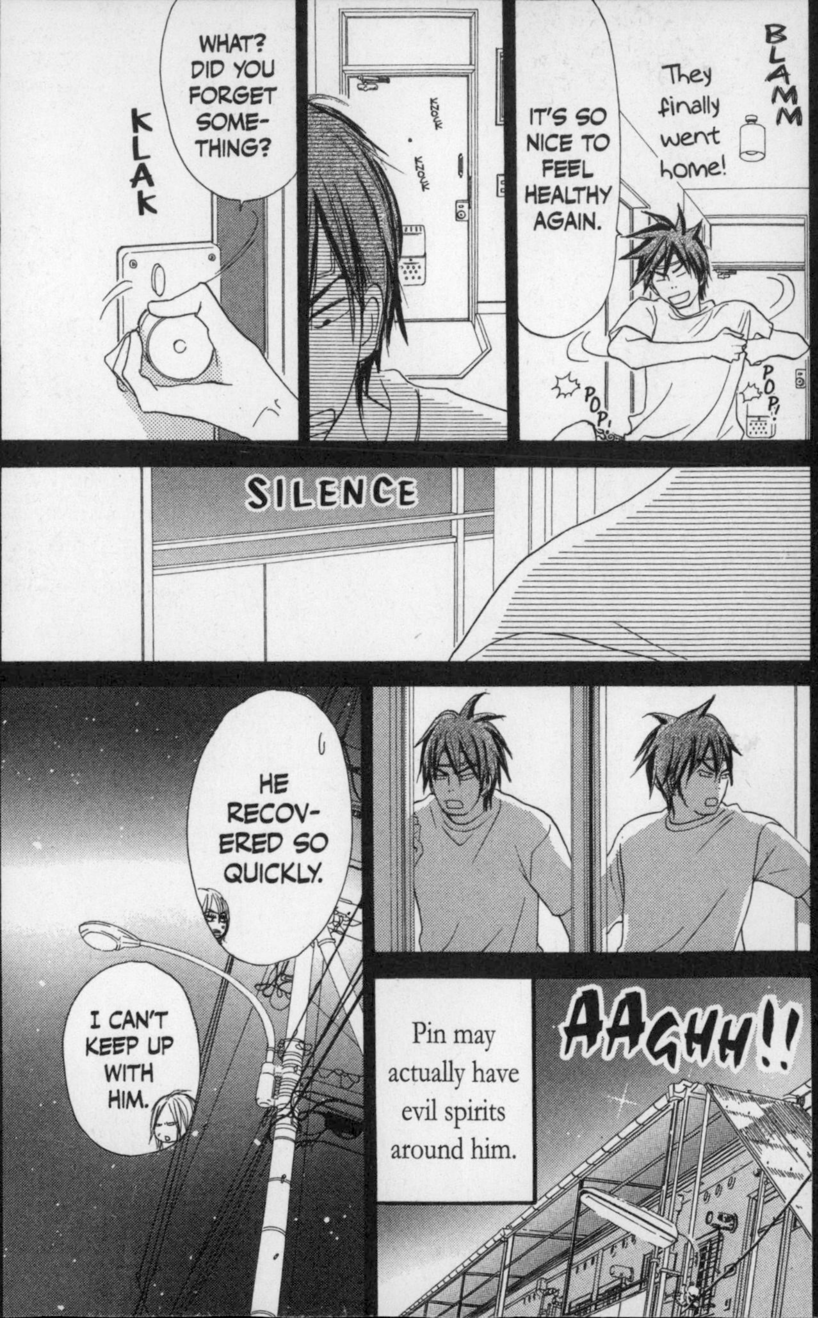
BLAMM
They finally went home!
IT'S SO NICE TO FEEL HEALTHY AGAIN.
POP!
POP!
KNOCK
KNOCK
WHAT? DID YOU FORGET SOME-THING?
KLAK
SILENCE
AAGHH!!
Pin may actually have evil spirits around him.
HE RECOV-ERED SO QUICKLY.
I CAN'T KEEP UP WITH HIM.

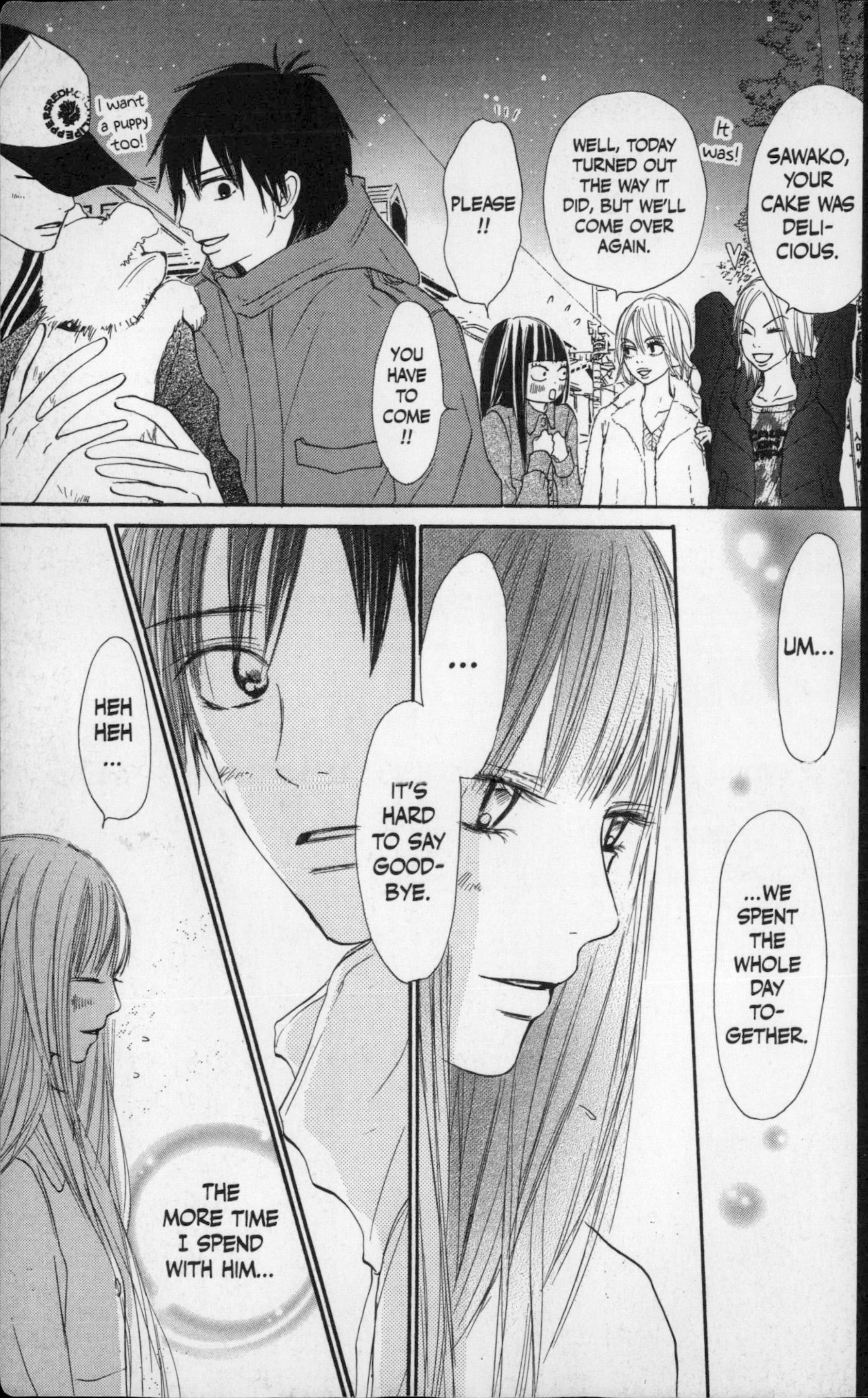
SAWAKO, YOUR CAKE WAS DELI-CIOUS.
It was!
WELL, TODAY TURNED OUT THE WAY IT DID, BUT WE'LL COME OVER AGAIN.
PLEASE !!
YOU HAVE TO COME !!
I want a puppy too!
UM...
...WE SPENT THE WHOLE DAY TO-GETHER.
...
IT'S HARD TO SAY GOOD-BYE.
HEH HEH ...
THE MORE TIME I SPEND WITH HIM...

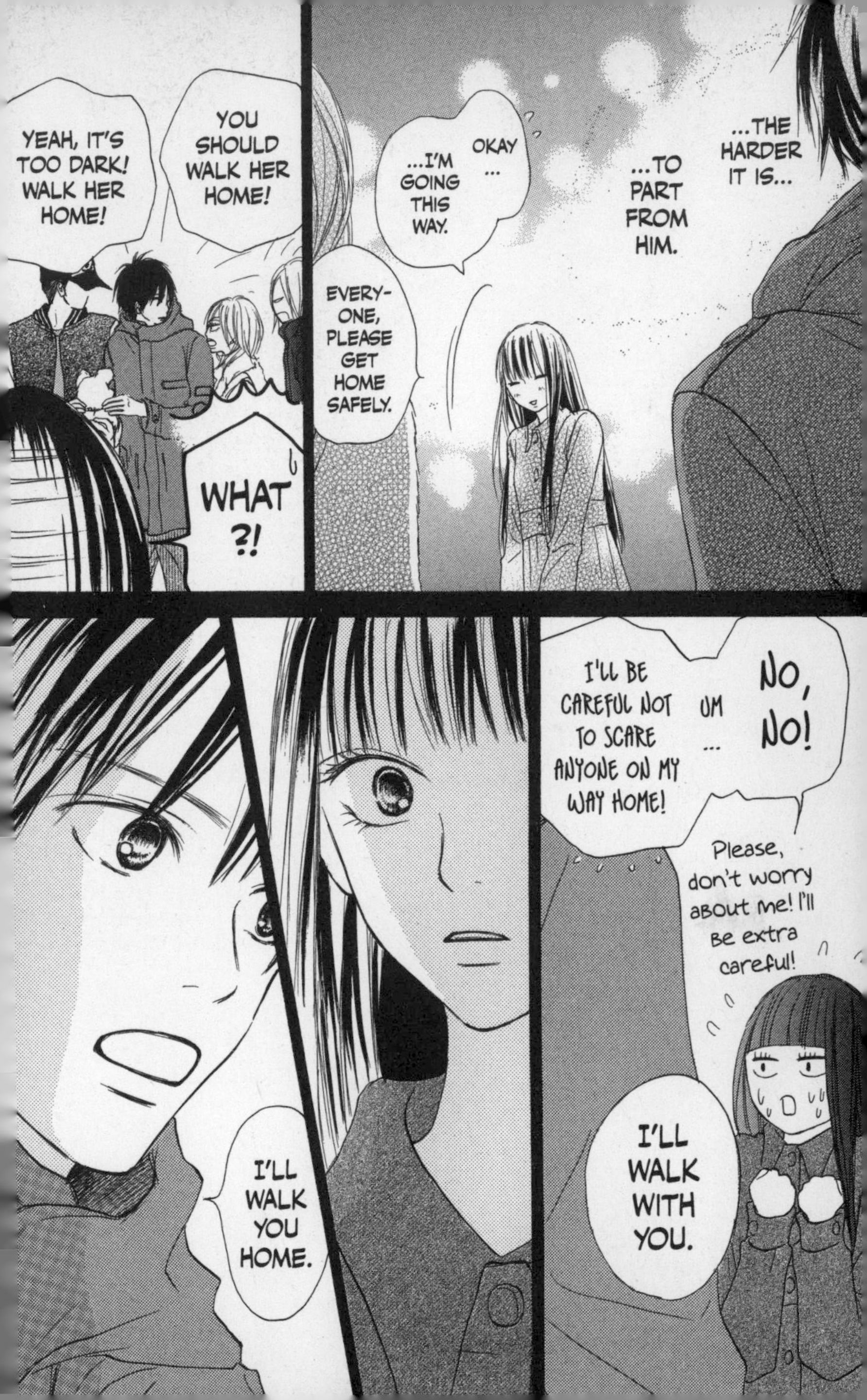
...THE HARDER IT IS...
...TO PART FROM HIM.
OKAY ...
...I'M GOING THIS WAY.
EVERY-ONE, PLEASE GET HOME SAFELY.
YOU SHOULD WALK HER HOME!
YEAH, IT'S TOO DARK! WALK HER HOME!
WHAT ?!
NO, NO!
UM ...
I'LL BE CAREFUL NOT TO SCARE ANYONE ON MY WAY HOME!
Please, don't worry about me! I'll be extra careful!
I'LL WALK WITH YOU.
I'LL WALK YOU HOME.

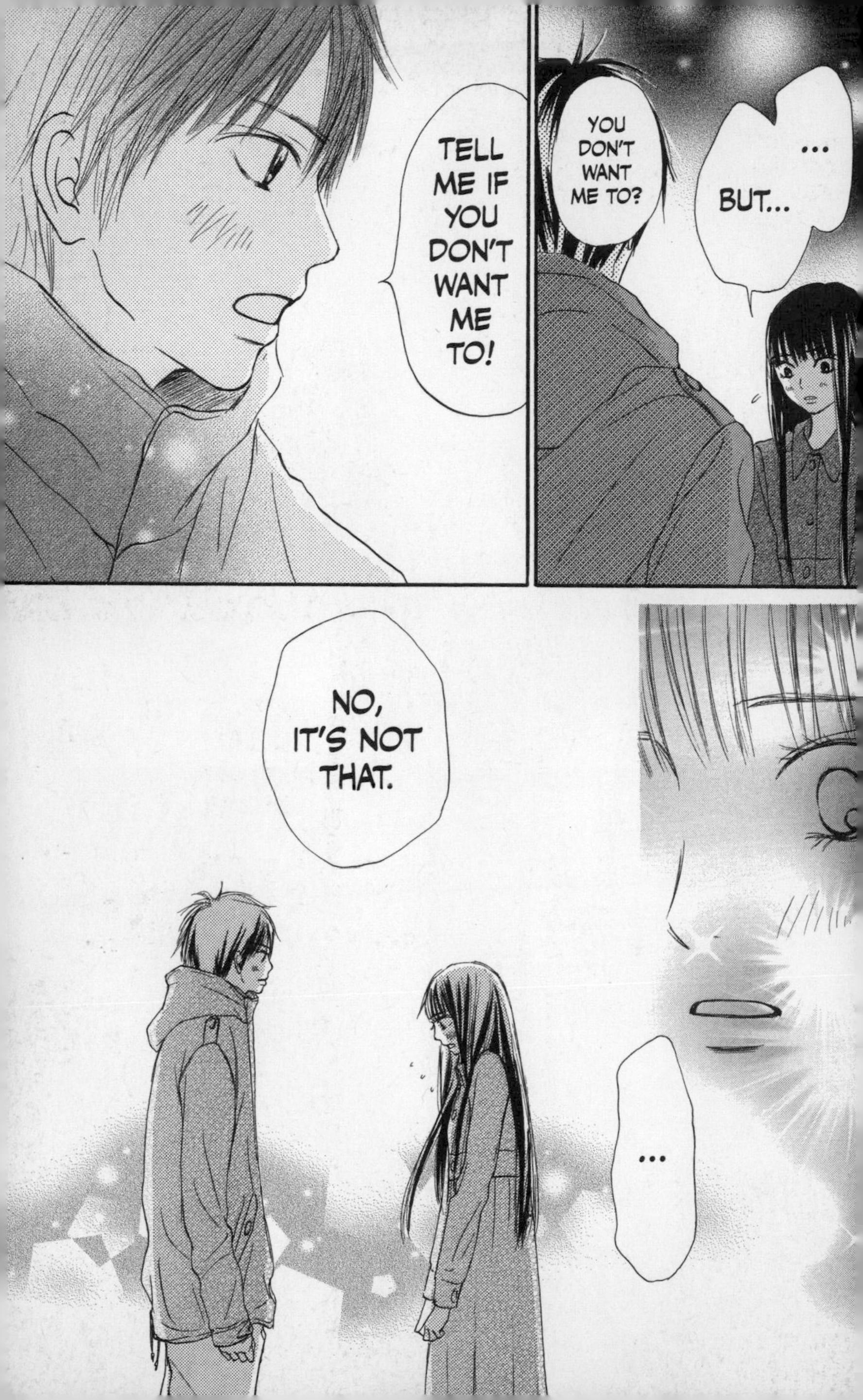
... BUT...
YOU DON'T WANT ME TO?
TELL ME IF YOU DON'T WANT ME TO!
...
NO, IT'S NOT THAT.

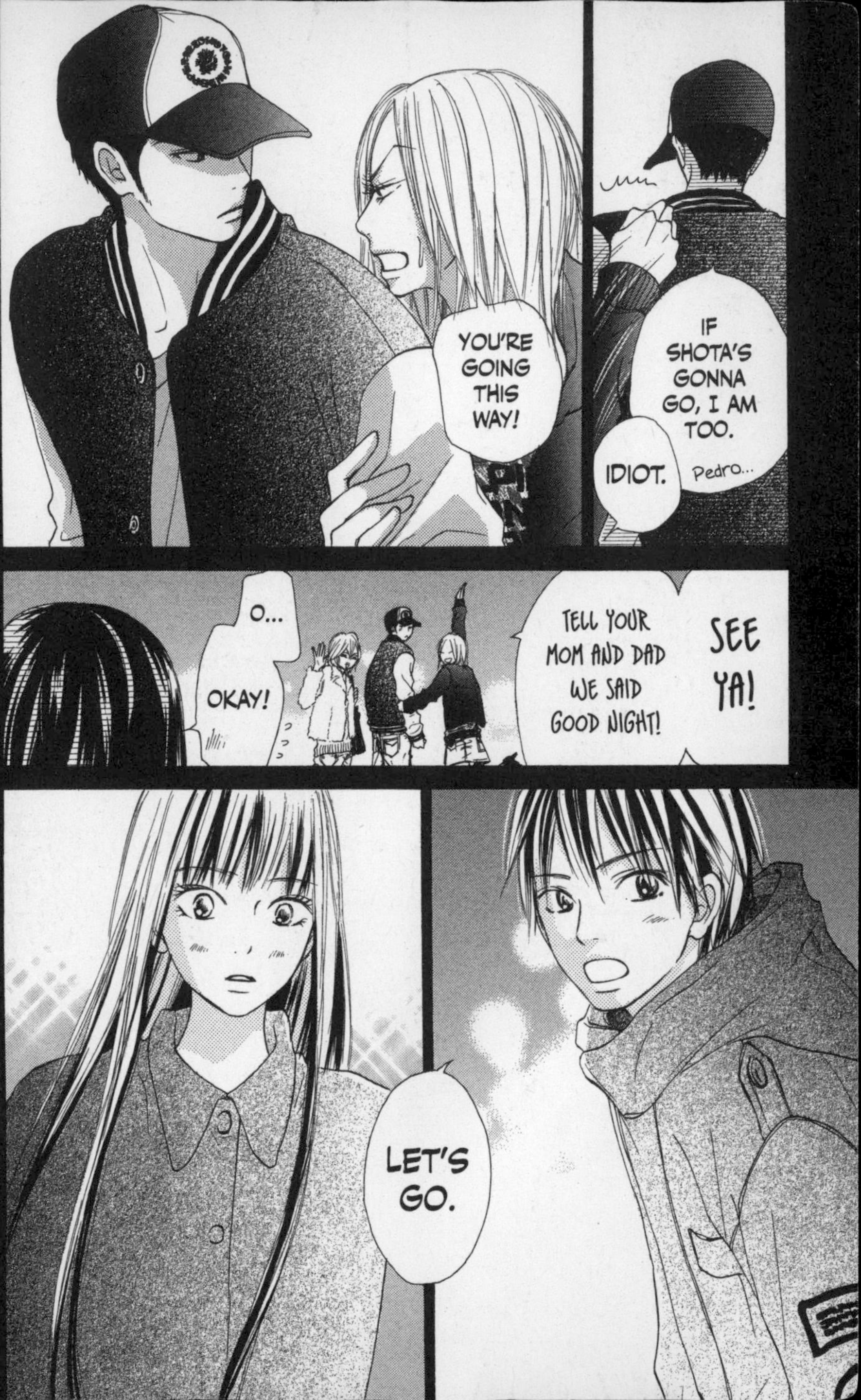
IF SHOTA'S GONNA GO, I AM TOO.
Pedro...
IDIOT.
YOU'RE GOING THIS WAY!
SEE YA!
TELL YOUR MOM AND DAD WE SAID GOOD NIGHT!
O...
OKAY!
LET'S GO.

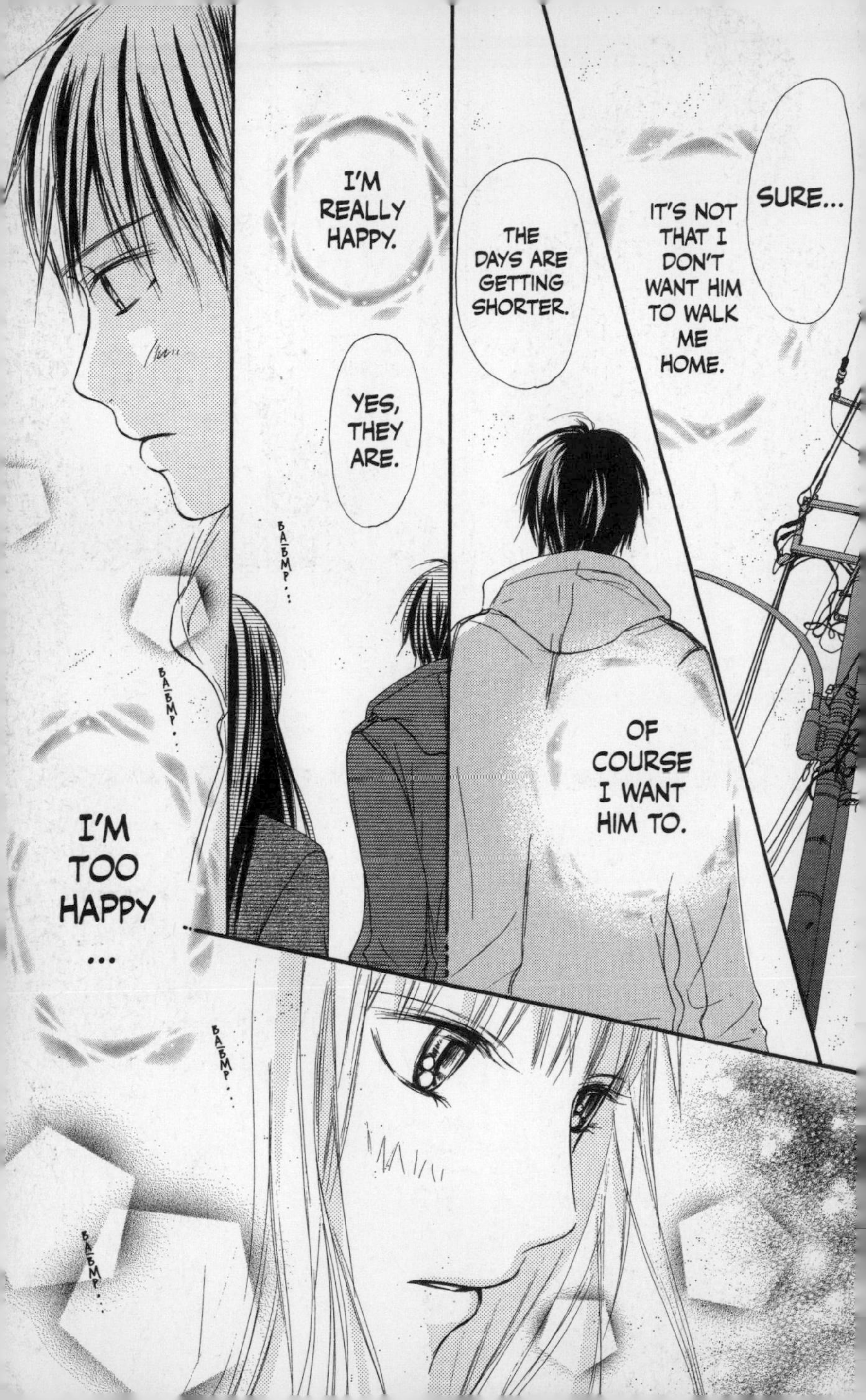
SURE...
IT'S NOT THAT I DON'T WANT HIM TO WALK ME HOME.
OF COURSE I WANT HIM TO.
THE DAYS ARE GETTING SHORTER.
I'M REALLY HAPPY.
YES, THEY ARE.
BA-BMP...
BA-BMP...
I'M TOO HAPPY...
BA-BMP...
BA-BMP...

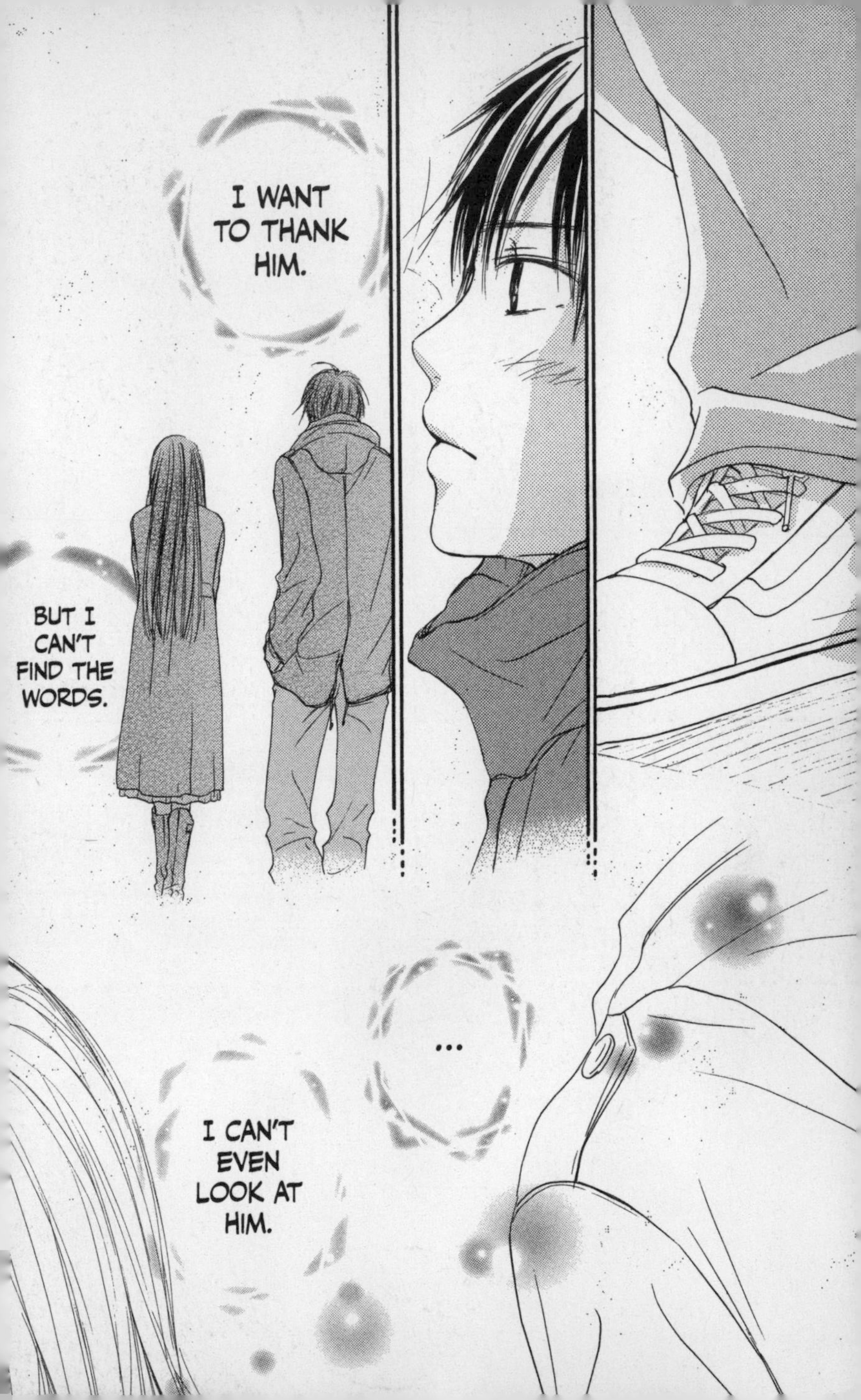
I WANT TO THANK HIM.
BUT I CAN'T FIND THE WORDS.
...
I CAN'T EVEN LOOK AT HIM.

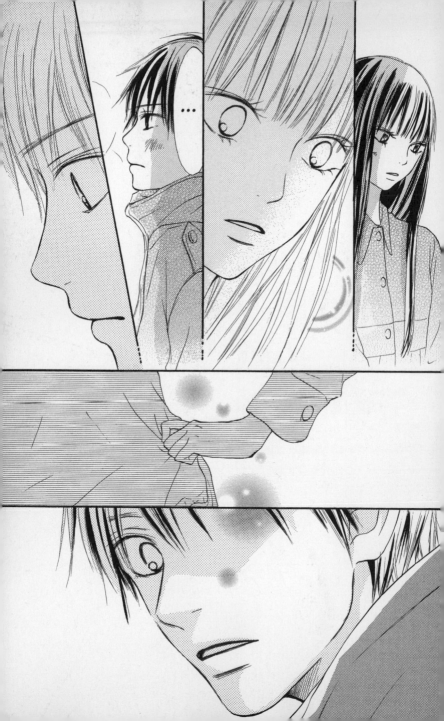

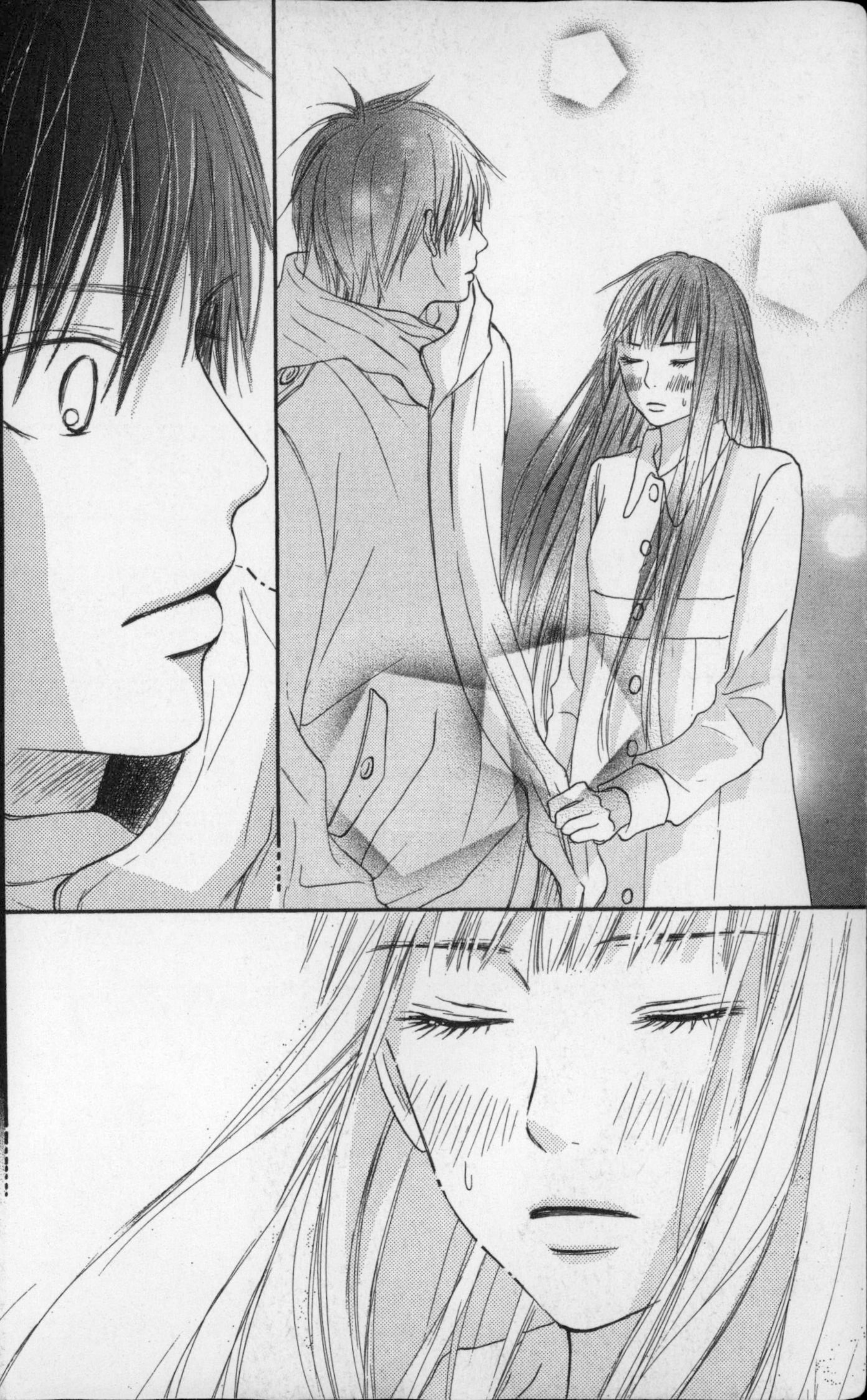

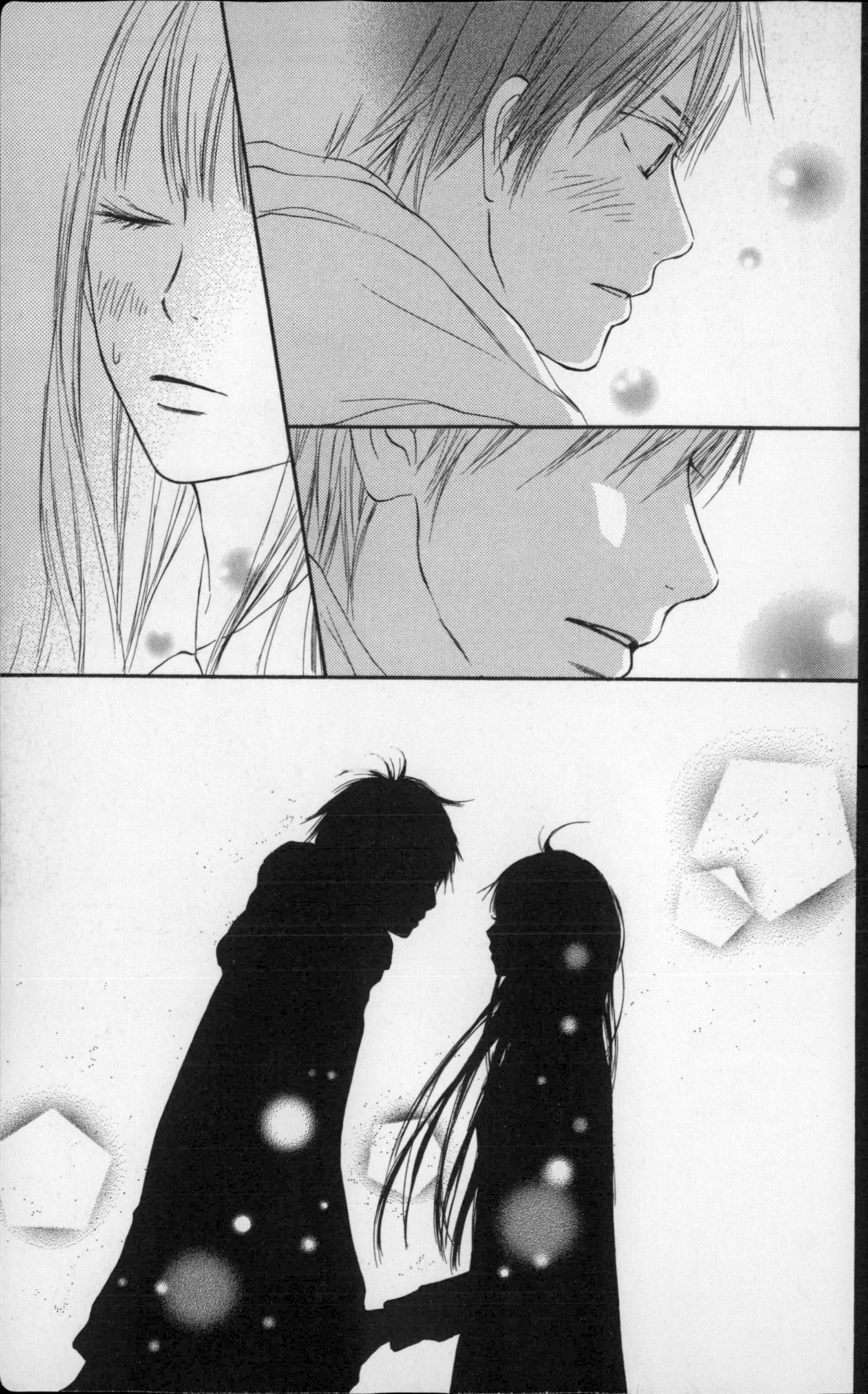

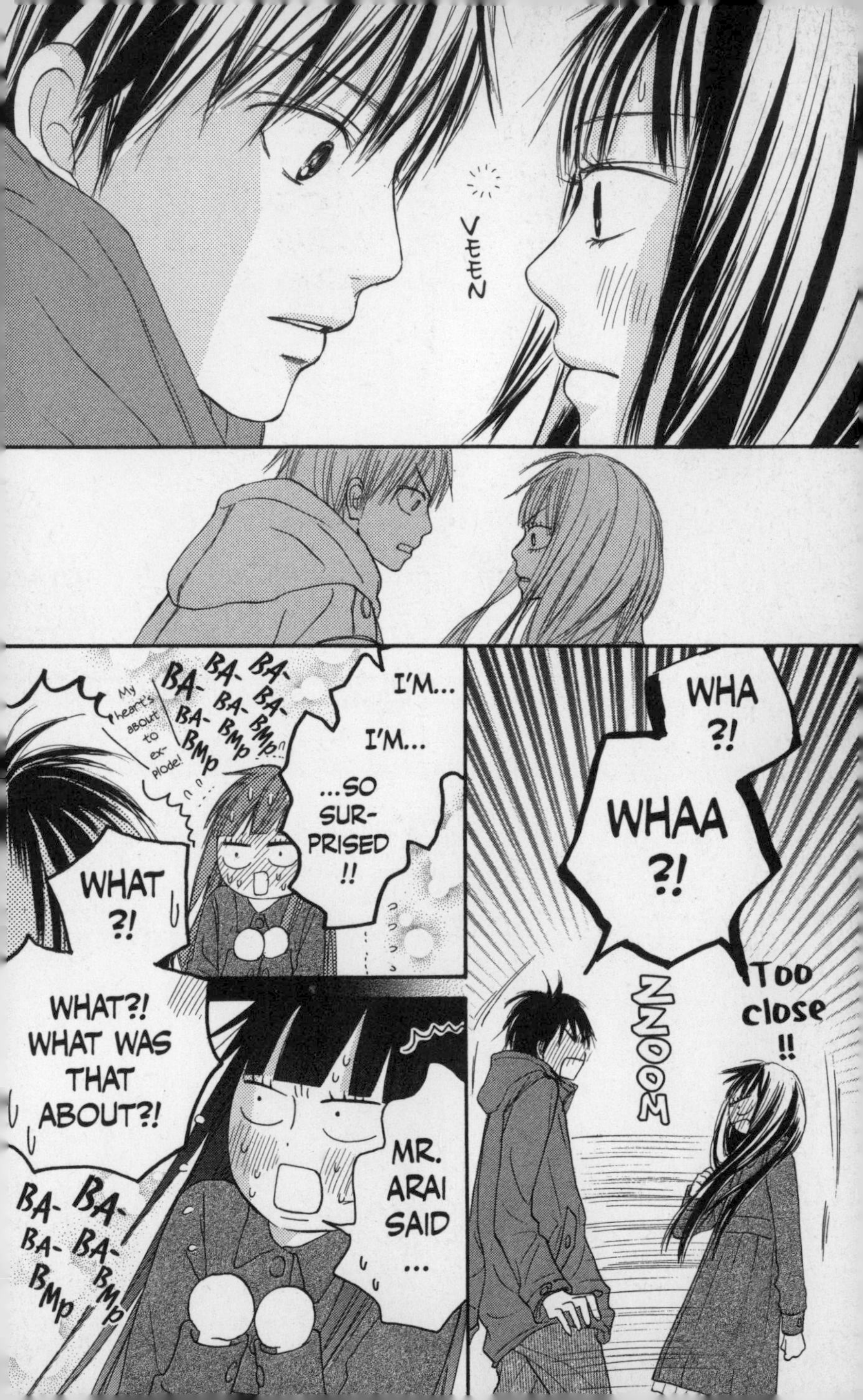
VEEN
WHA ?!
WHAA ?!
Too close !!
ZZOOM
I'M...
I'M...
...SO SURPRISED !!
BA-BA-BA-BMp
BA-BA-BA-BMp
My heart's about to explode!
WHAT ?!
MR. ARAI SAID ...
WHAT?! WHAT WAS THAT ABOUT?!
BA-BA-BMp
BA-BA-BMp

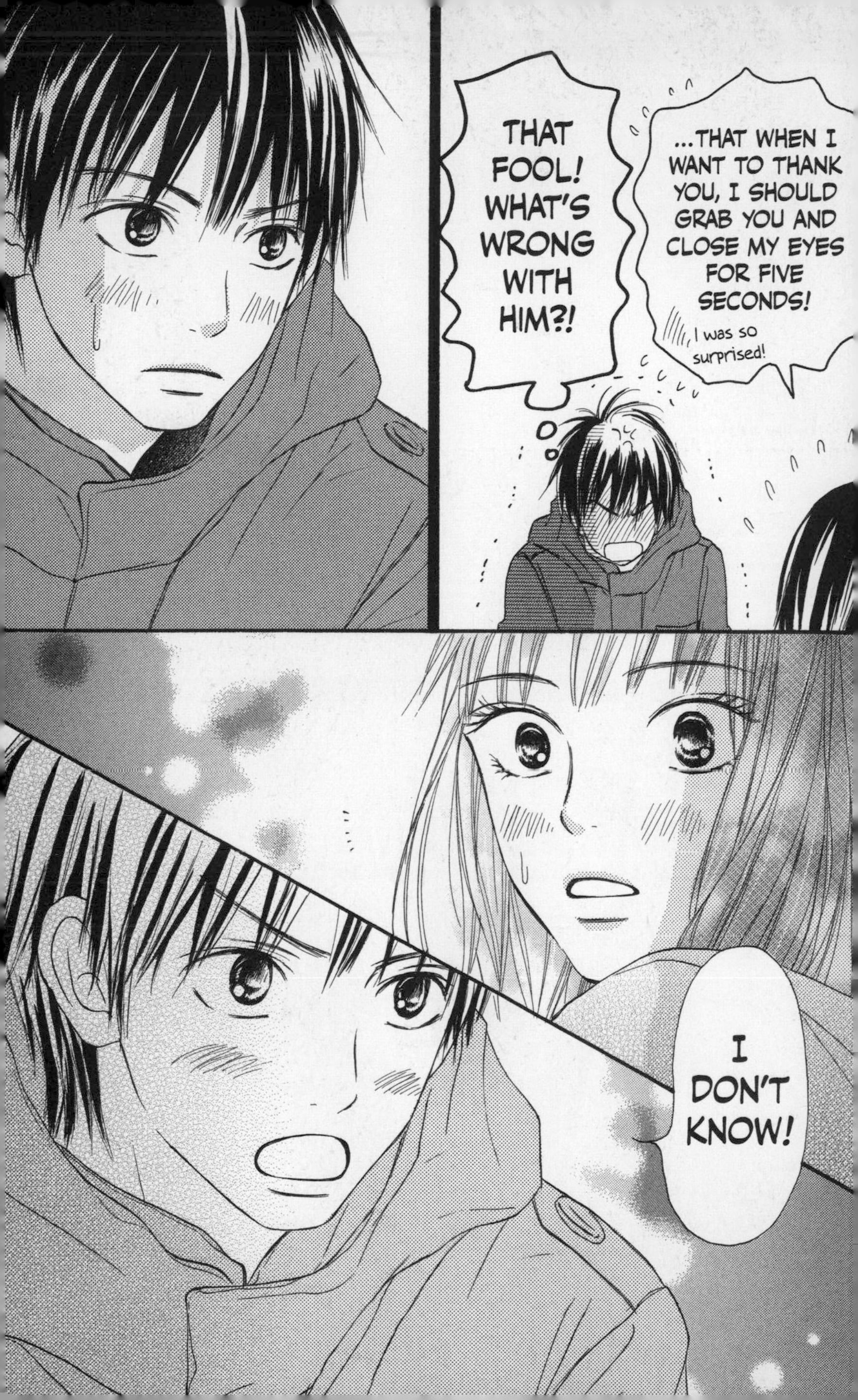
...THAT WHEN I WANT TO THANK YOU, I SHOULD GRAB YOU AND CLOSE MY EYES FOR FIVE SECONDS!
I was so surprised!
THAT FOOL! WHAT'S WRONG WITH HIM?!
I DON'T KNOW!

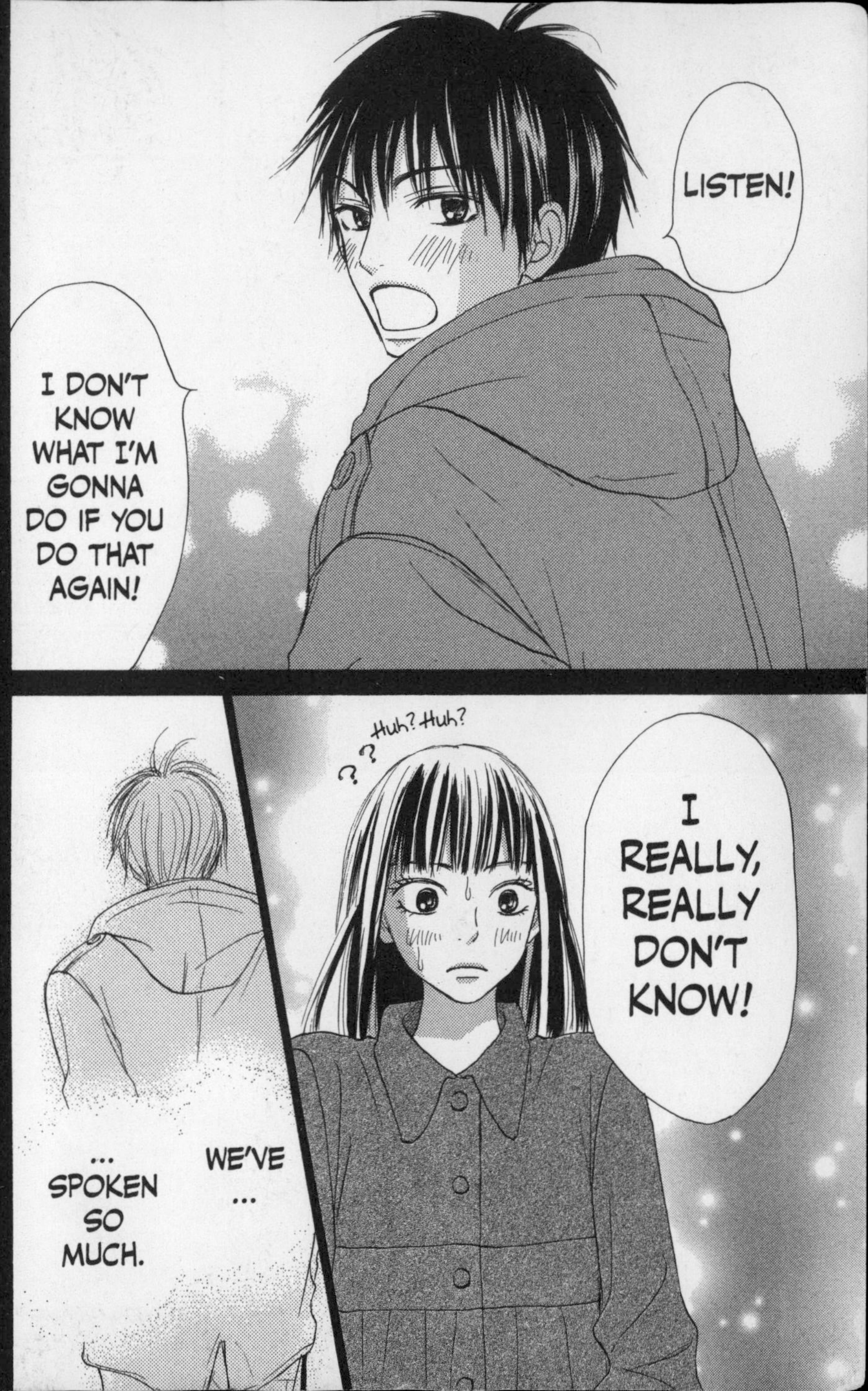
LISTEN!
I DON'T KNOW WHAT I'M GONNA DO IF YOU DO THAT AGAIN!
Huh? Huh?
I REALLY, REALLY DON'T KNOW!
WE'VE ...
... SPOKEN SO MUCH.

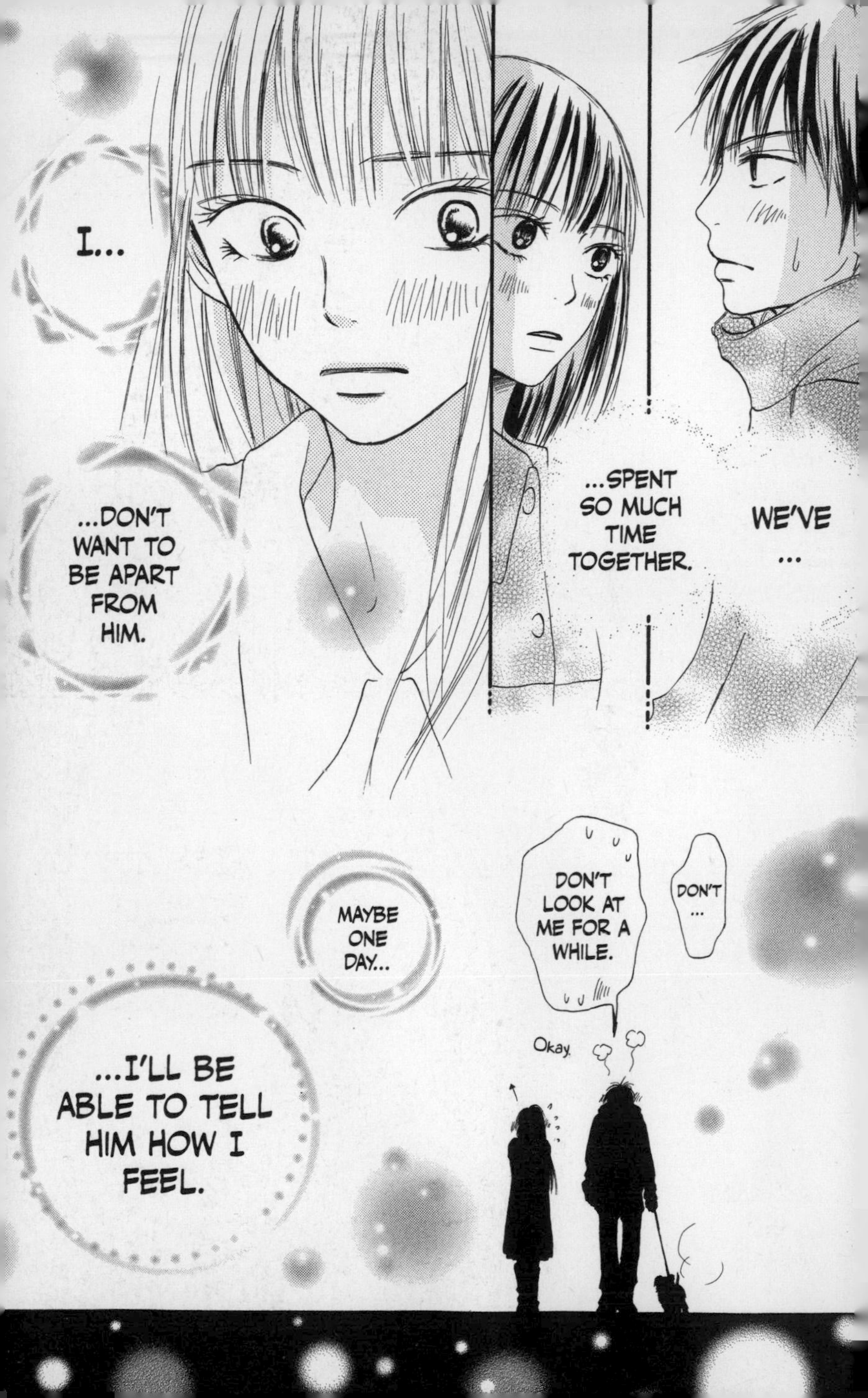

WE'VE ...
...SPENT SO MUCH TIME TOGETHER.
I...
...DON'T WANT TO BE APART FROM HIM.
DON'T ...
DON'T LOOK AT ME FOR A WHILE.
Okay.
MAYBE ONE DAY...
...I'LL BE ABLE TO TELL HIM HOW I FEEL.

Episode 19: Chizuru's Crush

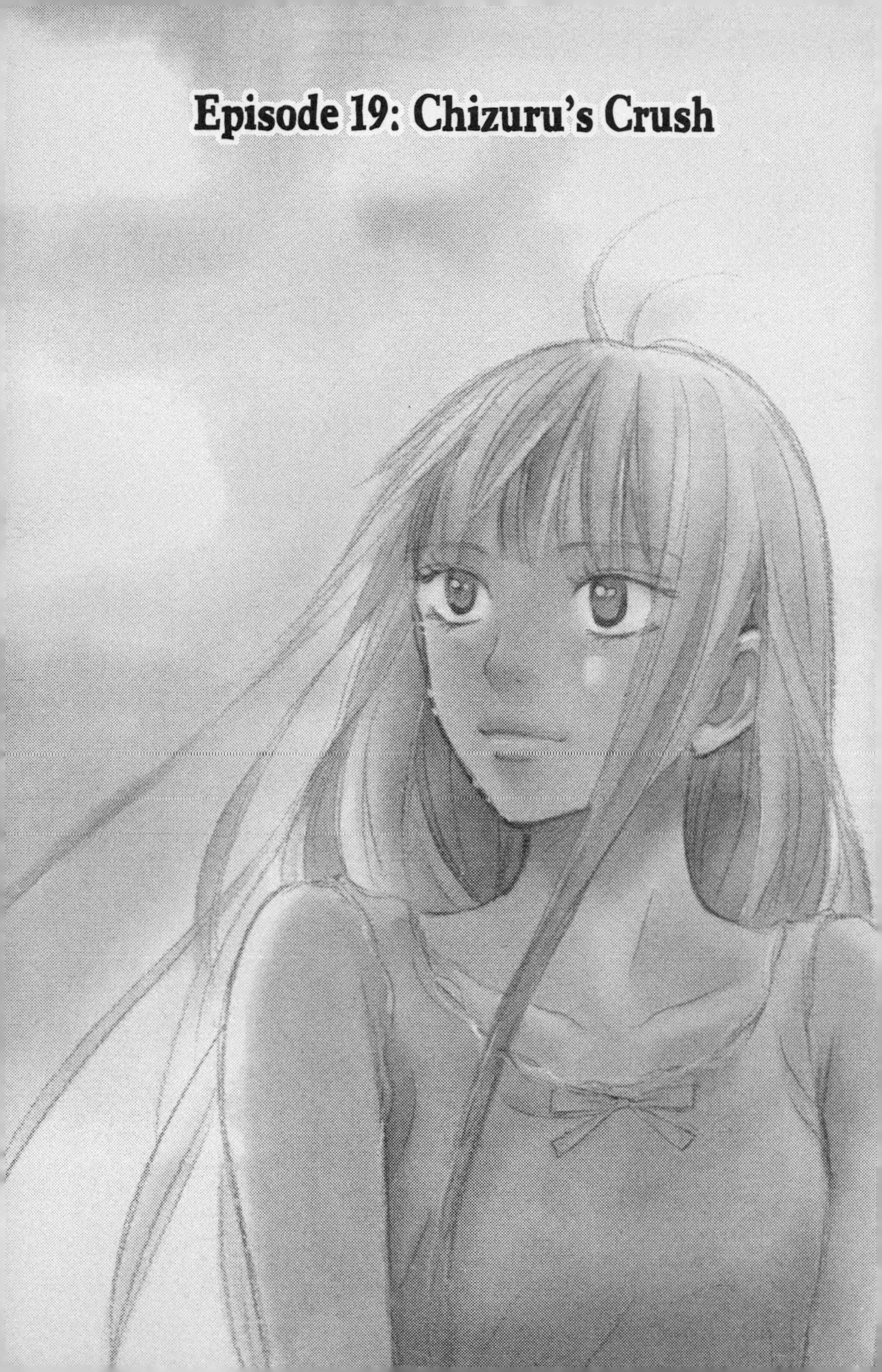

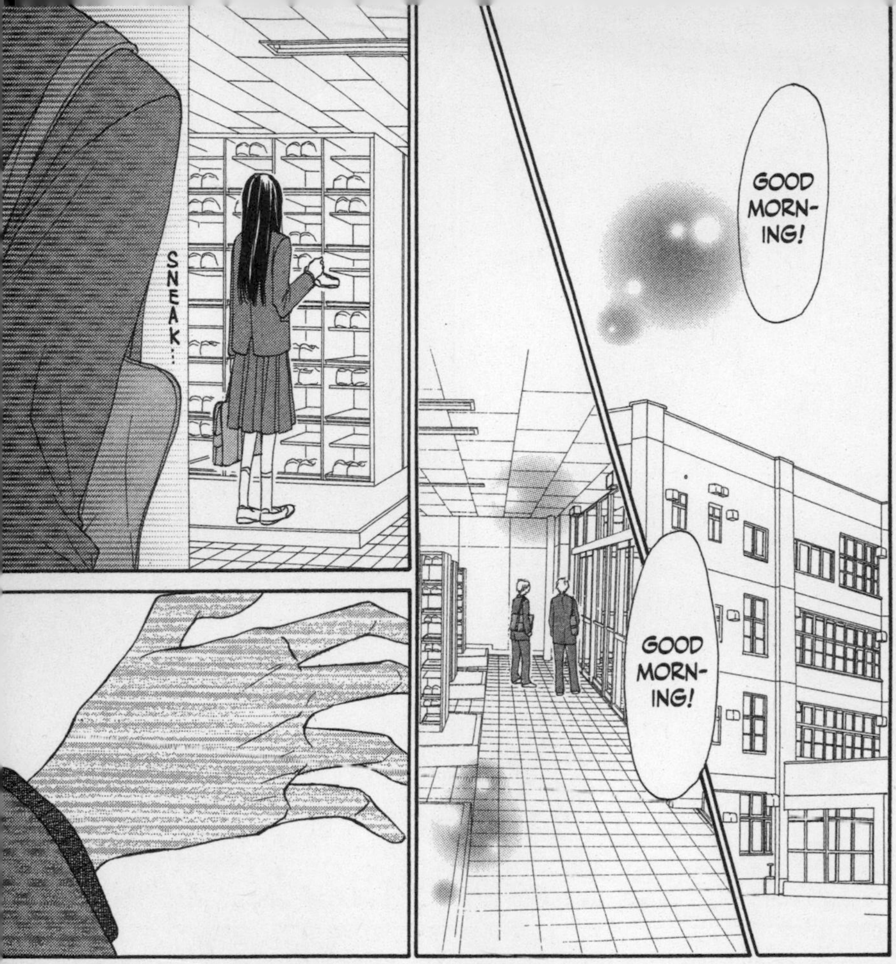
GOOD MORN-ING!
GOOD MORN-ING!
SNEAK...

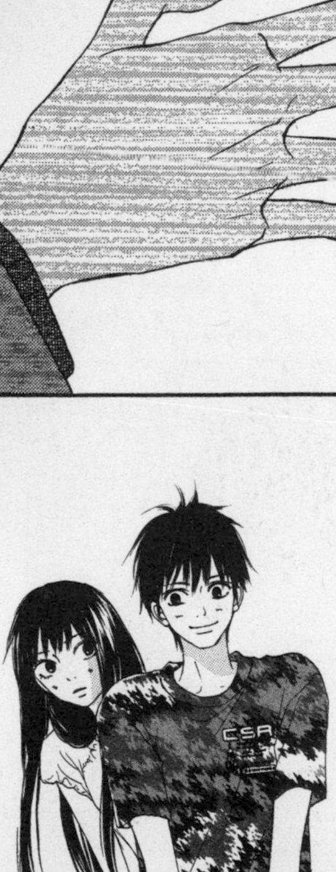

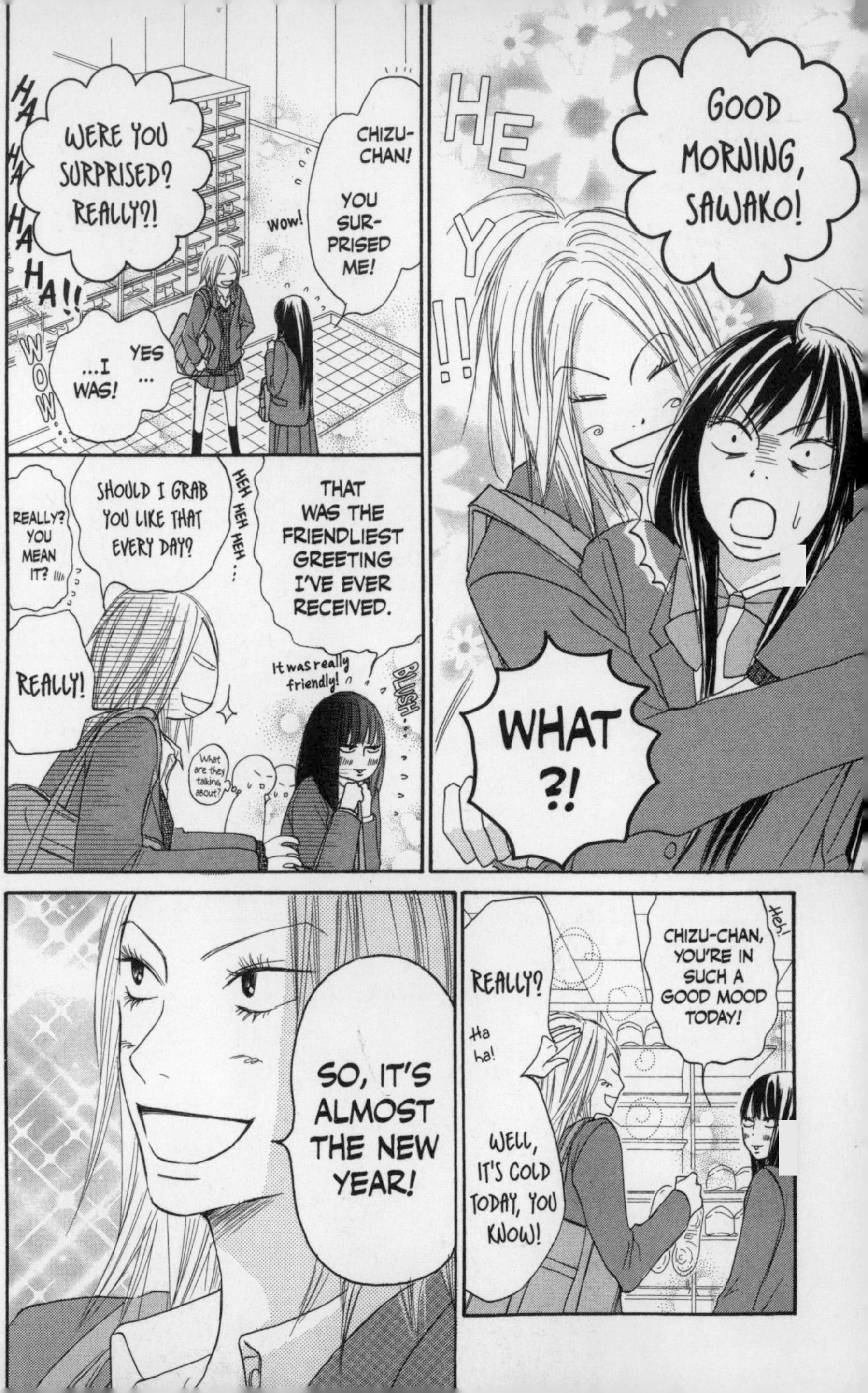
GOOD MORNING, SAWAKO!
HEY!!
WHAT?!
CHIZU-CHAN! YOU SURPRISED ME!
WOW!
WERE YOU SURPRISED? REALLY?!
HA HA HA HA HA!!
YES ... ...I WAS!
WOW...
THAT WAS THE FRIENDLIEST GREETING I'VE EVER RECEIVED.
HEH HEH HEH...
SHOULD I GRAB YOU LIKE THAT EVERY DAY?
REALLY? YOU MEAN IT?
It was really friendly!
BLUSH...
REALLY!
What are they talking about?
Heh!
CHIZU-CHAN, YOU'RE IN SUCH A GOOD MOOD TODAY!
REALLY?
Ha ha!
WELL, IT'S COLD TODAY, YOU KNOW!
SO, IT'S ALMOST THE NEW YEAR!

KARUPIN on JAPAN 3

Sawako stamp ②

This is a Sawako stamp that a reader sent us. It's so well made. She's much more beautiful than the Sawako I draw! You should be happy, Sawako!

Wow!

I'm so happy!

This one is also made out of an eraser, and it's really well made!

The stamp part is made out of an eraser.

The handle is made of wood!

It's so amazing!

The opposite side has the stamp design on it too!

This is a handmade stamp bag!

The bag is also really cute.

E.I.-san, thank you so much!
I'll treasure them!

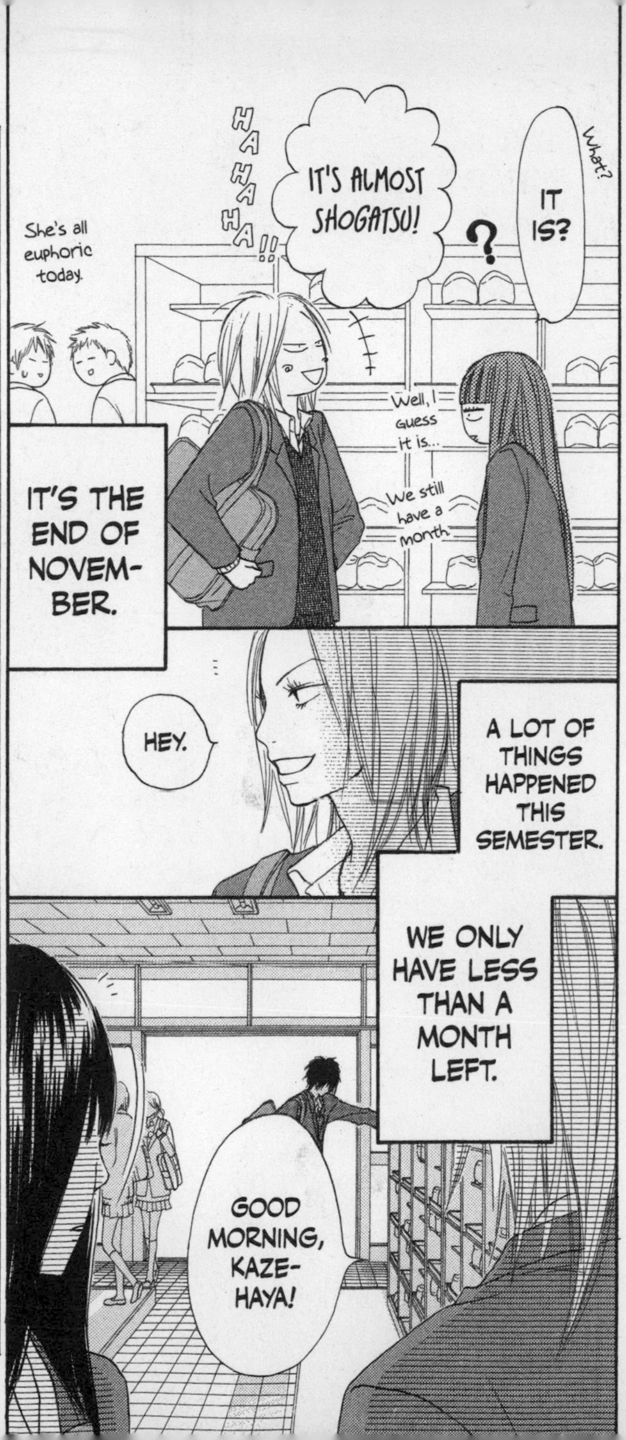
HAHAHAHA!!
IT'S ALMOST SHOGATSU!
She's all euphoric today.
?
What?
IT IS?
Well, I guess it is...
We still have a month.
IT'S THE END OF NOVEMBER.
A LOT OF THINGS HAPPENED THIS SEMESTER.
HEY.
WE ONLY HAVE LESS THAN A MONTH LEFT.
GOOD MORNING, KAZEHAYA!

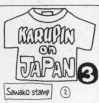

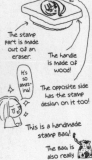

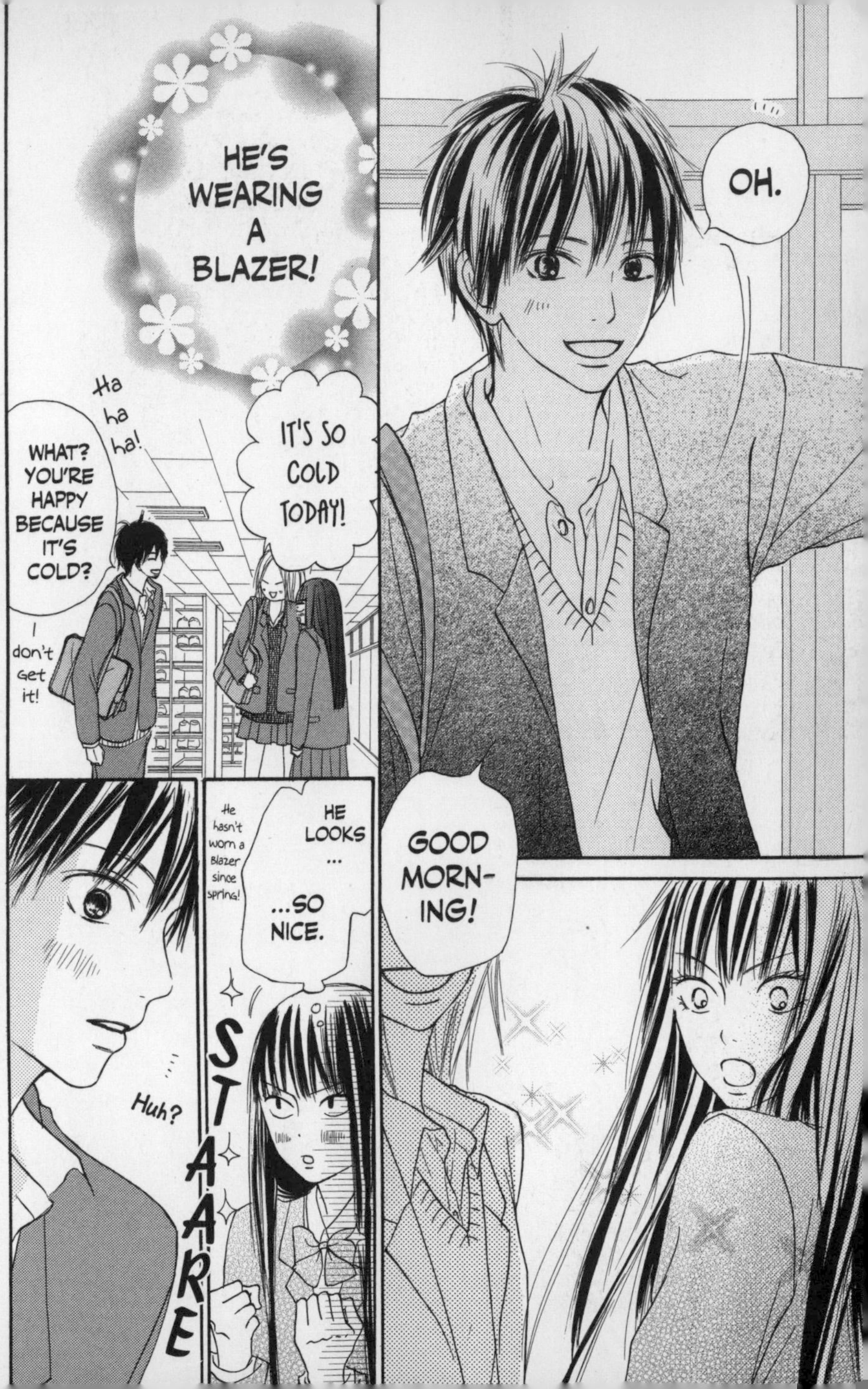

OH.
GOOD MORNING!
HE'S WEARING A BLAZER!
IT'S SO COLD TODAY!
Ha ha ha!
WHAT? YOU'RE HAPPY BECAUSE IT'S COLD?
I don't get it!
HE LOOKS ...
...SO NICE.
He hasn't worn a blazer since spring!
STAARE
Huh?

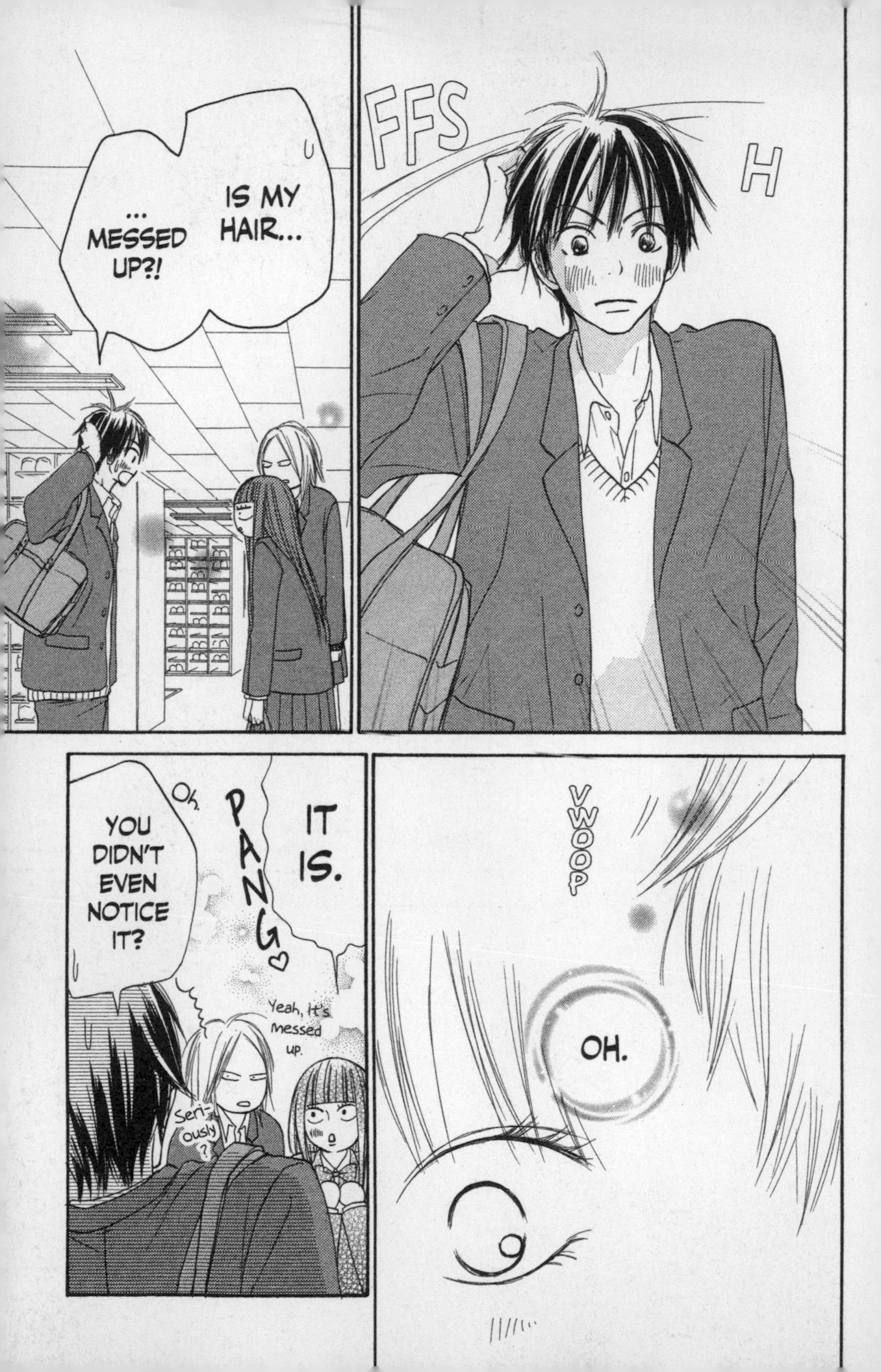
FFS
H
IS MY HAIR...
... MESSED UP?!
VWOOP
OH.
IT IS.
PANG♡
Oh.
YOU DIDN'T EVEN NOTICE IT?
Yeah, it's messed up.
Seri-ously?

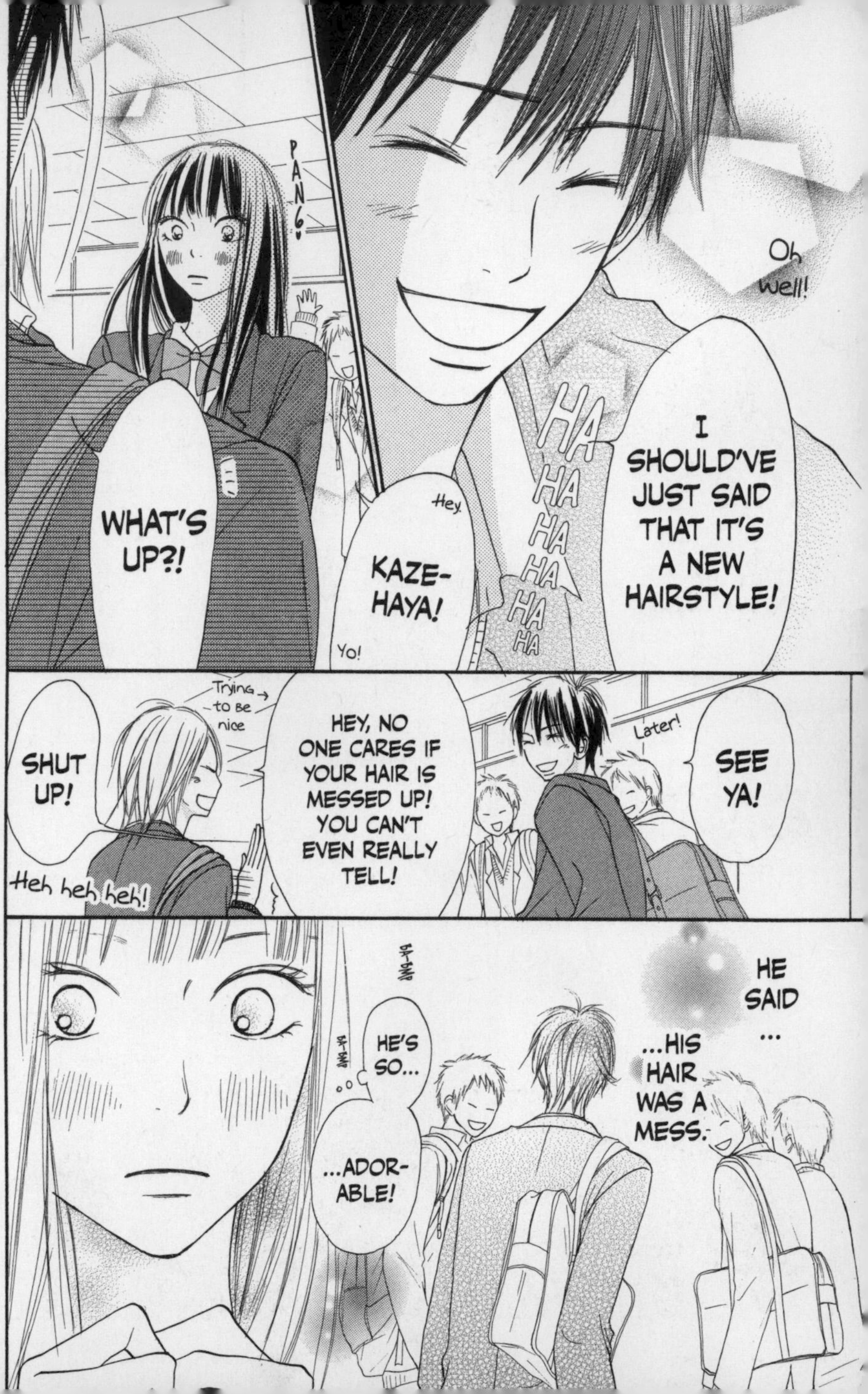
Oh well!
I SHOULD'VE JUST SAID THAT IT'S A NEW HAIRSTYLE!
HA HA HA HA HA HA HA HA
Hey.
KAZE-HAYA!
Yo!
PANG
WHAT'S UP?!
Later!
SEE YA!
HEY, NO ONE CARES IF YOUR HAIR IS MESSED UP! YOU CAN'T EVEN REALLY TELL!
Trying to be nice
SHUT UP!
Heh heh heh!
HE SAID ...
...HIS HAIR WAS A MESS.
BA-DMP
BA-DMP
HE'S SO...
...ADOR-ABLE!

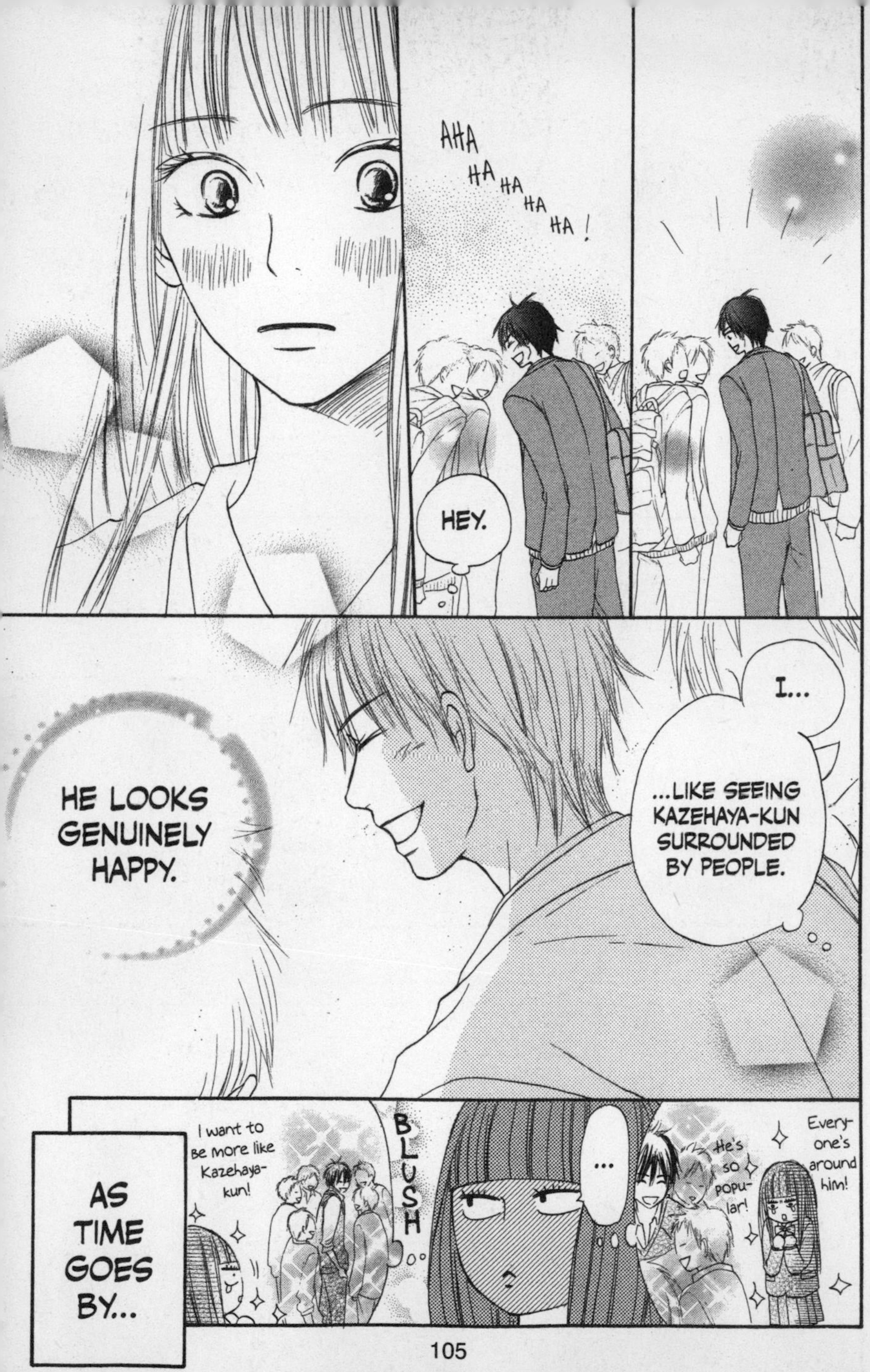
AHA HA HA HA HA!
HEY.
I...
...LIKE SEEING KAZEHAYA-KUN SURROUNDED BY PEOPLE.
HE LOOKS GENUINELY HAPPY.
Every-one's around him!
He's so popu-lar!
...
BLUSH
I want to be more like Kazehaya-kun!
AS TIME GOES BY...

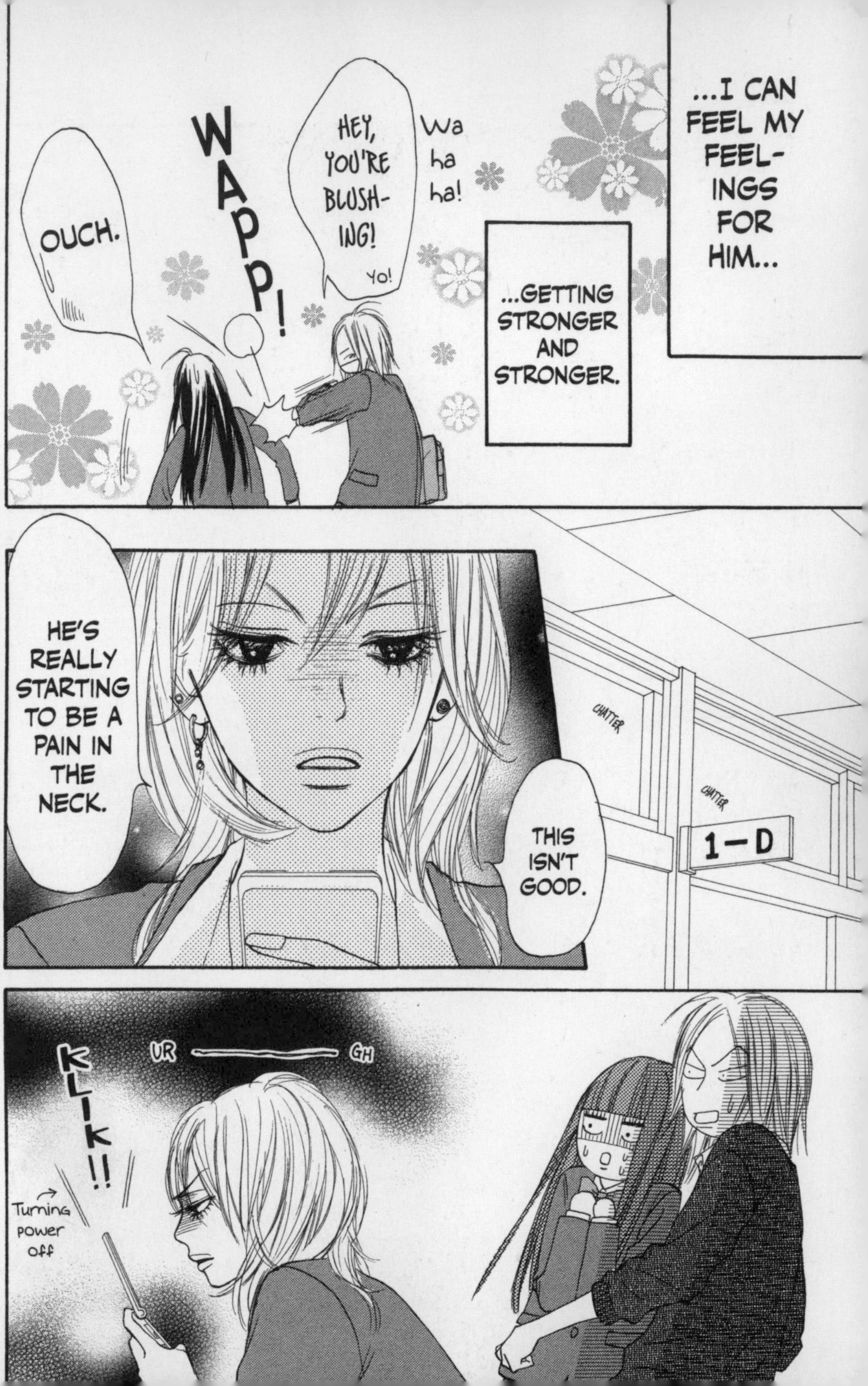
...I CAN FEEL MY FEEL-INGS FOR HIM...
...GETTING STRONGER AND STRONGER.
Wa ha ha!
HEY, YOU'RE BLUSH-ING!
Yo!
WAPP!
OUCH.
CHATTER
CHATTER
1-D
THIS ISN'T GOOD.
HE'S REALLY STARTING TO BE A PAIN IN THE NECK.
UR———GH
KLIK!!
Turning power off

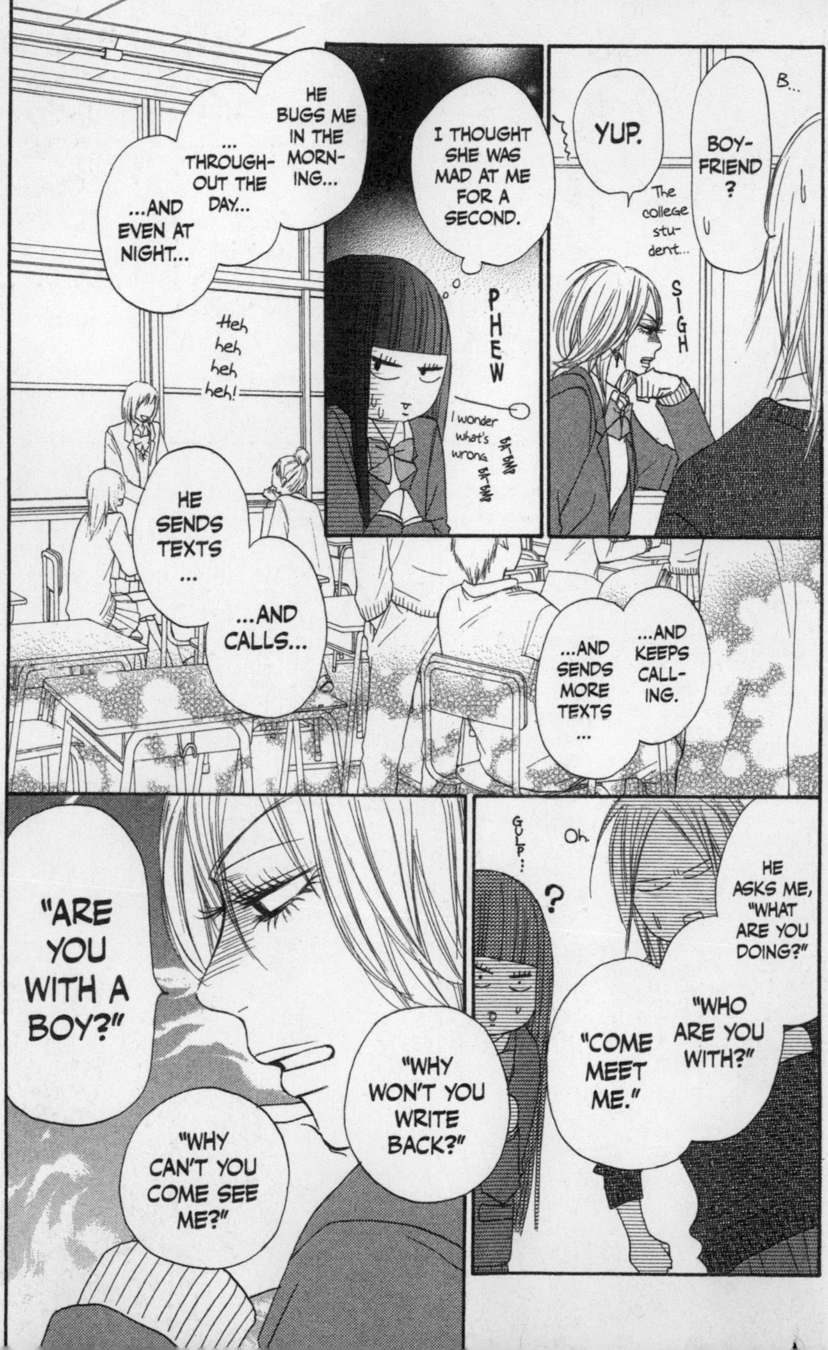
B...
BOY-FRIEND?
YUP.
The college student...
SIGH
I THOUGHT SHE WAS MAD AT ME FOR A SECOND.
PHEW
I wonder what's wrong
BA-BMP BA-BMP
HE BUGS ME IN THE MORNING...
...THROUGH-OUT THE DAY...
...AND EVEN AT NIGHT...
Heh heh heh heh!
HE SENDS TEXTS...
...AND CALLS...
...AND KEEPS CALL-ING.
...AND SENDS MORE TEXTS...
GULP...
Oh.
?
HE ASKS ME, "WHAT ARE YOU DOING?"
"WHO ARE YOU WITH?"
"COME MEET ME."
"WHY WON'T YOU WRITE BACK?"
"ARE YOU WITH A BOY?"
"WHY CAN'T YOU COME SEE ME?"

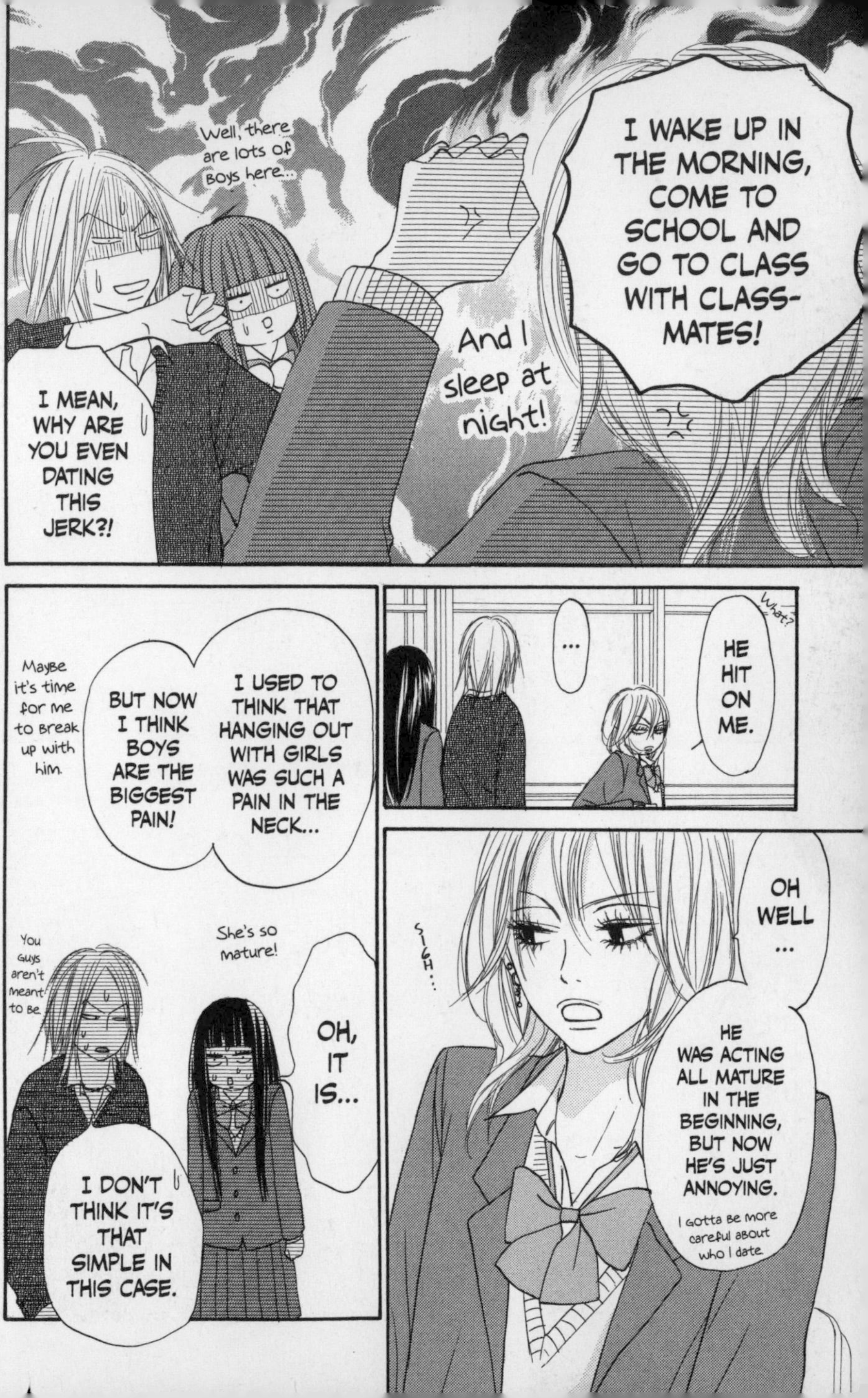
I WAKE UP IN THE MORNING, COME TO SCHOOL AND GO TO CLASS WITH CLASS-MATES!
And I sleep at night!
Well, there are lots of Boys here...
I MEAN, WHY ARE YOU EVEN DATING THIS JERK?!
What?
...
HE HIT ON ME.
OH WELL ...
SIGH...
HE WAS ACTING ALL MATURE IN THE BEGINNING, BUT NOW HE'S JUST ANNOYING.
I Gotta be more careful about who I date.
I USED TO THINK THAT HANGING OUT WITH GIRLS WAS SUCH A PAIN IN THE NECK...
BUT NOW I THINK BOYS ARE THE BIGGEST PAIN!
Maybe it's time for me to Break up with him.
She's so mature!
OH, IT IS...
You Guys aren't meant to Be.
I DON'T THINK IT'S THAT SIMPLE IN THIS CASE.

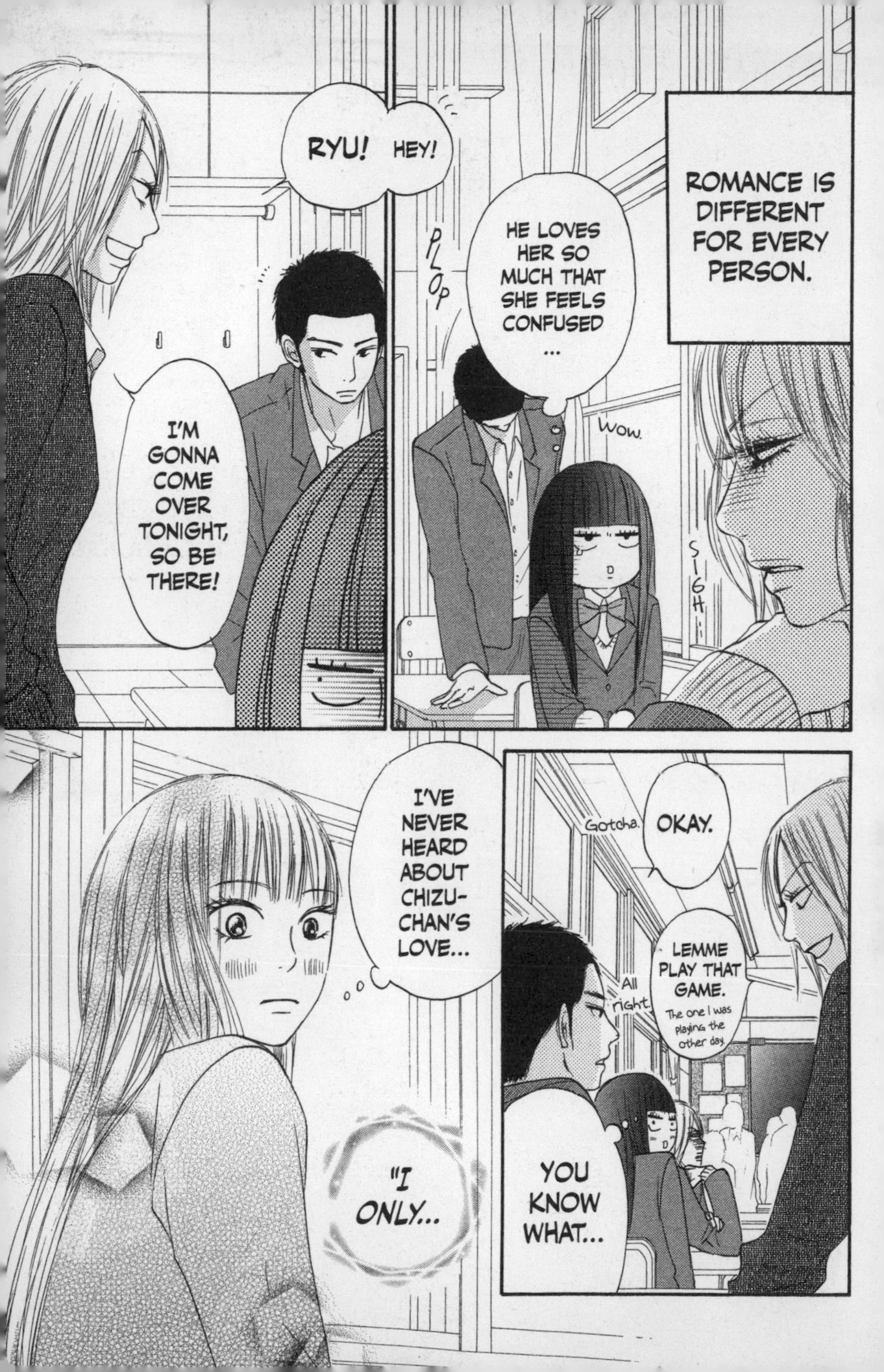
ROMANCE IS DIFFERENT FOR EVERY PERSON.
HE LOVES HER SO MUCH THAT SHE FEELS CONFUSED ...
PLOP
WOW.
SIGH...
HEY!
RYU!
I'M GONNA COME OVER TONIGHT, SO BE THERE!
OKAY.
Gotcha.
LEMME PLAY THAT GAME.
The one I was playing the other day.
All right.
YOU KNOW WHAT...
I'VE NEVER HEARD ABOUT CHIZU-CHAN'S LOVE...
"I ONLY...

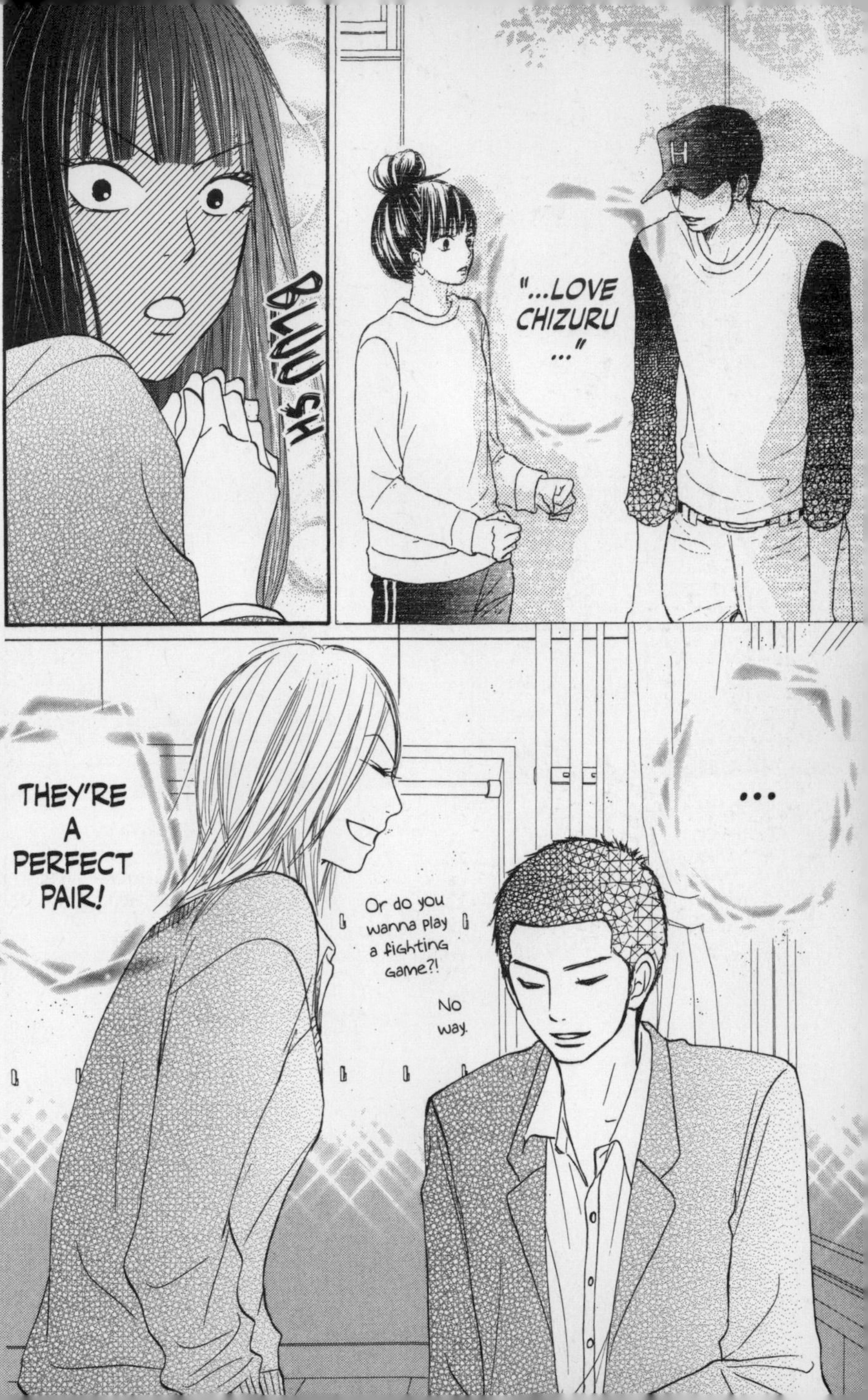
"...LOVE CHIZURU ..."
BLUUSH
...
Or do you wanna play a fighting game?!
No way.
THEY'RE A PERFECT PAIR!

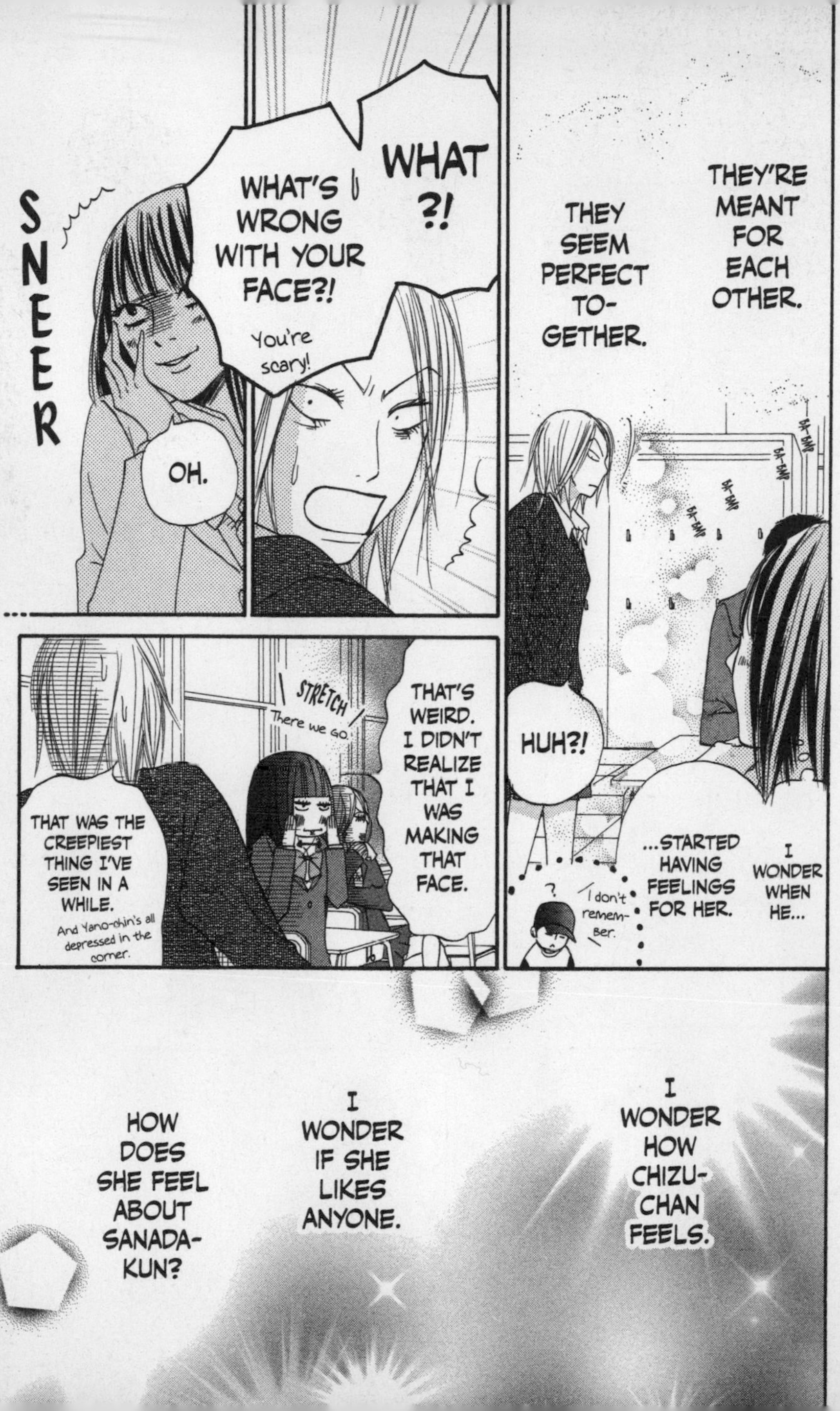
THEY'RE MEANT FOR EACH OTHER.
THEY SEEM PERFECT TO-GETHER.
HUH?!
I WONDER WHEN HE...
...STARTED HAVING FEELINGS FOR HER.
I don't remem-ber.
WHAT?!
WHAT'S WRONG WITH YOUR FACE?!
You're scary!
SNEER
OH.
THAT'S WEIRD. I DIDN'T REALIZE THAT I WAS MAKING THAT FACE.
STRETCH
There we go.
THAT WAS THE CREEPIEST THING I'VE SEEN IN A WHILE.
And Yano-chin's all depressed in the corner.
I WONDER HOW CHIZU-CHAN FEELS.
I WONDER IF SHE LIKES ANYONE.
HOW DOES SHE FEEL ABOUT SANADA-KUN?

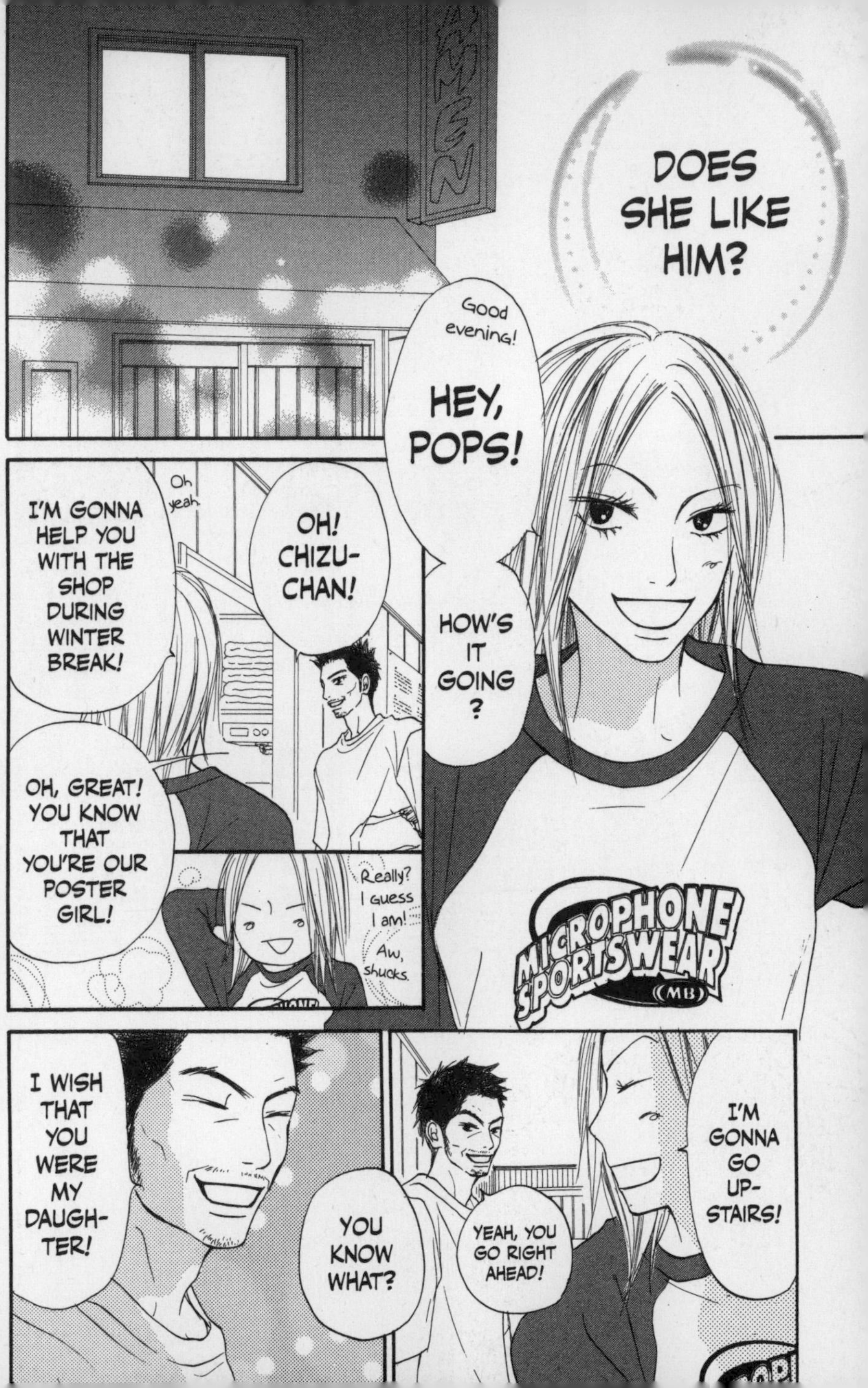
DOES SHE LIKE HIM?
Good evening!
HEY, POPS!
HOW'S IT GOING?
MICROPHONE! SPORTSWEAR
(MB)
OH! CHIZU-CHAN!
Oh yeah.
I'M GONNA HELP YOU WITH THE SHOP DURING WINTER BREAK!
OH, GREAT! YOU KNOW THAT YOU'RE OUR POSTER GIRL!
Really? I guess I am!
Aw, shucks.
I'M GONNA GO UP-STAIRS!
YEAH, YOU GO RIGHT AHEAD!
YOU KNOW WHAT?
I WISH THAT YOU WERE MY DAUGH-TER!

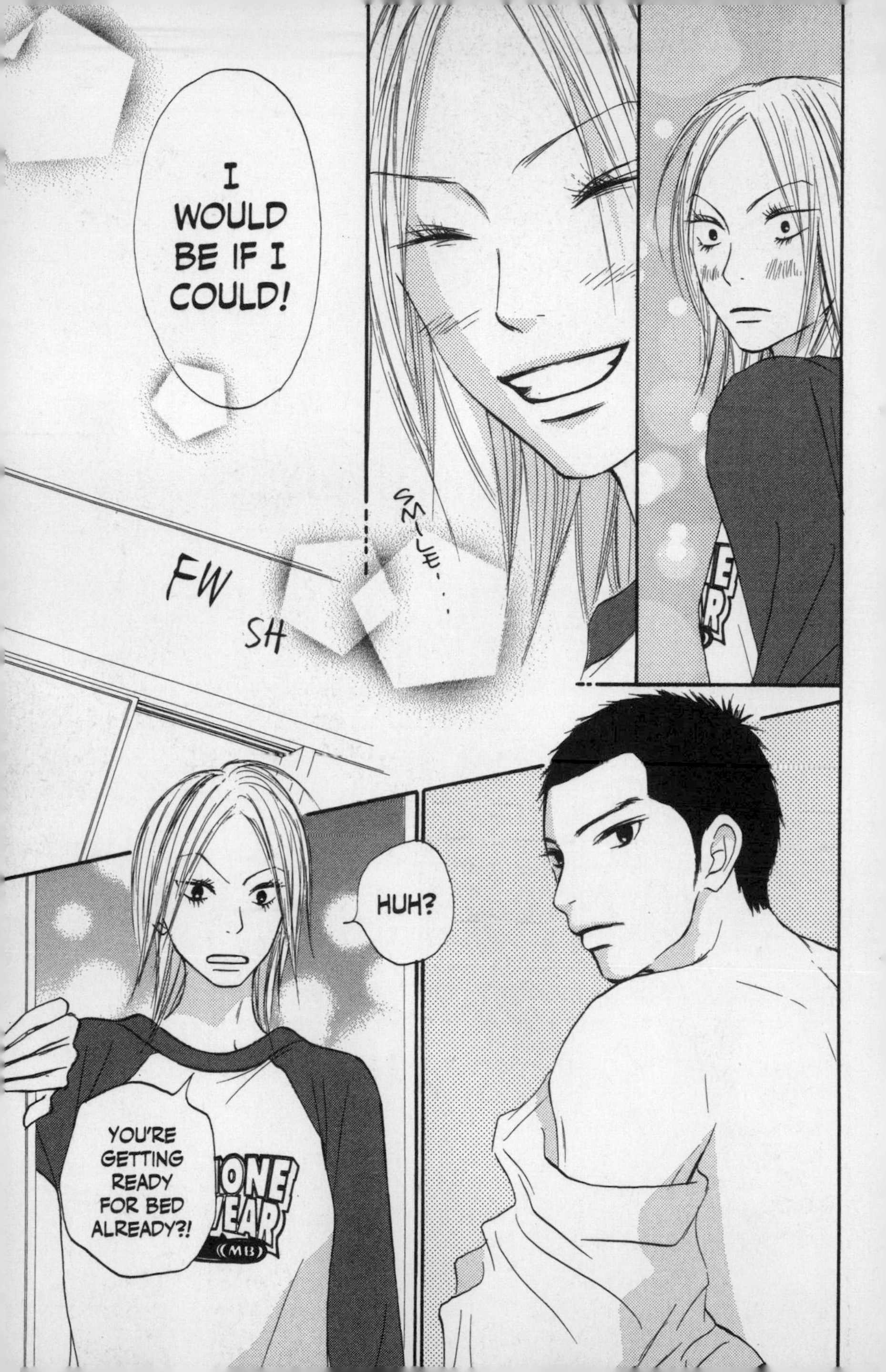
SMILE...
I WOULD BE IF I COULD!
FW
SH
HUH?
YOU'RE GETTING READY FOR BED ALREADY?!

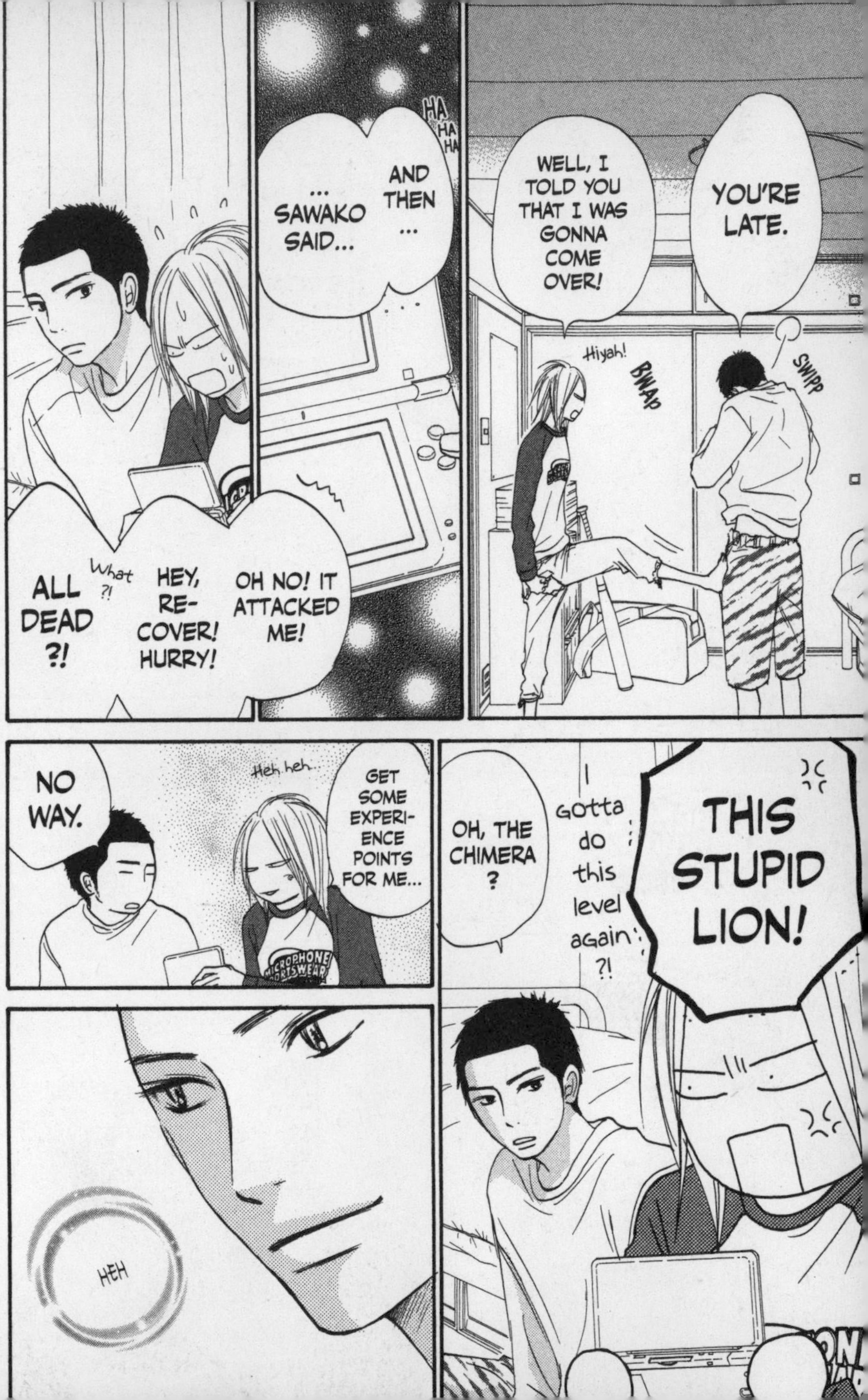
YOU'RE LATE.
WELL, I TOLD YOU THAT I WAS GONNA COME OVER!
Hiyah!
BWAP
SWIPP
AND THEN ...
... SAWAKO SAID...
HA HA HA
OH NO! IT ATTACKED ME!
HEY, RE-COVER! HURRY!
What ?!
ALL DEAD ?!
THIS STUPID LION!
I gotta do this level again ?!
OH, THE CHIMERA ?
GET SOME EXPERI-ENCE POINTS FOR ME...
Heh heh..
NO WAY.
HEH

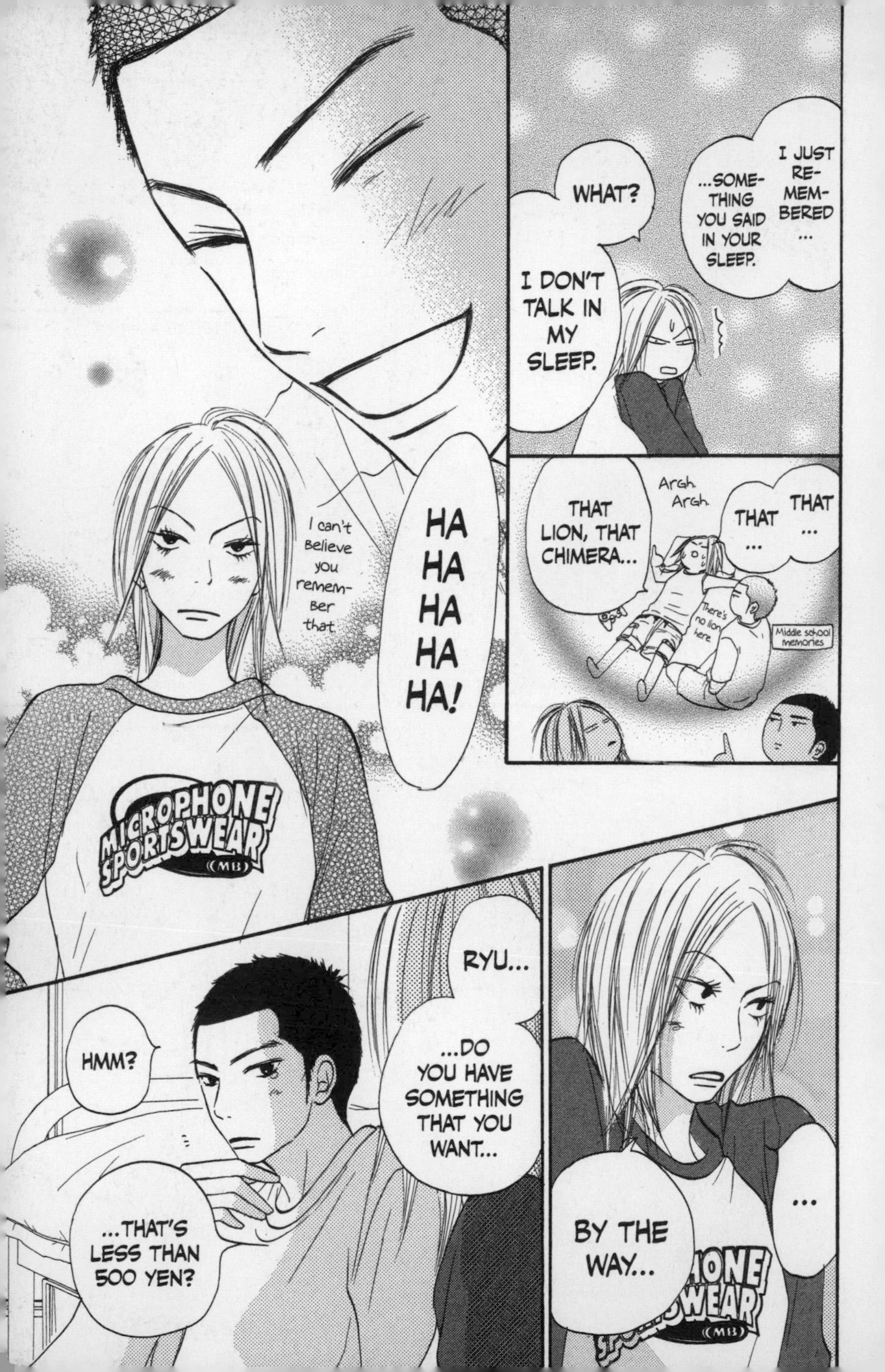
I JUST RE-MEM-BERED...
...SOME-THING YOU SAID IN YOUR SLEEP.
WHAT?
I DON'T TALK IN MY SLEEP.
THAT...
THAT...
Argh. Argh.
THAT LION, THAT CHIMERA...
There's no lion here
Middle school memories
HA HA HA HA HA HA!
I can't Believe you remem-Ber that.
MICROPHONE SPORTSWEAR
MB
...
BY THE WAY...
RYU...
...DO YOU HAVE SOMETHING THAT YOU WANT...
HMM?
...THAT'S LESS THAN 500 YEN?

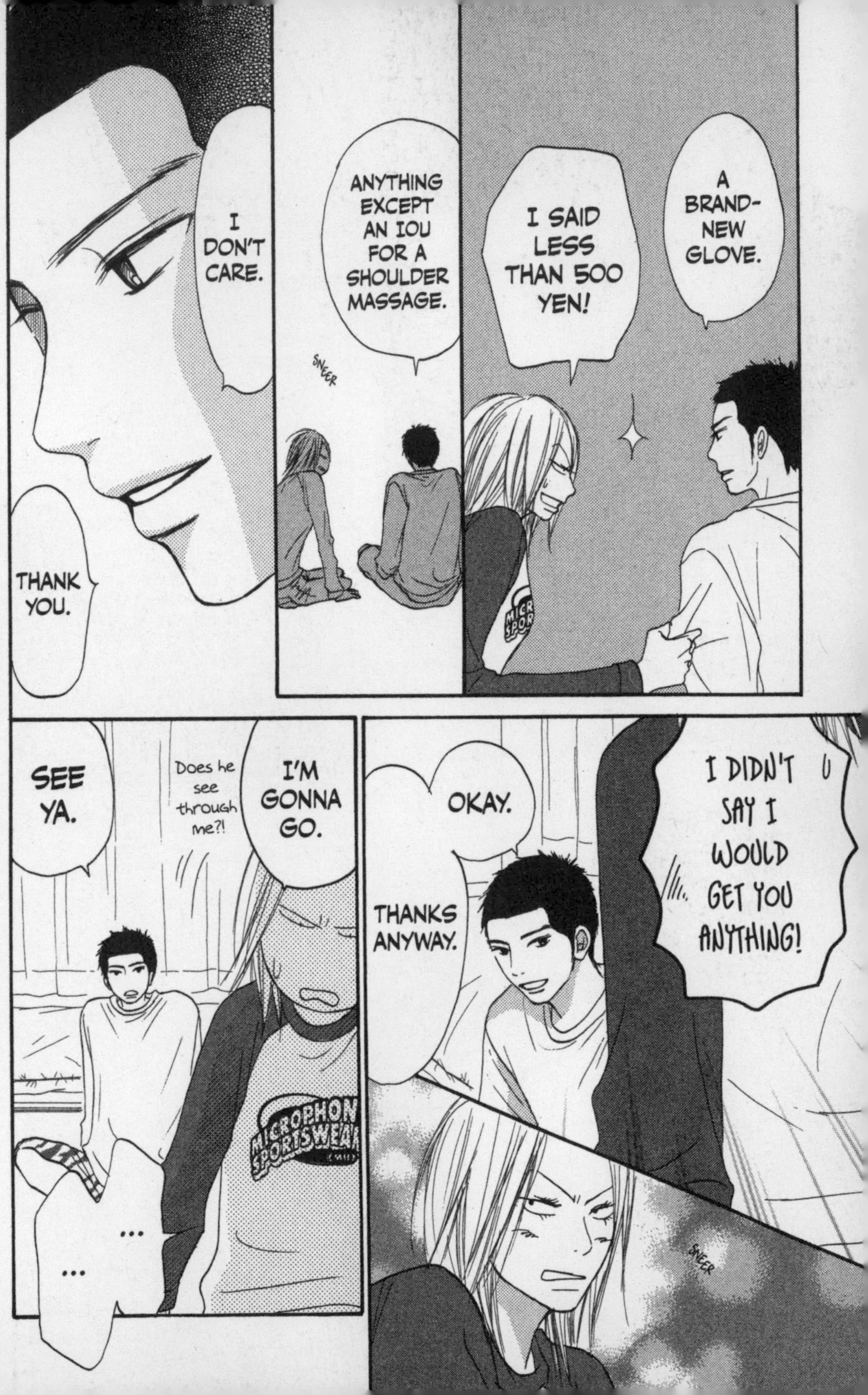
A BRAND-NEW GLOVE.
I SAID LESS THAN 500 YEN!
ANYTHING EXCEPT AN IOU FOR A SHOULDER MASSAGE.
SNEER
I DON'T CARE.
THANK YOU.
I DIDN'T SAY I WOULD GET YOU ANYTHING!
OKAY.
THANKS ANYWAY.
SNEER
I'M GONNA GO.
Does he see through me?!
SEE YA.
...
...

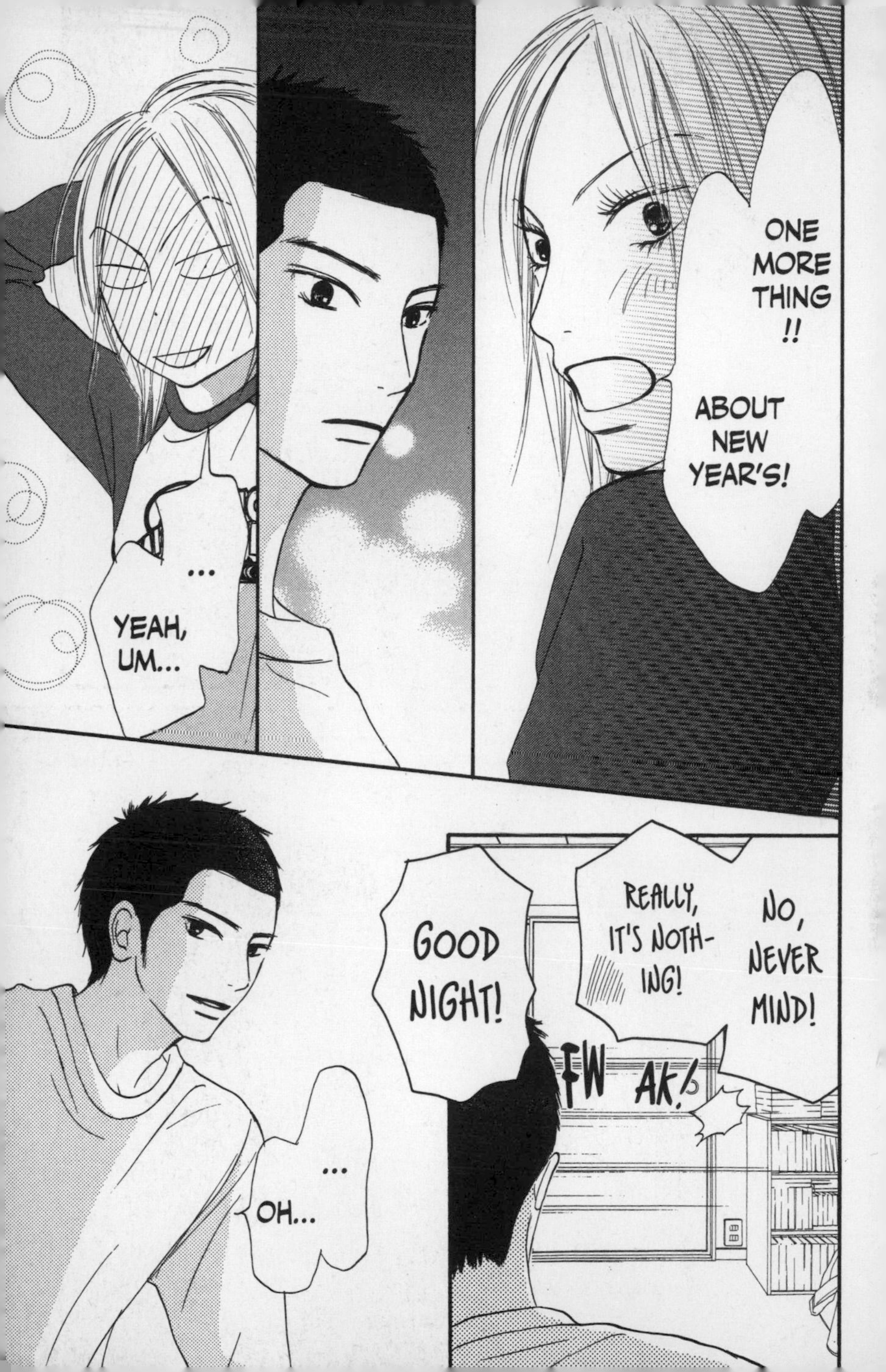
ONE MORE THING!!
ABOUT NEW YEAR'S!
...
YEAH, UM...
NO, NEVER MIND!
REALLY, IT'S NOTH-ING!
GOOD NIGHT!
FWAK!
...
OH...

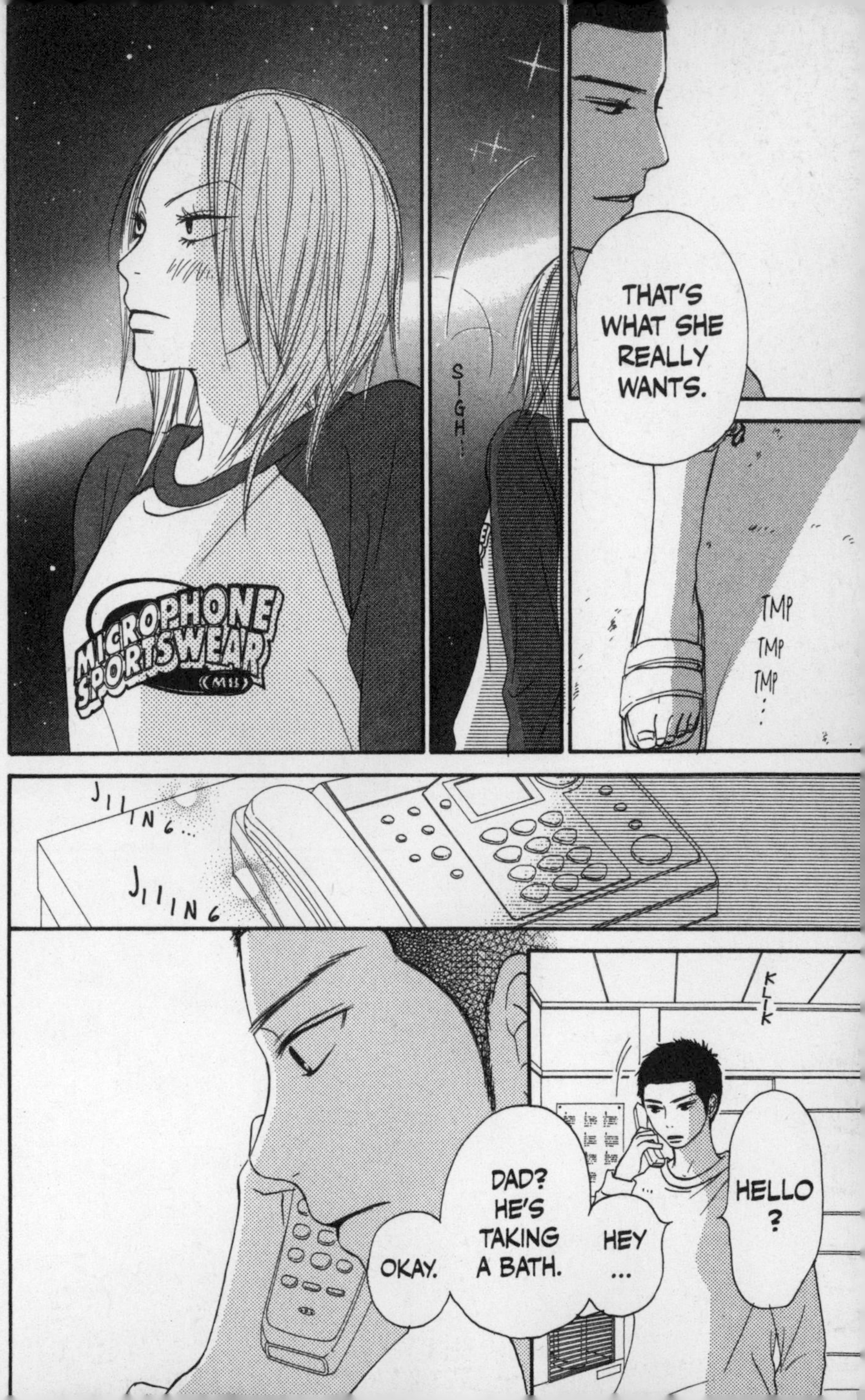
THAT'S WHAT SHE REALLY WANTS.
TMP
TMP
TMP...
SIGH...
MICROPHONE SPORTSWEAR
JIIING...
JIIING
KLIK
HELLO?
...
HEY...
DAD? HE'S TAKING A BATH.
OKAY.

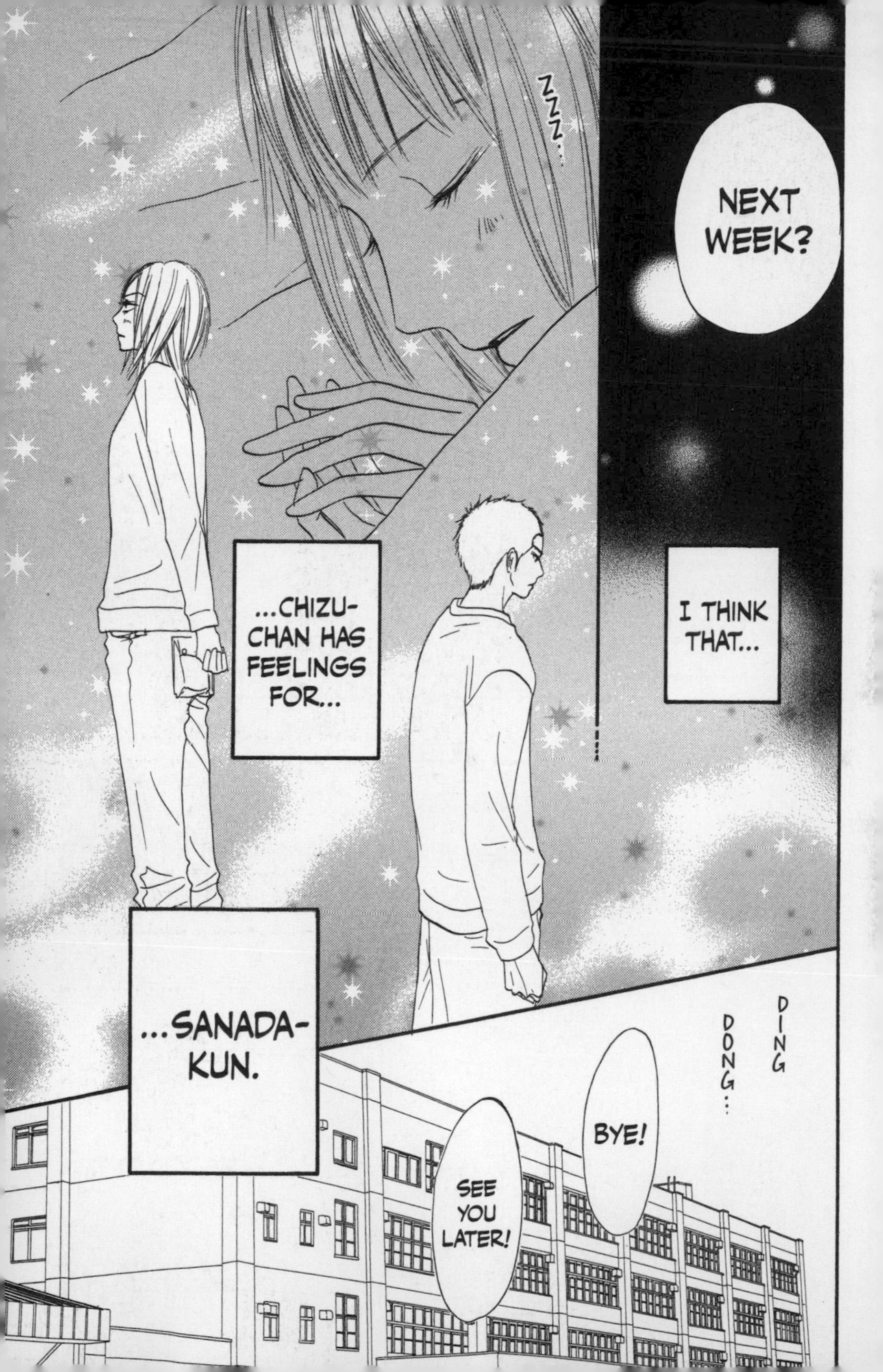
NEXT WEEK?
I THINK THAT...
ZZZ...
...CHIZU-CHAN HAS FEELINGS FOR...
...SANADA-KUN.
DING DONG...
BYE!
SEE YOU LATER!

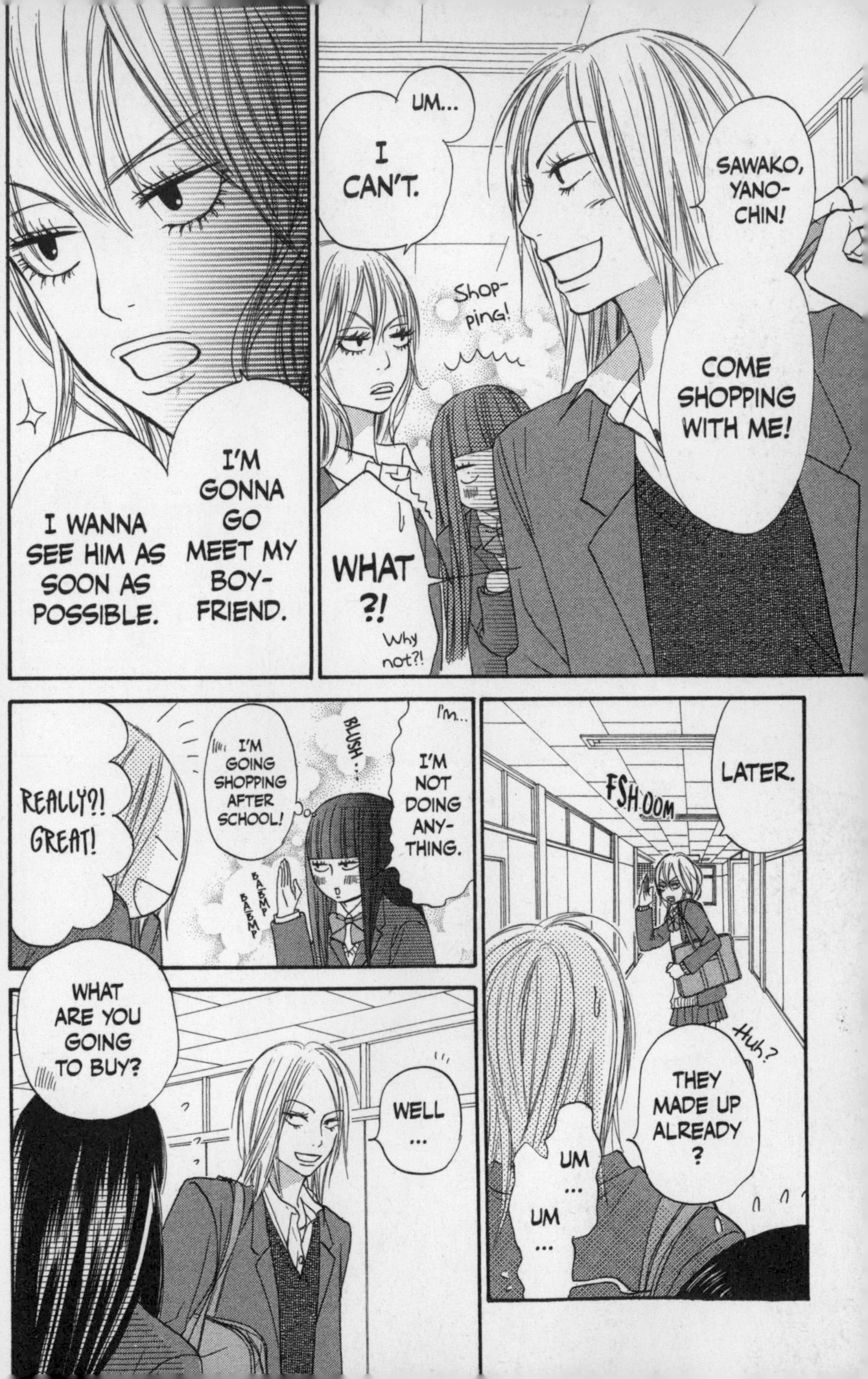
SAWAKO, YANO-CHIN!
COME SHOPPING WITH ME!
UM... I CAN'T.
Shop-ping!
WHAT?!
Why not?!
I'M GONNA GO MEET MY BOY-FRIEND.
I WANNA SEE HIM AS SOON AS POSSIBLE.
LATER.
FSHOOM
Huh?
THEY MADE UP ALREADY?
UM...
UM...
I'm...
I'M NOT DOING ANY-THING.
BLUSH...
I'M GOING SHOPPING AFTER SCHOOL!
BA-BMP BA-BMP
REALLY?! GREAT!
WELL...
WHAT ARE YOU GOING TO BUY?

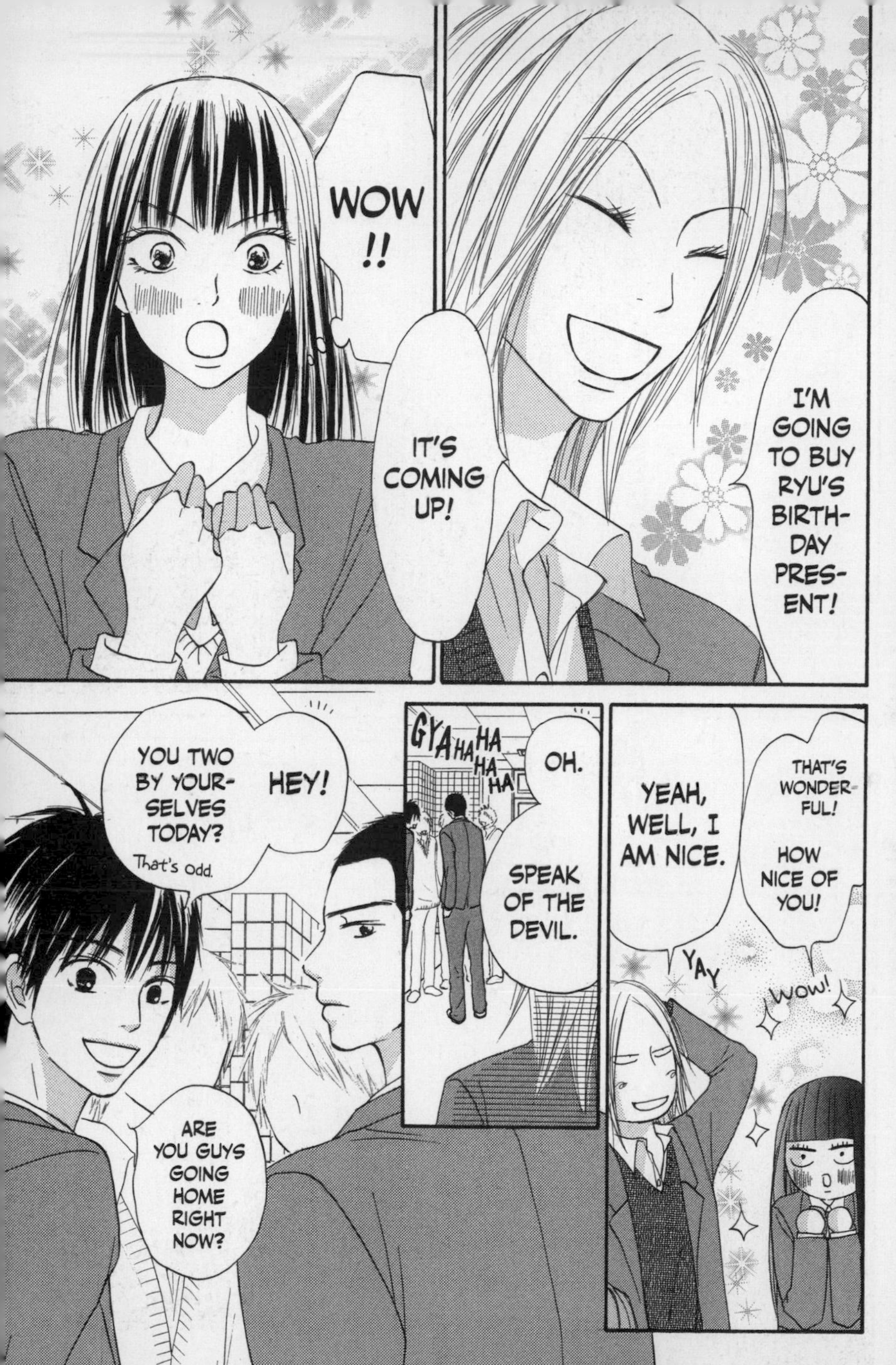
I'M GOING TO BUY RYU'S BIRTHDAY PRESENT!
IT'S COMING UP!
WOW !!
THAT'S WONDERFUL! HOW NICE OF YOU!
YEAH, WELL, I AM NICE.
YAY
WOW!
GYAHAHAHAHAHA
OH.
SPEAK OF THE DEVIL.
HEY!
YOU TWO BY YOURSELVES TODAY?
That's odd.
ARE YOU GUYS GOING HOME RIGHT NOW?

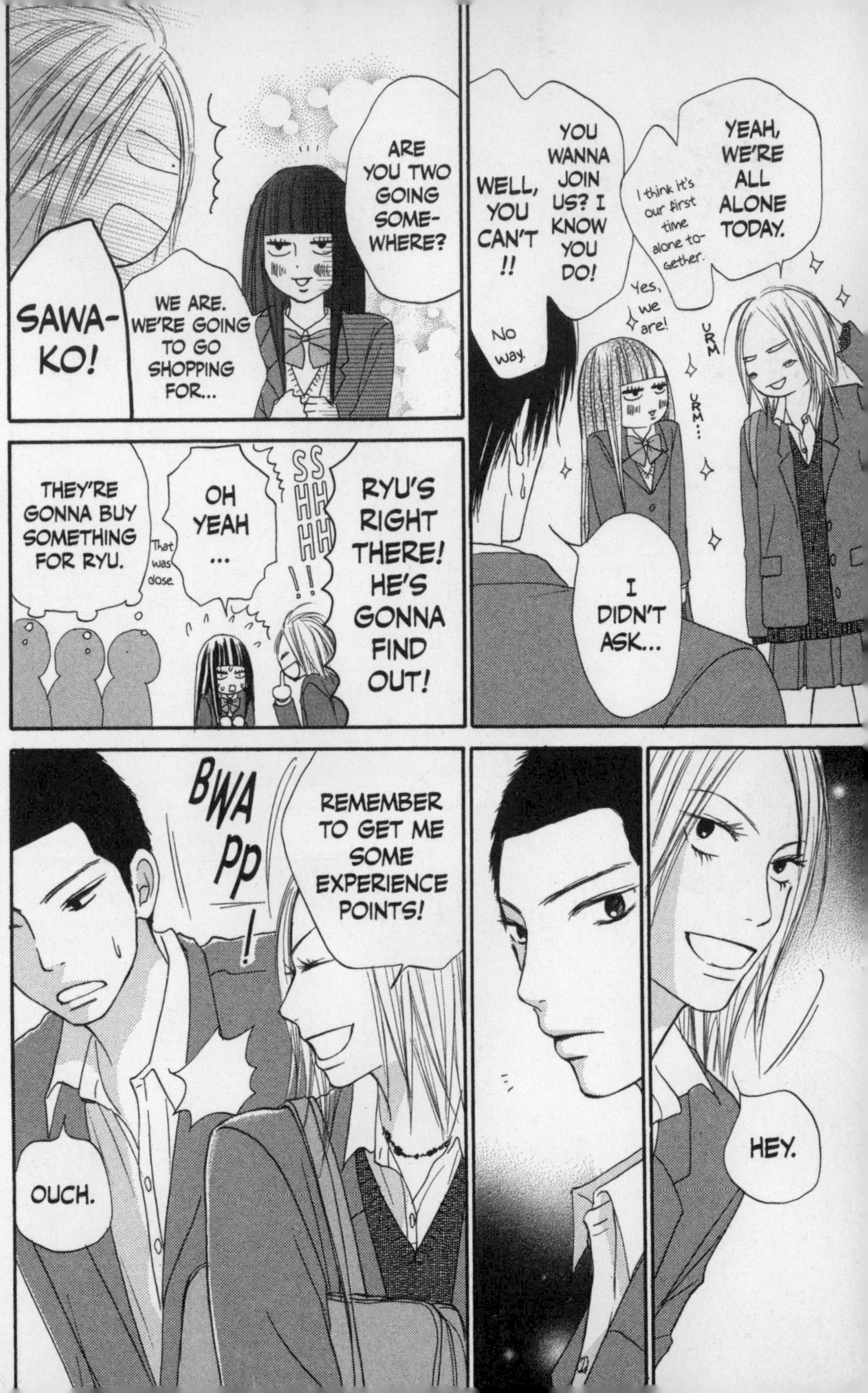
YEAH, WE'RE ALL ALONE TODAY.
I think it's our first time alone together.
URM URM...
YOU WANNA JOIN US? I KNOW YOU DO!
Yes, we are!
WELL, YOU CAN'T!!
No way.
I DIDN'T ASK...
ARE YOU TWO GOING SOMEWHERE?
WE ARE. WE'RE GOING TO GO SHOPPING FOR...
SAWAKO!
RYU'S RIGHT THERE! HE'S GONNA FIND OUT!
SSHHHHH!!
OH YEAH...
That was close.
THEY'RE GONNA BUY SOMETHING FOR RYU.
HEY.
REMEMBER TO GET ME SOME EXPERIENCE POINTS!
BWAPP!
OUCH.

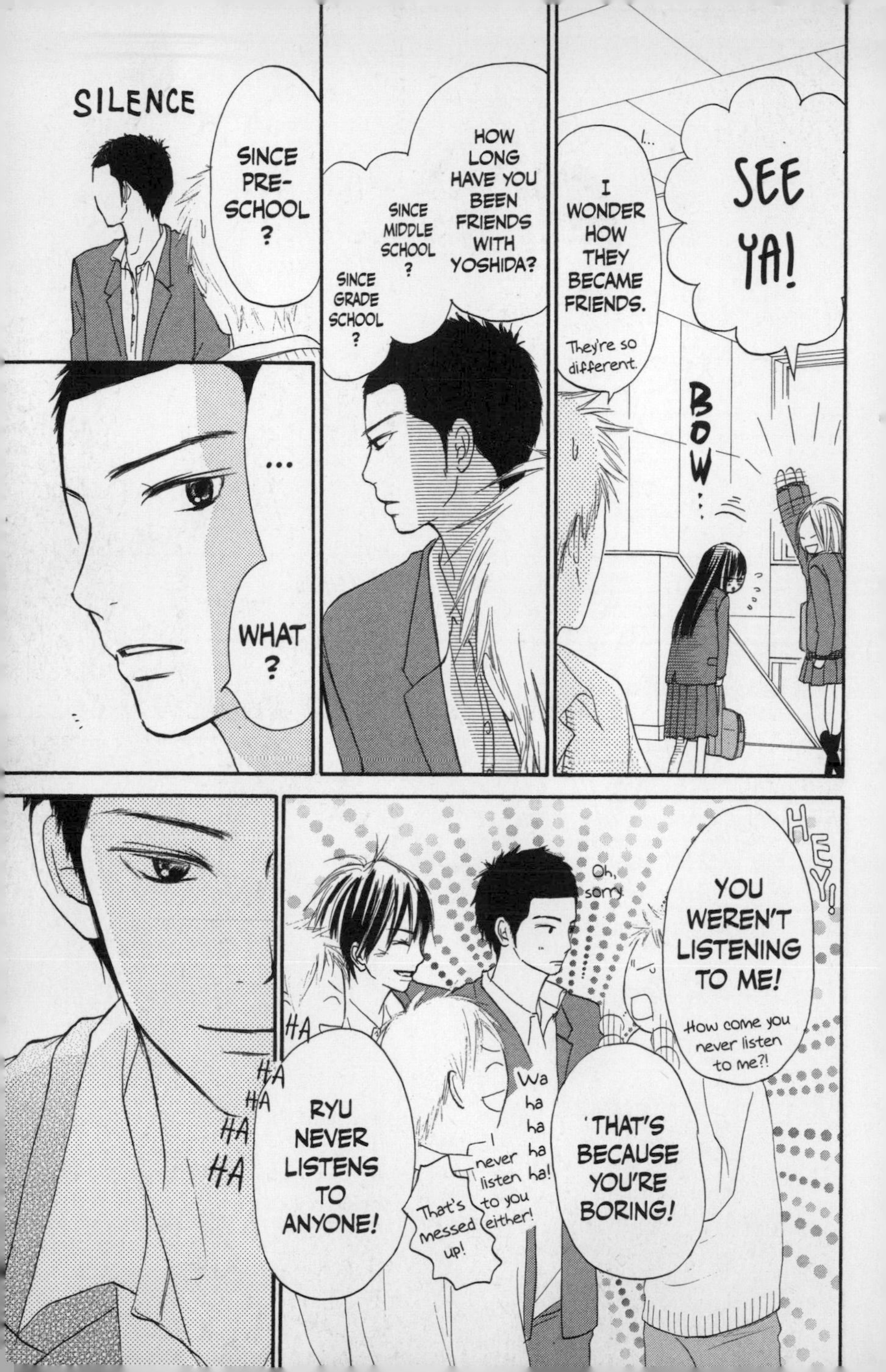
SEE YA!
I...
I WONDER HOW THEY BECAME FRIENDS.
They're so different.
BOW...
HOW LONG HAVE YOU BEEN FRIENDS WITH YOSHIDA?
SINCE MIDDLE SCHOOL?
SINCE GRADE SCHOOL?
SILENCE
SINCE PRE-SCHOOL?
...
WHAT?
HEY!
YOU WEREN'T LISTENING TO ME!
How come you never listen to me?!
Oh, sorry.
'THAT'S BECAUSE YOU'RE BORING!
Wa ha ha ha ha!
I never listen to you either!
That's messed up!
RYU NEVER LISTENS TO ANYONE!
HA HA HA HA HA

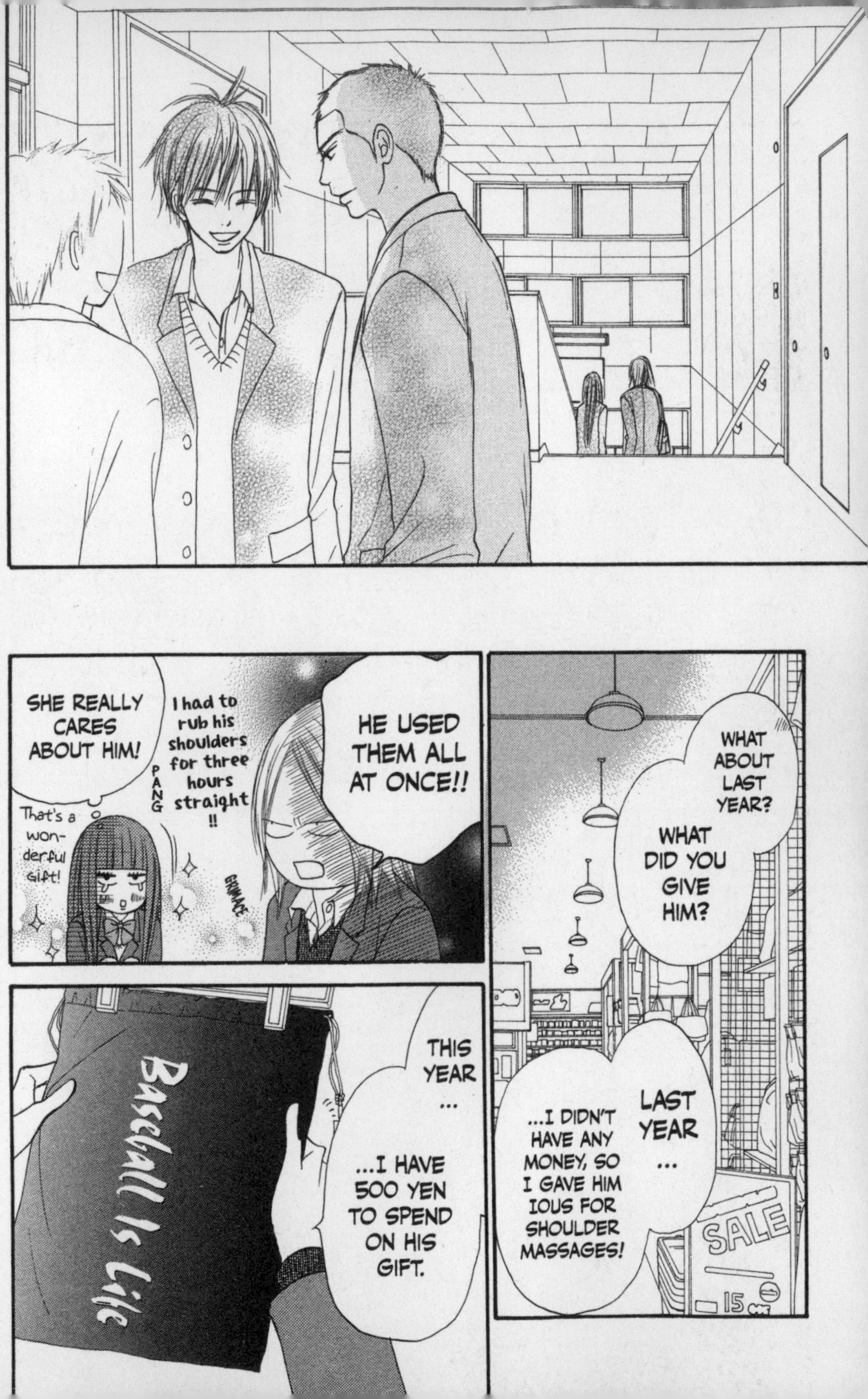
WHAT ABOUT LAST YEAR?
WHAT DID YOU GIVE HIM?
LAST YEAR...
...I DIDN'T HAVE ANY MONEY, SO I GAVE HIM IOUS FOR SHOULDER MASSAGES!
SALE
HE USED THEM ALL AT ONCE!!
I had to rub his shoulders for three hours straight!!
PANG
GRIMACE
SHE REALLY CARES ABOUT HIM!
That's a wonderful gift!
THIS YEAR...
...I HAVE 500 YEN TO SPEND ON HIS GIFT.
Baseball Is Life

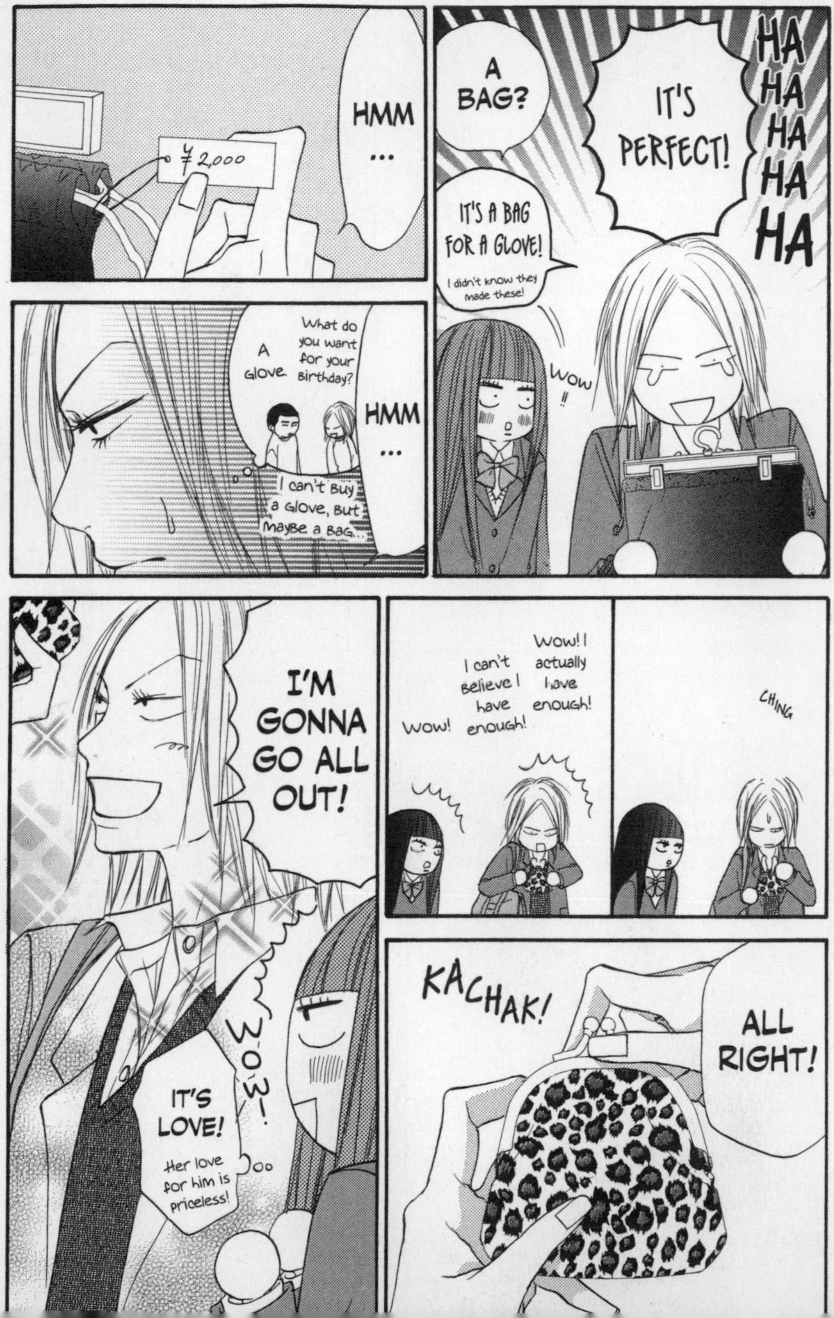
HA HA HA HA HA
IT'S PERFECT!
A BAG?
IT'S A BAG FOR A GLOVE!
I didn't know they made these!
WOW !!
HMM ...
¥2,000
HMM ...
What do you want for your Birthday?
A Glove.
I can't Buy a Glove, But maybe a Bag...
CHING
Wow! I actually have enough!
I can't Believe I have enough!
Wow!
ALL RIGHT!
KACHAK!
I'M GONNA GO ALL OUT!
WOW!
IT'S LOVE!
Her love for him is priceless!

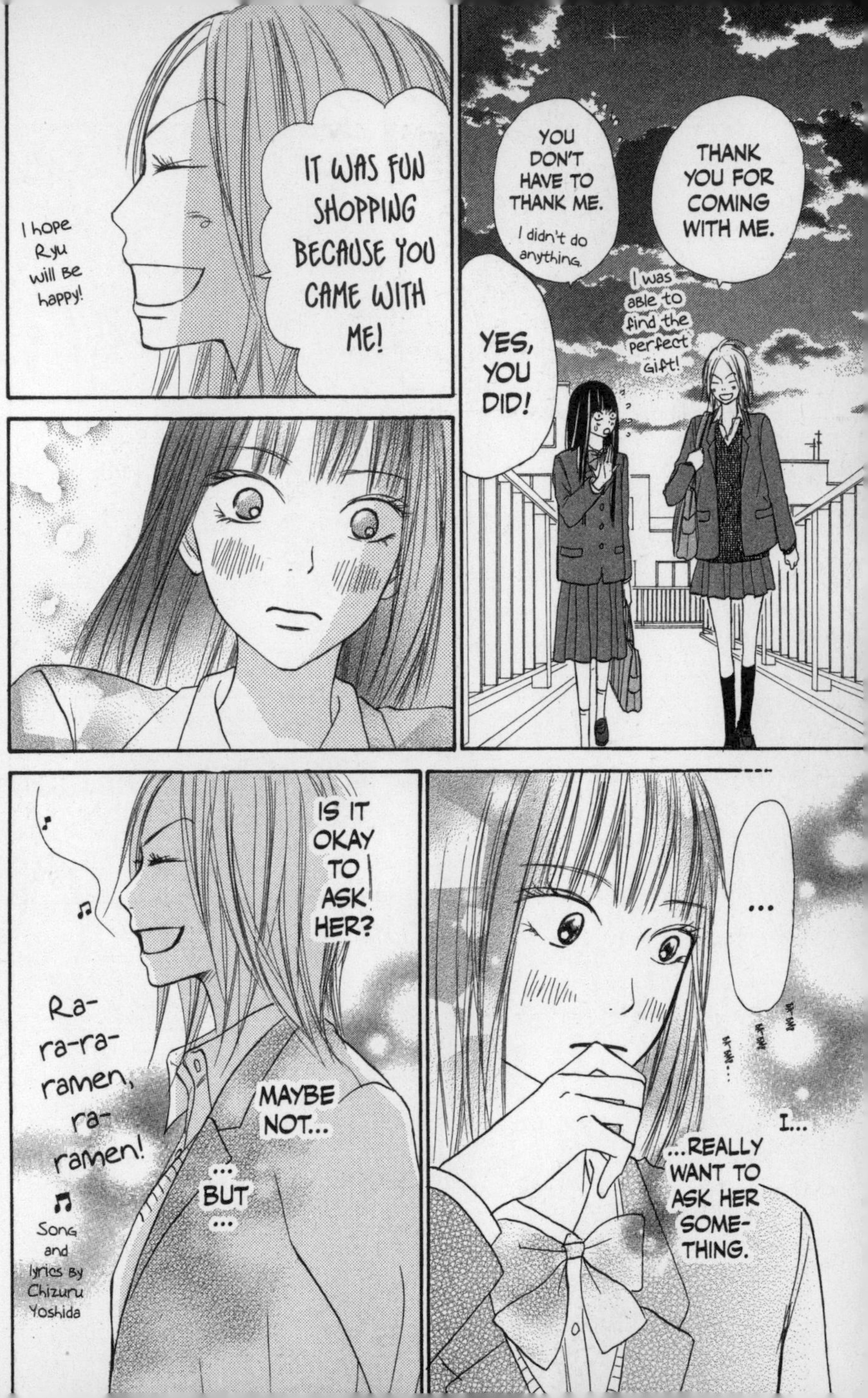
THANK YOU FOR COMING WITH ME.
I was able to find the perfect gift!
YOU DON'T HAVE TO THANK ME.
I didn't do anything.
YES, YOU DID!
IT WAS FUN SHOPPING BECAUSE YOU CAME WITH ME!
I hope Ryu will be happy!
...
I...
...REALLY WANT TO ASK HER SOME-THING.
IS IT OKAY TO ASK HER?
MAYBE NOT...
...BUT...
Ra-ra-ra-ramen, ra-ramen!
Song and lyrics by Chizuru Yoshida

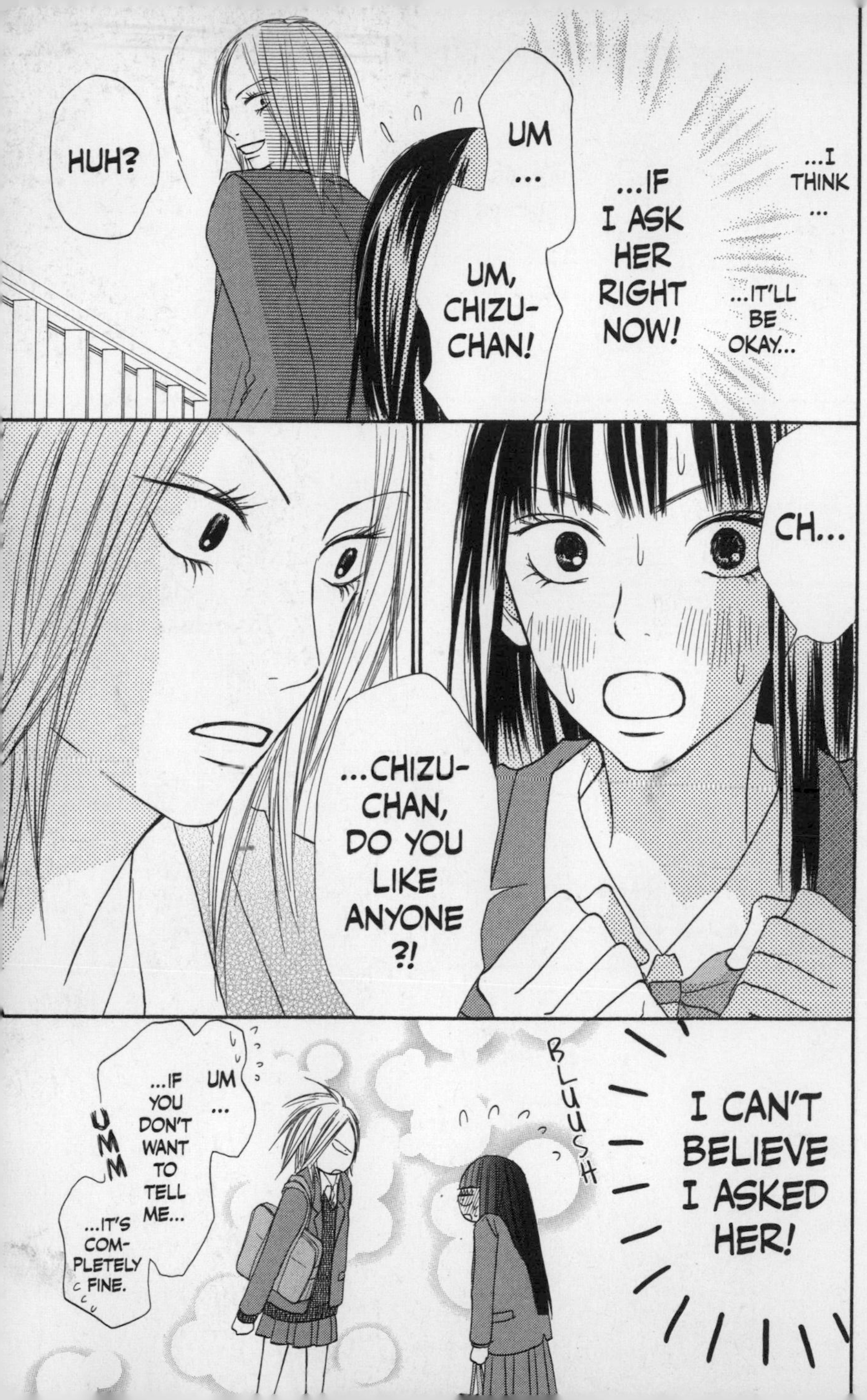
...I THINK ...
...IT'LL BE OKAY...
...IF I ASK HER RIGHT NOW!
UM ...
UM, CHIZU-CHAN!
HUH?
CH...
...CHIZU-CHAN, DO YOU LIKE ANYONE ?!
I CAN'T BELIEVE I ASKED HER!
BLUUSH
UM ...
...IF YOU DON'T WANT TO TELL ME...
UMM
...IT'S COMPLETELY FINE.

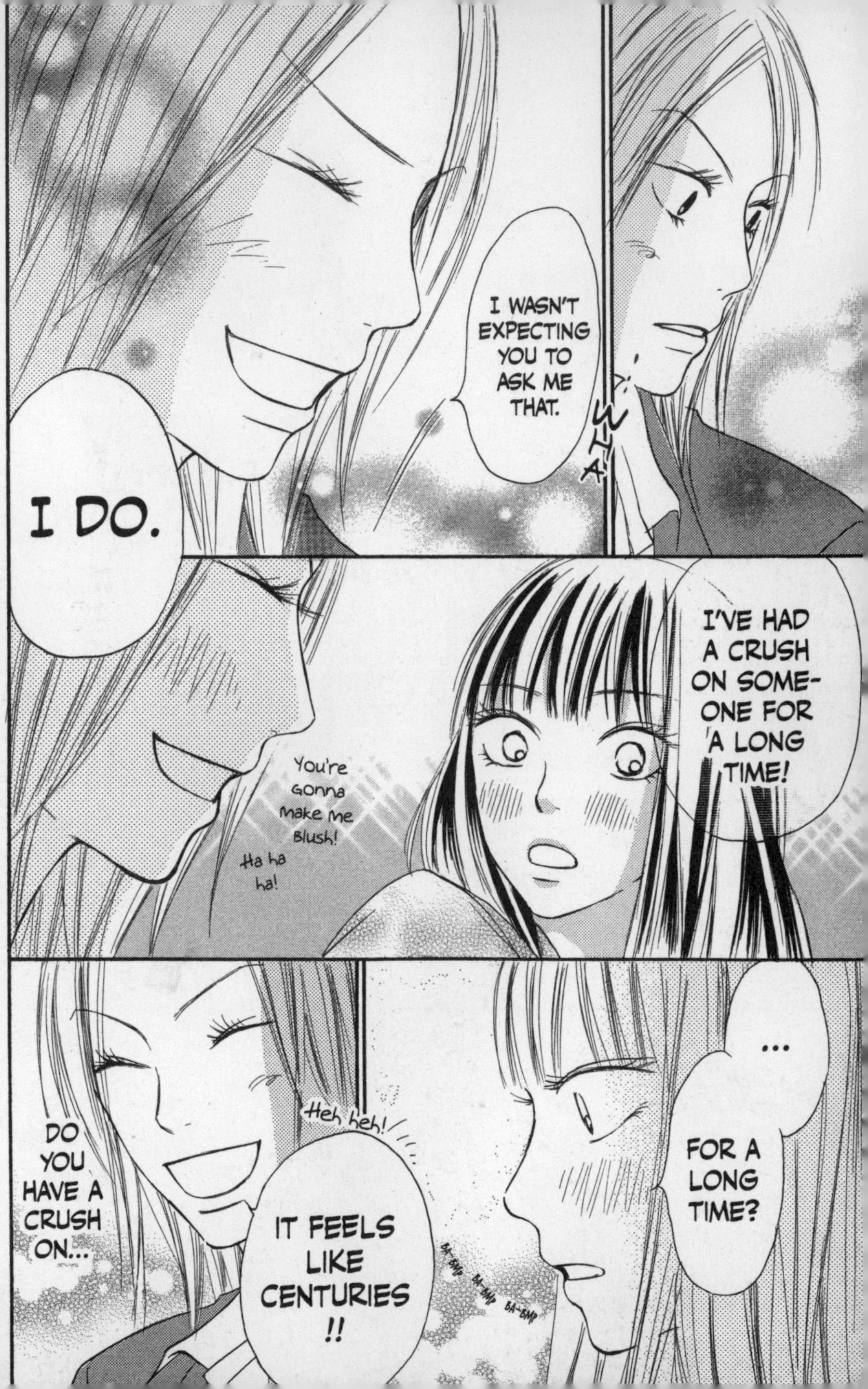
WHA
I WASN'T EXPECTING YOU TO ASK ME THAT.
I DO.
I'VE HAD A CRUSH ON SOME-ONE FOR A LONG TIME!
You're gonna make me blush!
Ha ha ha!
...
FOR A LONG TIME?
BA-BMP BA-BMP BA-BMP
Heh heh!
IT FEELS LIKE CENTURIES !!
DO YOU HAVE A CRUSH ON...

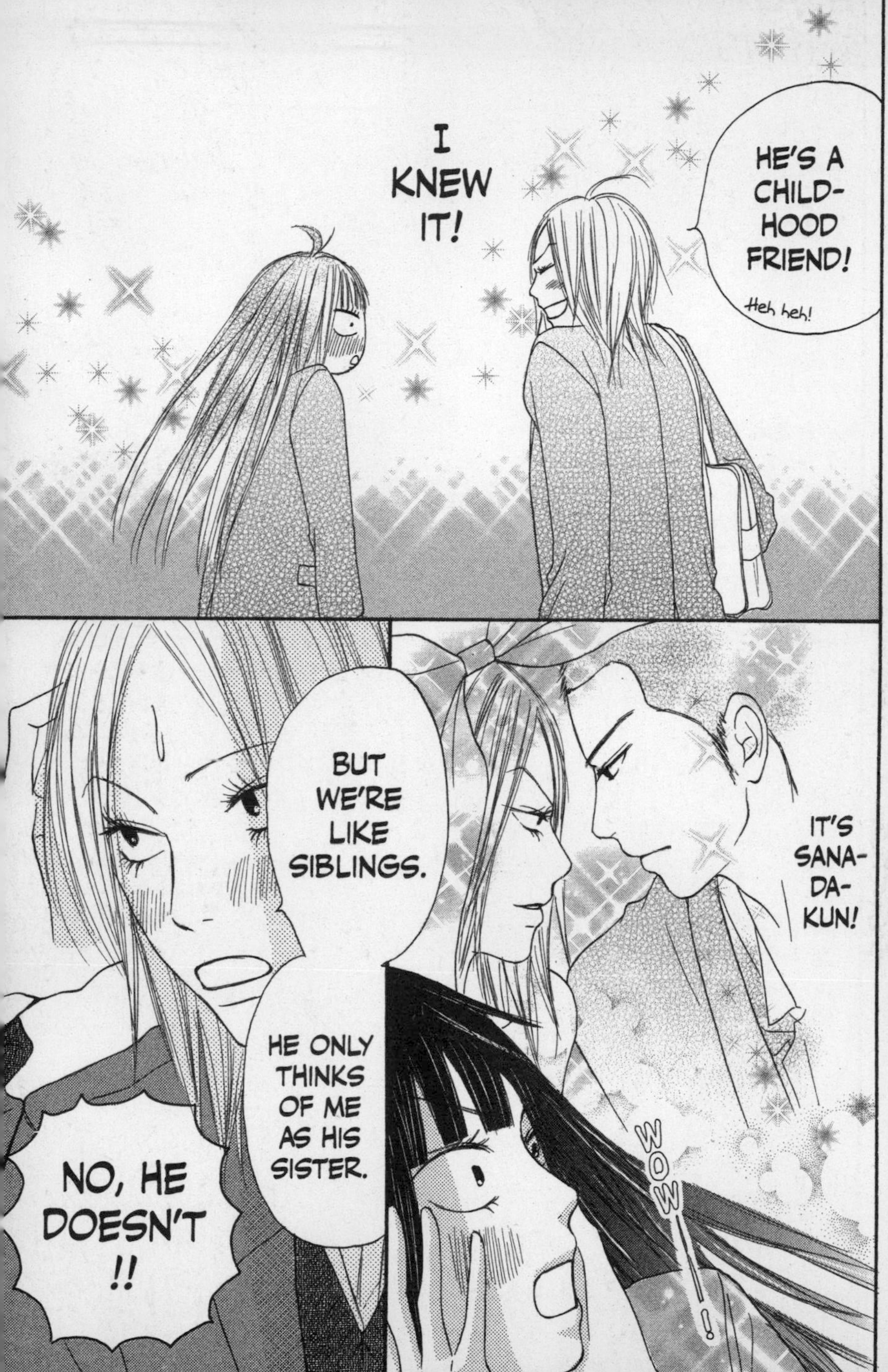
HE'S A CHILD-HOOD FRIEND!
Heh heh!
I KNEW IT!
IT'S SANA-DA-KUN!
WOW—!
BUT WE'RE LIKE SIBLINGS.
HE ONLY THINKS OF ME AS HIS SISTER.
NO, HE DOESN'T !!

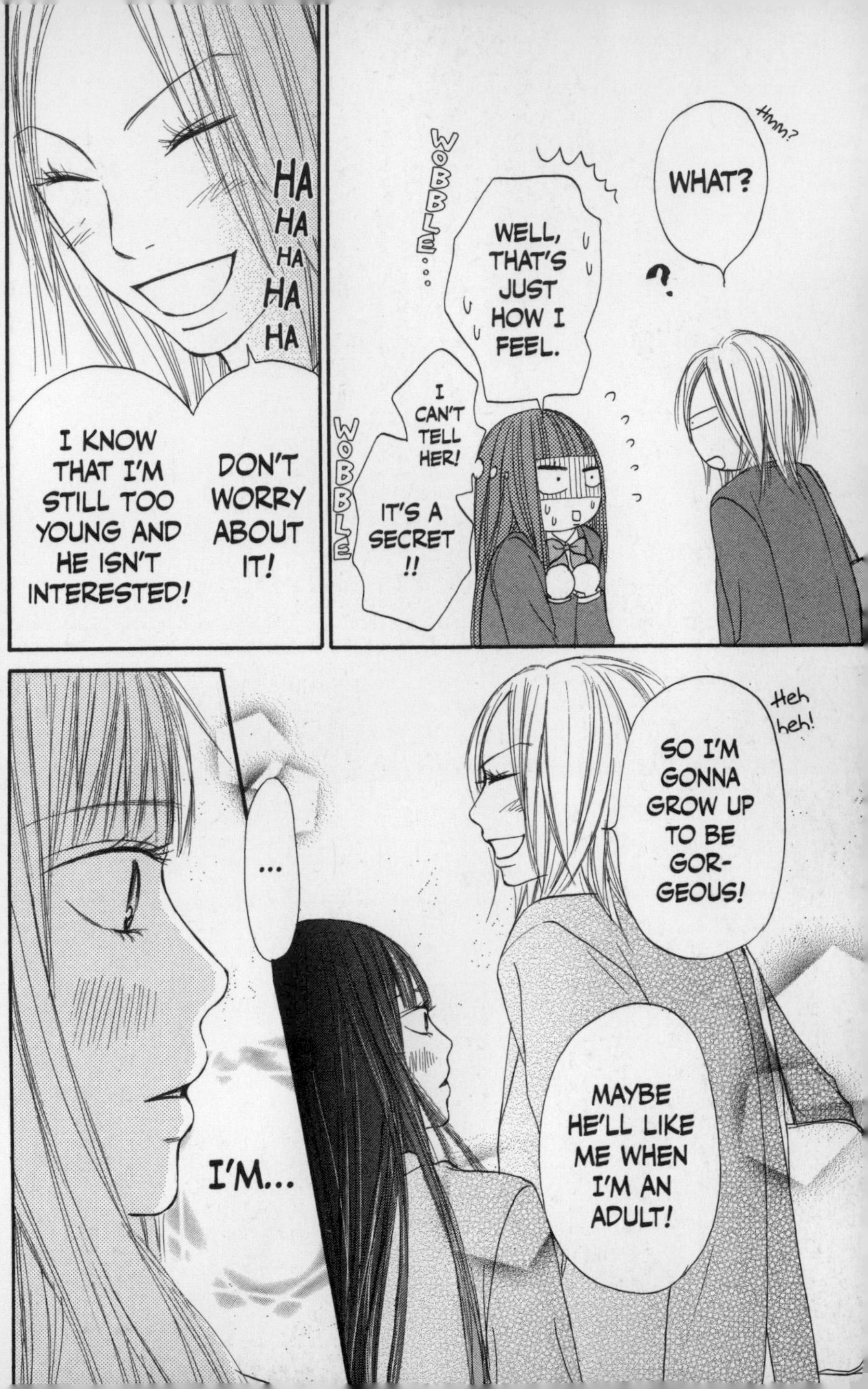
Hmm?
WHAT?
?
WOBBLE...
WELL, THAT'S JUST HOW I FEEL.
I CAN'T TELL HER!
IT'S A SECRET!!
WOBBLE
HA HA HA HA HA
DON'T WORRY ABOUT IT!
I KNOW THAT I'M STILL TOO YOUNG AND HE ISN'T INTERESTED!
Heh heh!
SO I'M GONNA GROW UP TO BE GOR-GEOUS!
MAYBE HE'LL LIKE ME WHEN I'M AN ADULT!
...
I'M...

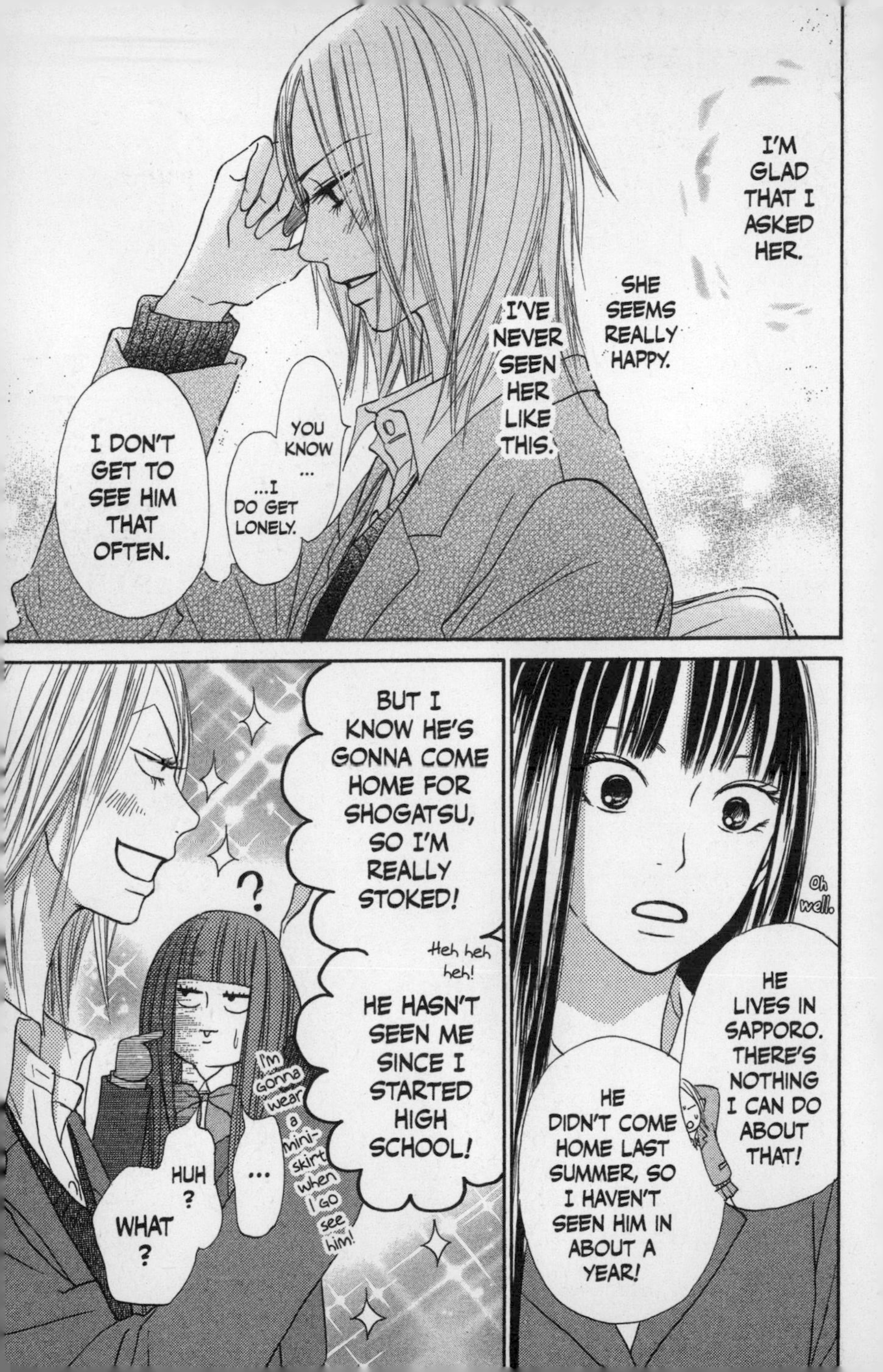
I'M GLAD THAT I ASKED HER.
SHE SEEMS REALLY HAPPY.
I'VE NEVER SEEN HER LIKE THIS.
YOU KNOW ...
...I DO GET LONELY.
I DON'T GET TO SEE HIM THAT OFTEN.
Oh well.
HE LIVES IN SAPPORO. THERE'S NOTHING I CAN DO ABOUT THAT!
HE DIDN'T COME HOME LAST SUMMER, SO I HAVEN'T SEEN HIM IN ABOUT A YEAR!
BUT I KNOW HE'S GONNA COME HOME FOR SHOGATSU, SO I'M REALLY STOKED!
Heh heh heh!
HE HASN'T SEEN ME SINCE I STARTED HIGH SCHOOL!
I'm gonna wear a mini-skirt when I go see him!
...
HUH?
WHAT?

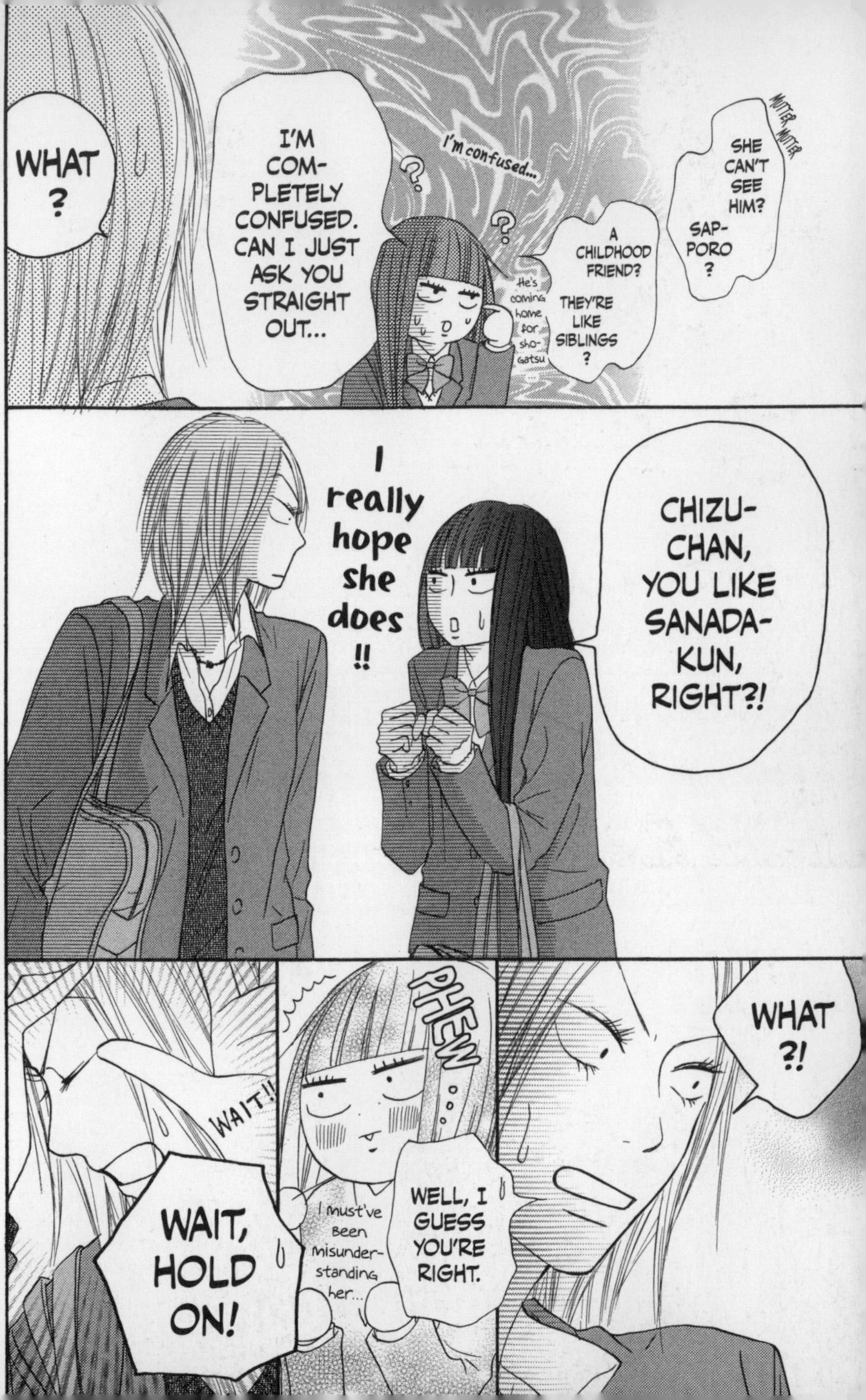
MUTTER MUTTER
SHE CAN'T SEE HIM?
SAPPORO?
A CHILDHOOD FRIEND?
THEY'RE LIKE SIBLINGS?
He's coming home for sho-gatsu...
I'm confused...
I'M COMPLETELY CONFUSED. CAN I JUST ASK YOU STRAIGHT OUT...
WHAT?
CHIZU-CHAN, YOU LIKE SANADA-KUN, RIGHT?!
I really hope she does!!
WHAT?!
PHEW
WELL, I GUESS YOU'RE RIGHT.
I must've been misunderstanding her...
WAIT!!
WAIT, HOLD ON!

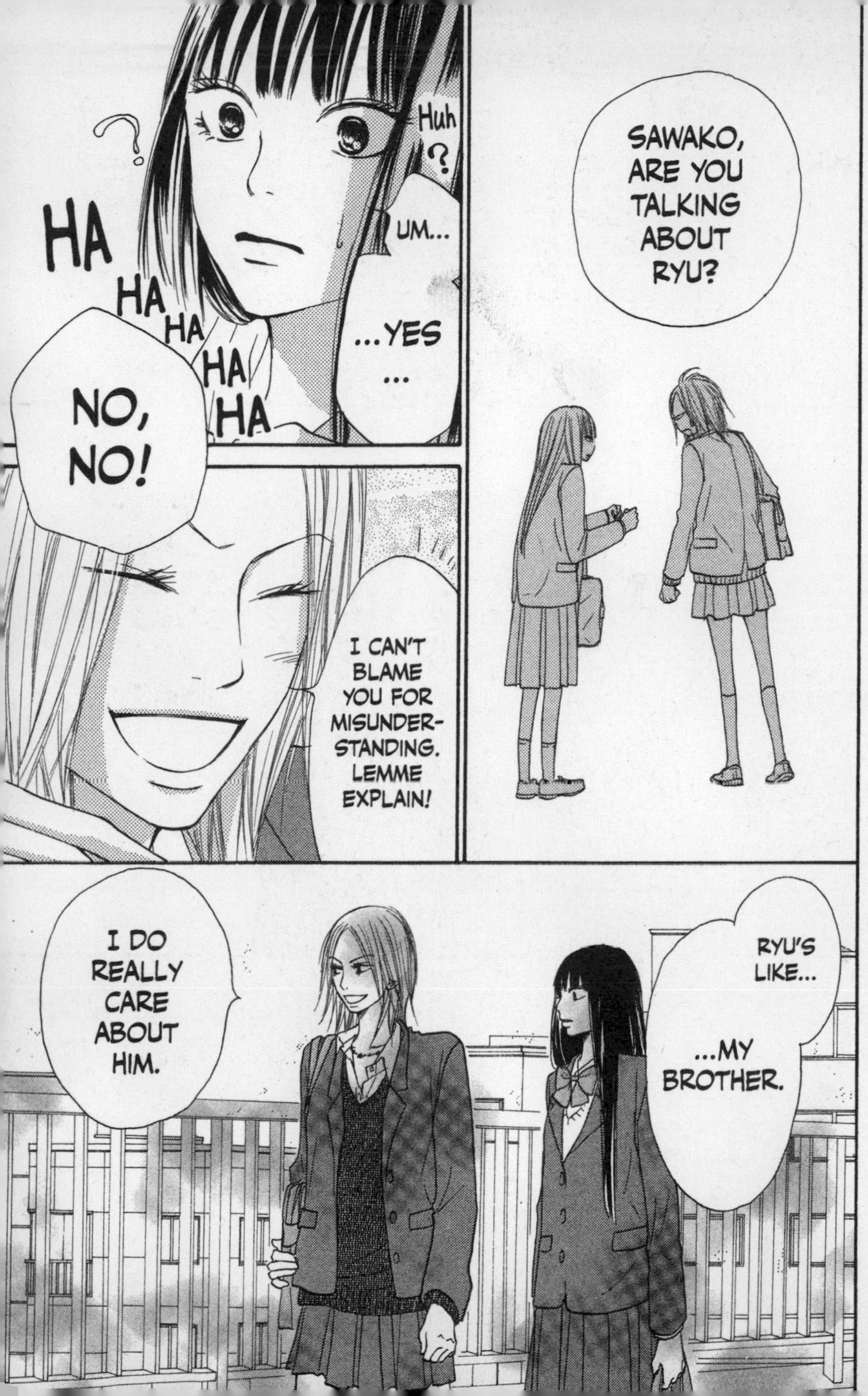
SAWAKO, ARE YOU TALKING ABOUT RYU?
Huh?
UM...
...YES...
HA HA HA HA HA
NO, NO!
I CAN'T BLAME YOU FOR MISUNDER-STANDING. LEMME EXPLAIN!
RYU'S LIKE...
...MY BROTHER.
I DO REALLY CARE ABOUT HIM.

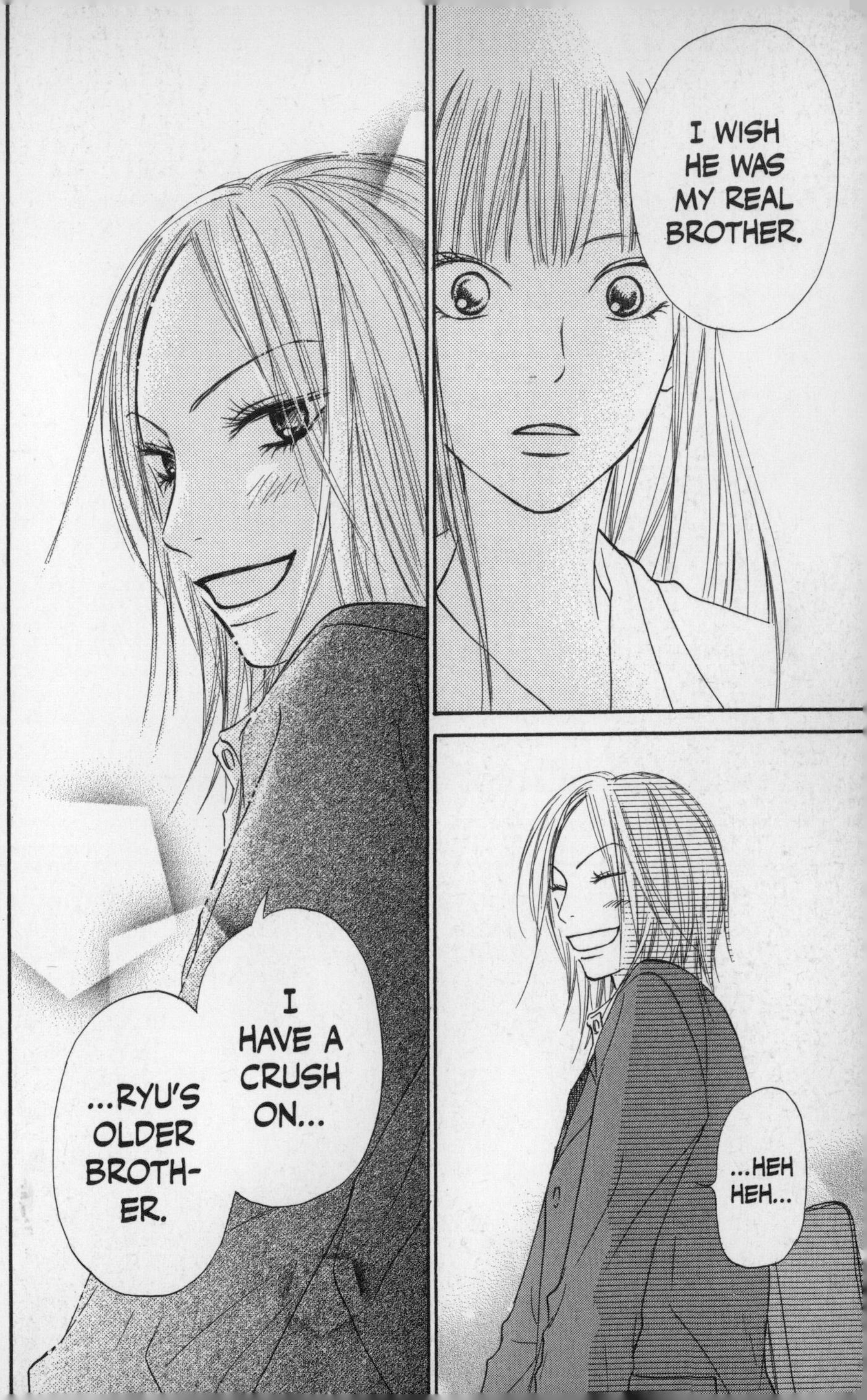
I WISH HE WAS MY REAL BROTHER.
...HEH HEH...
I HAVE A CRUSH ON...
...RYU'S OLDER BROTH-ER.

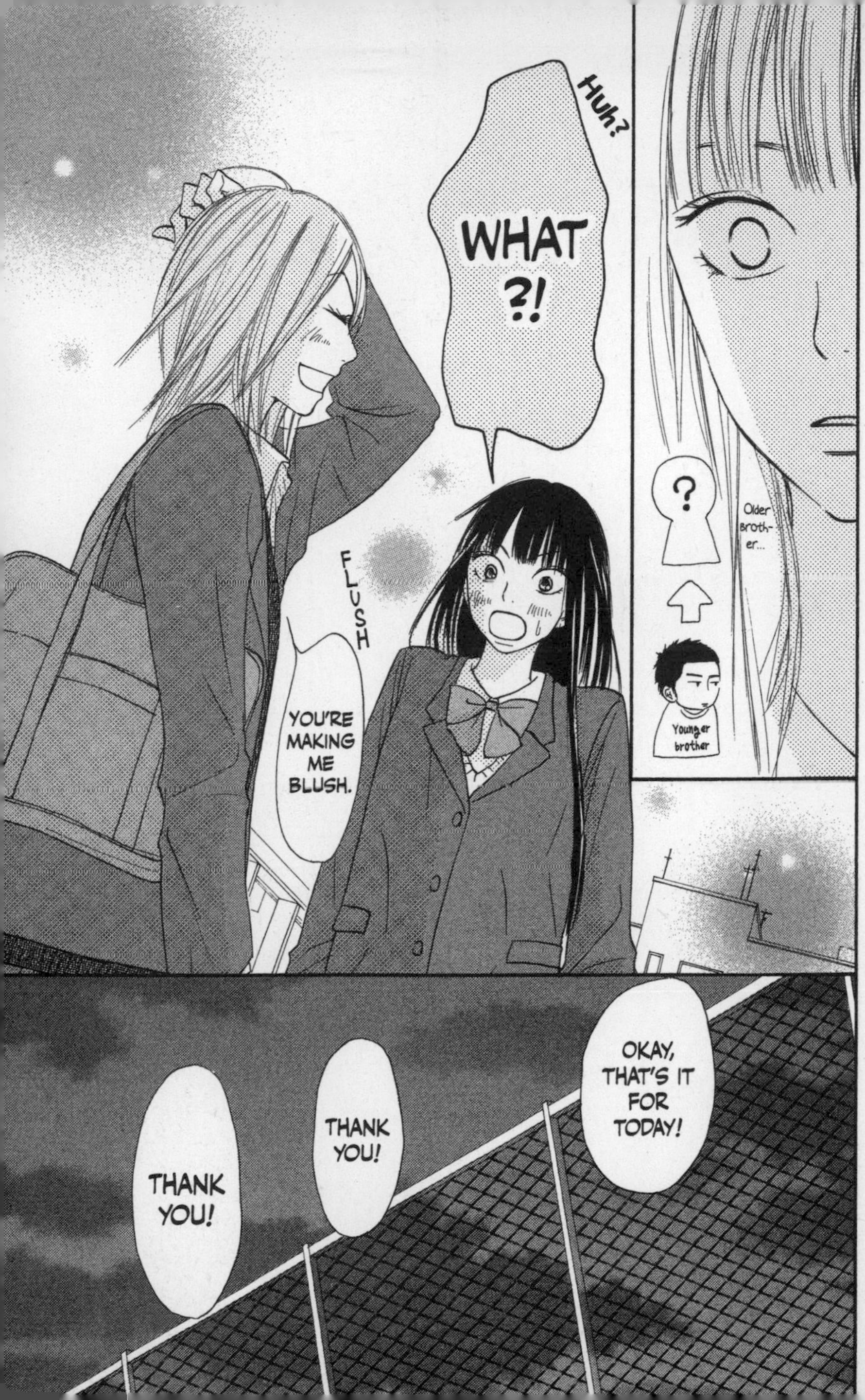
Older broth-er...
?
Younger brother
Huh?
WHAT ?!
FLUSH
YOU'RE MAKING ME BLUSH.
OKAY, THAT'S IT FOR TODAY!
THANK YOU!
THANK YOU!

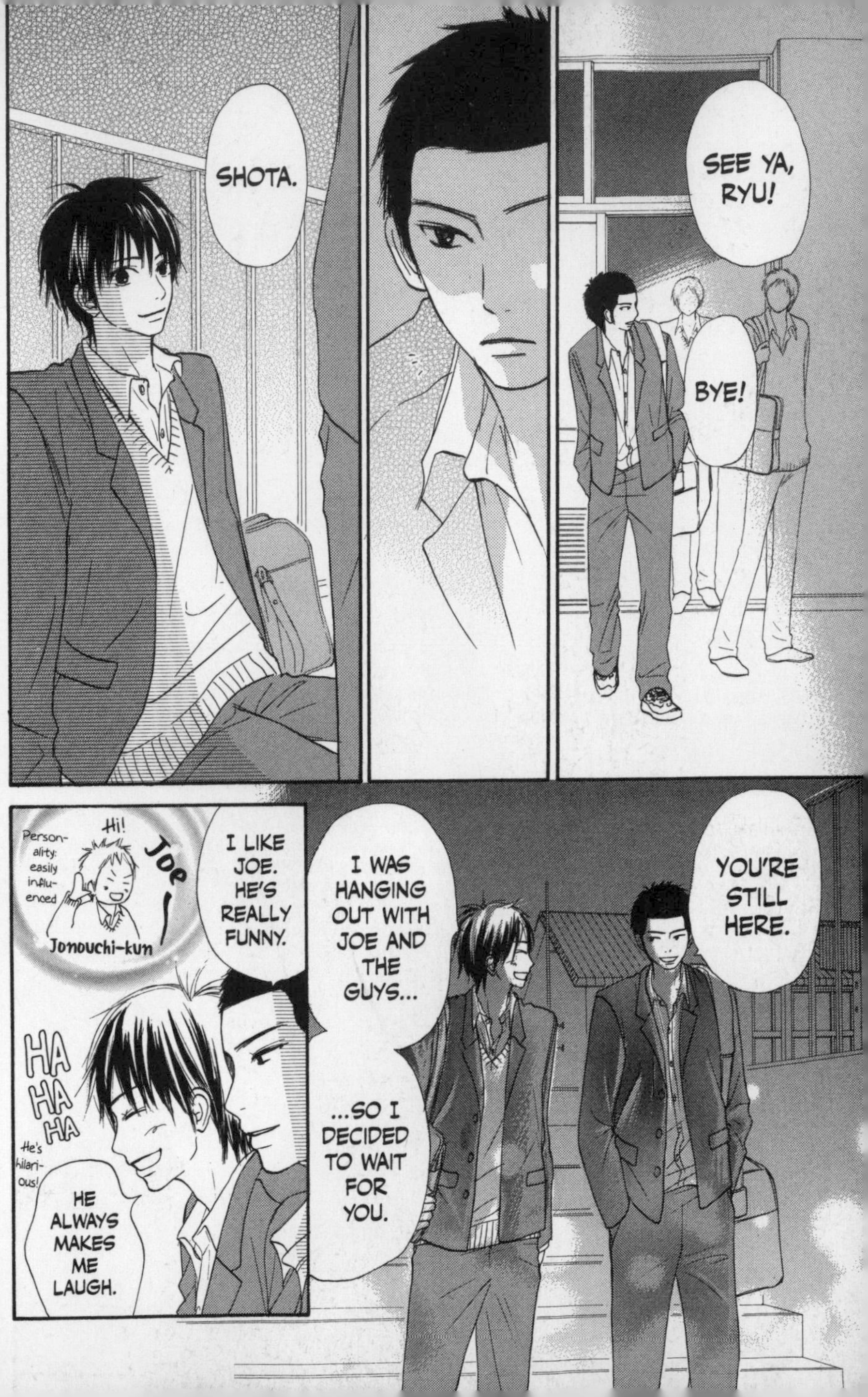
SEE YA, RYU!
BYE!
SHOTA.
YOU'RE STILL HERE.
I WAS HANGING OUT WITH JOE AND THE GUYS...
...SO I DECIDED TO WAIT FOR YOU.
I LIKE JOE. HE'S REALLY FUNNY.
Joe
Hi!
Personality: easily influenced
Jonouchi-kun
HA HA HA
He's hilarious!
HE ALWAYS MAKES ME LAUGH.

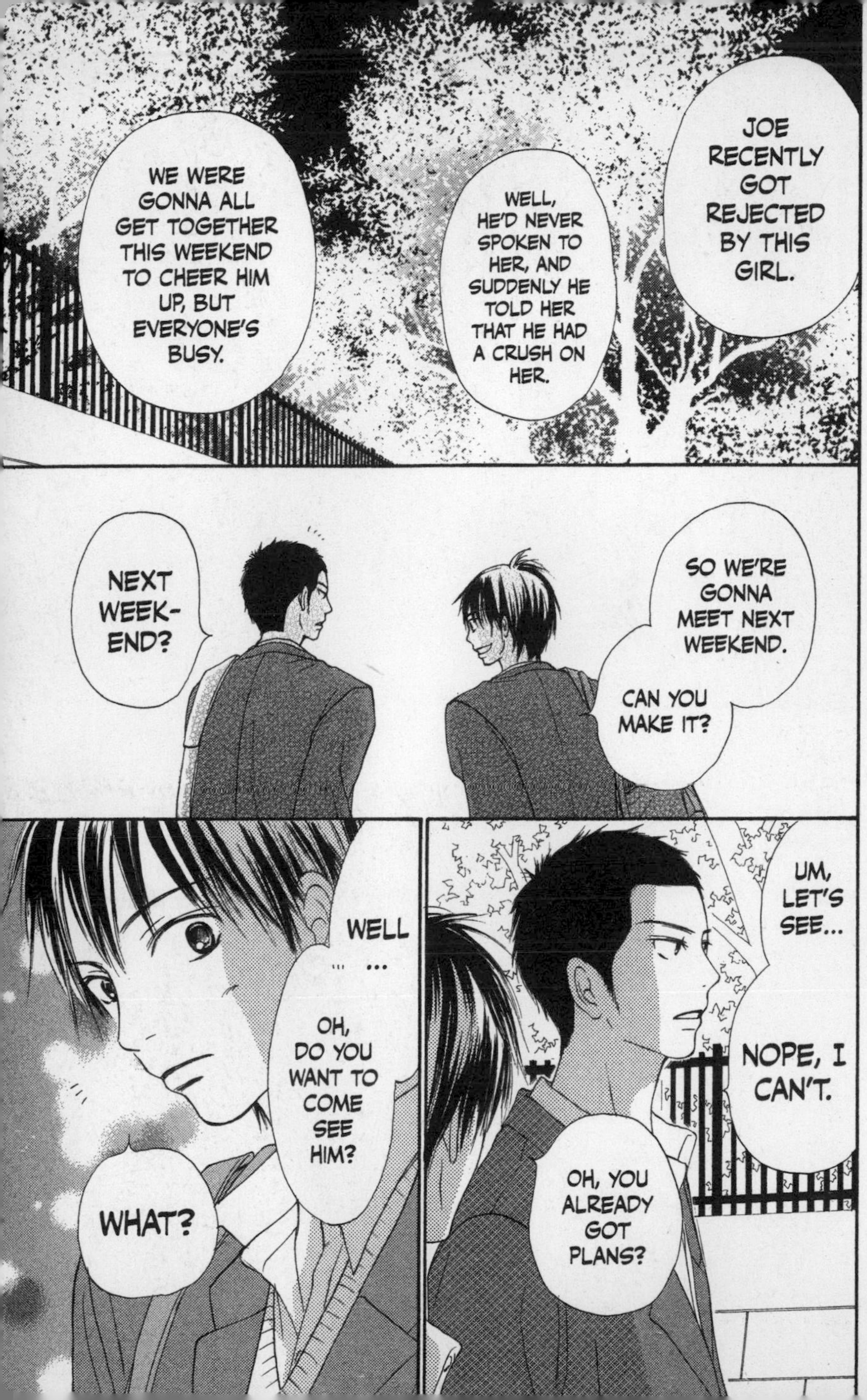
JOE RECENTLY GOT REJECTED BY THIS GIRL.
WELL, HE'D NEVER SPOKEN TO HER, AND SUDDENLY HE TOLD HER THAT HE HAD A CRUSH ON HER.
WE WERE GONNA ALL GET TOGETHER THIS WEEKEND TO CHEER HIM UP, BUT EVERYONE'S BUSY.
SO WE'RE GONNA MEET NEXT WEEKEND.
CAN YOU MAKE IT?
NEXT WEEK-END?
UM, LET'S SEE...
NOPE, I CAN'T.
OH, YOU ALREADY GOT PLANS?
WELL
... ...
OH, DO YOU WANT TO COME SEE HIM?
WHAT?

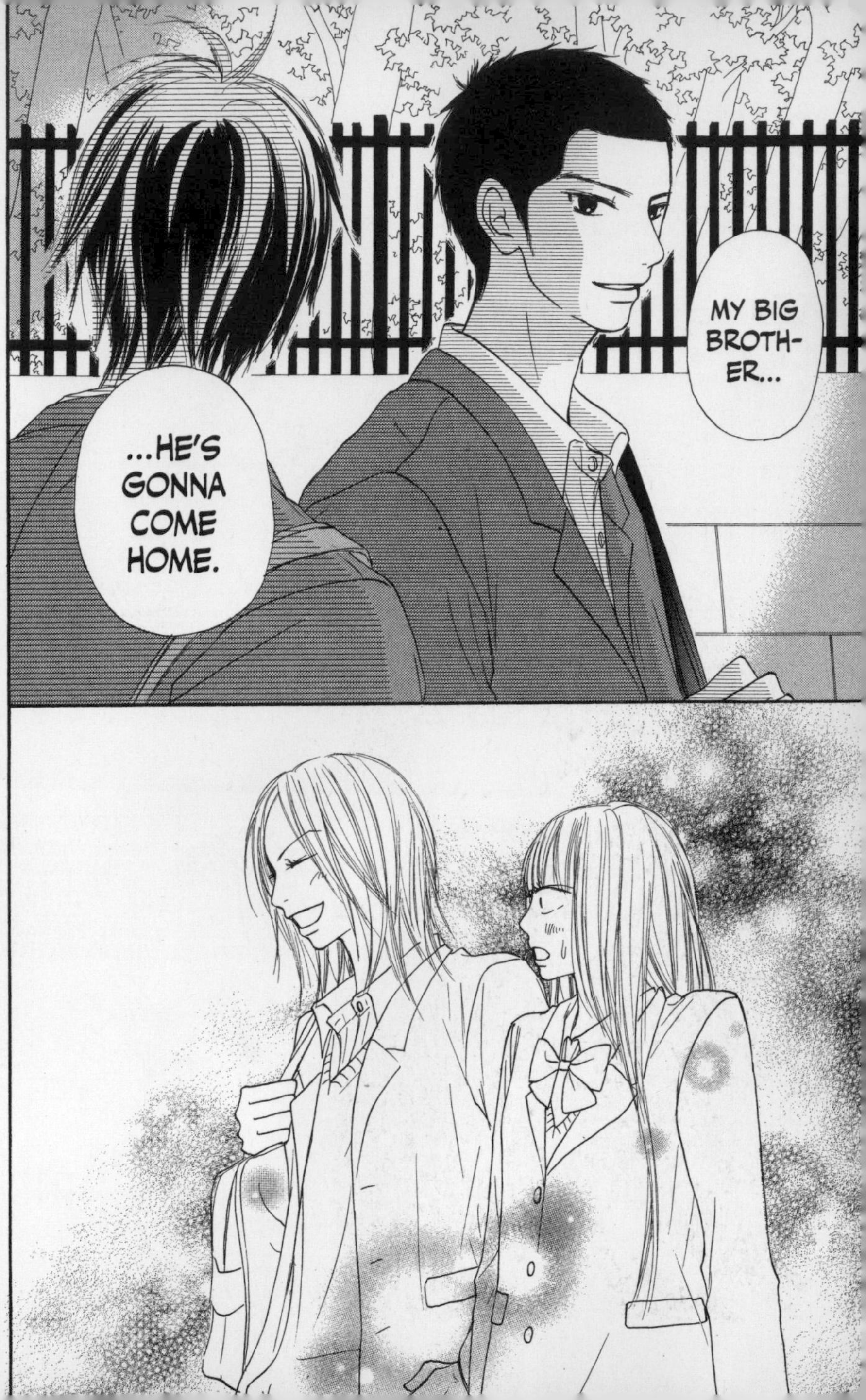
MY BIG BROTHER...
...HE'S GONNA COME HOME.

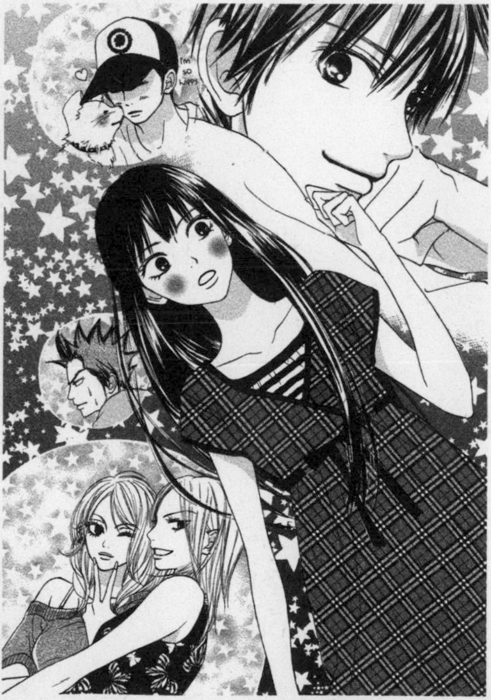
I'm so happy

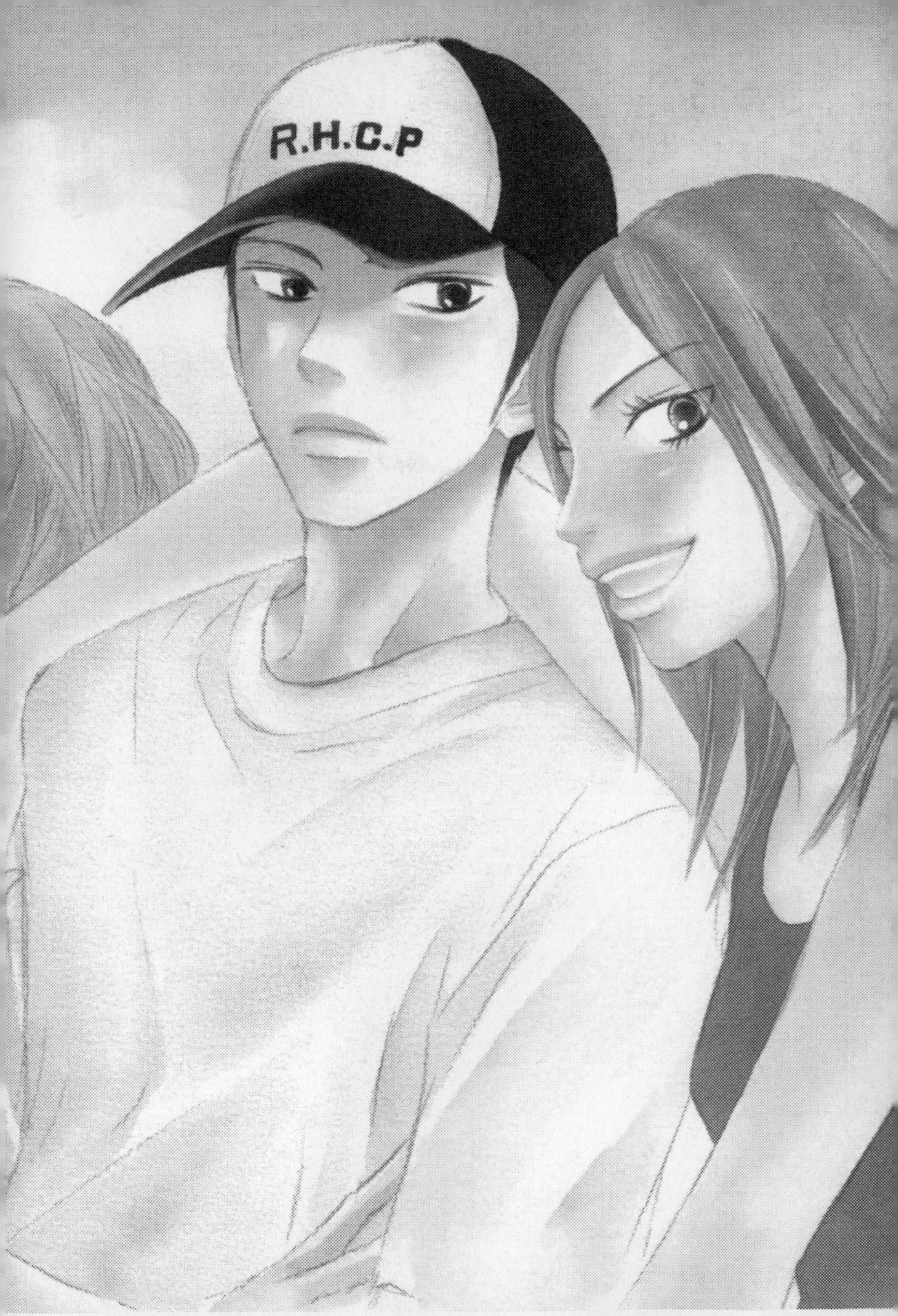
R.H.C.P

Episode 20: Big Brother's Homecoming

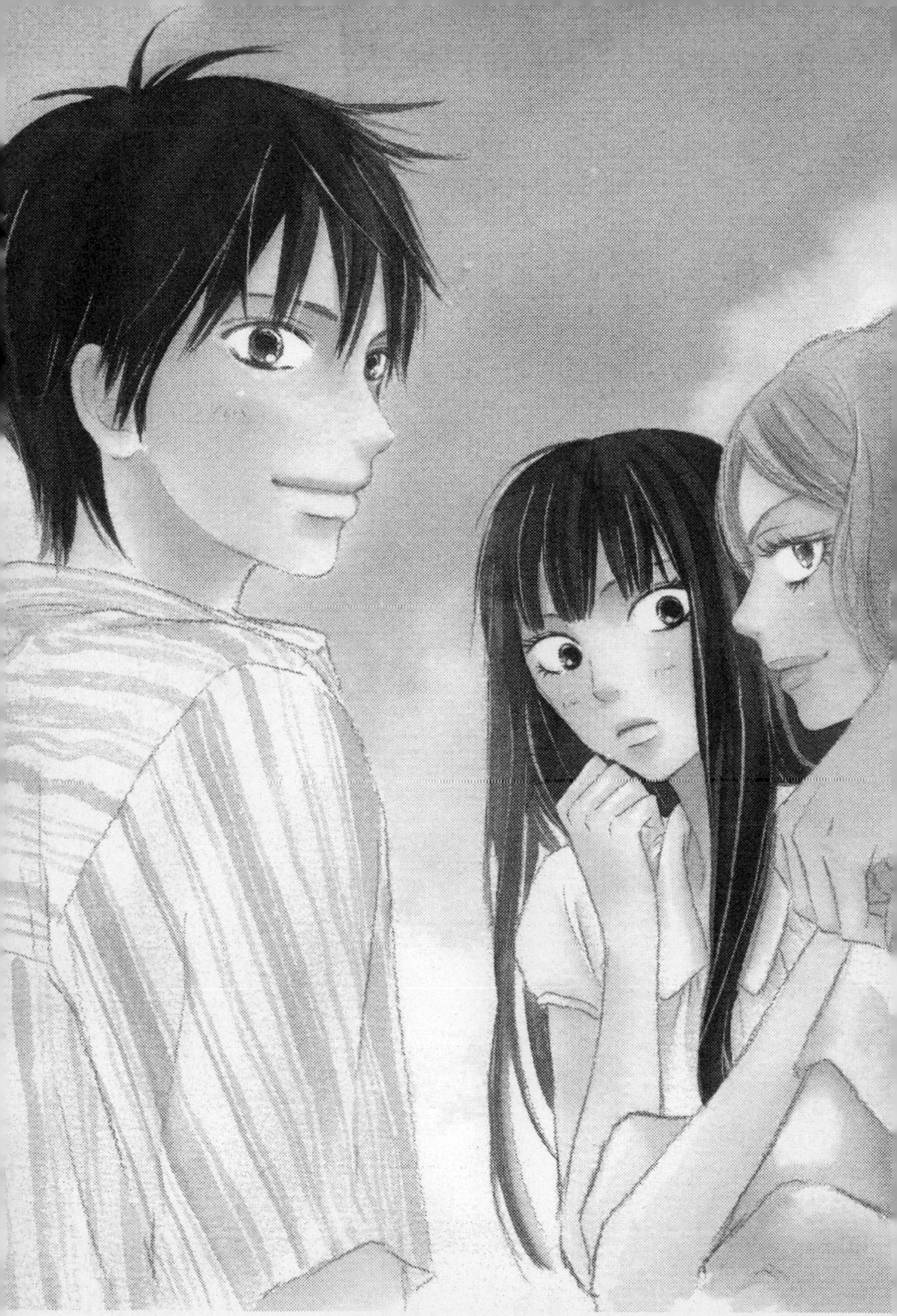

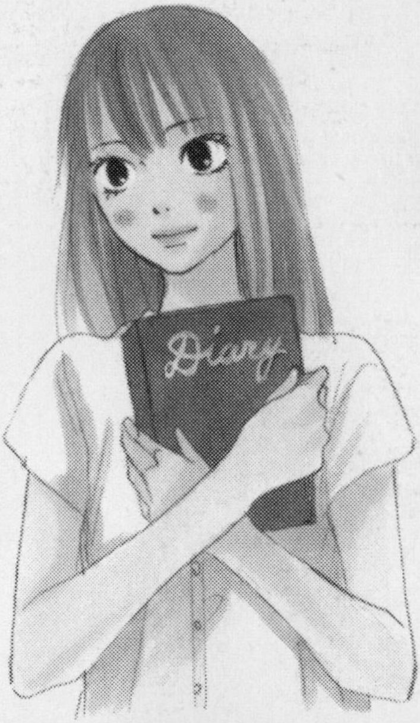
Diary

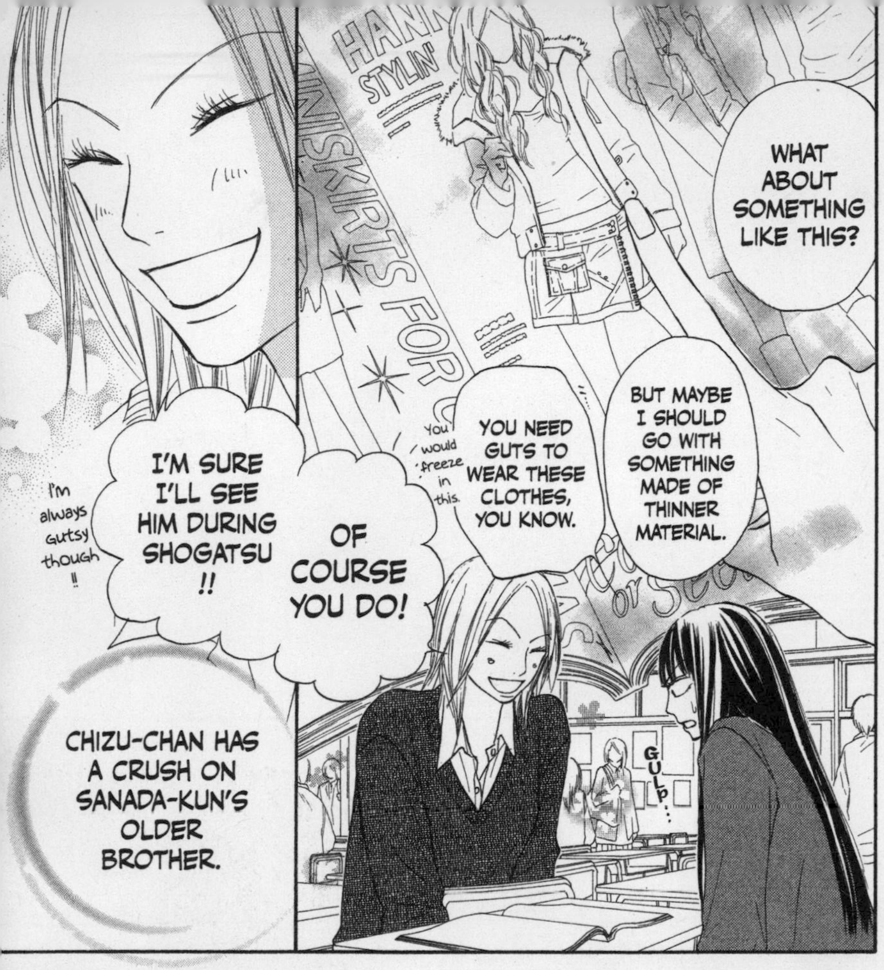
STYLIN'
WHAT ABOUT SOMETHING LIKE THIS?
BUT MAYBE I SHOULD GO WITH SOMETHING MADE OF THINNER MATERIAL.
YOU NEED GUTS TO WEAR THESE CLOTHES, YOU KNOW.
You would freeze in this.
GULP...
OF COURSE YOU DO!
I'M SURE I'LL SEE HIM DURING SHOGATSU !!
I'm always Gutsy though !!
CHIZU-CHAN HAS A CRUSH ON SANADA-KUN'S OLDER BROTHER.

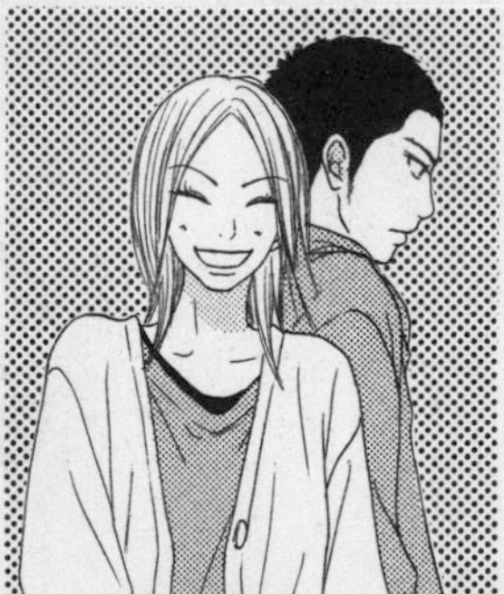

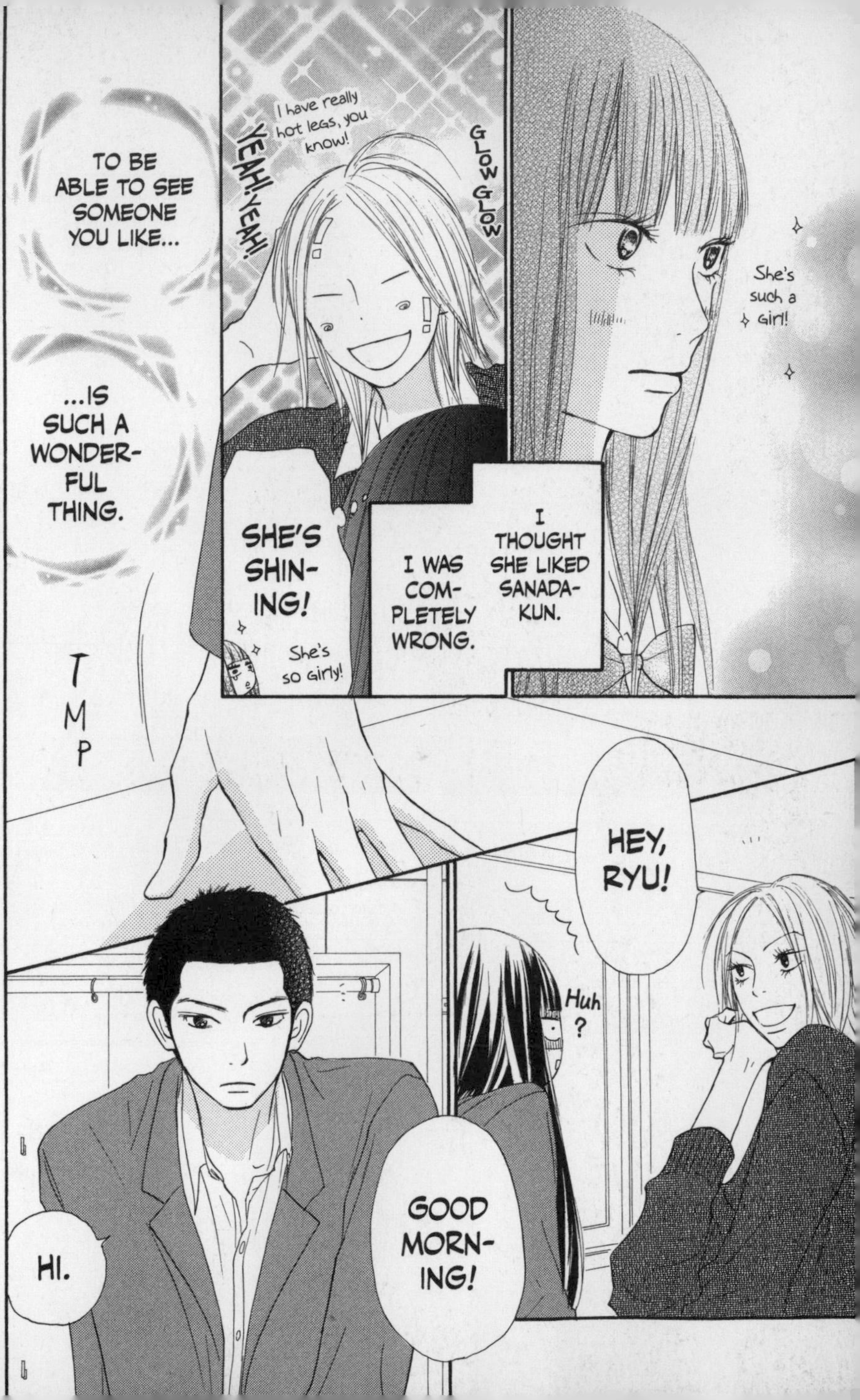

She's such a girl!
I THOUGHT SHE LIKED SANADA-KUN.
I WAS COMPLETELY WRONG.
GLOW GLOW
I have really hot legs, you know!
YEAH! YEAH!
SHE'S SHINING!
She's so girly!
TO BE ABLE TO SEE SOMEONE YOU LIKE...
...IS SUCH A WONDERFUL THING.
TMP
HEY, RYU!
Huh?
GOOD MORNING!
HI.

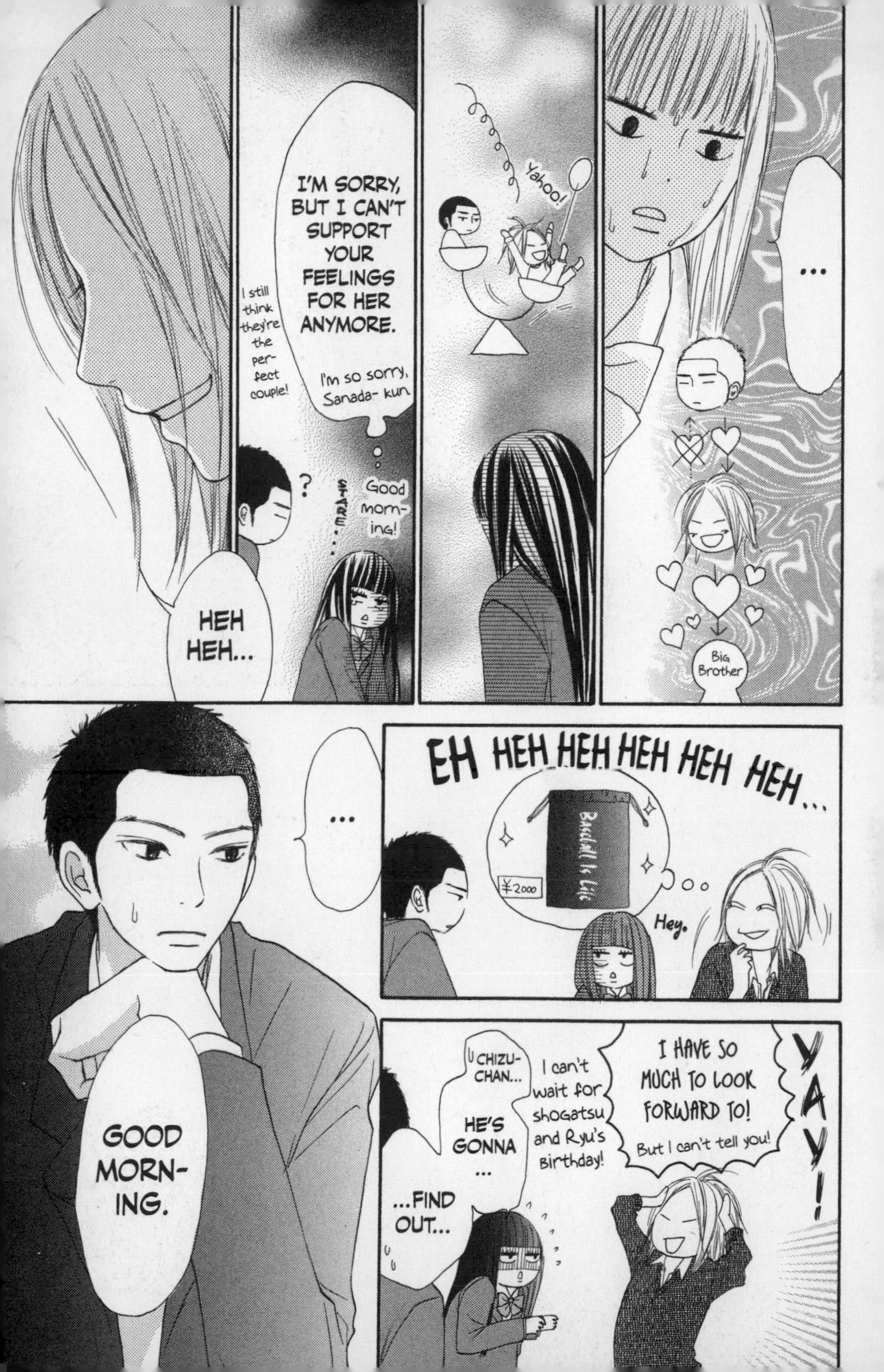
...
Big Brother
Yahoo!
I'M SORRY, BUT I CAN'T SUPPORT YOUR FEELINGS FOR HER ANYMORE.
I'm so sorry, Sanada-kun.
I still think they're the perfect couple!
Good morning!
STARE...
?
HEH HEH...
EH HEH HEH HEH HEH HEH...
Baseball Is Life
¥2000
Hey.
YAY!
I HAVE SO MUCH TO LOOK FORWARD TO!
But I can't tell you!
I can't wait for shogatsu and Ryu's birthday!
CHIZU-CHAN...
HE'S GONNA ...
...FIND OUT...
...
GOOD MORNING.

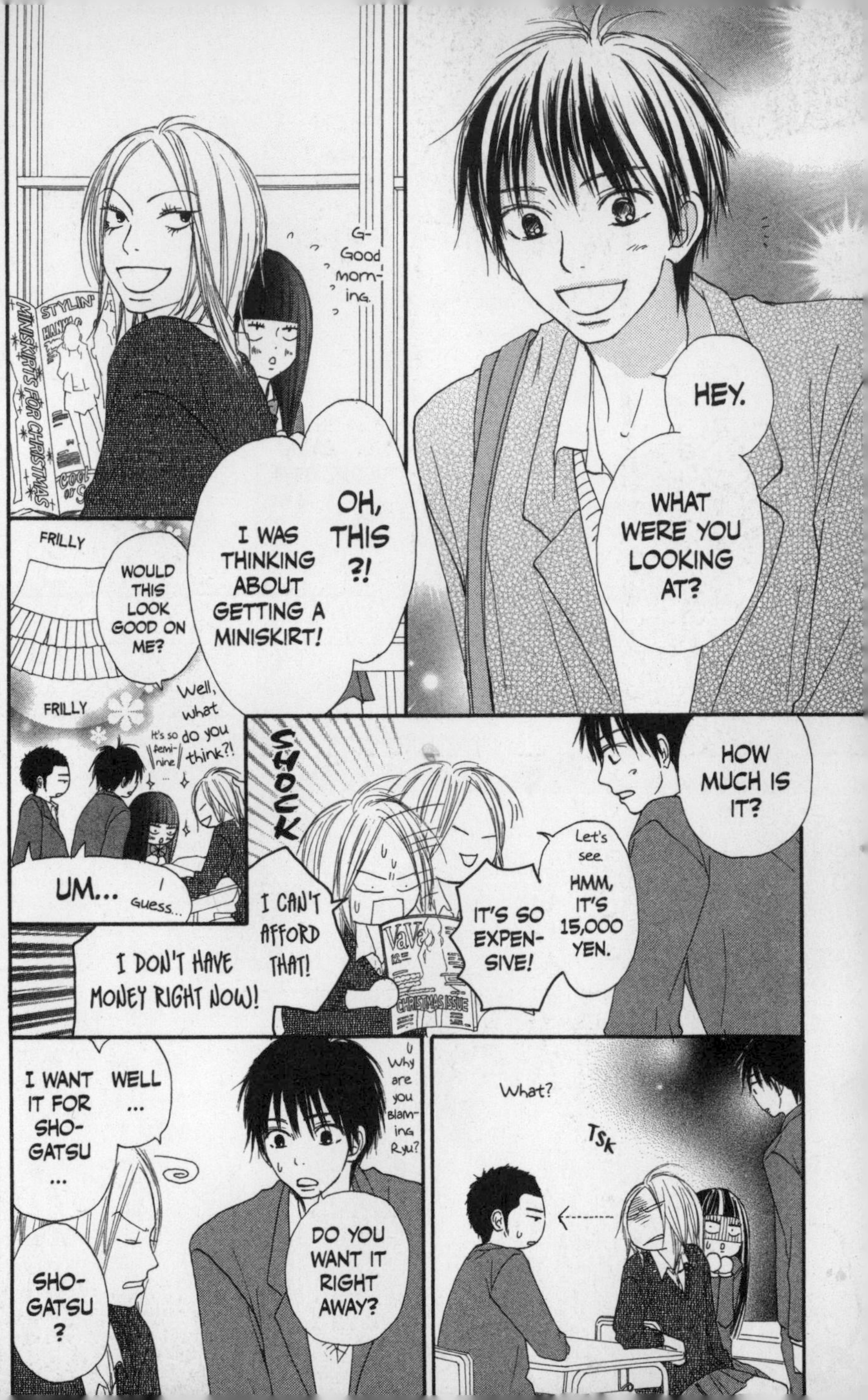
HEY.
WHAT WERE YOU LOOKING AT?
G-Good morn-ing.
STYLIN'
MINISKIRTS FOR CHRISTMAS
OH, THIS?! I WAS THINKING ABOUT GETTING A MINISKIRT!
FRILLY
FRILLY
WOULD THIS LOOK GOOD ON ME?
Well, what do you think?!
It's so femi-nine...
UM...
I guess...
HOW MUCH IS IT?
Let's see. HMM, IT'S 15,000 YEN.
IT'S SO EXPEN-SIVE!
SHOCK
CHRISTMAS ISSUE
I CAN'T AFFORD THAT!
I DON'T HAVE MONEY RIGHT NOW!
What?
TSK
Why are you blam-ing Ryu?
DO YOU WANT IT RIGHT AWAY?
WELL...
I WANT IT FOR SHO-GATSU...
SHO-GATSU?

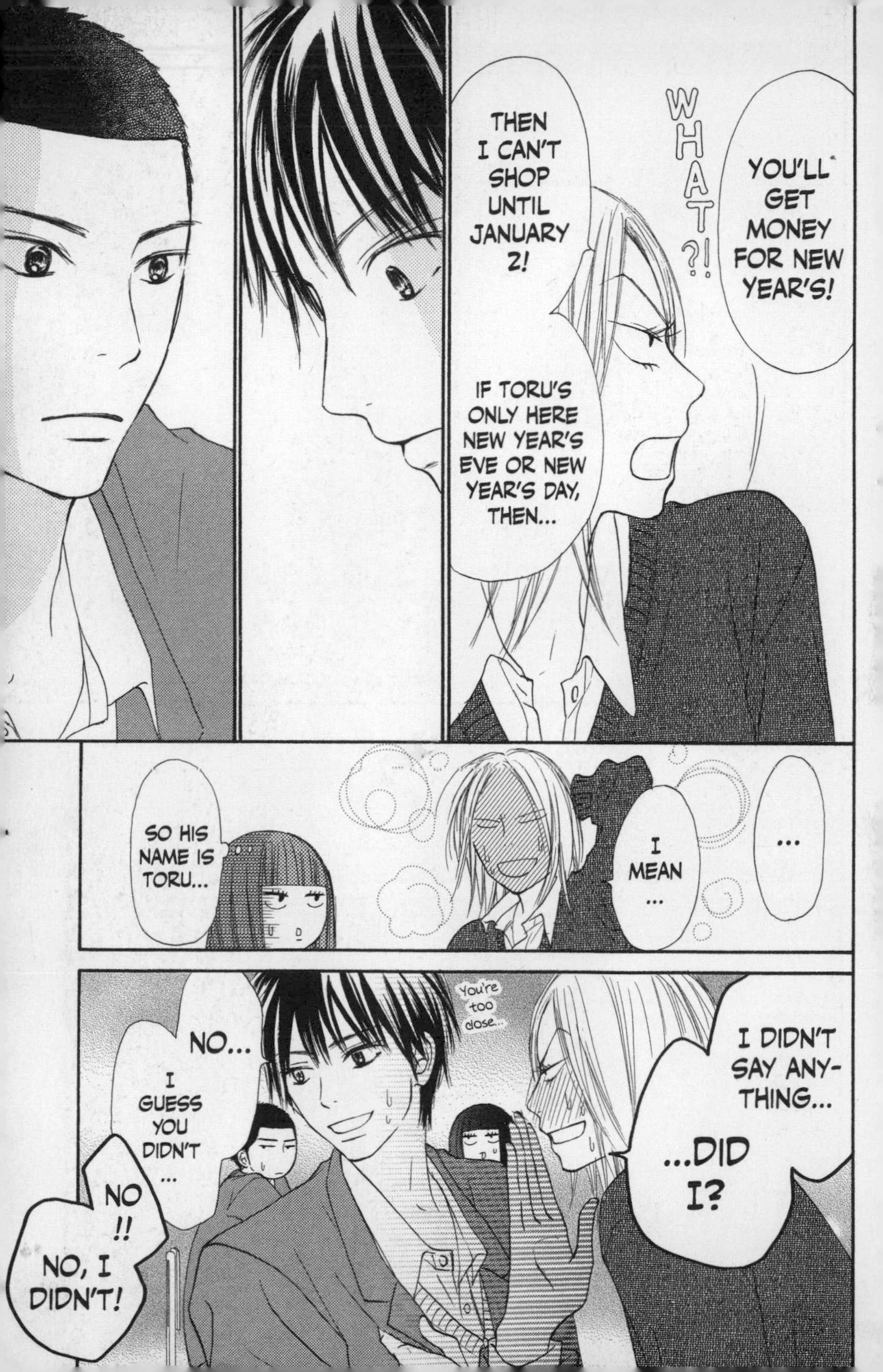
YOU'LL GET MONEY FOR NEW YEAR'S!
WHAT?!
THEN I CAN'T SHOP UNTIL JANUARY 2!
IF TORU'S ONLY HERE NEW YEAR'S EVE OR NEW YEAR'S DAY, THEN...
...
I MEAN ...
SO HIS NAME IS TORU...
I DIDN'T SAY ANY-THING...
...DID I?
You're too close...
NO...
I GUESS YOU DIDN'T ...
NO!!
NO, I DIDN'T!

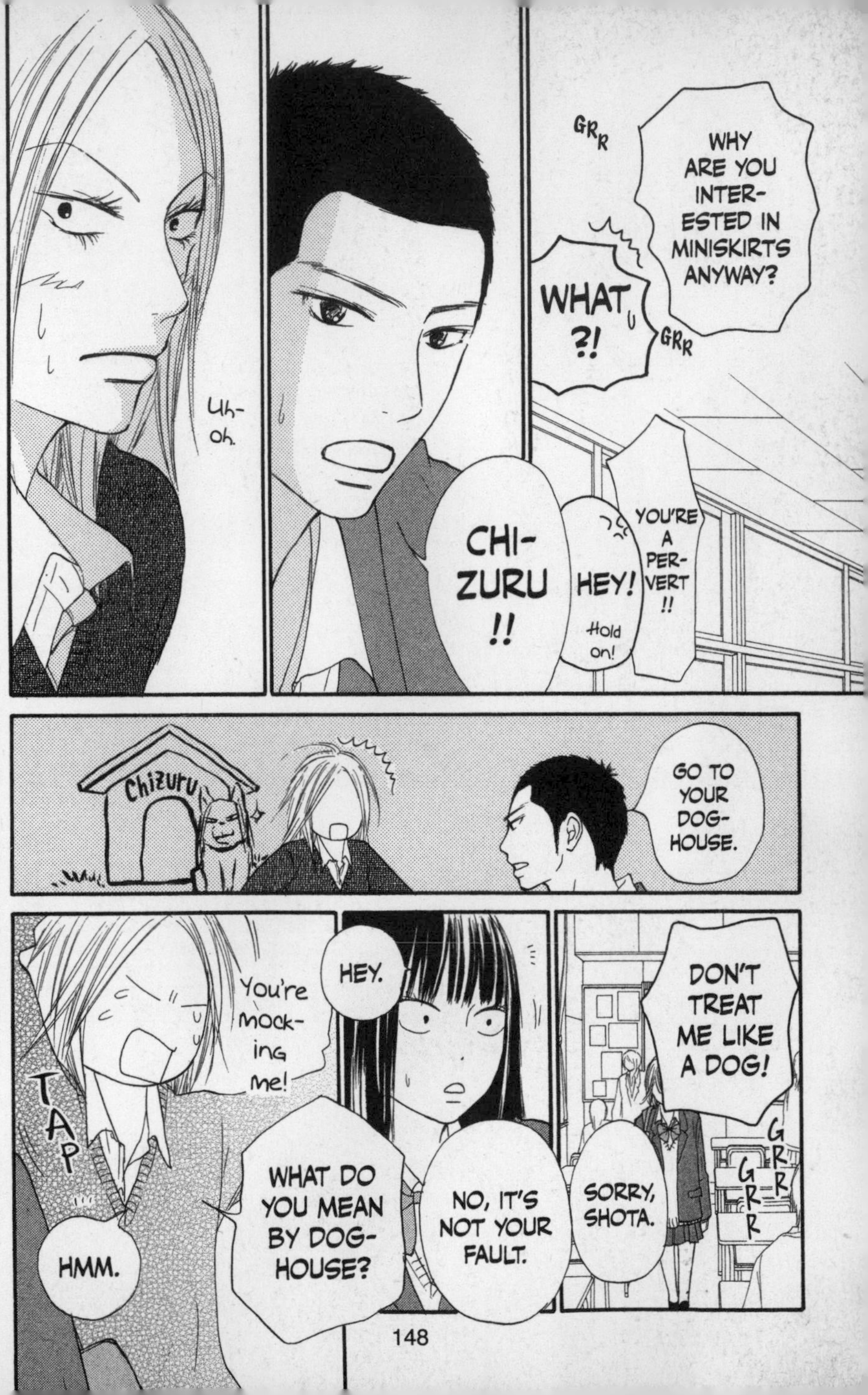
WHY ARE YOU INTER-ESTED IN MINISKIRTS ANYWAY?
GRR
WHAT?!
GRR
YOU'RE A PER-VERT!!
HEY!
Hold on!
CHI-ZURU!!
Uh-oh.
GO TO YOUR DOG-HOUSE.
Chizuru
DON'T TREAT ME LIKE A DOG!
GRR
GRR
SORRY, SHOTA.
HEY.
NO, IT'S NOT YOUR FAULT.
WHAT DO YOU MEAN BY DOG-HOUSE?
You're mock-ing me!
TAP
HMM.

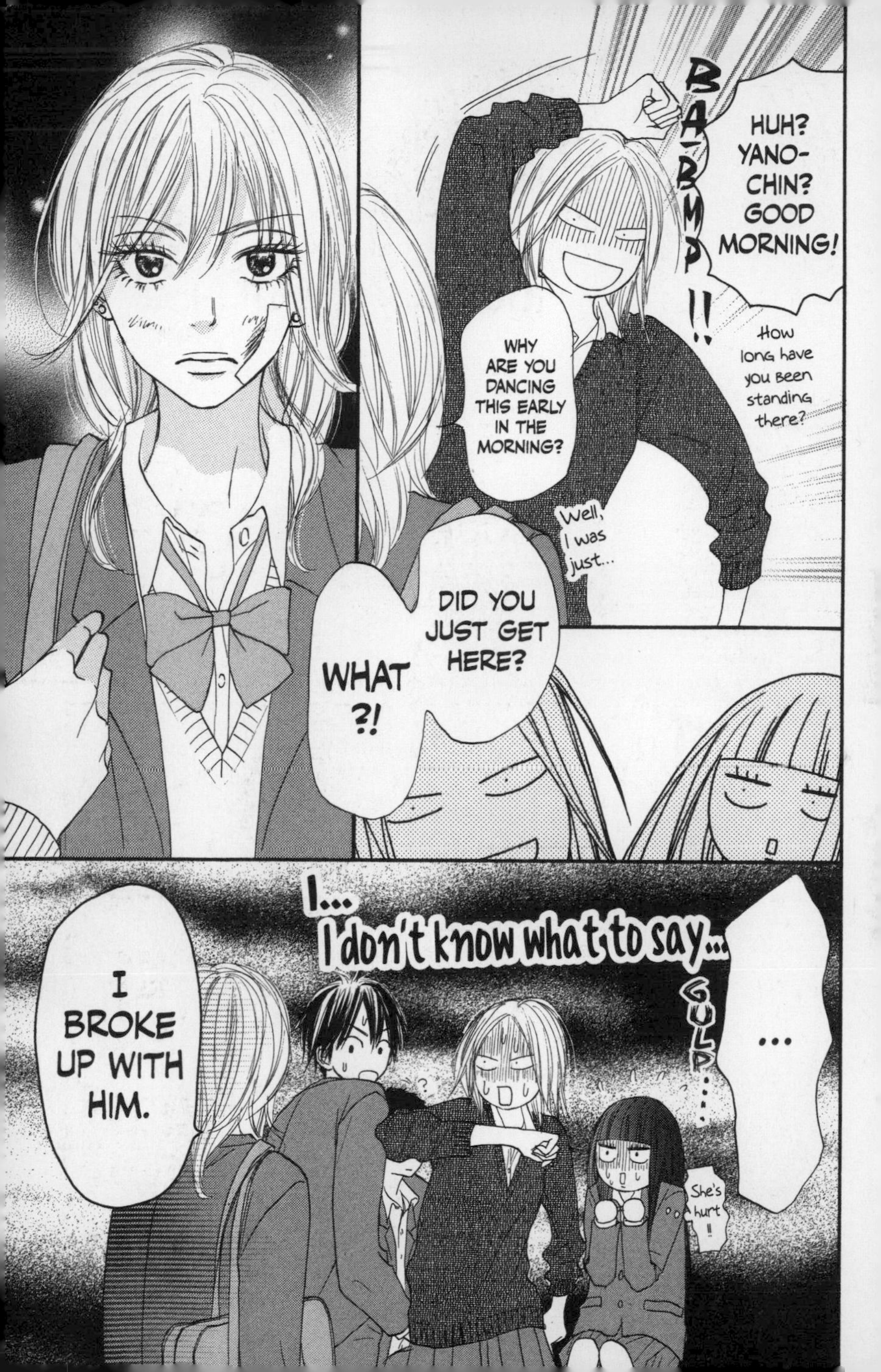
BARUMP!!
HUH? YANO-CHIN? GOOD MORNING!
How long have you been standing there?
WHY ARE YOU DANCING THIS EARLY IN THE MORNING?
Well, I was just...
DID YOU JUST GET HERE?
WHAT?!
...
GULP...
I... I don't know what to say...
She's hurt!!
I BROKE UP WITH HIM.

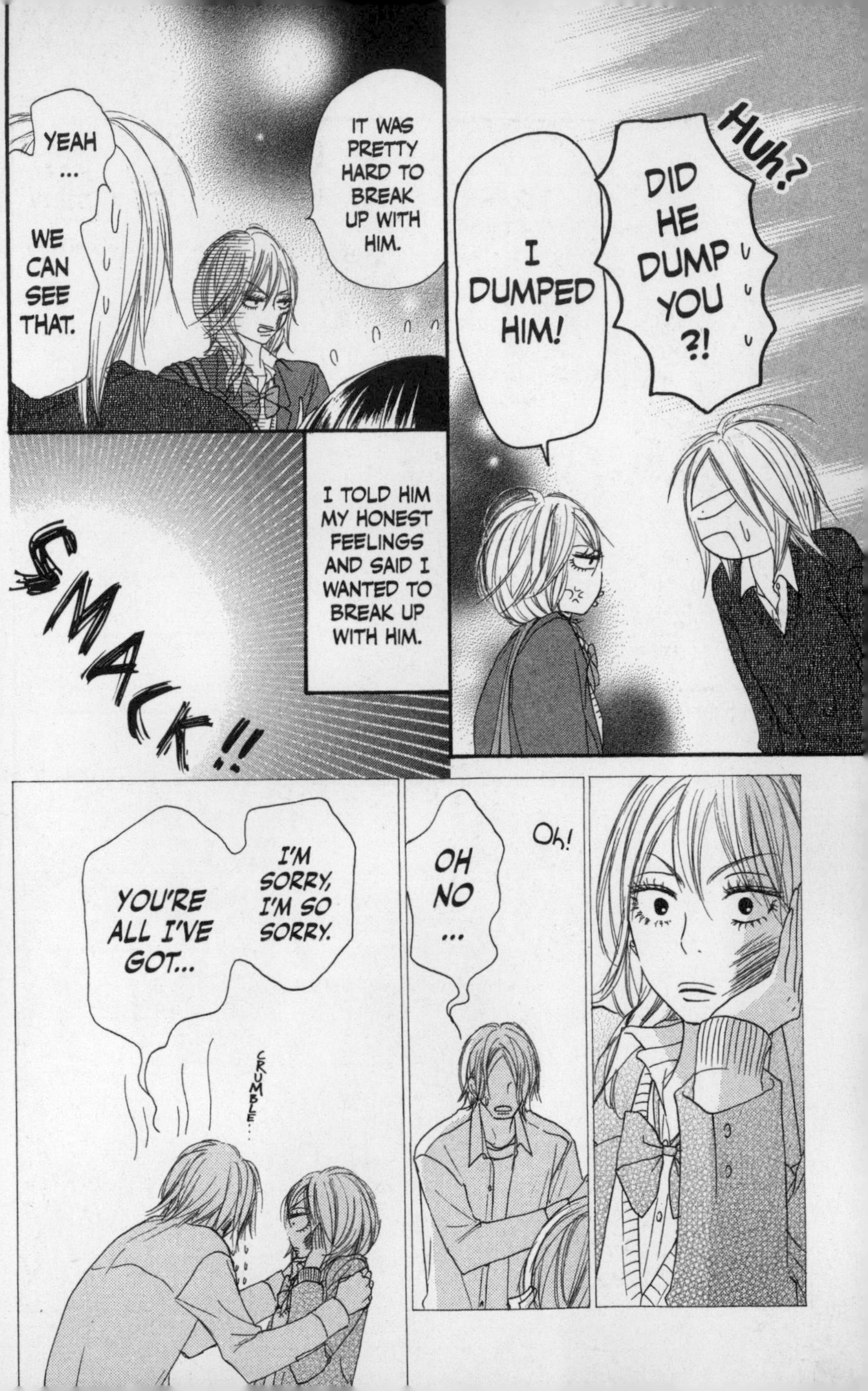
Huh?
DID HE DUMP YOU ?!
I DUMPED HIM!
IT WAS PRETTY HARD TO BREAK UP WITH HIM.
YEAH ... WE CAN SEE THAT.
I TOLD HIM MY HONEST FEELINGS AND SAID I WANTED TO BREAK UP WITH HIM.
SMACK!!
Oh!
OH NO ...
I'M SORRY, I'M SO SORRY.
YOU'RE ALL I'VE GOT...
CRUMBLE...

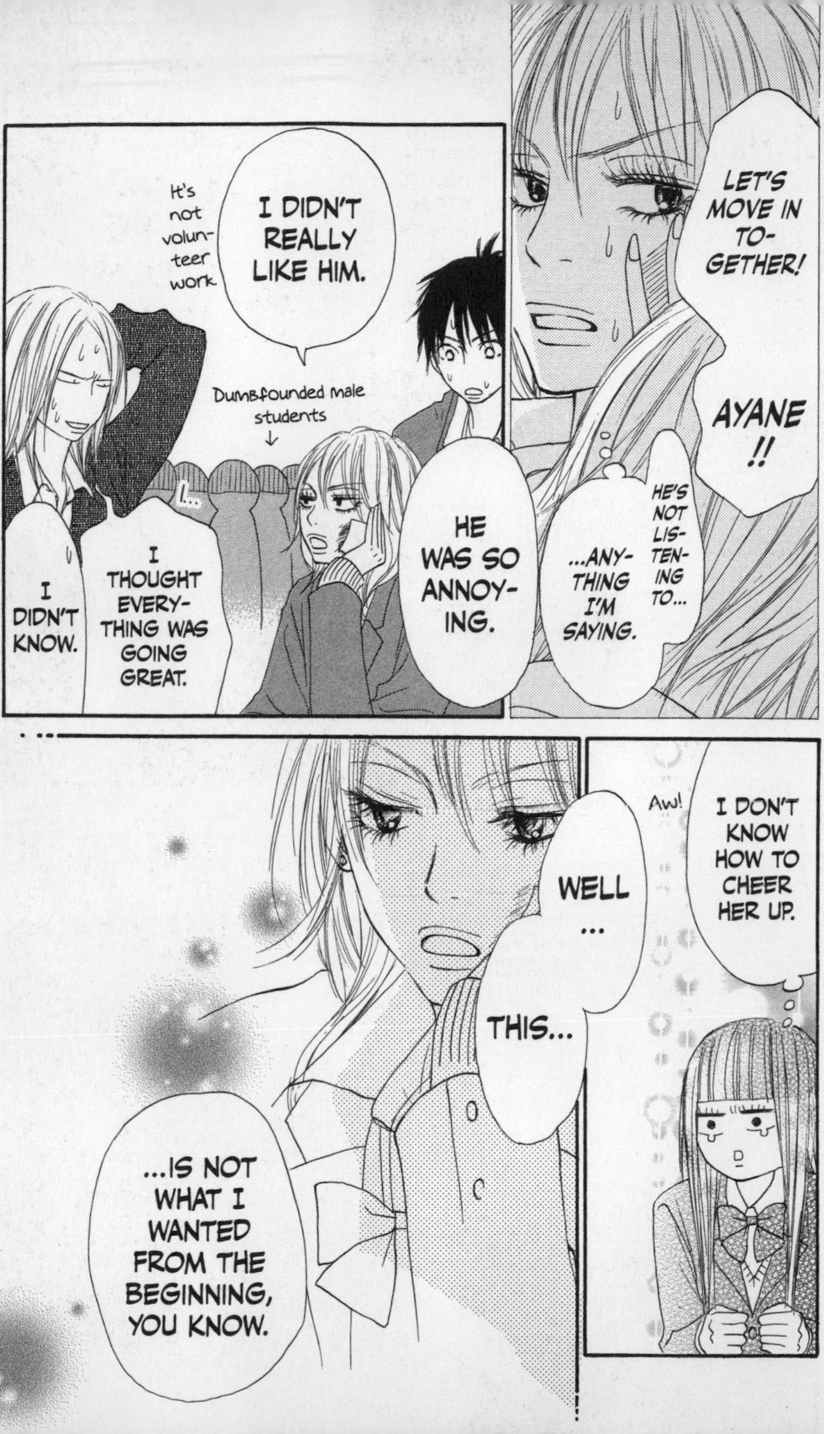
LET'S MOVE IN TO-GETHER!
AYANE !!
HE'S NOT LIS-TEN-ING TO...
...ANY-THING I'M SAYING.
HE WAS SO ANNOY-ING.
I DIDN'T REALLY LIKE HIM.
It's not volun-teer work.
Dumbfounded male students ↓
I...
I THOUGHT EVERY-THING WAS GOING GREAT.
I DIDN'T KNOW.
I DON'T KNOW HOW TO CHEER HER UP.
Aw!
WELL ...
THIS...
...IS NOT WHAT I WANTED FROM THE BEGINNING, YOU KNOW.

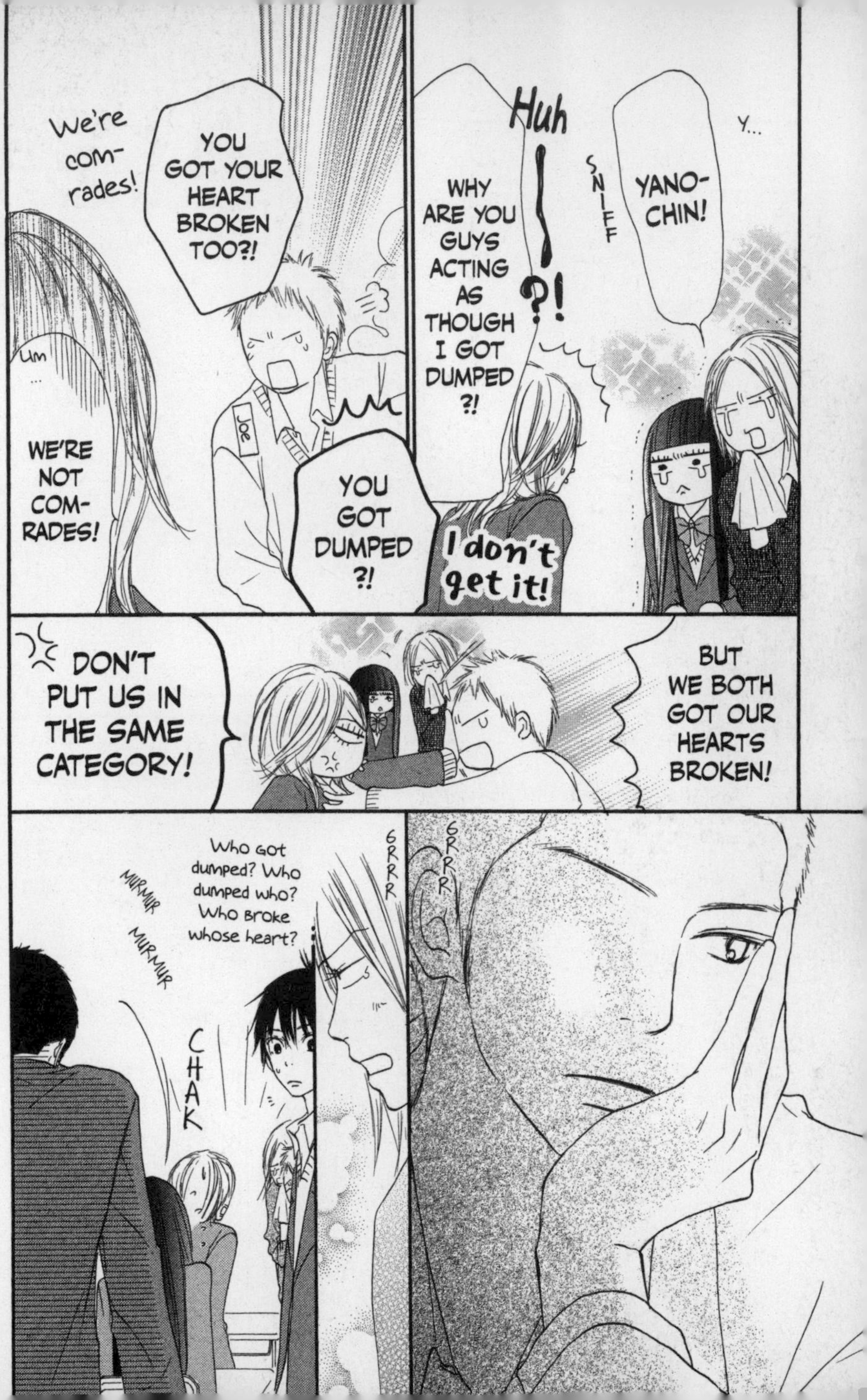
Y...
YANO-CHIN!
SNIFF
Huh ?!
WHY ARE YOU GUYS ACTING AS THOUGH I GOT DUMPED ?!
I don't get it!
YOU GOT DUMPED ?!
YOU GOT YOUR HEART BROKEN TOO?!
We're com-rades!
Um...
WE'RE NOT COM-RADES!
BUT WE BOTH GOT OUR HEARTS BROKEN!
DON'T PUT US IN THE SAME CATEGORY!
GRRR
GRRR
Who got dumped? Who dumped who? Who broke whose heart?
MURMUR
MURMUR
CHAK

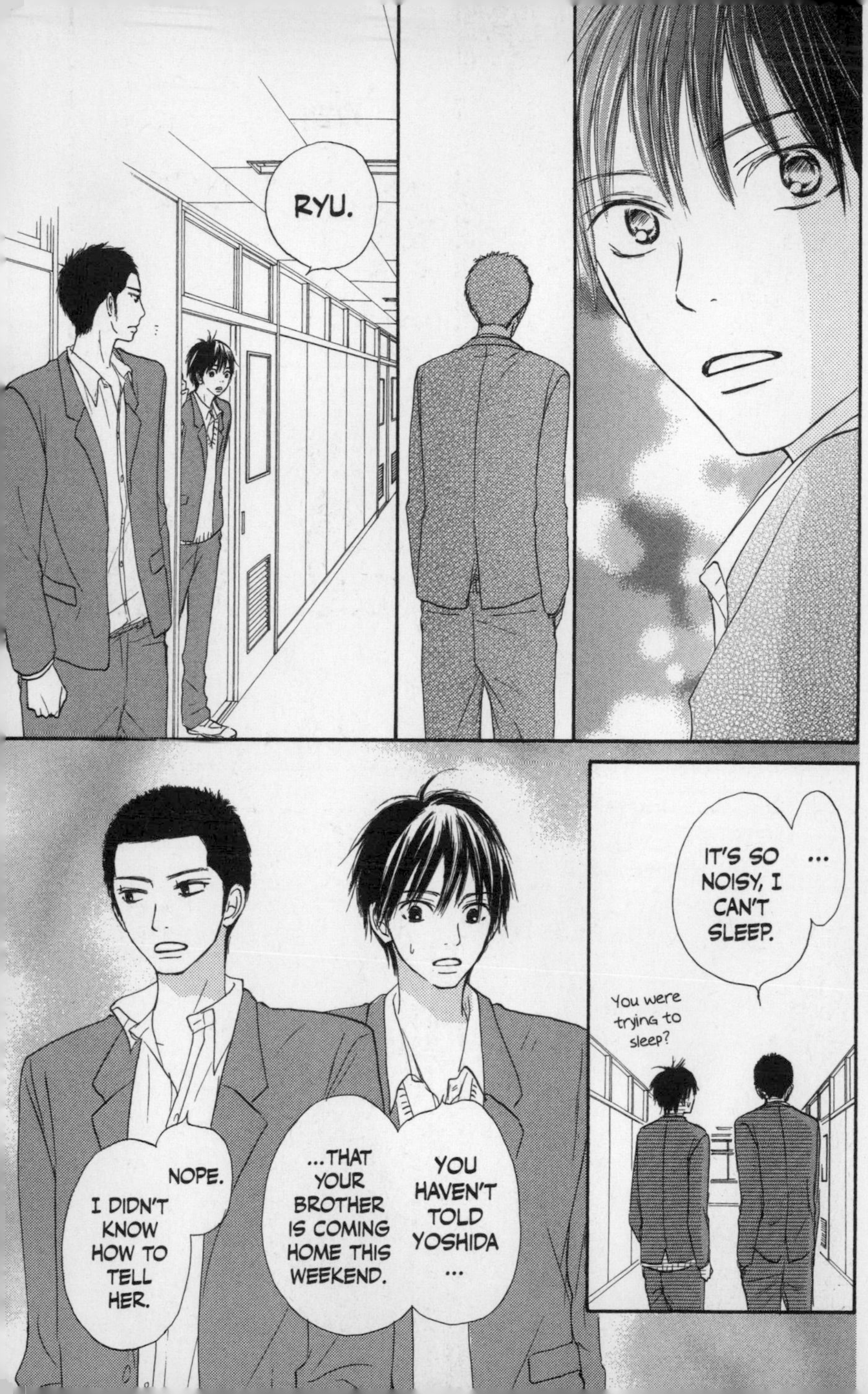
RYU.
... IT'S SO NOISY, I CAN'T SLEEP.
You were trying to sleep?
YOU HAVEN'T TOLD YOSHIDA ...
...THAT YOUR BROTHER IS COMING HOME THIS WEEKEND.
NOPE.
I DIDN'T KNOW HOW TO TELL HER.

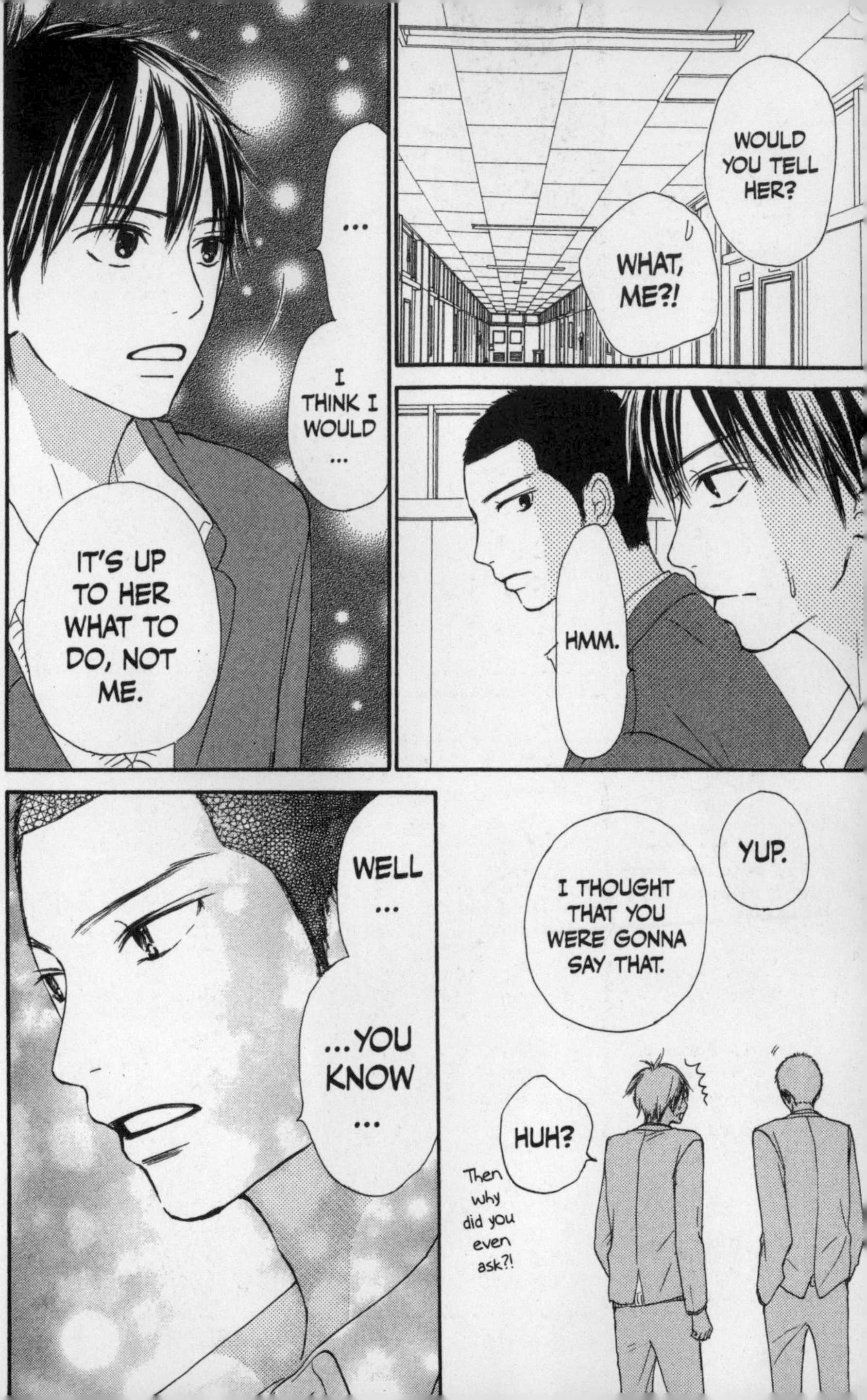
WOULD YOU TELL HER?
WHAT, ME?!
HMM.
...
I THINK I WOULD ...
IT'S UP TO HER WHAT TO DO, NOT ME.
YUP.
I THOUGHT THAT YOU WERE GONNA SAY THAT.
HUH?
Then why did you even ask?!
WELL ...
...YOU KNOW ...

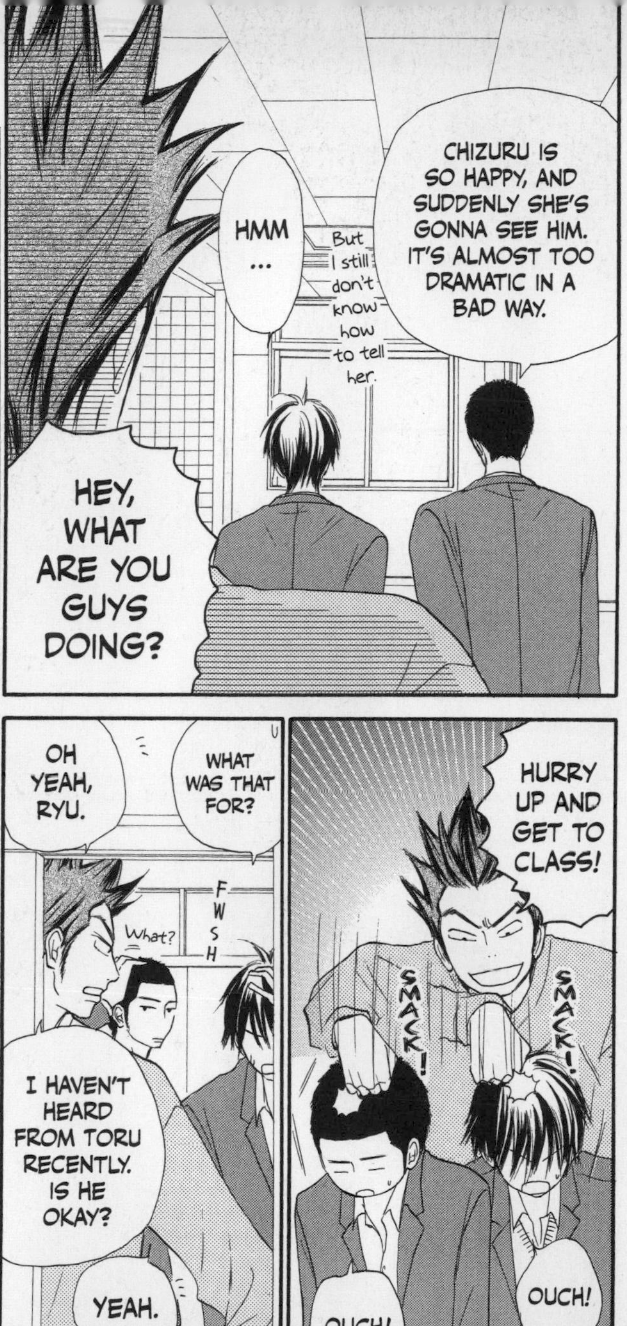
CHIZURU IS SO HAPPY, AND SUDDENLY SHE'S GONNA SEE HIM. IT'S ALMOST TOO DRAMATIC IN A BAD WAY.
But I still don't know how to tell her.
HMM ...
HEY, WHAT ARE YOU GUYS DOING?
HURRY UP AND GET TO CLASS!
SMACK!
SMACK!
OUCH!
OUCH!
WHAT WAS THAT FOR?
OH YEAH, RYU.
FWSH
What?
I HAVEN'T HEARD FROM TORU RECENTLY. IS HE OKAY?
YEAH.

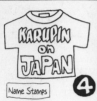

KARUPIN on JAPAN 4

Name Stamps

← Kimi ni Todoke stamp

Karuho stamp → ("Karu" for "Karuho")

↑ Shota stamp ("Shi" for "Shota") ♥

↑ Sawako stamp ("Sa" for "Sawako") ♥

I received these stamps from the publisher. They're made out of stone! They're amazing!

Wow!

They said it took a long time to make them! Of course it did! I'm sure!

I will definitely use them! Thank you!

I'm so happy!

That's it for this round! I'll see you again.

Karuho Shiina

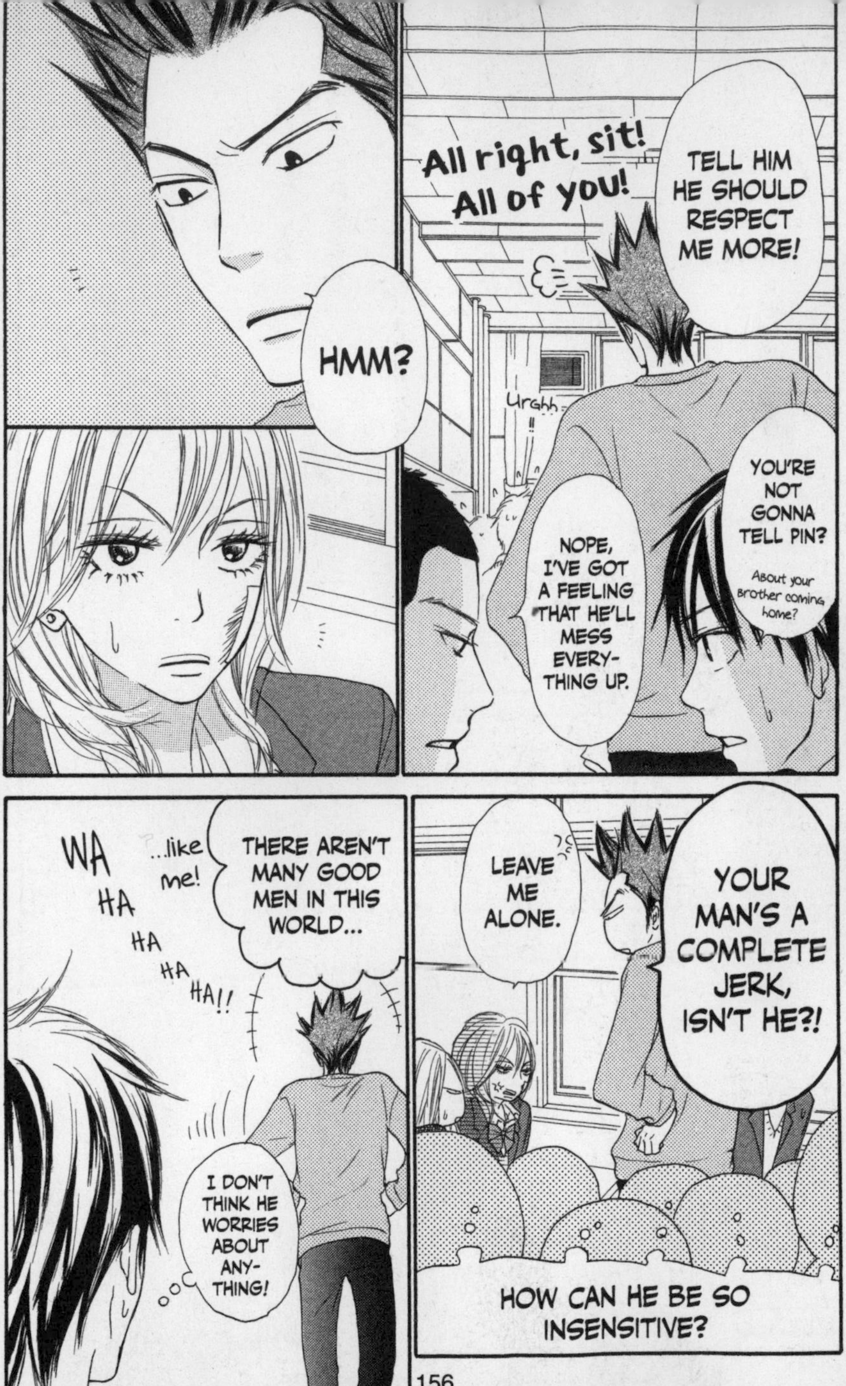
TELL HIM HE SHOULD RESPECT ME MORE!
All right, sit! All of you!
Urghh
YOU'RE NOT GONNA TELL PIN?
About your brother coming home?
NOPE, I'VE GOT A FEELING THAT HE'LL MESS EVERYTHING UP.
HMM?
YOUR MAN'S A COMPLETE JERK, ISN'T HE?!
LEAVE ME ALONE.
HOW CAN HE BE SO INSENSITIVE?
THERE AREN'T MANY GOOD MEN IN THIS WORLD...
...like me!
WA HA HA HA HA!!
I DON'T THINK HE WORRIES ABOUT ANYTHING!

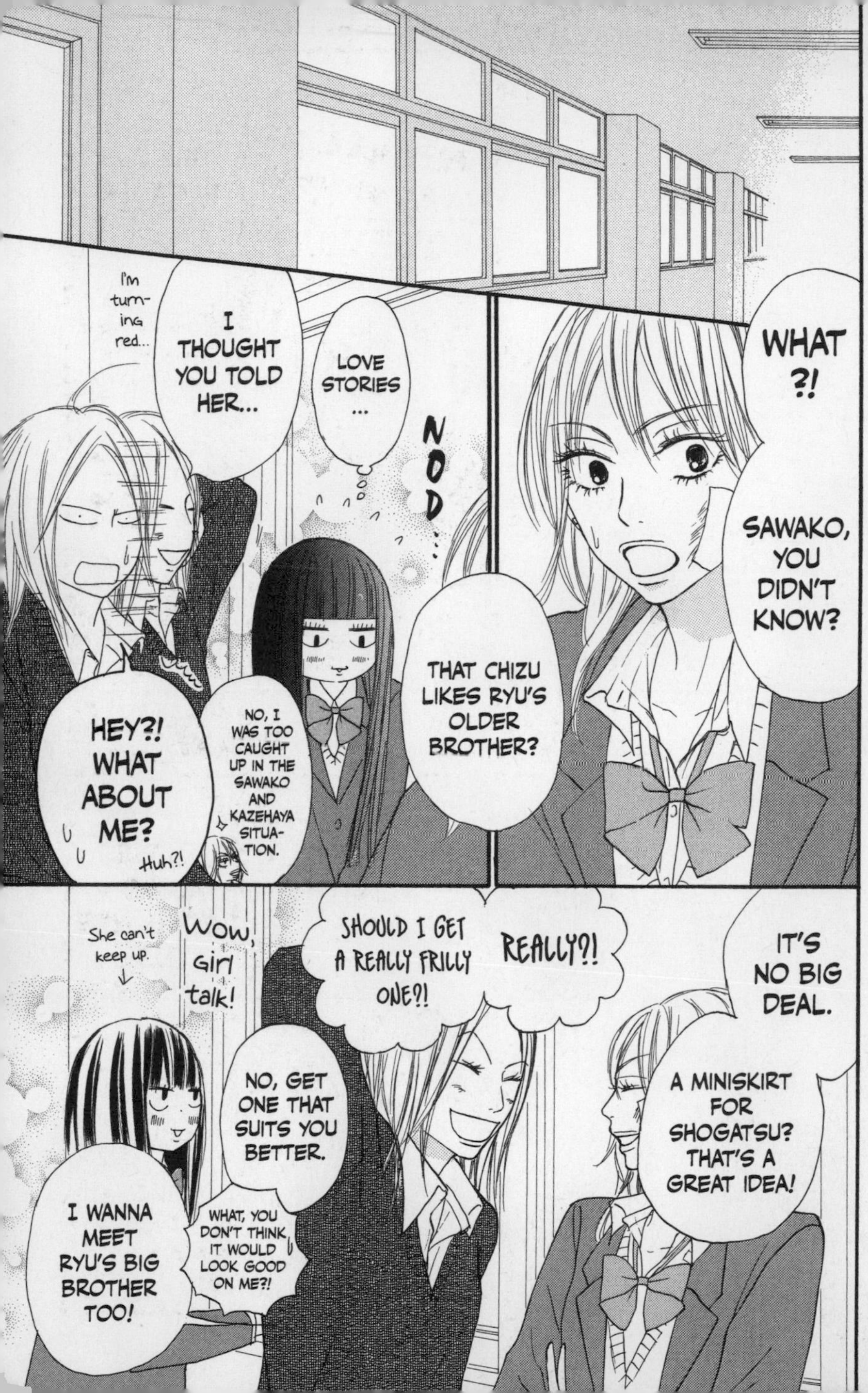
WHAT?!
SAWAKO, YOU DIDN'T KNOW?
THAT CHIZU LIKES RYU'S OLDER BROTHER?
LOVE STORIES...
NOD...
I THOUGHT YOU TOLD HER...
I'm turning red...
NO, I WAS TOO CAUGHT UP IN THE SAWAKO AND KAZEHAYA SITUATION.
HEY?! WHAT ABOUT ME?
Huh?!
IT'S NO BIG DEAL.
A MINISKIRT FOR SHOGATSU? THAT'S A GREAT IDEA!
REALLY?!
SHOULD I GET A REALLY FRILLY ONE?!
NO, GET ONE THAT SUITS YOU BETTER.
WHAT, YOU DON'T THINK IT WOULD LOOK GOOD ON ME?!
Wow, girl talk!
She can't keep up.
I WANNA MEET RYU'S BIG BROTHER TOO!

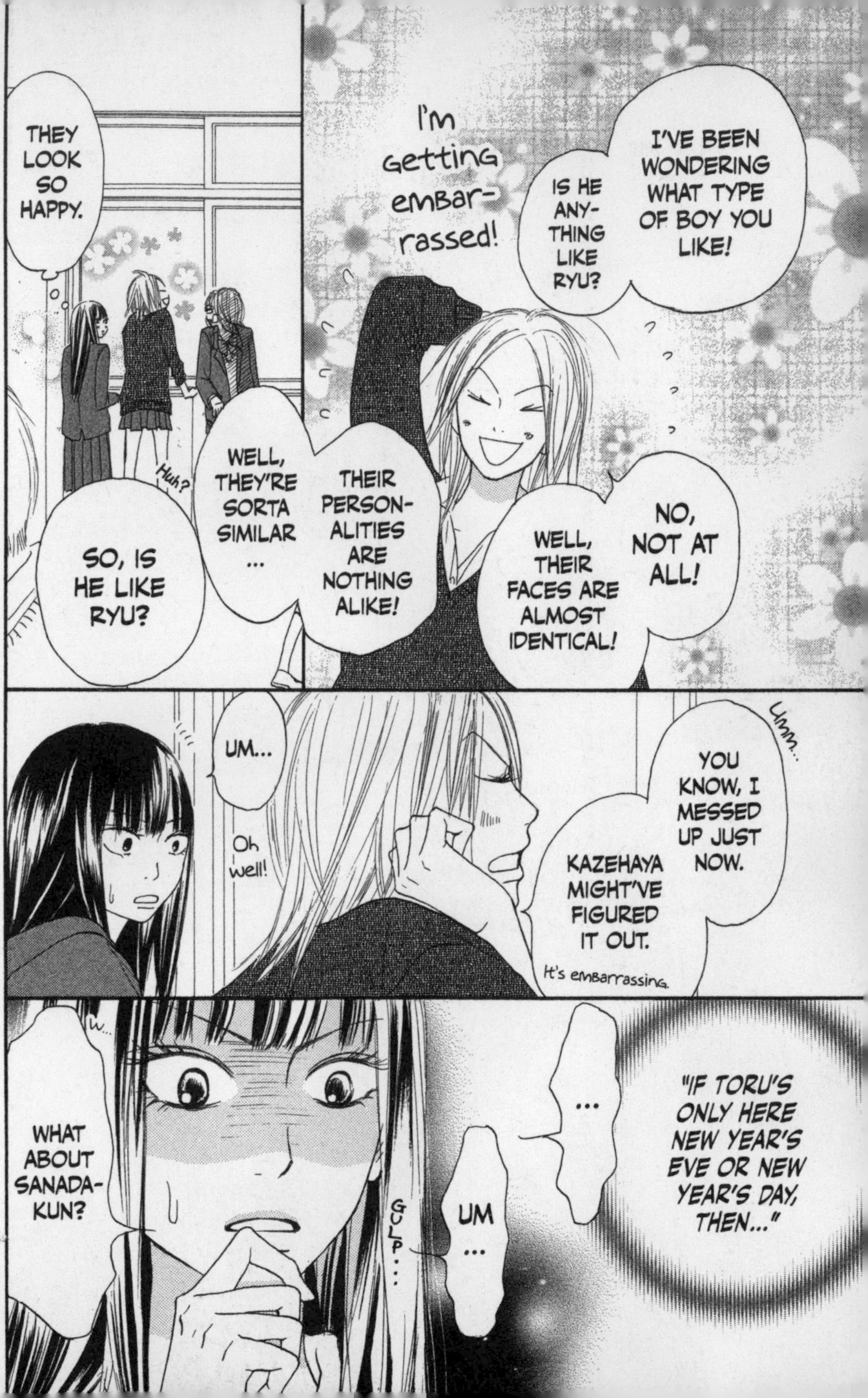
I'VE BEEN WONDERING WHAT TYPE OF BOY YOU LIKE!
IS HE ANYTHING LIKE RYU?
I'm getting embarrassed!
NO, NOT AT ALL!
WELL, THEIR FACES ARE ALMOST IDENTICAL!
THEIR PERSONALITIES ARE NOTHING ALIKE!
WELL, THEY'RE SORTA SIMILAR ...
THEY LOOK SO HAPPY.
Huh?
SO, IS HE LIKE RYU?
Umm...
YOU KNOW, I MESSED UP JUST NOW.
KAZEHAYA MIGHT'VE FIGURED IT OUT.
It's embarrassing.
UM...
Oh well!
"IF TORU'S ONLY HERE NEW YEAR'S EVE OR NEW YEAR'S DAY, THEN..."
...
UM ...
GULP...
W...
WHAT ABOUT SANADA-KUN?

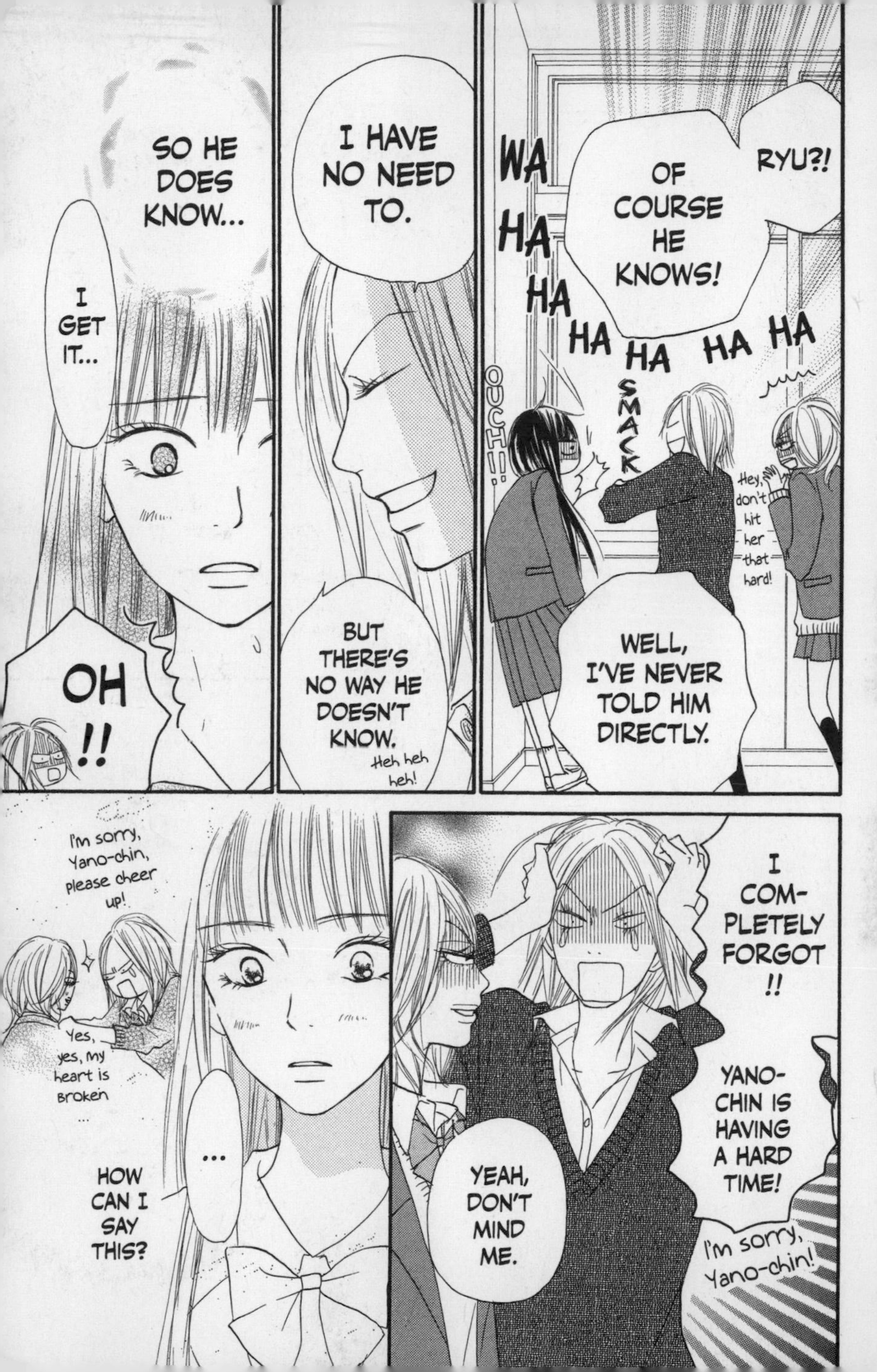
RYU?!
OF COURSE HE KNOWS!
WA HA HA HA HA HA HA HA
OUCH!!
SMACK
Hey, don't hit her that hard!
WELL, I'VE NEVER TOLD HIM DIRECTLY.
I HAVE NO NEED TO.
BUT THERE'S NO WAY HE DOESN'T KNOW.
Heh heh heh!
SO HE DOES KNOW...
I GET IT...
OH!!
I COM-PLETELY FORGOT!!
YANO-CHIN IS HAVING A HARD TIME!
I'm sorry, Yano-chin!
YEAH, DON'T MIND ME.
I'm sorry, Yano-chin, please cheer up!
Yes, yes, my heart is broken...
...
HOW CAN I SAY THIS?

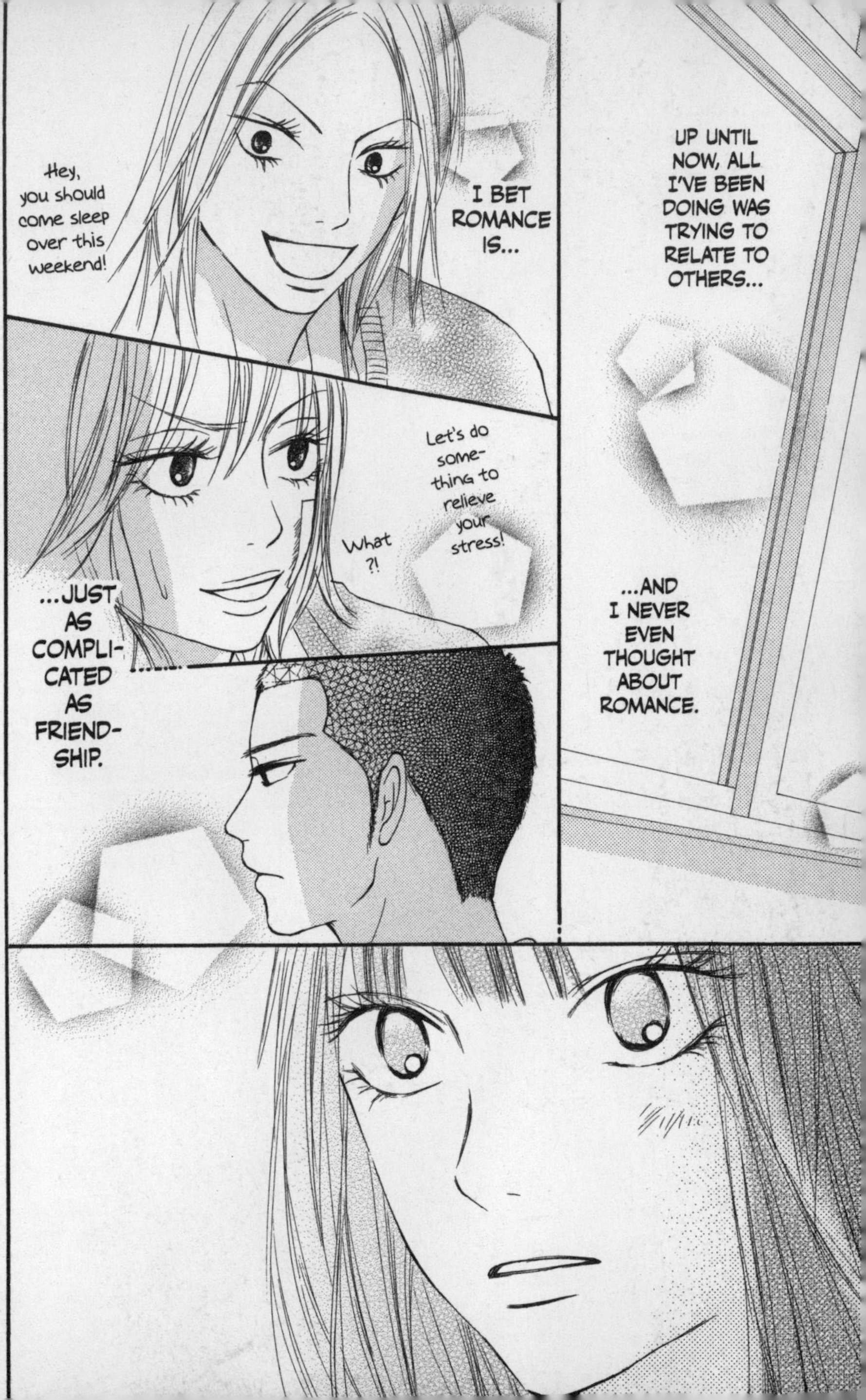
UP UNTIL NOW, ALL I'VE BEEN DOING WAS TRYING TO RELATE TO OTHERS...
...AND I NEVER EVEN THOUGHT ABOUT ROMANCE.
I BET ROMANCE IS...
Hey, you should come sleep over this weekend!
Let's do something to relieve your stress!
What?!
...JUST AS COMPLICATED AS FRIENDSHIP.

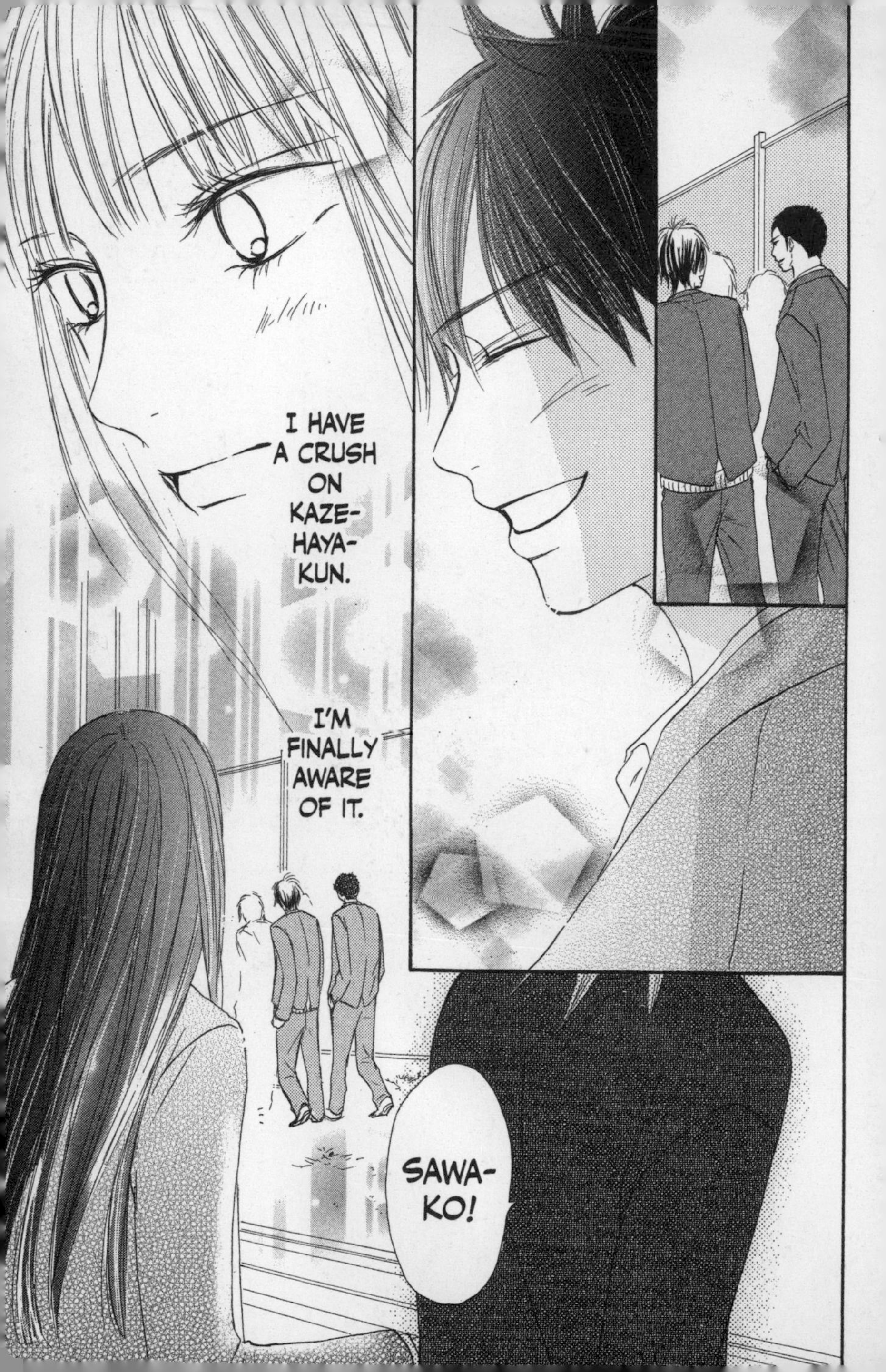
I HAVE A CRUSH ON KAZE-HAYA-KUN.
I'M FINALLY AWARE OF IT.
SAWA-KO!

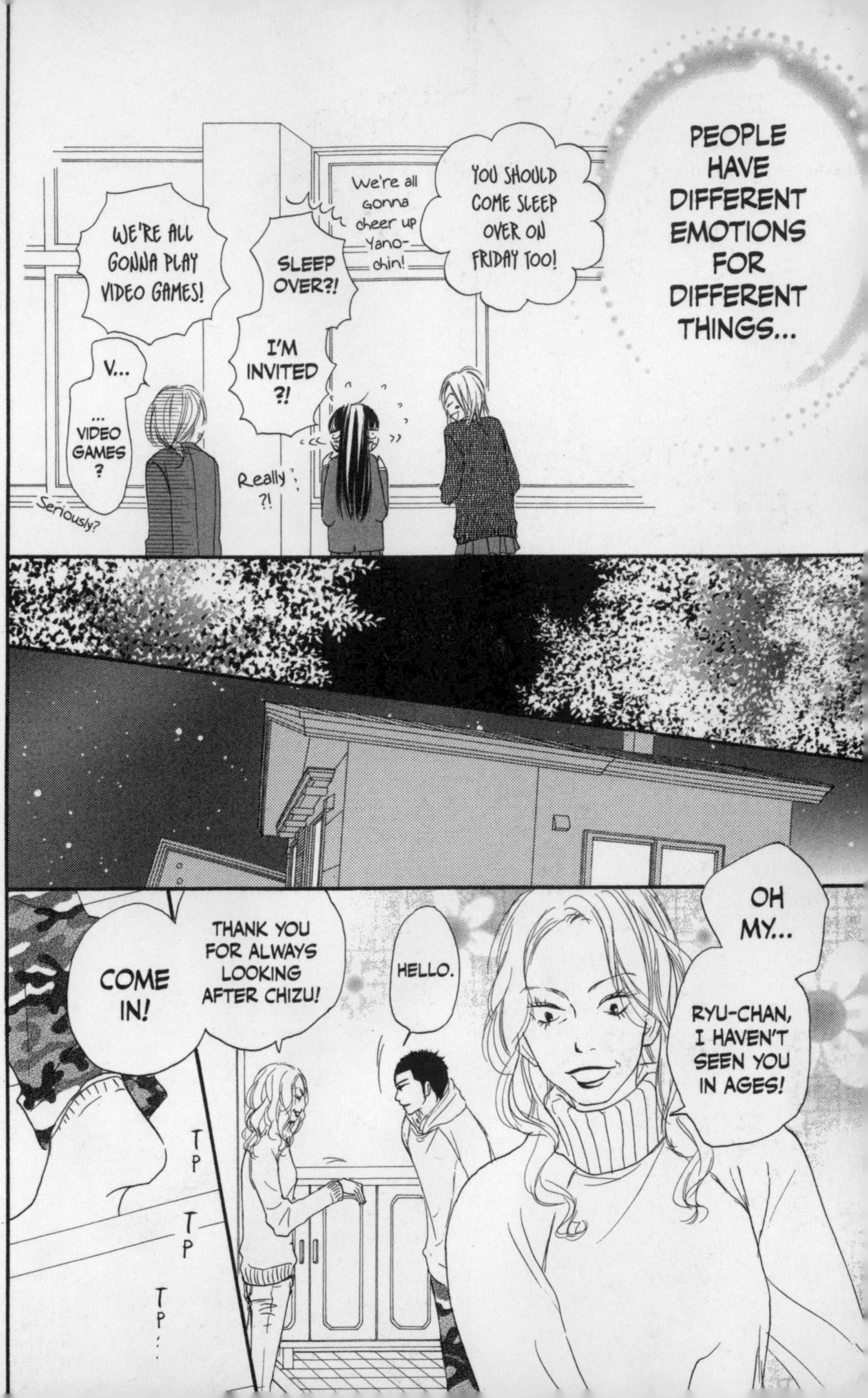
PEOPLE HAVE DIFFERENT EMOTIONS FOR DIFFERENT THINGS...
YOU SHOULD COME SLEEP OVER ON FRIDAY TOO!
We're all gonna cheer up Yano-chin!
SLEEP OVER?!
I'M INVITED ?!
Really ?!
WE'RE ALL GONNA PLAY VIDEO GAMES!
V...
... VIDEO GAMES ?
Seriously?
OH MY...
RYU-CHAN, I HAVEN'T SEEN YOU IN AGES!
HELLO.
THANK YOU FOR ALWAYS LOOKING AFTER CHIZU!
COME IN!
TP
TP
TP...

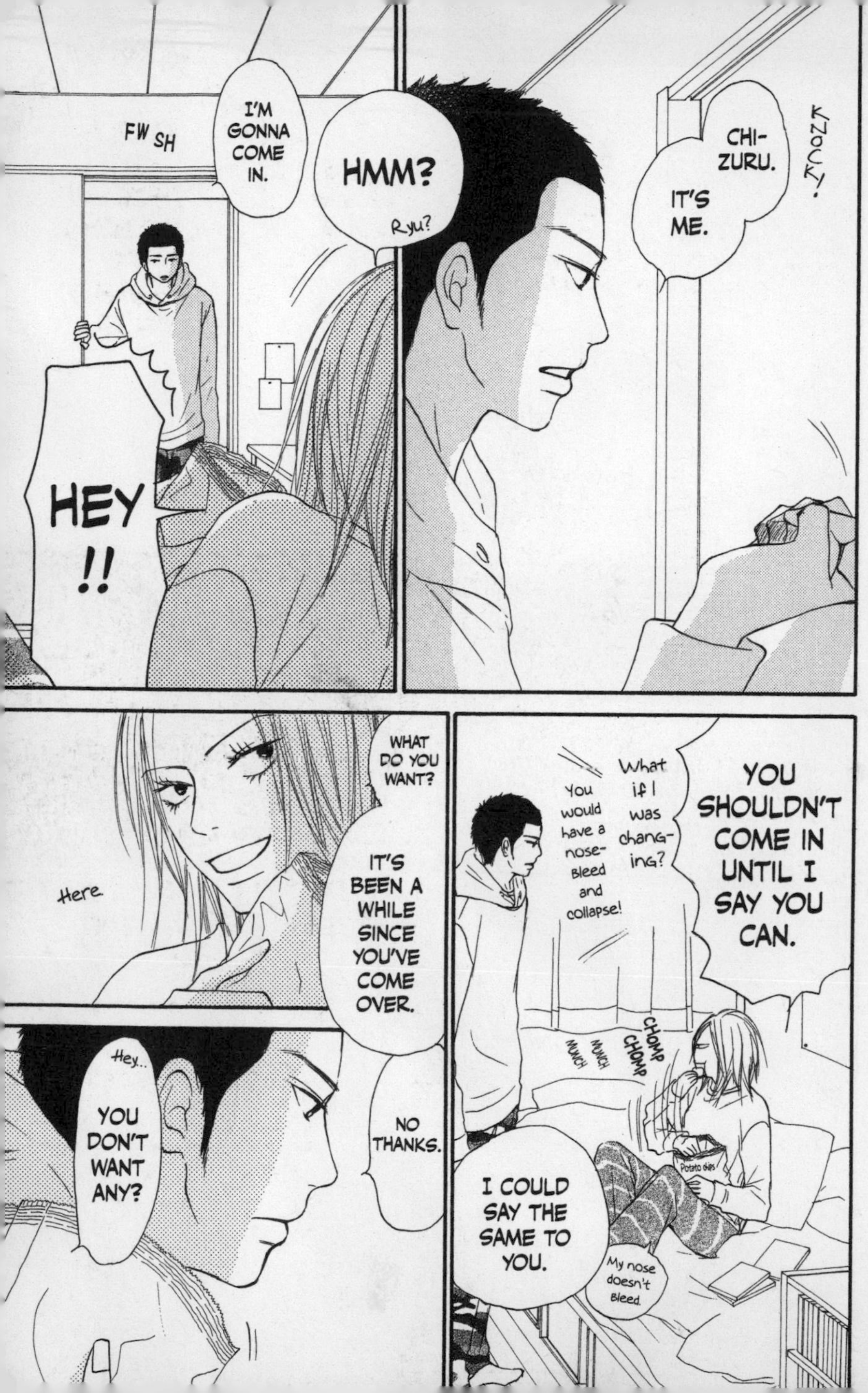
KNOCK!
CHI-ZURU.
IT'S ME.
HMM?
Ryu?
I'M GONNA COME IN.
FW SH
HEY!!
YOU SHOULDN'T COME IN UNTIL I SAY YOU CAN.
What if I was changing?
You would have a nose-bleed and collapse!
CHOMP CHOMP
MUNCH MUNCH
I COULD SAY THE SAME TO YOU.
My nose doesn't bleed.
WHAT DO YOU WANT?
IT'S BEEN A WHILE SINCE YOU'VE COME OVER.
Here.
Hey...
YOU DON'T WANT ANY?
NO THANKS.

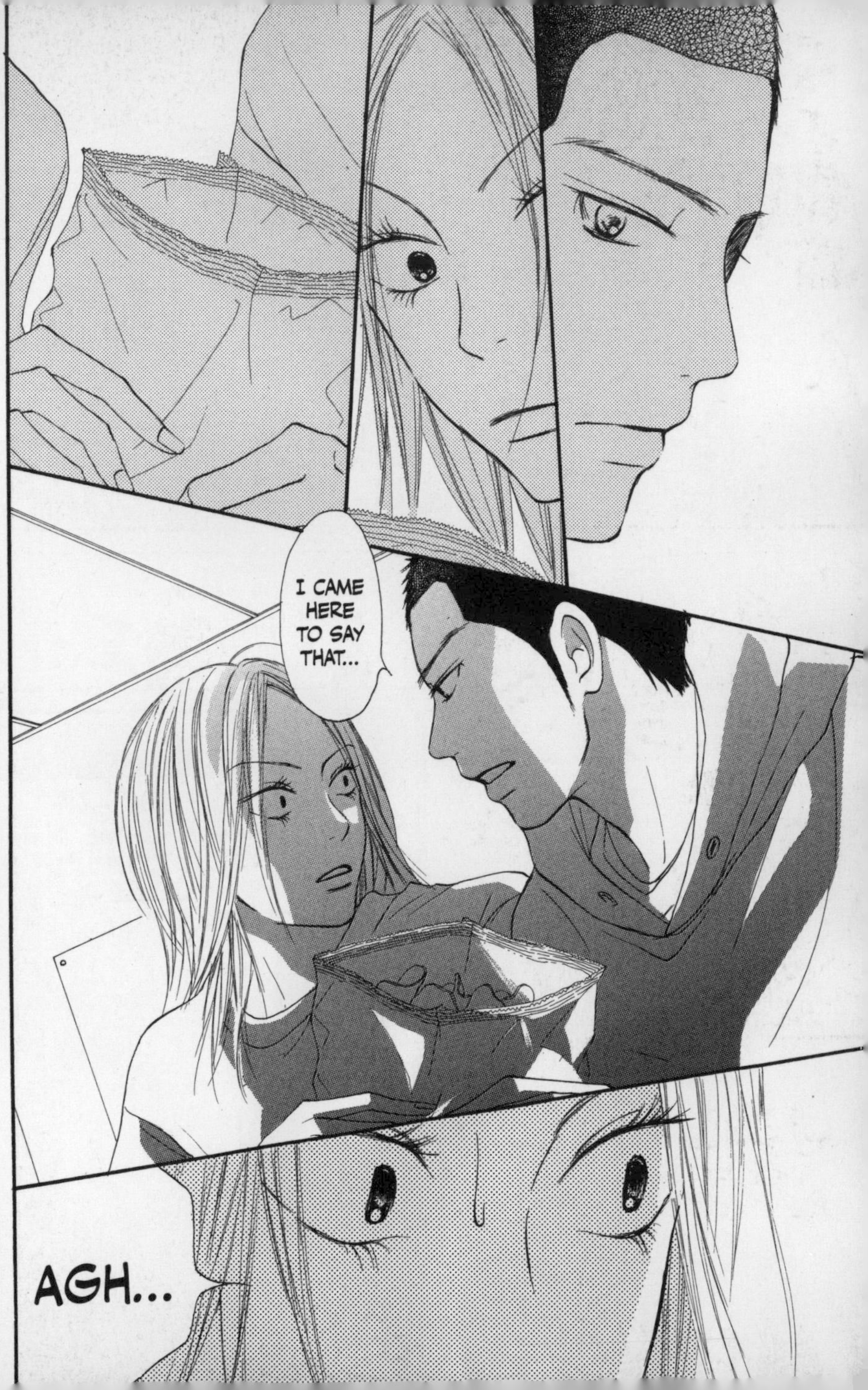
I CAME HERE TO SAY THAT...
AGH...

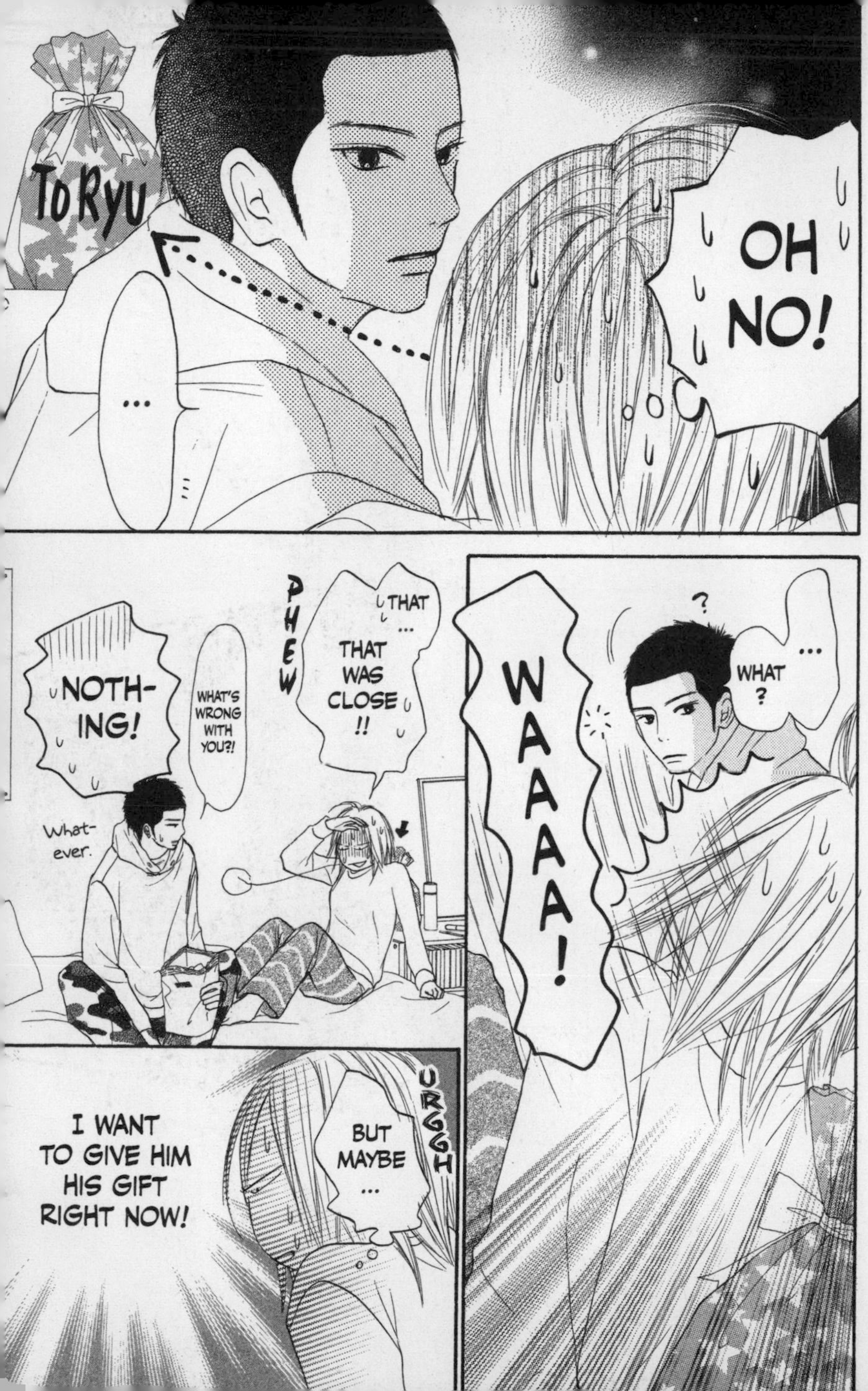
OH NO!
To Ryu
...
...
WHAT?
WAAAA!
THAT... THAT WAS CLOSE!!
PHEW
WHAT'S WRONG WITH YOU?!
NOTH-ING!
What-ever.
URGGH
BUT MAYBE...
I WANT TO GIVE HIM HIS GIFT RIGHT NOW!

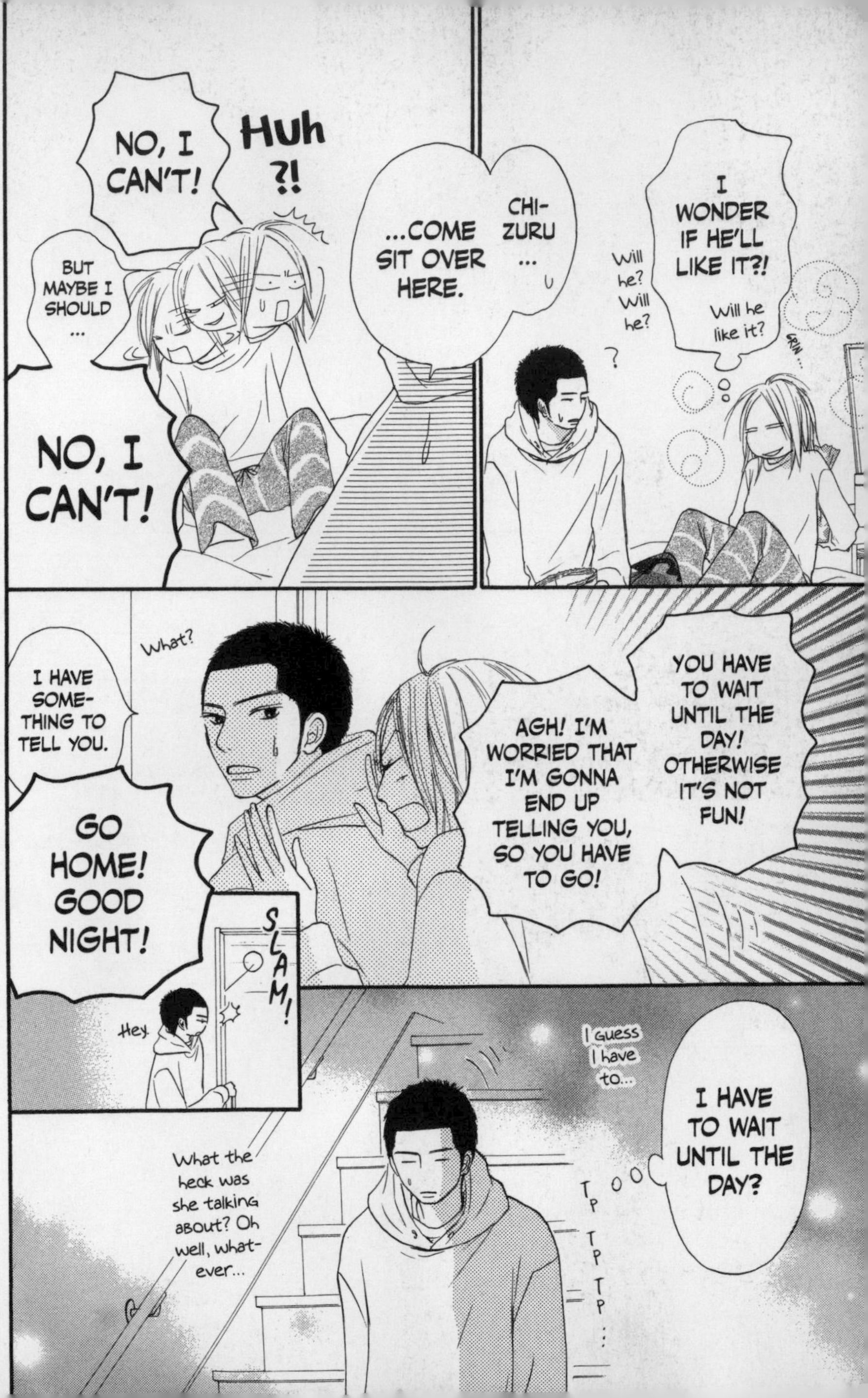
I WONDER IF HE'LL LIKE IT?!
Will he like it?
GRIN...
Will he? Will he?
?
CHI-ZURU ...
...COME SIT OVER HERE.
Huh ?!
NO, I CAN'T!
BUT MAYBE I SHOULD ...
NO, I CAN'T!
YOU HAVE TO WAIT UNTIL THE DAY! OTHERWISE IT'S NOT FUN!
AGH! I'M WORRIED THAT I'M GONNA END UP TELLING YOU, SO YOU HAVE TO GO!
What?
I HAVE SOME-THING TO TELL YOU.
GO HOME! GOOD NIGHT!
SLAM!
Hey.
I HAVE TO WAIT UNTIL THE DAY?
I guess I have to...
TP TP TP...
What the heck was she talking about? Oh well, what-ever...

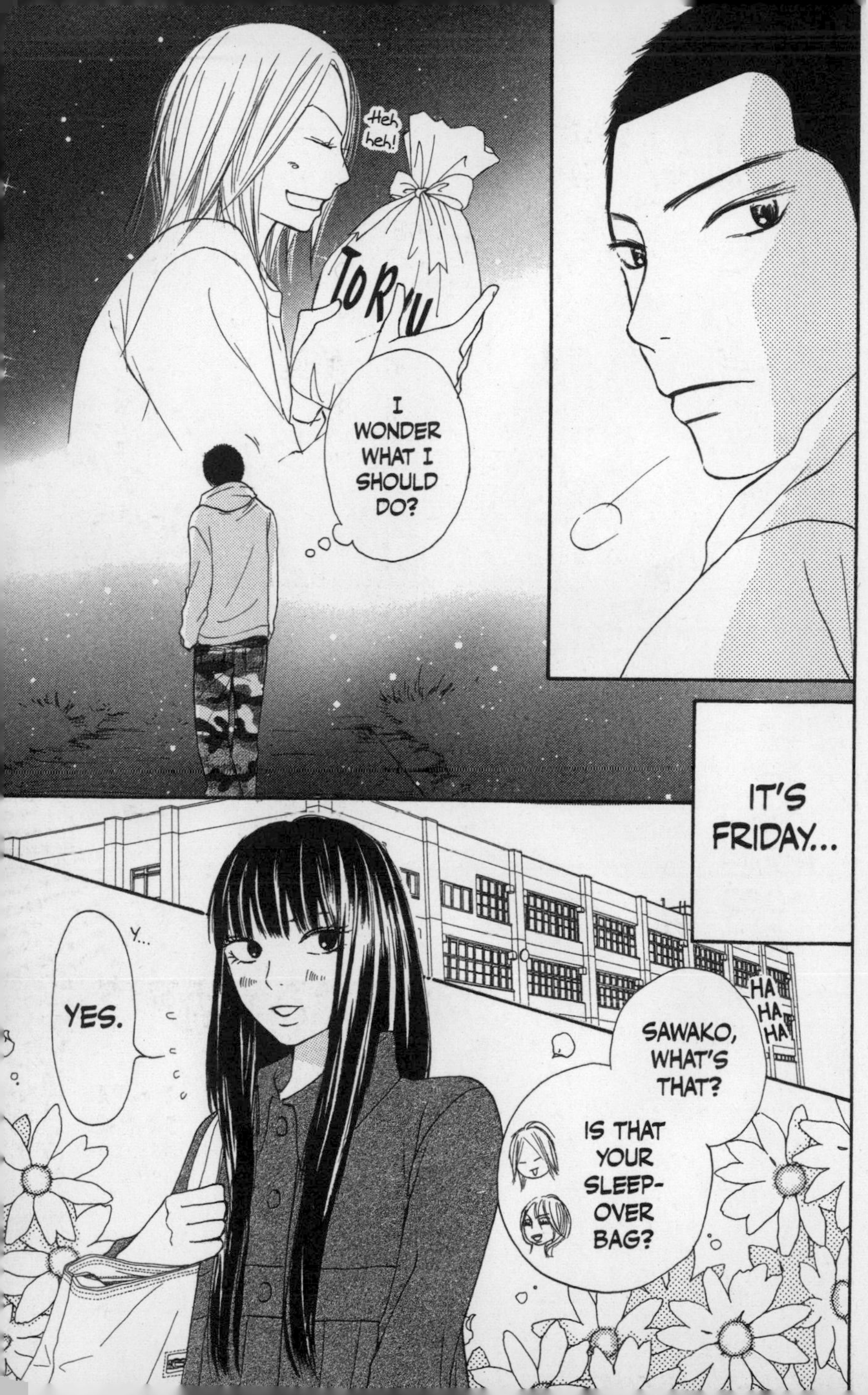
Heh heh!
TORYU
I WONDER WHAT I SHOULD DO?
IT'S FRIDAY...
HA HA HA
SAWAKO, WHAT'S THAT?
IS THAT YOUR SLEEP-OVER BAG?
Y... YES.

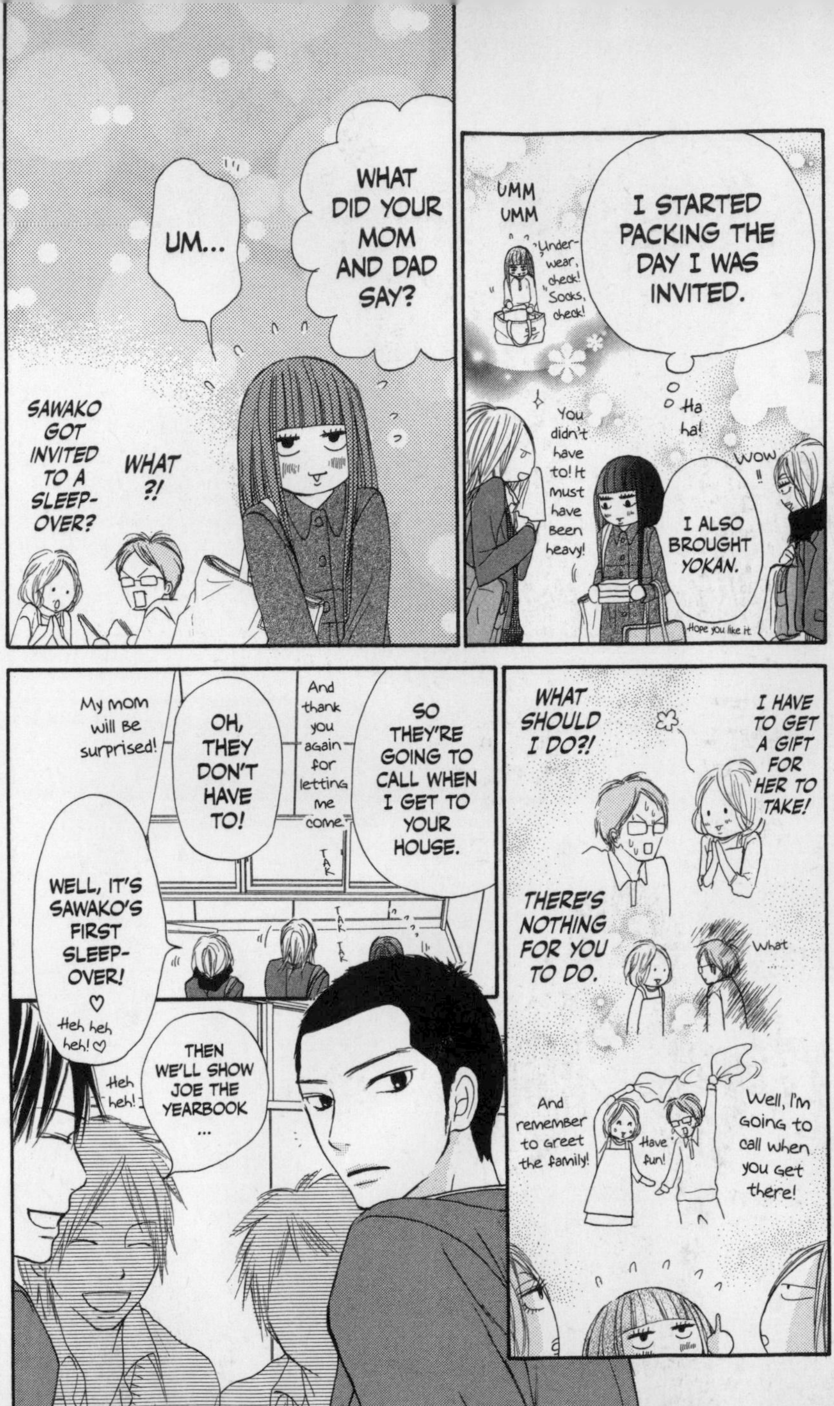
I STARTED PACKING THE DAY I WAS INVITED.
UMM UMM
Underwear, check! Socks, check!
Ha ha!
WOW!!
I ALSO BROUGHT YOKAN.
Hope you like it
You didn't have to! It must have been heavy!
WHAT DID YOUR MOM AND DAD SAY?
UM...
WHAT ?!
SAWAKO GOT INVITED TO A SLEEP-OVER?
I HAVE TO GET A GIFT FOR HER TO TAKE!
WHAT SHOULD I DO?!
What...
THERE'S NOTHING FOR YOU TO DO.
Well, I'm going to call when you get there!
Have fun!
And remember to greet the family!
SO THEY'RE GOING TO CALL WHEN I GET TO YOUR HOUSE.
And thank you again for letting me come.
OH, THEY DON'T HAVE TO!
My mom will be surprised!
TAK
TAK TAK
WELL, IT'S SAWAKO'S FIRST SLEEP-OVER! ♡
Heh heh heh! ♡
THEN WE'LL SHOW JOE THE YEARBOOK ...
Heh heh!

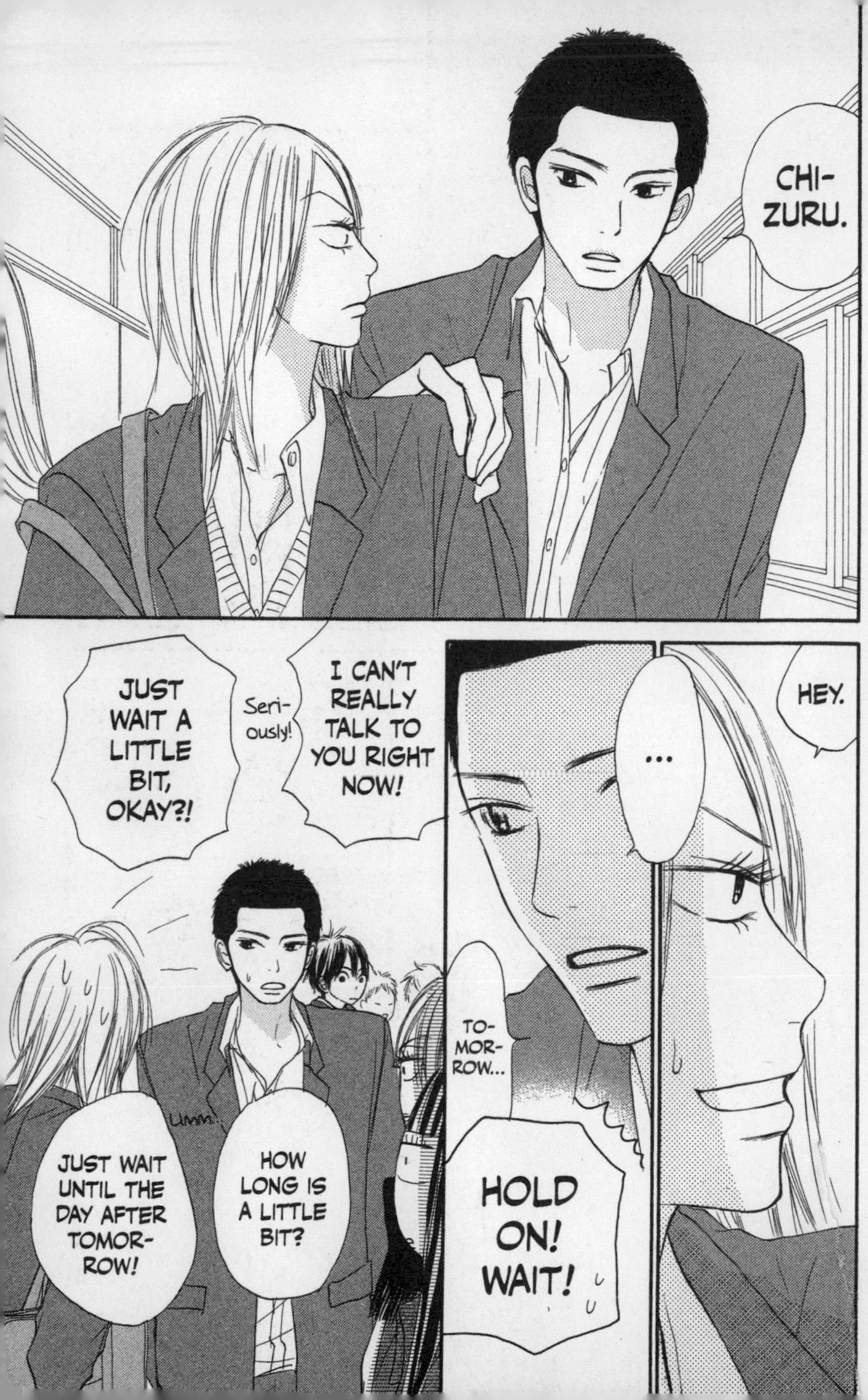
CHI-ZURU.
HEY.
...
TO-MOR-ROW...
HOLD ON! WAIT!
I CAN'T REALLY TALK TO YOU RIGHT NOW!
Seri-ously!
JUST WAIT A LITTLE BIT, OKAY?!
Umm...
HOW LONG IS A LITTLE BIT?
JUST WAIT UNTIL THE DAY AFTER TOMOR-ROW!

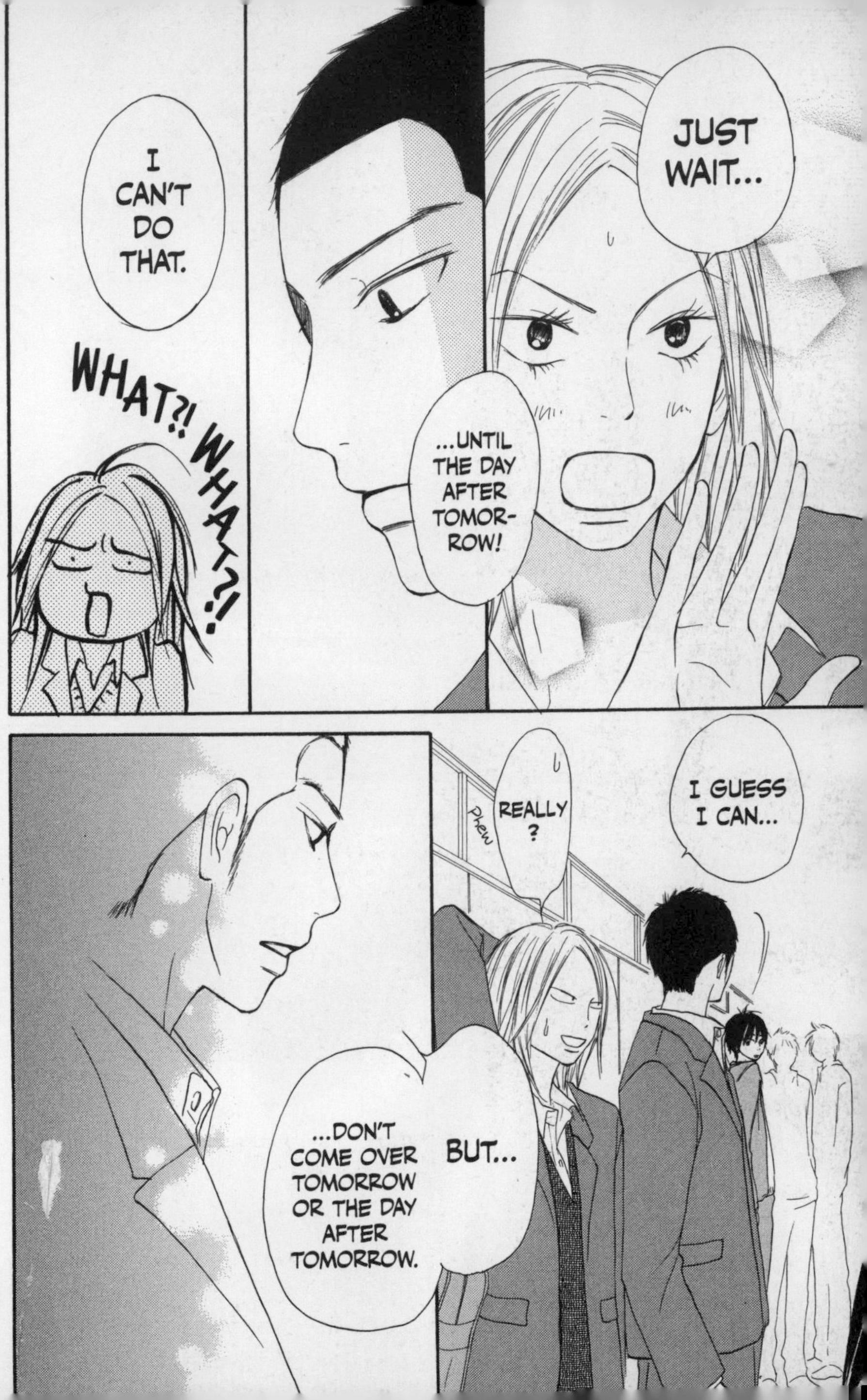
JUST WAIT...
...UNTIL THE DAY AFTER TOMOR-ROW!
I CAN'T DO THAT.
WHAT?! WHAT?!
I GUESS I CAN...
Phew
REALLY?
BUT...
...DON'T COME OVER TOMORROW OR THE DAY AFTER TOMORROW.

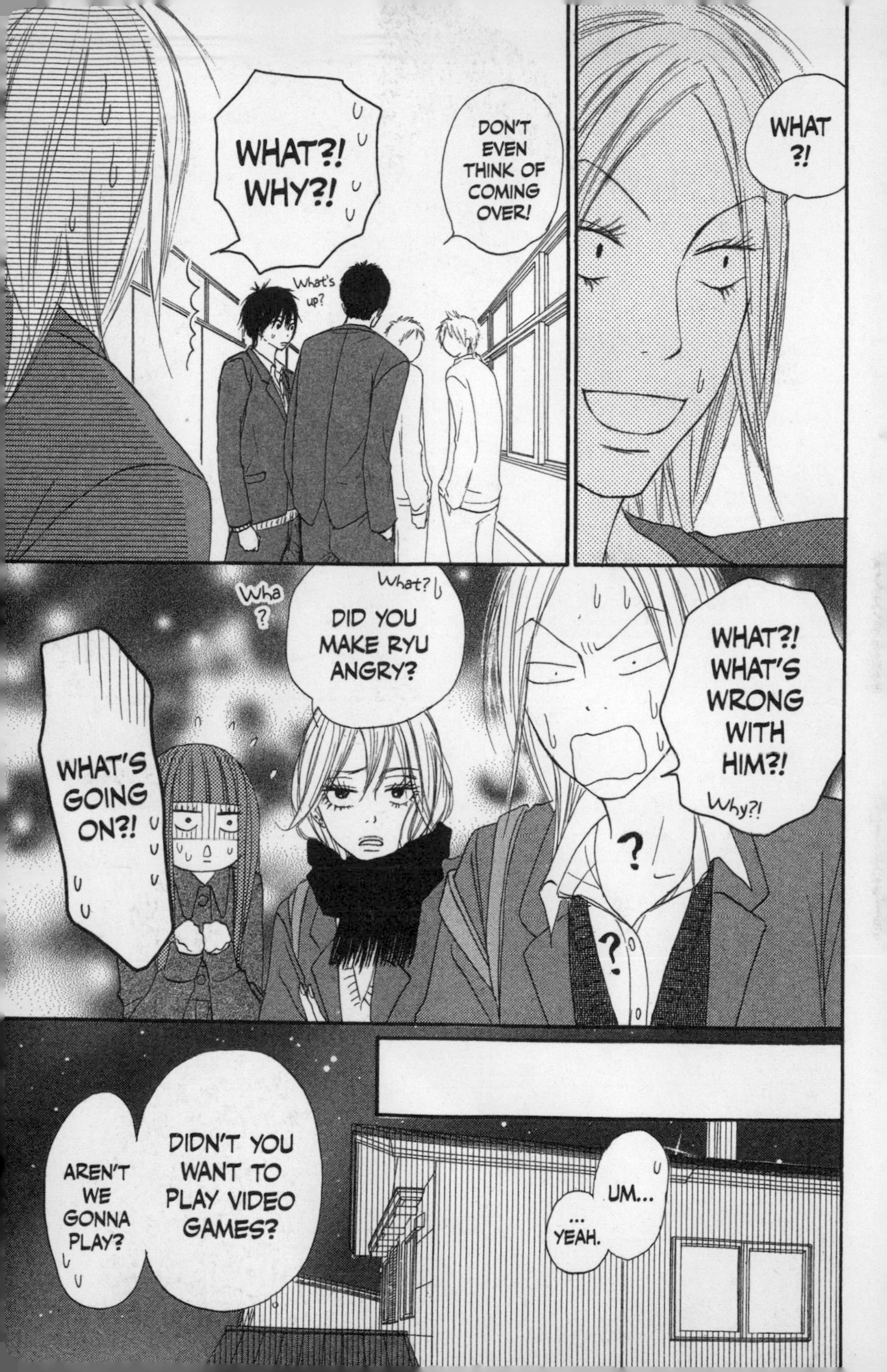
WHAT ?!
DON'T EVEN THINK OF COMING OVER!
WHAT?! WHY?!
What's up?
WHAT?! WHAT'S WRONG WITH HIM?!
Why?!
What?
DID YOU MAKE RYU ANGRY?
Wha ?
WHAT'S GOING ON?!
UM... ... YEAH.
DIDN'T YOU WANT TO PLAY VIDEO GAMES?
AREN'T WE GONNA PLAY?

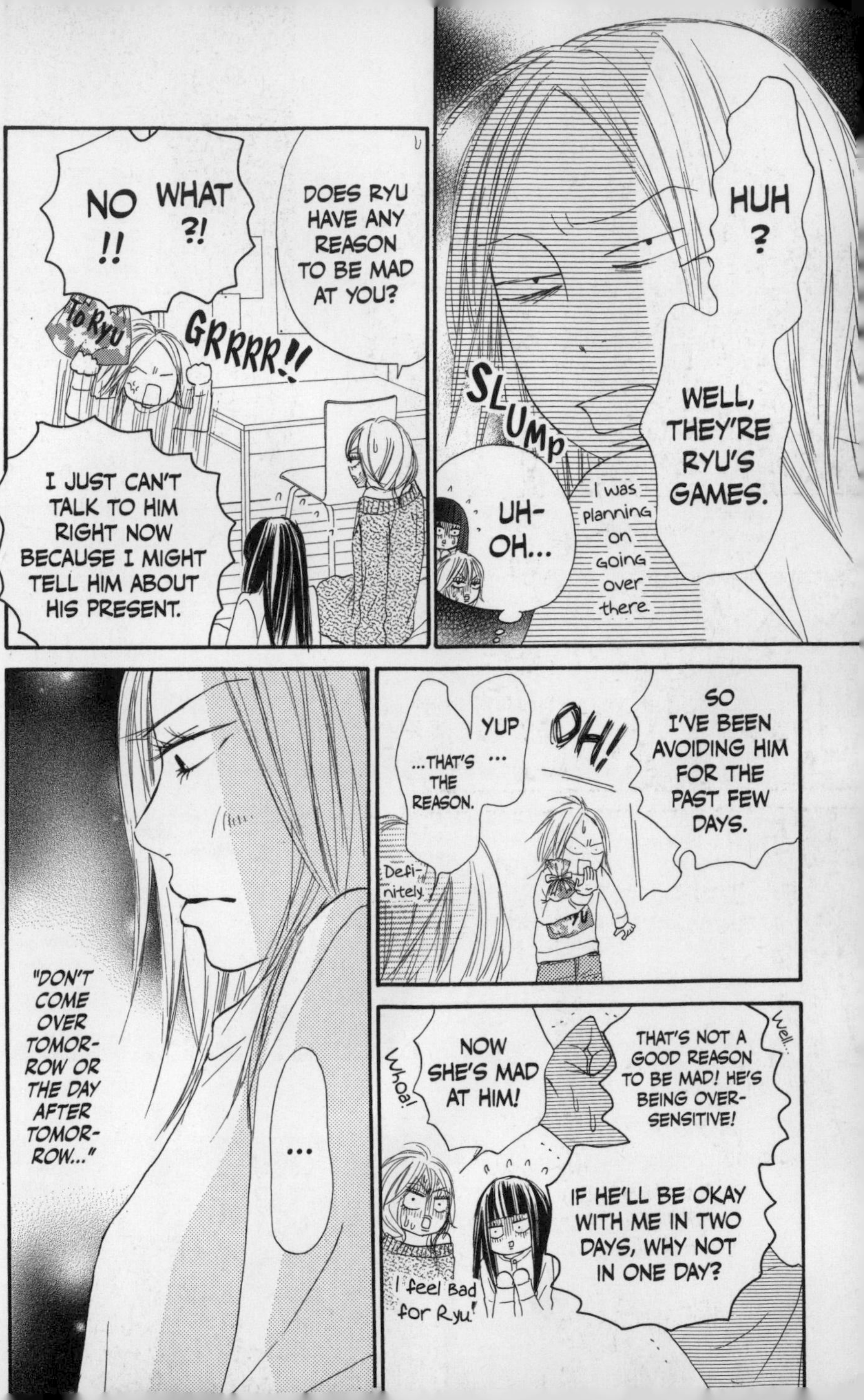
HUH ?
WELL, THEY'RE RYU'S GAMES.
SLUMP
UH-OH...
I was planning on going over there.
DOES RYU HAVE ANY REASON TO BE MAD AT YOU?
WHAT ?!
NO !!
GRRRR!!
To Ryu
I JUST CAN'T TALK TO HIM RIGHT NOW BECAUSE I MIGHT TELL HIM ABOUT HIS PRESENT.
SO I'VE BEEN AVOIDING HIM FOR THE PAST FEW DAYS.
OH!
YUP ...
...THAT'S THE REASON.
Definitely.
Well...
THAT'S NOT A GOOD REASON TO BE MAD! HE'S BEING OVER-SENSITIVE!
NOW SHE'S MAD AT HIM!
Whoa!
IF HE'LL BE OKAY WITH ME IN TWO DAYS, WHY NOT IN ONE DAY?
I feel Bad for Ryu!
...
"DON'T COME OVER TOMORROW OR THE DAY AFTER TOMORROW..."

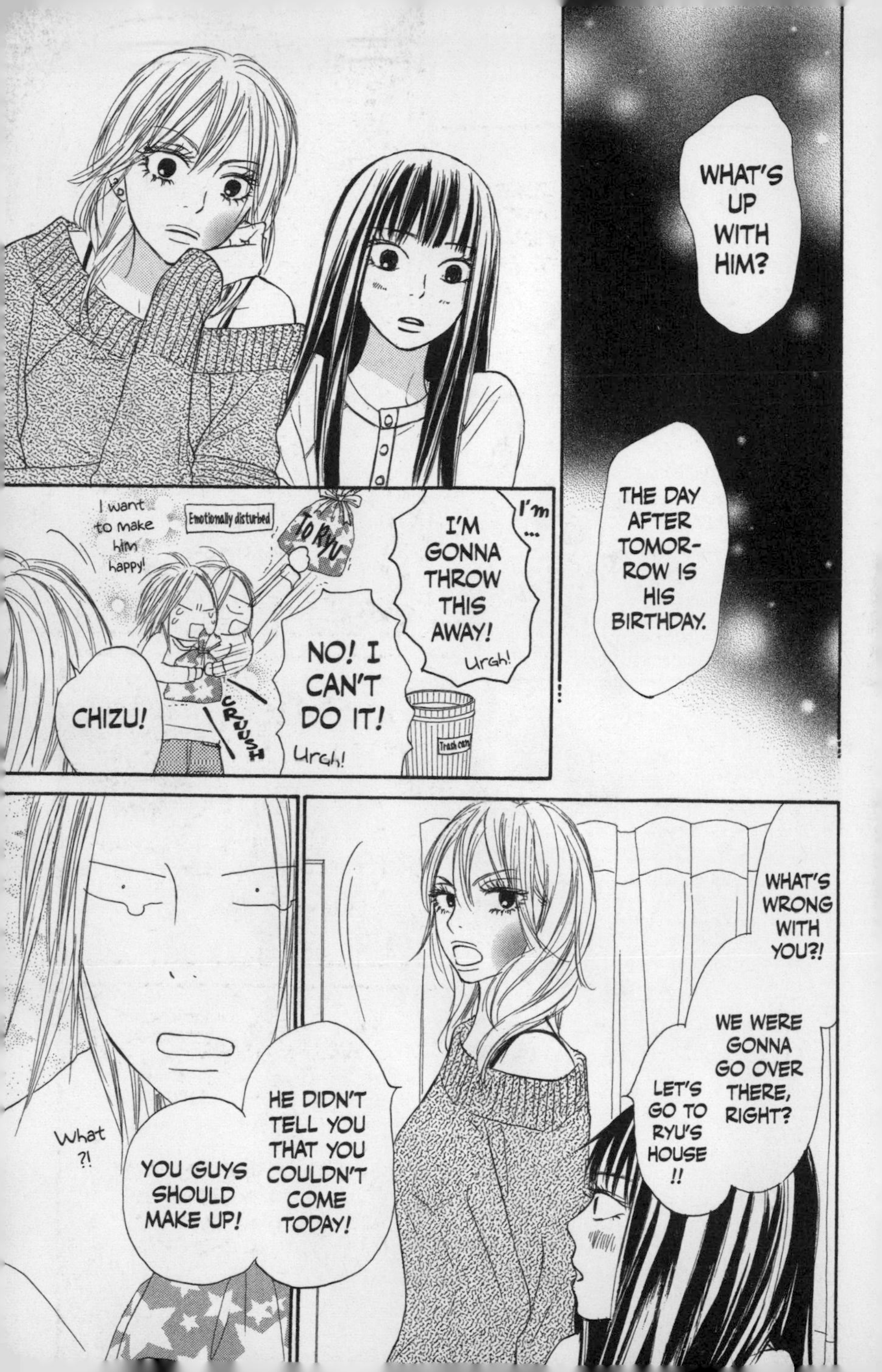
WHAT'S UP WITH HIM?
THE DAY AFTER TOMORROW IS HIS BIRTHDAY.
I'm...
I'M GONNA THROW THIS AWAY!
Urgh!
To Ryu
Emotionally disturbed
I want to make him happy!
Trash can
NO! I CAN'T DO IT!
Urgh!
CRUUSH
CHIZU!
WHAT'S WRONG WITH YOU?!
WE WERE GONNA GO OVER THERE, RIGHT?
LET'S GO TO RYU'S HOUSE!!
HE DIDN'T TELL YOU THAT YOU COULDN'T COME TODAY!
YOU GUYS SHOULD MAKE UP!
What?!

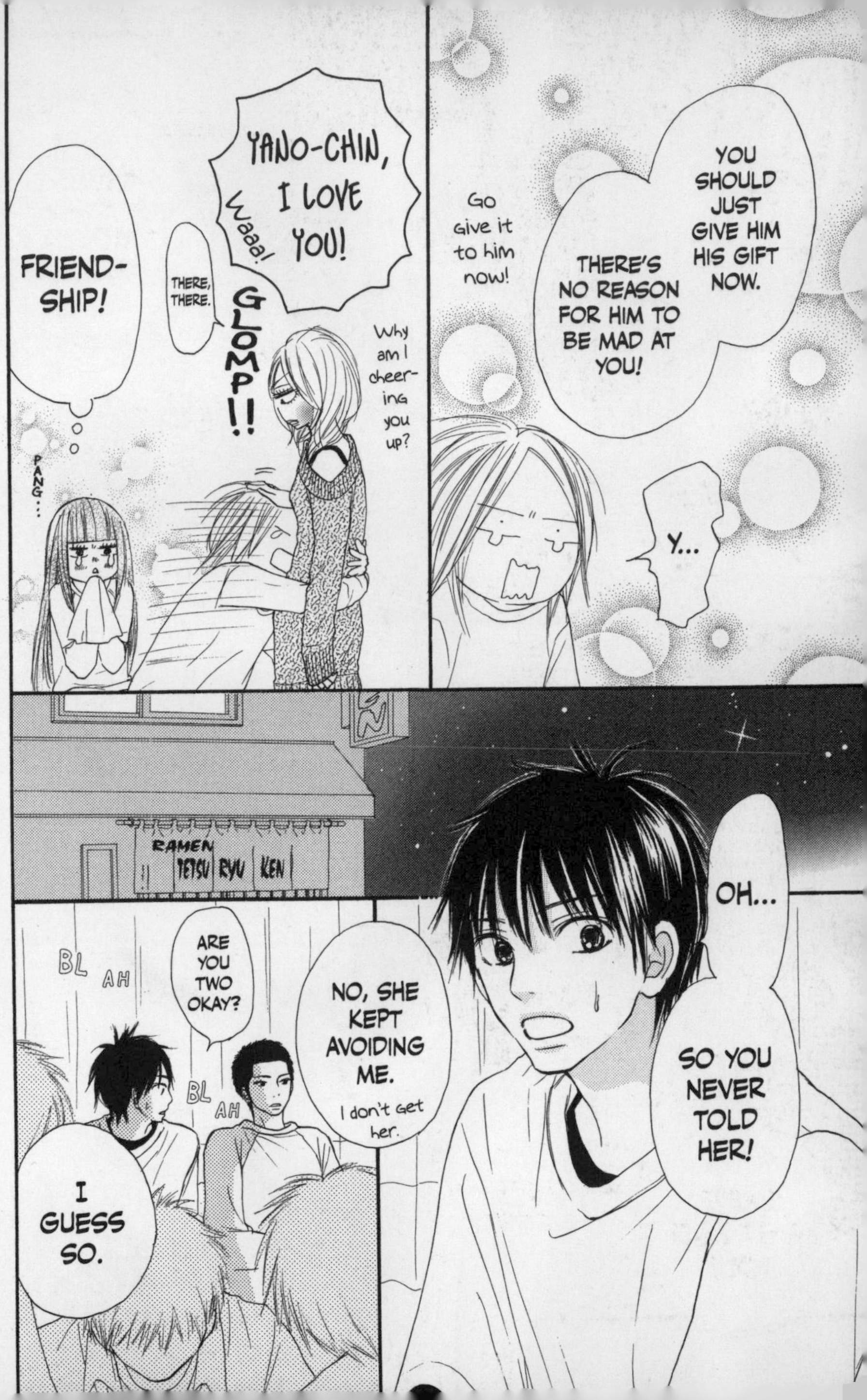
YOU SHOULD JUST GIVE HIM HIS GIFT NOW.
THERE'S NO REASON FOR HIM TO BE MAD AT YOU!
Go give it to him now!
Y...
YANO-CHIN, I LOVE YOU!
Waaa!
Why am I cheering you up?
GLOMP!!
THERE, THERE.
FRIEND-SHIP!
PANG...
OH...
SO YOU NEVER TOLD HER!
RAMEN
TETSU RYU KEN
NO, SHE KEPT AVOIDING ME.
I don't get her.
ARE YOU TWO OKAY?
BLAH
BLAH
I GUESS SO.

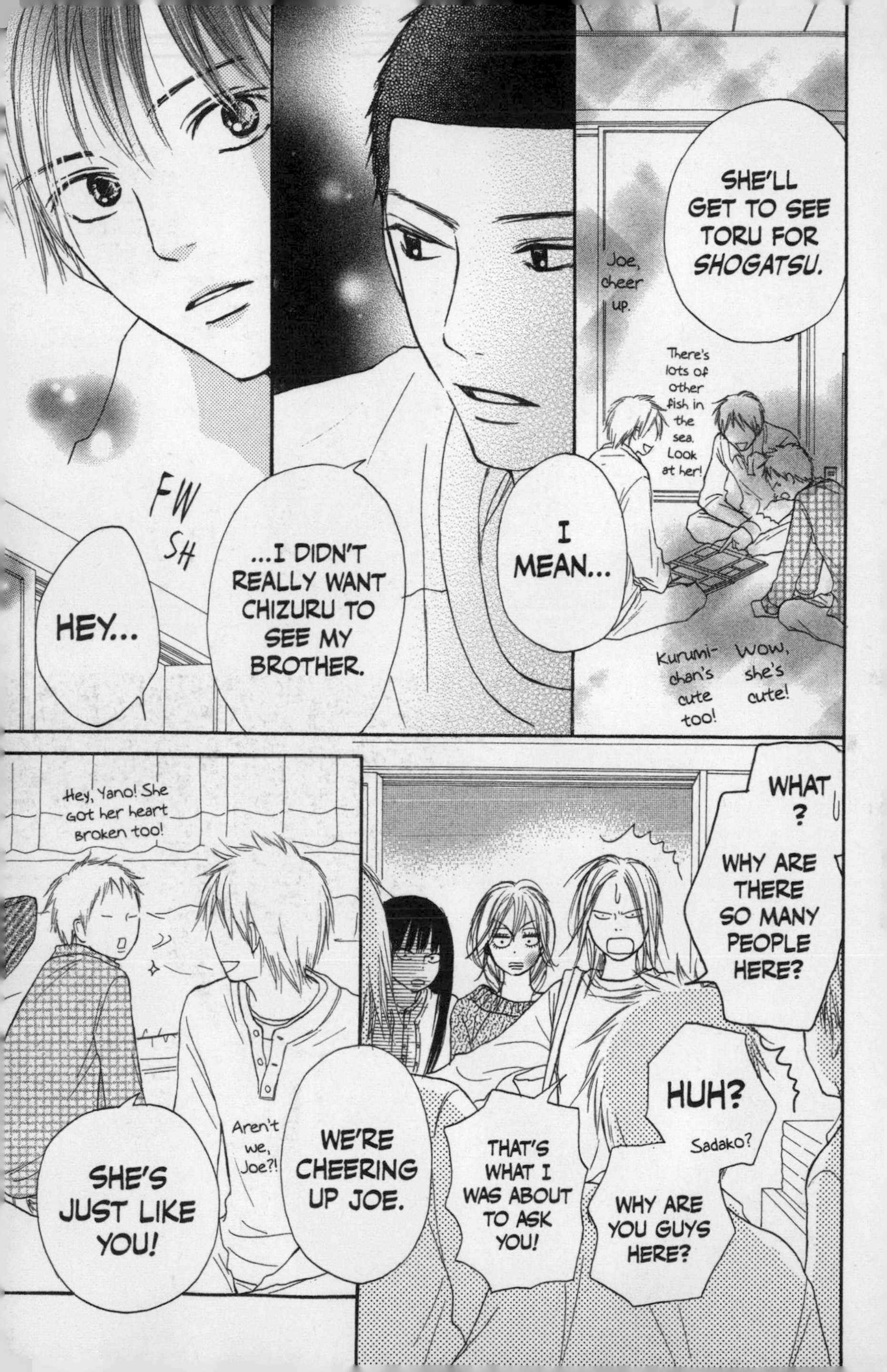
SHE'LL GET TO SEE TORU FOR SHOGATSU.
Joe, cheer up.
There's lots of other fish in the sea. Look at her!
Wow, she's cute!
Kurumi-chan's cute too!
I MEAN...
...I DIDN'T REALLY WANT CHIZURU TO SEE MY BROTHER.
FWSH
HEY...
WHAT?
WHY ARE THERE SO MANY PEOPLE HERE?
HUH?
Sadako?
WHY ARE YOU GUYS HERE?
THAT'S WHAT I WAS ABOUT TO ASK YOU!
WE'RE CHEERING UP JOE.
Aren't we, Joe?!
Hey, Yano! She got her heart broken too!
SHE'S JUST LIKE YOU!

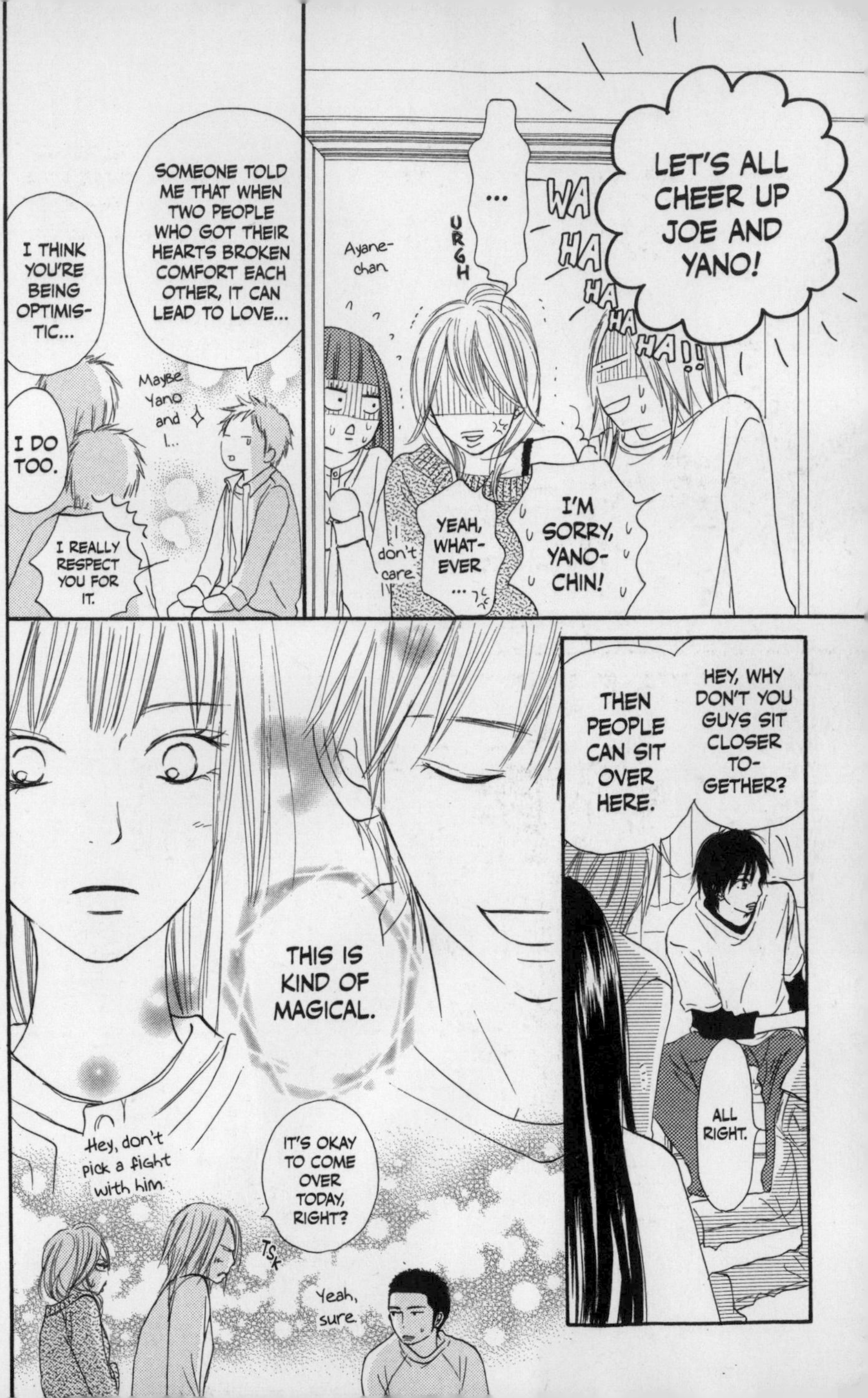
LET'S ALL CHEER UP JOE AND YANO!
WA HA HA HA HA!!
URGH
...
Ayane-chan
I'M SORRY, YANO-CHIN!
YEAH, WHATEVER...
I don't care.
SOMEONE TOLD ME THAT WHEN TWO PEOPLE WHO GOT THEIR HEARTS BROKEN COMFORT EACH OTHER, IT CAN LEAD TO LOVE...
I THINK YOU'RE BEING OPTIMISTIC...
Maybe Yano and I...
I DO TOO.
I REALLY RESPECT YOU FOR IT.
HEY, WHY DON'T YOU GUYS SIT CLOSER TOGETHER?
THEN PEOPLE CAN SIT OVER HERE.
ALL RIGHT.
THIS IS KIND OF MAGICAL.
IT'S OKAY TO COME OVER TODAY, RIGHT?
TSK
Hey, don't pick a fight with him.
Yeah, sure.

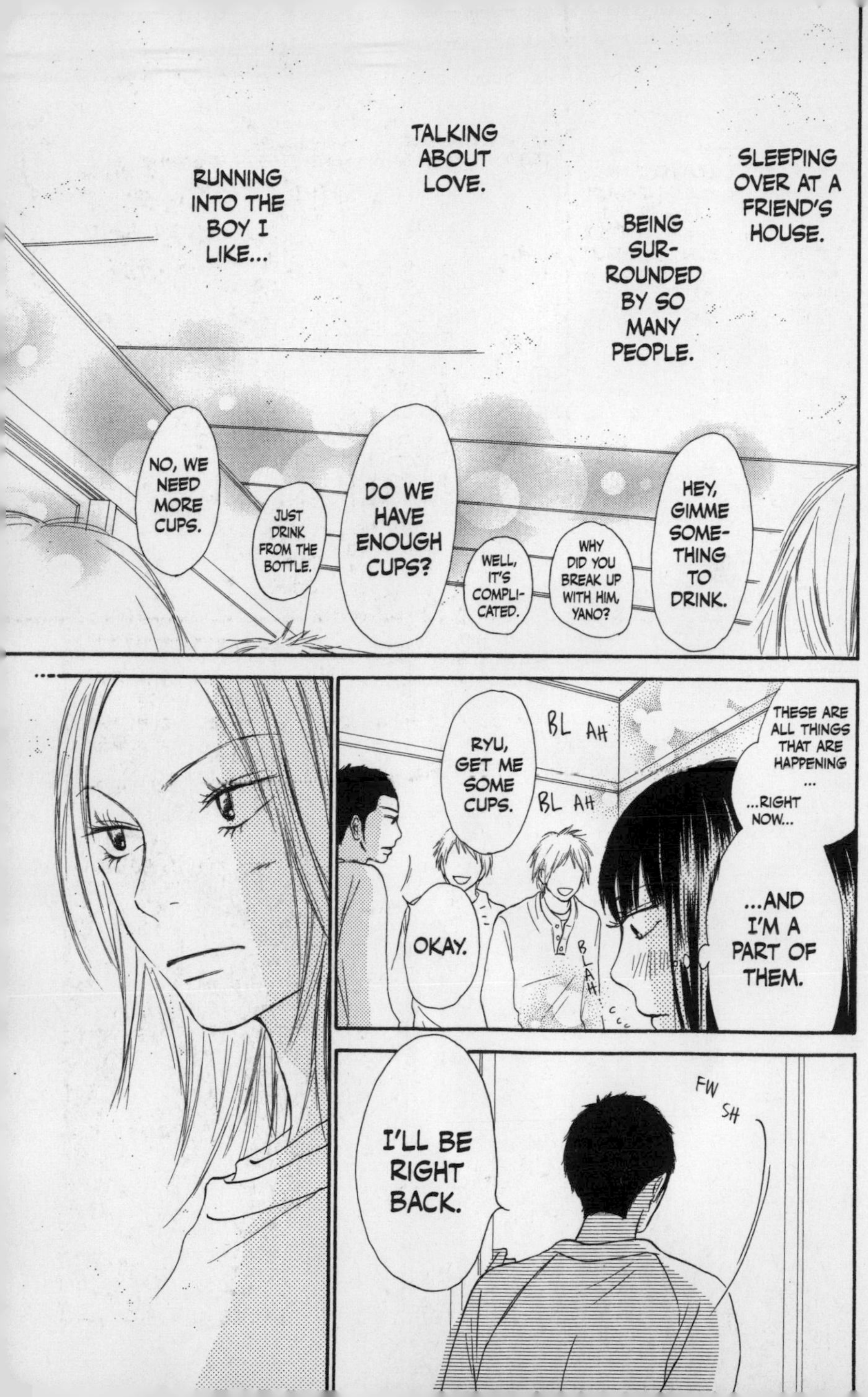
SLEEPING OVER AT A FRIEND'S HOUSE.
BEING SUR-ROUNDED BY SO MANY PEOPLE.
TALKING ABOUT LOVE.
RUNNING INTO THE BOY I LIKE...
HEY, GIMME SOME-THING TO DRINK.
WHY DID YOU BREAK UP WITH HIM, YANO?
WELL, IT'S COMPLI-CATED.
DO WE HAVE ENOUGH CUPS?
JUST DRINK FROM THE BOTTLE.
NO, WE NEED MORE CUPS.
THESE ARE ALL THINGS THAT ARE HAPPENING ...
...RIGHT NOW...
...AND I'M A PART OF THEM.
BL AH
BL AH
RYU, GET ME SOME CUPS.
BLAH
OKAY.
FW SH
I'LL BE RIGHT BACK.

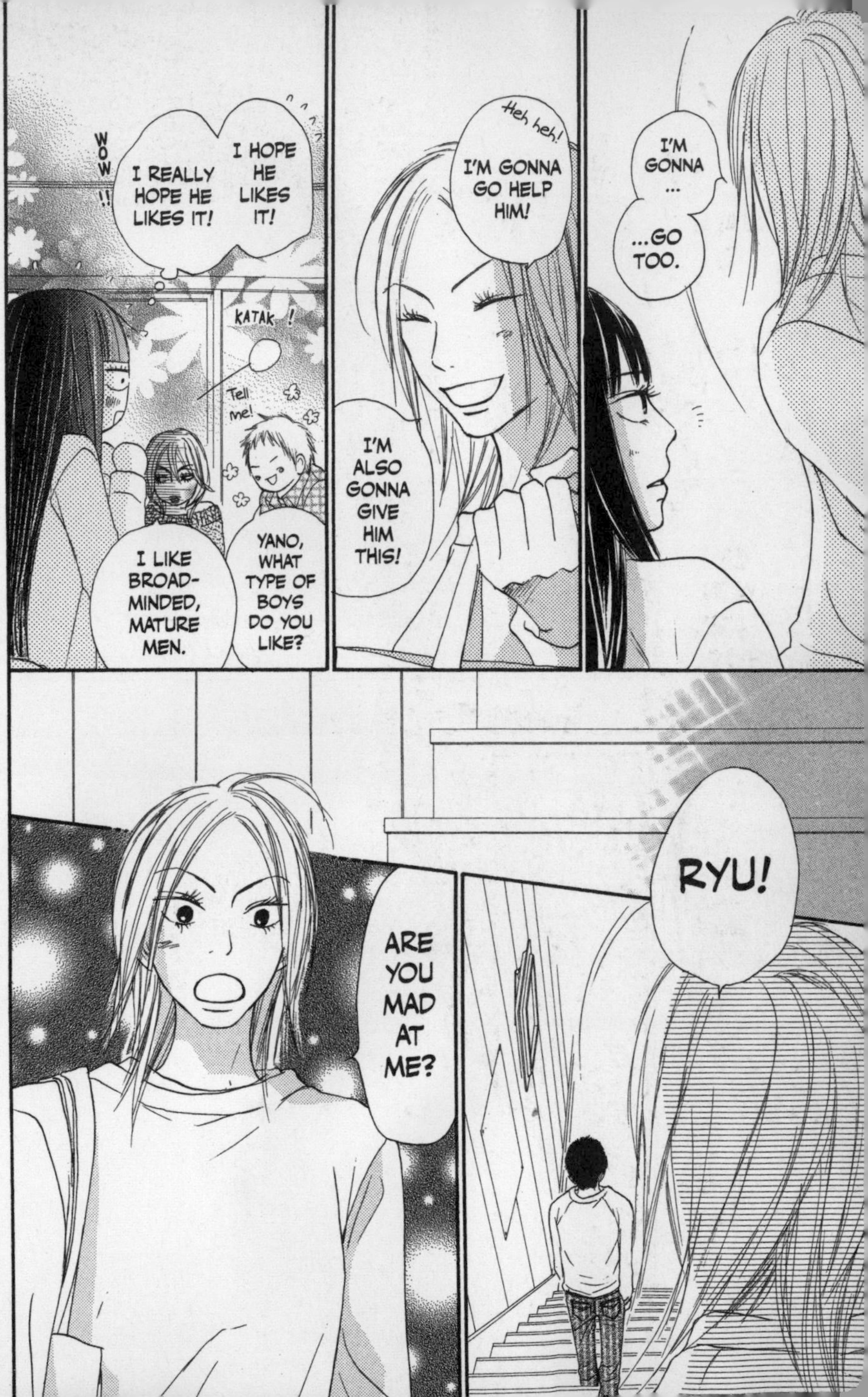
I'M GONNA ...
...GO TOO.
Heh heh!
I'M GONNA GO HELP HIM!
I'M ALSO GONNA GIVE HIM THIS!
I HOPE HE LIKES IT!
I REALLY HOPE HE LIKES IT!
WOW!!
KATAK!
Tell me!
YANO, WHAT TYPE OF BOYS DO YOU LIKE?
I LIKE BROAD-MINDED, MATURE MEN.
RYU!
ARE YOU MAD AT ME?

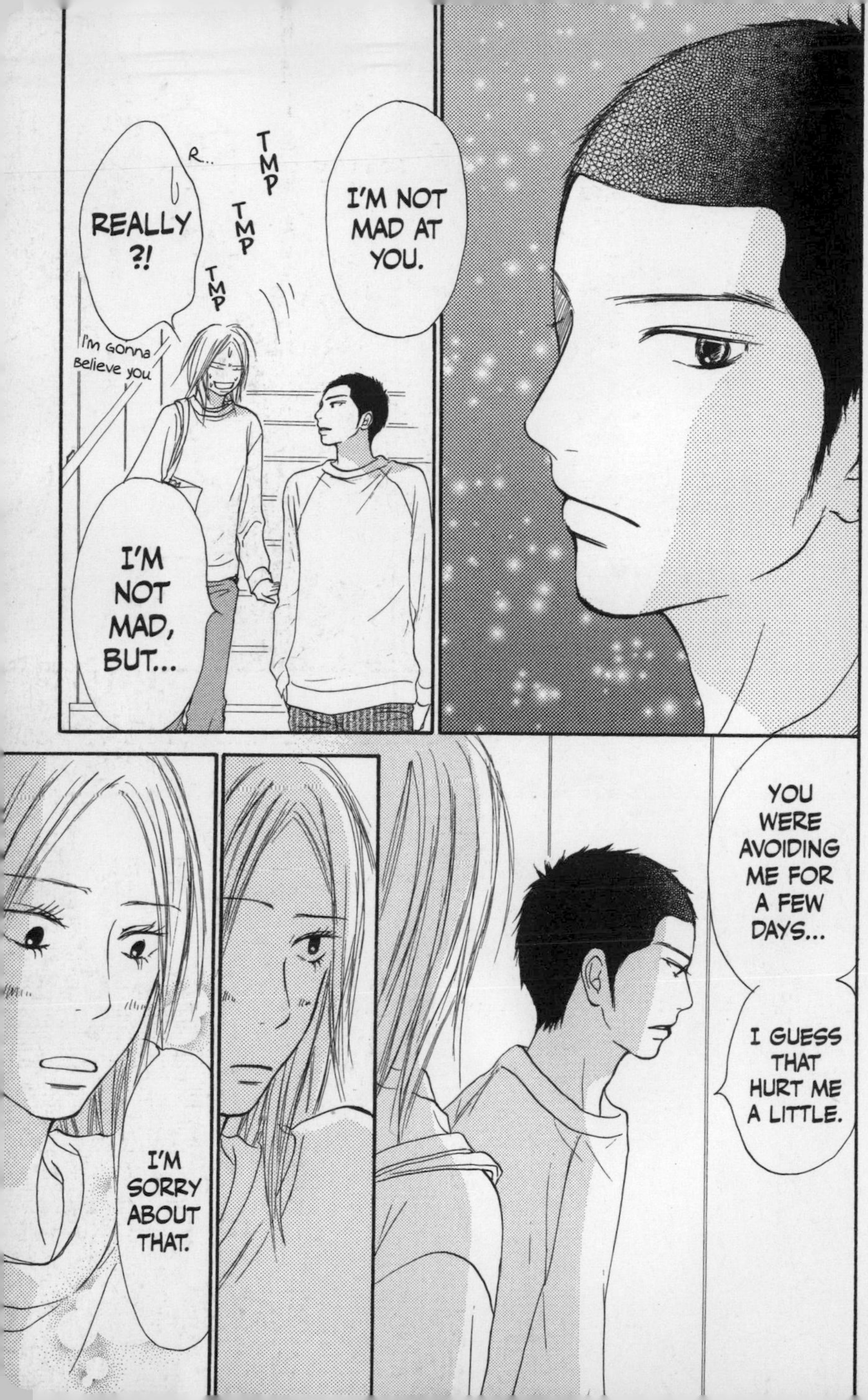
I'M NOT MAD AT YOU.
TMP
TMP
TMP
R.. REALLY ?!
I'm Gonna Believe you
I'M NOT MAD, BUT...
YOU WERE AVOIDING ME FOR A FEW DAYS...
I GUESS THAT HURT ME A LITTLE.
I'M SORRY ABOUT THAT.

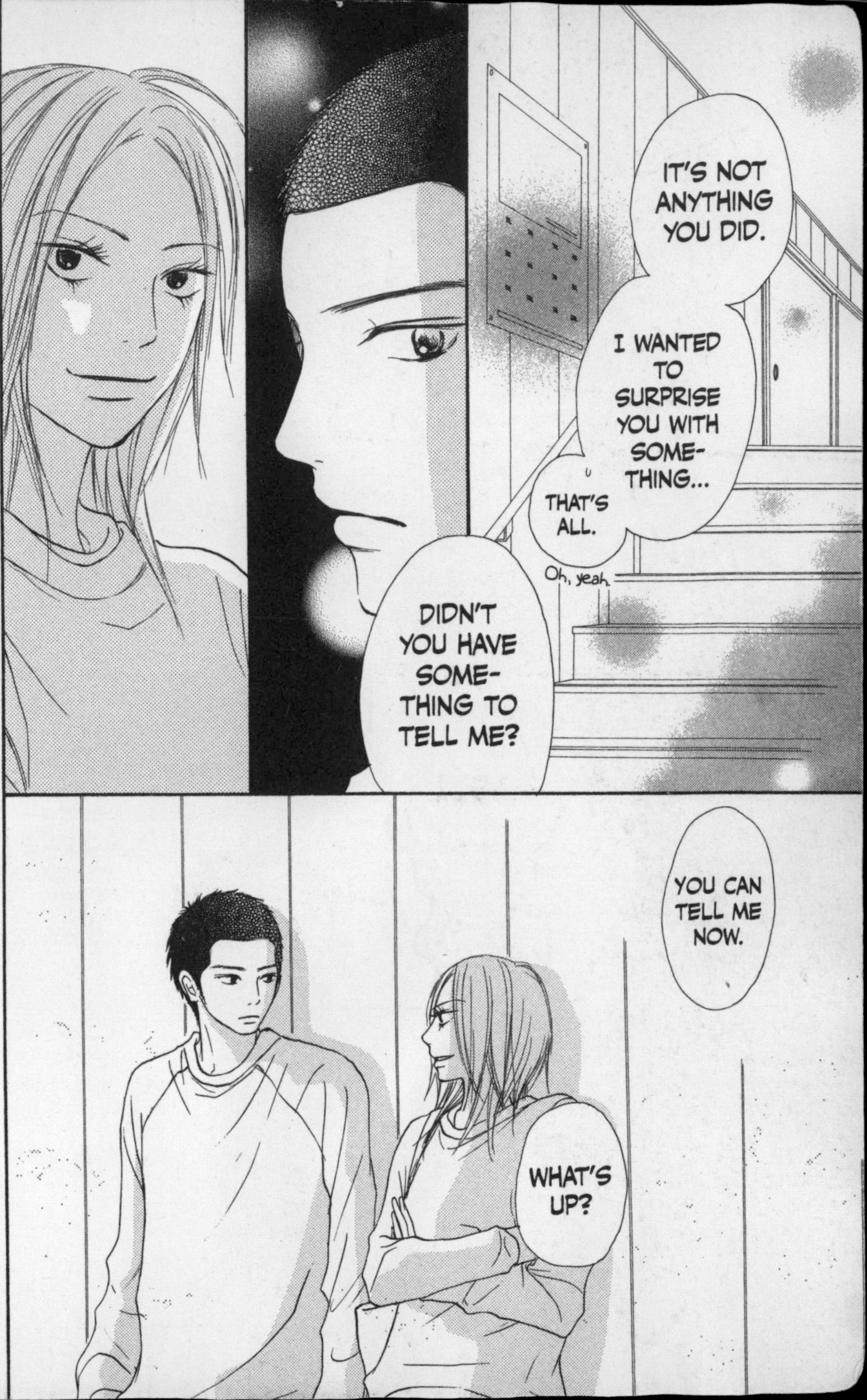
IT'S NOT ANYTHING YOU DID.
I WANTED TO SURPRISE YOU WITH SOME-THING...
THAT'S ALL.
Oh, yeah.
DIDN'T YOU HAVE SOME-THING TO TELL ME?
YOU CAN TELL ME NOW.
WHAT'S UP?

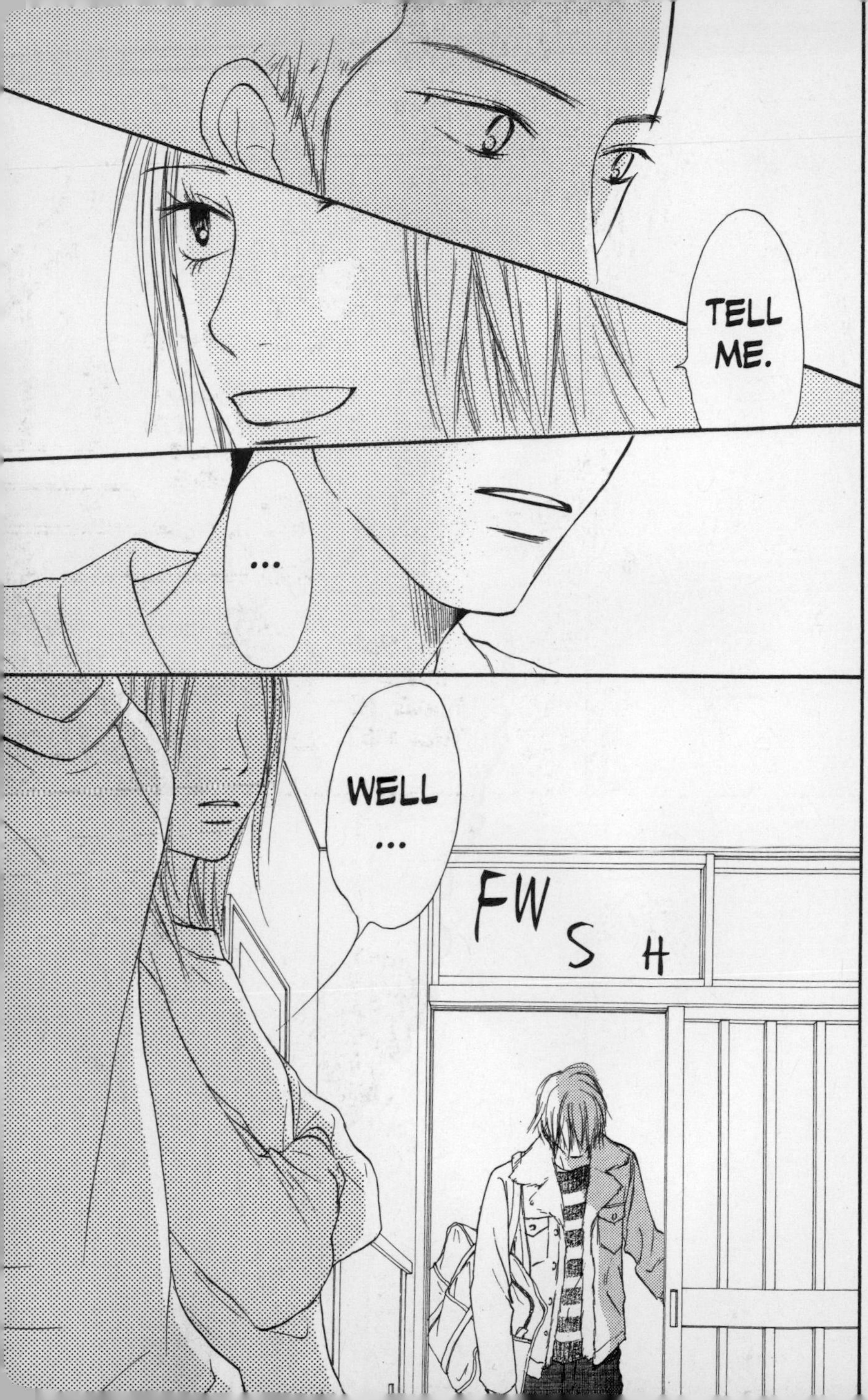
TELL ME.
...
WELL ...
FWSH

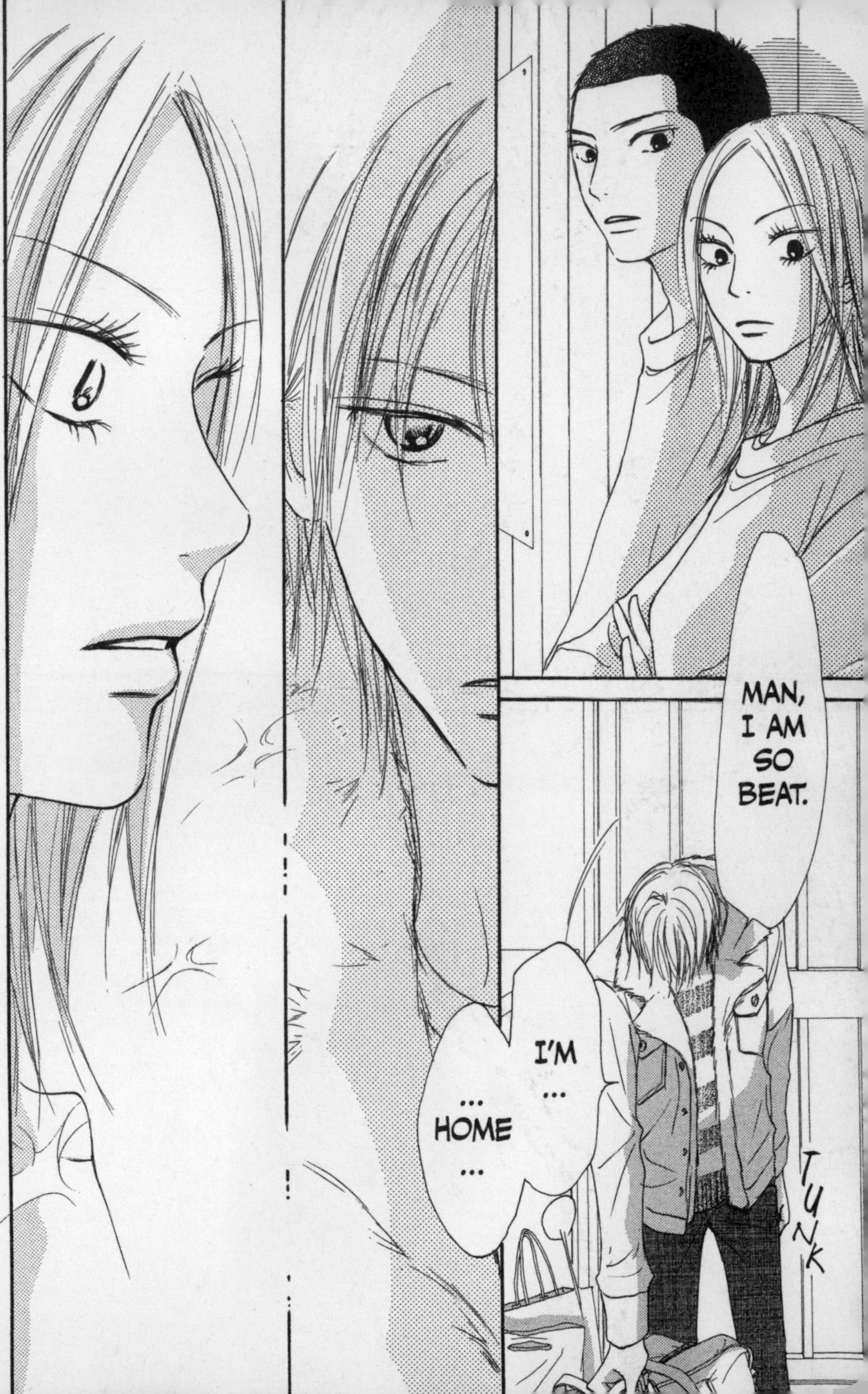
MAN, I AM SO BEAT.
I'M ... ... HOME ...
TUNK

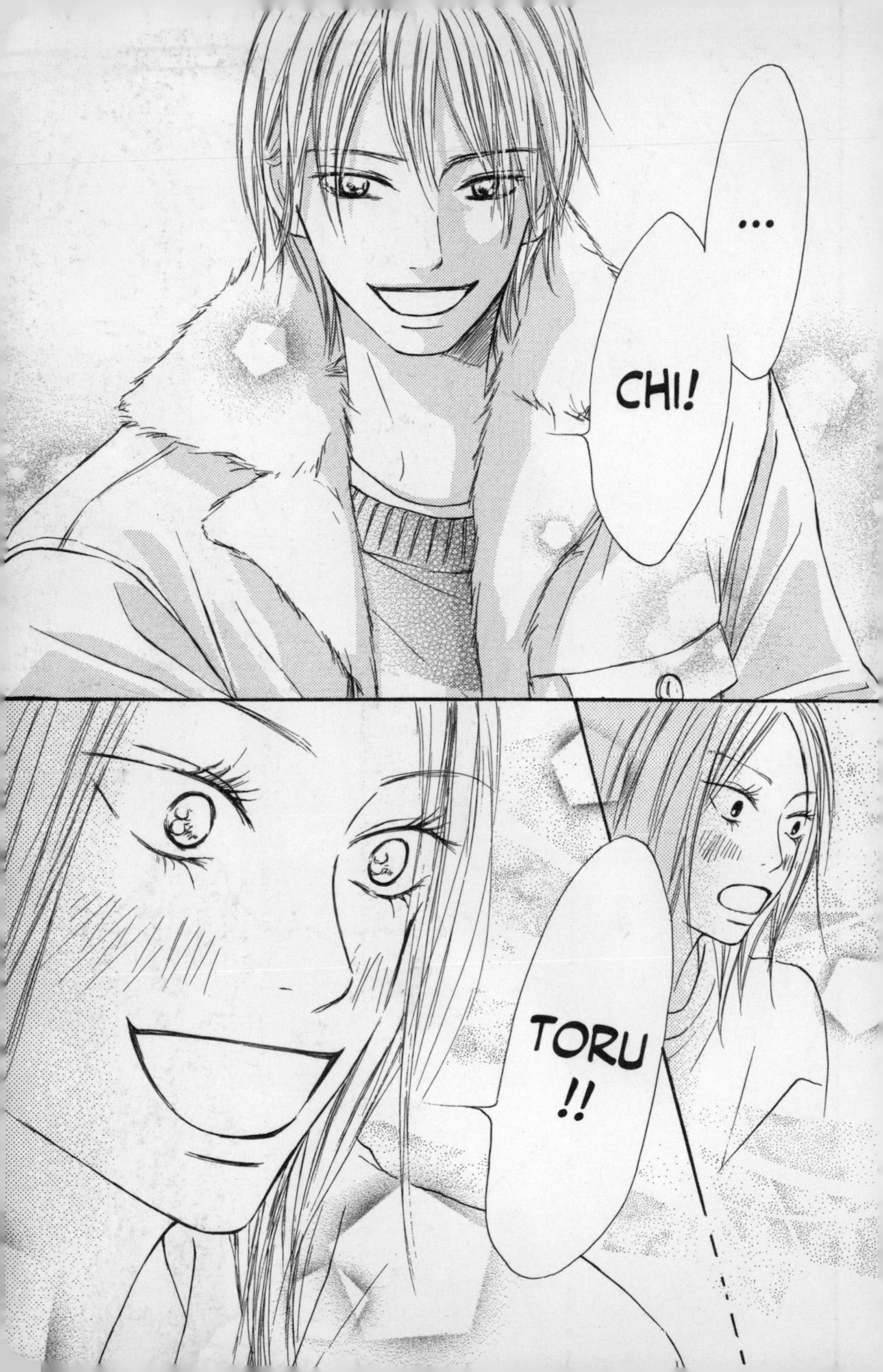
...
CHI!
TORU !!

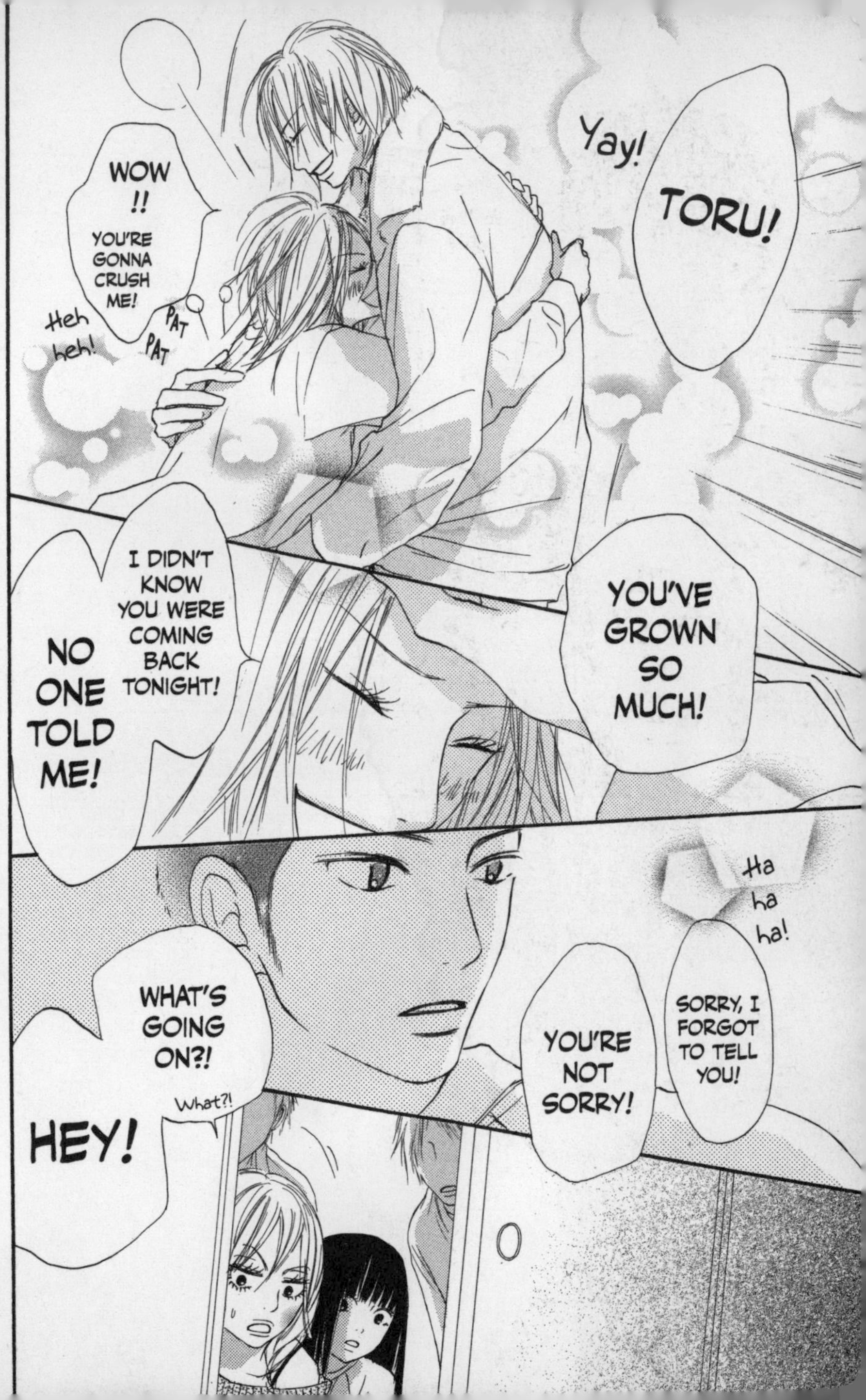
Yay!
TORU!
WOW !! YOU'RE GONNA CRUSH ME!
PAT PAT
Heh heh!
YOU'VE GROWN SO MUCH!
I DIDN'T KNOW YOU WERE COMING BACK TONIGHT!
NO ONE TOLD ME!
Ha ha ha!
SORRY, I FORGOT TO TELL YOU!
YOU'RE NOT SORRY!
WHAT'S GOING ON?!
What?!
HEY!

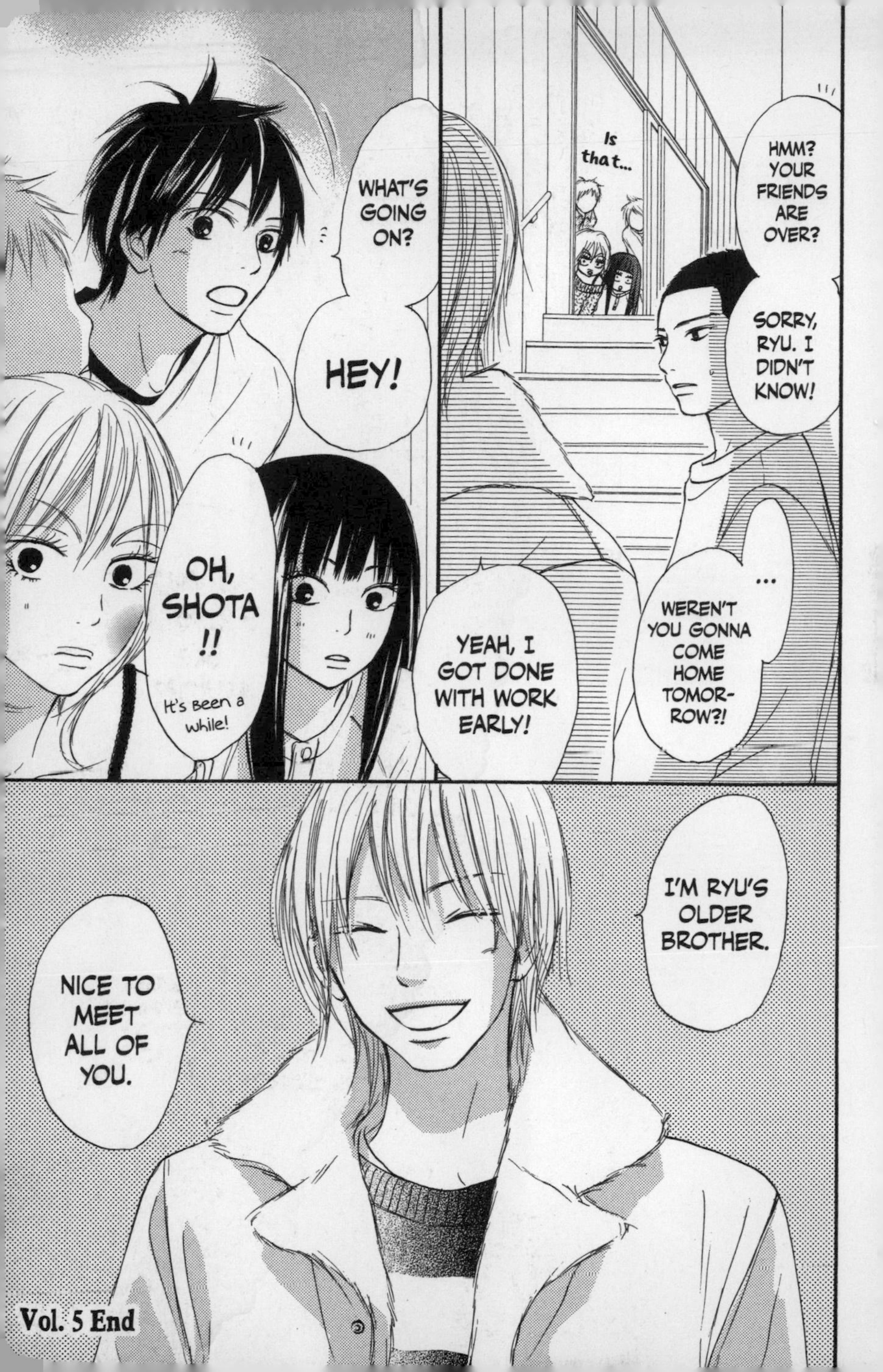
HMM? YOUR FRIENDS ARE OVER?
Is that...
SORRY, RYU. I DIDN'T KNOW!
...
WEREN'T YOU GONNA COME HOME TOMOR-ROW?!
YEAH, I GOT DONE WITH WORK EARLY!
WHAT'S GOING ON?
HEY!
OH, SHOTA!!
It's been a while!
I'M RYU'S OLDER BROTHER.
NICE TO MEET ALL OF YOU.

Vol. 5 End

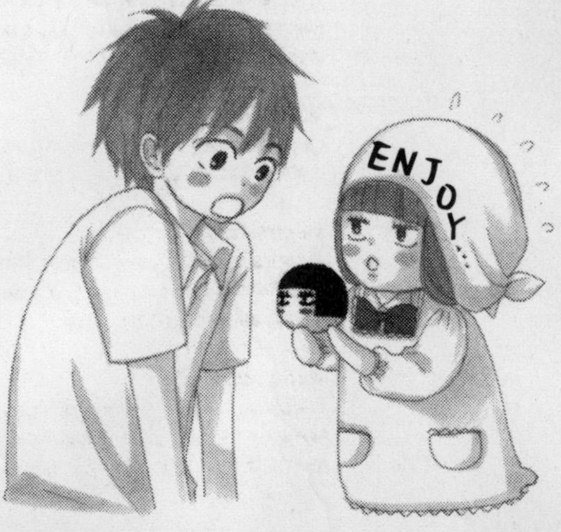
ENJOY

From me (the editor) to you (the reader).

Here are some Japanese culture explanations that will help you better understand the references in the *Kimi ni Todoke* world.

Honorifics:
When saying someone's name in Japanese, a suffix is often attached to indicate how familiar the speaker is with the person. Some are more polite and respectful, while others are endearing. Calling someone by just their first name is the most informal.
-kun is used for young men or boys, usually someone you are familiar with.
-chan is used for young women, girls or young children and can be used as a term of endearment.
-san is used for someone you respect or are not close to, or to be polite.

Page 67, salt water:
Japanese superstition holds that salt can ward off unwanted spirits.

Page 100, New Year:
The New Year's holiday, *shogatsu*, is the most important holiday in Japan, traditionally spent with one's family.

Page 131, Sapporo:
Sapporo is the capital of Hokkaido Prefecture. It's located in northern Japan.

Page 147, money:
Children typically receive gifts of money, called *otoshidama*, from their older relatives on New Year's Day.

Page 168, yokan:
Yokan is a traditional Japanese dessert made of red bean paste, agar and sugar. It's usually packaged in blocks and eaten in slices.

These are cookies, rice balls and a chestnut
creme cake that caterers and our editors
made for a magazine photo shoot. The cake
was considered to be too much and wasn't
used, but I personally like it! They're all
so cute!! Just look at the Ryu cookie!! He's
laughing!!

--Karuho Shiina

Karuho Shiina was born and raised in
Hokkaido, Japan. Though *Kimi ni Todoke*
is only her second series following many
one-shot stories, it has already racked up
accolades from various "Best Manga of the
Year" lists. Winner of the 2008 Kodansha
Manga Award for the shojo category, *Kimi
ni Todoke* also placed fifth in the first-
ever Manga Taisho (Cartoon Grand Prize)
contest in 2008. An animated TV series
debuted in October 2009 in Japan.

Kimi ni Todoke
VOL. 5

Shojo Beat Edition

STORY AND ART BY
KARUHO SHIINA

Translation/Koichiro Kensho Nishimura, HC Language Solutions, Inc.
Touch-up Art & Lettering/Vanessa Satone
Design/Yukiko Whitley
Editor/Carrie Shepherd

KIMI NI TODOKE © 2005 by Karuho Shiina
All rights reserved. First published in Japan in 2005 by SHUEISHA Inc.,
Tokyo. English translation rights arranged by SHUEISHA Inc.

Printed in the U.S.A.

Published by VIZ Media, LLC
P.O. Box 77010
San Francisco, CA 94107

10 9 8 7 6 5 4 3 2
First printing, August 2010
Second printing, September 2010

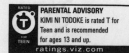

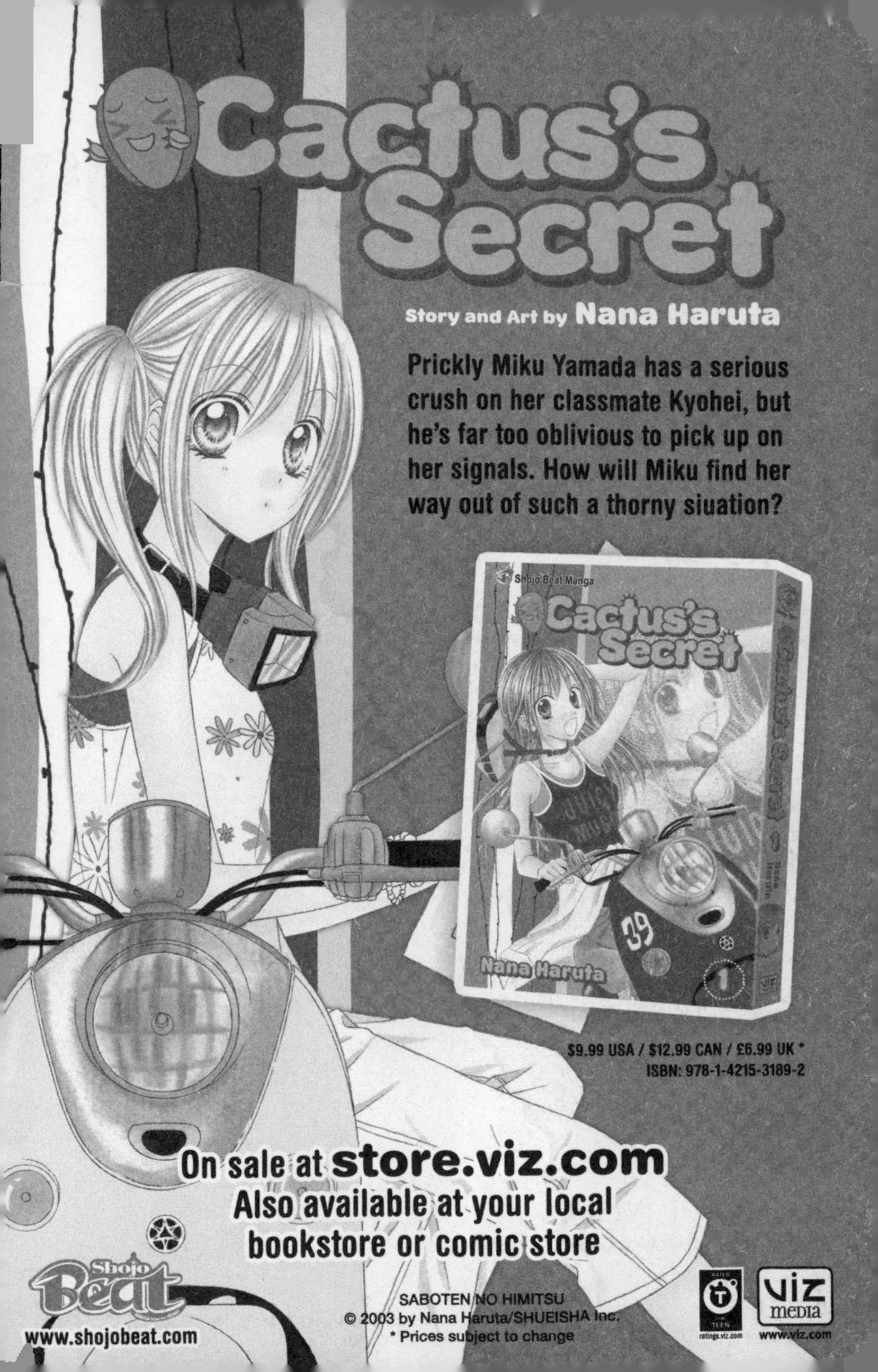

Cactus's Secret
Story and Art by Nana Haruta
Prickly Miku Yamada has a serious crush on her classmate Kyohei, but he's far too oblivious to pick up on her signals. How will Miku find her way out of such a thorny siuation?
Shojo Beat Manga
Cactus's Secret
Nana Haruta
1
$9.99 USA / $12.99 CAN / £6.99 UK *
ISBN: 978-1-4215-3189-2
On sale at store.viz.com
Also available at your local bookstore or comic store
Shojo Beat
www.shojobeat.com
SABOTEN NO HIMITSU
© 2003 by Nana Haruta/SHUEISHA Inc.
* Prices subject to change
RATED T TEEN
ratings.viz.com
VIZ media
www.viz.com

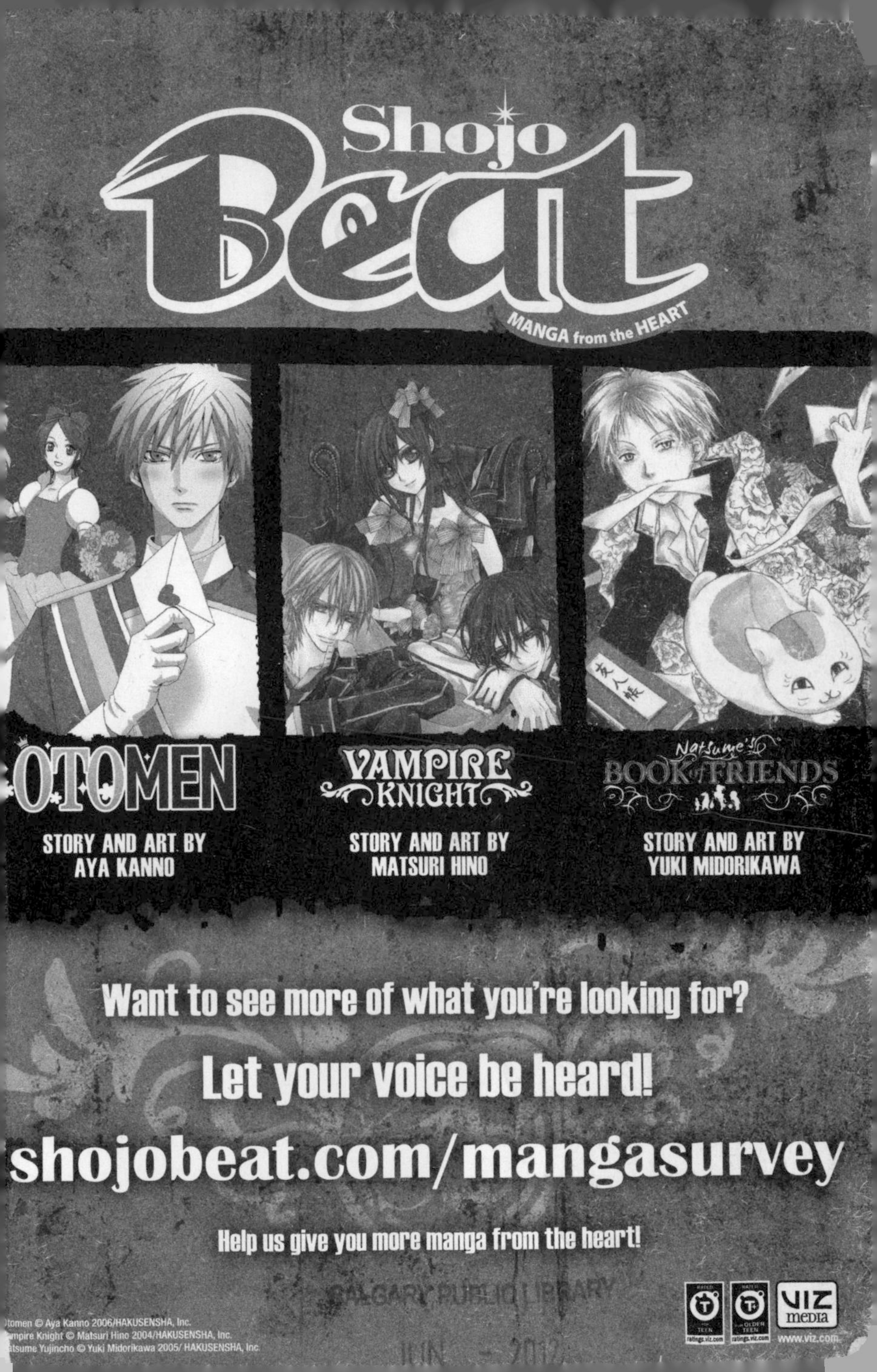
Shojo Beat
MANGA from the HEART
OTOMEN
STORY AND ART BY
AYA KANNO
VAMPIRE KNIGHT
STORY AND ART BY
MATSURI HINO
Natsume's BOOK of FRIENDS
STORY AND ART BY
YUKI MIDORIKAWA
Want to see more of what you're looking for?
Let your voice be heard!
shojobeat.com/mangasurvey
Help us give you more manga from the heart!
Otomen © Aya Kanno 2006/HAKUSENSHA, Inc.
Vampire Knight © Matsuri Hino 2004/HAKUSENSHA, Inc.
Natsume Yujincho © Yuki Midorikawa 2005/ HAKUSENSHA, Inc.
RATED T FOR TEEN ratings.viz.com
RATED T+ FOR OLDER TEEN ratings.viz.com
VIZ media
www.viz.com
CALGARY PUBLIC LIBRARY
JUN - 2012